COURAGE IN COMBAT

COURAGE IN COMBAT

Stories By and About Recipients of the
Nation's Highest Decorations

COMPILED AND EDITED BY
RICHARD J. RINALDO

FOREWORD BY JOSEPH L. GALLOWAY

CASEMATE | publishers
Philadelphia & Oxford

Published in the United States of America and Great Britain in 2017 by
CASEMATE PUBLISHERS
1950 Lawrence Road, Havertown, PA 19083, USA
and
The Old Music Hall, 106–108 Cowley Road, Oxford OX4 1JE, UK

Paperback Edition: ISBN 978-1-61200-456-3
Digital Edition: ISBN 978-1-61200-457-0

A CIP record for this book is available from the British Library and the Library of Congress

Printed and bound in the United States of America
Typeset in India by Lapiz Digital Services, Chennai

For a complete list of Casemate titles, please contact:

CASEMATE PUBLISHERS (US)
Telephone (610) 853-9131
Fax (610) 853-9146
Email: casemate@casematepublishers.com
www.casematepublishers.com

CASEMATE PUBLISHERS (UK)
Telephone (01865) 241249
Fax (01865) 794449
Email: casemate-uk@casematepublishers.co.uk
www.casematepublishers.co.uk

DEDICATION

To the select few who earned the Nation's highest awards for valor and received them and the many that earned them but did not.

War is the province of danger, and therefore courage above
all things is the first quality of the warrior.

Carl von Clausewitz

And dearer yet the Brotherhood
That binds the brave of all the earth.

Henry Newbolt

The secret of happiness is freedom,
and the secret of freedom is a brave heart.

Pericles

CONTENTS

FOREWORD

Joseph L. Galloway

Between the covers of this remarkable book are individual stories of incredible bravery in the face of death; stories that will make you proud to be an American; stories that will make your blood run cold.

In four decades of reporting from America's battlefields from Vietnam to the Persian Gulf to Iraq I have been a witness to acts of stunning heroism time and time again. In one battle, in the Ia Drang Valley in November of 1965, three men received the nation's highest award for heroism, the Medal of Honor.

You cannot predict who will risk or lay down his life in an act of bravery and self-sacrifice. These are decisions made in a split-second to risk everything to save a brother, or to save an entire unit of brothers in dire danger under the enemy guns.

Those decisions are made almost without thought because there is no time for thinking, for rationalizing, for reckoning the odds of success or death. The need for action is there and one soldier, airman, sailor or Marine answers the call.

Afterward those who wear the Medal of Honor, the Distinguished Service Cross, Navy Cross, or Air Force Cross are unanimous in declaring "I was just doing my job." They will add that they wear the medal on behalf of all the others who deserved it just as much but whose heroism wasn't seen or written up.

When North Vietnamese machine guns, well protected in bunkers, were chewing up his Marine company, Karl Marlantes—who had wanted to be a hero ever since he saw his father's medals from World War II—left a safe position to rescue one of the wounded men trapped under the guns, then watched that man die. The next day, faced with another line of enemy machine guns, Marlantes simply got up and charged alone into the hail of bullets. Faced with his example, his Marine platoon got up and followed him.

Former Senator and Marine Captain James Webb has a bone to pick with any who lionize the Greatest Generation of World War II and denigrate the heroism of those who fought the Vietnam War, his generation and his war. "Those who believe that it was a "dirty little war" where the bombs did all the work might contemplate that (Vietnam) was the most costly war the U.S. Marine Corps has ever fought," writes Webb, adding, "Five times as many dead as World War I, three times as many dead as in Korea, and more total killed and wounded than in all of World War II."

Twenty years ago at a book party in Los Angeles I ran into a former Army sergeant, Dan Garcia, who had served a tour in Vietnam with 2nd Battalion 7th Cavalry, 1st Cavalry Division. He spoke to me with great passion about a young infantry captain who took over his company after two predecessors were killed in combat. He told stories of incredible leadership in combat by the captain. Garcia, when asked, said he believed the captain was mortally wounded while leading a charge against enemy machine gun bunkers in the jungle. I asked the name of his brave captain. "His name was Barry McCaffrey," he replied. I was shocked for a long minute of silence, then said: "Your captain is alive and I have his phone number." I had ridden into battle with Major General Barry McCaffrey in the Persian Gulf War, by which time McCaffrey was a four-star general.

Garcia wrote a long letter to General McCaffrey about what he had meant to a beaten-down company of grunts whose daily sacrifices in combat were beyond belief. And McCaffrey wrote a long letter back. Their correspondence, which I can't read without tears, is included in these pages and I commend it to anyone who wants to know the raw truth about Vietnam and the brave men and officers who fought and died there.

I once wrote about marching with an infantry platoon in Vietnam, the soldiers weighed down with packs that totaled 60 or 70 pounds as they slogged through muddy paddies and into deep jungle under a blistering tropical sun. Men staggered under the weight and the sun, their eyes darting right and left searching for sign of an enemy ambush. I said they reminded me of a tree full of owls. When one of their number seemed likely to collapse they would quickly take his pack, share out the ammo he carried, and help him stumble along.

In my eyes they were all heroes, fighting in a war 12,000 miles from home—a war that was abandoned by the politicians who ordered it and, eventually, by the very people back home. The grunts soldiered on. If they couldn't fight for country and flag then, by God, they would fight and die for each other, and they did.

These are the stories of men who earned the nation's highest awards, and men who earned no awards at all. They may not all be the Greatest Generation but by God they are the greatest of their generation.

Joseph L. Galloway is the co-author of We Were Soldiers Once ... and Young, We Are Soldiers Still, *and* Triumph Without Victory: A History of the Persian Gulf War.

ACKNOWLEDGEMENTS

Just as in combat where there are many unsung heroes, when we write acknowledgements, there are many we know, and only God knows the rest. May His grace remind. But the music ends, and one leaves the stage frightened. If I missed you, forgive me. Likewise, if you are included generically among the mentioned groups.

All the contributors. Their names are listed in the book including those who serve the public in its domain and whose creative and competent efforts support our nation. Thanks also to those editors, publishers and others who have granted generous permissions, the *sine qua non* of getting stories to a wider audience, even when it was already wide enough.

Our then Adjutant Philip Conran for his patient and untiring devotion in support of this project and in all matters of the Legion of Valor.

Anonymous. We both know who you are among friends, mentors, teachers and former classmates. We keep secrets.

Our Board of Directors. They have vision and fight fiercely for the Legion of Valor.

Casemate Publishers. David Farnsworth for faith in signing on. Steve Smith for getting us started. Clare Litt, Tara Lichterman, Hannah McAdams, Ruth Sheppard for aid and comfort along the way.

Family. My wife Hermi, a "straw widow" who deserves more time and attention. My son Brian for advice and a keen sense of propriety. My granddaughter Angela for lots of important work and our great grandson Eli because he adds joy and meaning to the present and the future. Love.

Jill Jorden Spitz. Chief Editor of a newspaper, she volunteered her talents early and helped lastingly and when I was late. An honorable patriot who saw the value from the start.

Robert L. Tonsetic. He wrote a lot of books for Casemate. He was one of the best—smart and a kind gentleman, hero, warrior, friend and mentor. We will miss him.

PREFACE

Fighting our nation's battles demands a healthy dose of courage in combat. A relative handful of Americans fight—and die—for all of us.

Those of us left behind, service members and their supporters alike need to know their stories before it is too late. As of writing, in 2017 only around 400 members of the Legion of Valor of the United States of America, Inc. are still alive.

The idea for this anthology, in fact, comes from such stories told at the annual convention of the Legion of Valor held in Opelika/Auburn, Alabama in April 2013. This convention and other meetings and reunions of our organization over the years are at its core, its heart and soul. It is where we report our activities, make major decisions and plans, meet old friends, make new ones, and enjoy one another's company and that of our loved ones and others who join us.

At these gatherings we tell stories—true stories that many of us would not or could not tell elsewhere. For this reason perhaps, military writer Steven Coonts tells us in the introduction to his *New York Times* bestseller, *Victory: Call to Arms*: "Only in fiction can the essence of the human experience of war be laid bare." For sure, by creating plots and characters and allowing literary technique to heighten and illuminate experiences, there is great value in fiction. But with a little digging we find valuable non-fiction stories in books, articles and previously unpublished memoirs.

So, this book is an anthology about courage in combat. But it is more. It contains reflections about awards and decorations for our military. It relates personal accounts of combat and war as well as stories about the military and civilian lives of our members. It seeks to parse courage in combat, not so much by definition, as by aspects of the lives, thoughts, and actions of recipients of the Medal of Honor, the Distinguished Service Cross, the Navy Cross and the Air Force Cross. Those awards are our nation's highest military decorations.

All the stories and reflections in this collection are derived in one way or another from members of our association; included is a short history of this unique and relatively small group. We also award a Silver Cross for Valor to selected civilians to recognize actions involving saving or preservation of life at personal physical risk. We include stories about some of these award recipients. We have some honorary members also, and volunteers at our museum in Fresno, California. We would be remiss in not including some of their stories.

Yet, all of that begs the question. Why gather so much of this in one book? First, our motive is not money. The proceeds from the book will go into our already adequate coffers for general use. And these monies primarily come from member donations and bequests and careful investment. Of course, any association can make good use of more money. But that's not our main goal here. Second, it is not fame. We have among us plenty of that already. The answer lies in the objectives of our organization as listed in our Constitution and Bylaws. Several of them directly apply:

- To cherish the memories of the valiant deeds in arms for which the Congressional Medal of Honor, the Distinguished Service Cross, the Navy Cross, and the Air Force Cross are the insignia.
- To advance the best interests of members of the Armed Forces of the United States of America and to enhance their prestige and understanding by example and personal activity.
- To stimulate patriotism in the minds of our youth and to engender a national pride and interest in the Armed Forces of the United States.

Clearly, as long as the world is filled with jealousy and hatred, with political and religious intolerance, the security environment will present dangers to our nation. Our policies and active involvement in world affairs are not always welcomed. And if history is any guide, our military will continue to confront deadly enemies of our nation, and must be ready and willing, when directed, to seek them out and destroy them. We will go in ships, planes, tanks and on foot to find our enemies wherever they may be and defeat them. We will do so with air, naval and land power and with missiles, bombs, bullets, bayonets, rifle butts, and hand grenades. And sometimes, with stones.

INTRODUCTION

GOLDEN DEEDS

Courage is the footstool of the Virtues, upon which they stand.
                                              Robert Louis Stevenson

Count that day lost, whose low descending sun, views from thy hand no worthy action done.
                                              Staniford's Art of Reading

One of our more colorful members—a fierce fighter in combat, highly decorated, and poised to roar—likes to playfully greet newcomers by asking them, "Are you a fighter or a saver?"[*]

Some of our members clearly fit into one of those boxes—our medics, medevac and pararescue pilots, nurses and chaplains, for example. But many of them carried weapons onto the battlefield, if not for offense, then for self-protection, and they used them. The rest opted to fight and kill our enemies, to achieve assigned missions, while saving or protecting their comrades and others. So they are all both fighters and savers, just in different ways.

What they did may be called "Golden Deeds."

What is a "Golden Deed"? Charlotte M. Yonge answers in her 1864 collection, *A Book of Golden Deeds*: "It is that which makes the eye gleam and the heart throb, and bears us through the details of suffering, bloodshed, and even barbarity—feeling our spirt moved and elevated by contemplating the courage and endurance that they have called forth.... Such is the charm of brilliant valour..."

---

[*] Brigadier General John C. "Doc" Bahnsen USA Ret., Distinguished Service Cross.

Those involved will often simply say, "I was just doing my job." Sometimes they may be right, but more likely they did more, or did it when others did not, could not or would not. There is also some truth to the notion that the brave are thus because they might tolerate being afraid a little longer than others. Or maybe they're a bit crazy. You be the judge.

Is there a doctrine for this? A training program? How does one come to the barbarity of combat in sane fashion? Each conflict had its own special on-the-job training. Adaptability is now seen as critical to success in combat. Our military schools teach us techniques for killing and surviving. Still, there are more pieces to the puzzle.

This anthology is less a persuasion about courage than a description of it in varied times or circumstances, which reveal common threads woven into different fabrics. These are the virtues that guide and embolden action in dire conditions, like combat.

However, wars are the context of combat. The Vietnam War is a dire case in point. James Webb speaks eloquently and coherently about that in his contribution to this book. So does President Obama in comments inaugurating its 50th anniversary commemoration. Our Secretary of Defense then was Chuck Hagel, a former Army sergeant who served in the infantry in Vietnam, earning two Purple Hearts. (At least for a time, one of our sergeants, who could run companies of infantry and even bigger units, ran the Pentagon.) Joe Galloway revealed how he got along in combat. He was told, "Look for somebody with a lot of stripes on his sleeves, and do what he does!"

Context aside, this collection addresses combat itself. Webb in his novel about Vietnam, *Fields of Fire*, considered a classic of the genre, says, "It was all here, everything, and there was none of it there. All of life's compelling throbs condensed and honed each time a bullet flew: the pain, the brother love, and the sacrifice ... the heart-rending deaths. The successes ... all here. None of it there back in the bowels of the World."

Combat has plenty of contradictions. It's rare and common. Fight fiercely and live for days in the bush. Stand down bored for two weeks guarding the bunker line of a base camp. Or maybe sit on a road near the civilian population, where you can at least buy some ramen soup and a Coke.

It's old and new, part of the intercourse of the human race since the dawn of man, but fought with different weapons, styles and purposes— some good, some bad. It's violent and gentle, sometimes with ferocity toward brothers and kindness towards enemies. It's exhilarating and calming, like the "crack cocaine of all excitement highs" that Karl Marlantes talks about or sunning oneself on a bunker during a firefight, as a member of my rifle company confessed in a telephone call last year.

It's hard with deprivation and terror. It's easy, maybe too easy, when you have the enemy comfortably in your sights from a distance and can pick him off like in a turkey shoot. You might be isolated behind a log, seeing and hearing nothing but dust and loud noises with the bullets winging overhead. Or connected in a foxhole with your buddy. Or standing together at a memorial service to mourn the loss of friends.

It's punishing and forgiving; a piece of hot shrapnel might blind you or miss by mere inches to burn your earlobe, as it did mine. It's memorable and forgettable, gruesome and beautiful, and on and on. It will make you crazy and bring you back to reality in a flash.

Defenses against it all are the numerous virtues and qualities we teach our service members with courage being among the most important. It is, as Winston Churchill once said, "the first of human qualities… because it is the quality which guarantees all the others." But virtue, especially courage, needs to be practiced and exhibited in combat.

In a short phone interview, I asked one of my personal heroes about courage in combat. Retired Army Lieutenant General Samuel Wilson, who endured so much and fought so hard as a member of Merrill's Marauders in Burma during World War II, disavowed the idea of bravado, a false sense of one's power and courage. He talked instead of sustained courage, day in and out—something that springs from within, formed in belief and practice. This is a piece of the classic Greek Aristotelian notion of *eudaimonia*: right action.

Sam Wilson, Jr., his son, summed it up in talking about his father.

> Essence precedes being. Values precede action. That is the core truth of my father's reflections on the origins of his gifts, talents, and efforts. As an offspring who also resides in Southside Virginia, I can testify how deeply the quiet ethos of faith and service run in this region. It is largely unspoken but quietly evident

in the casual but warm way we greet friend and stranger alike; the stoicism with which disappointment and loss are greeted; the deflection of attention to oneself; the absolute determination to fulfill an obligation; the upholding of the standard "do it right." Here, we all, in one way or the other, attempt to "Mean, Speak, and Do Well." My father is a patriarch in that tradition.

Plato's *thymos* or "spiritedness" adds the dimension of shared sacrifice in risky work toward a greater good. Sebastian Junger in his book, *War*, described the loss some veterans felt for the camaraderie and sense of purpose they had in combat.

General Sam, as he later liked to be called, was assigned to the Infantry School and tasked to replace a great teacher of leadership at the podium. Despite his combat experience he felt inadequate to the task. As he said in an interview later:

> I talked to every successful platoon leader, company commander, battalion commander, regimental commander that I could find, and I took copious notes. I developed about 60 hours worth of lecture units based on finding people who had tried things that worked, trying to analyze them, put them together, group them, organize them…

To him, courage was fragile and its essence needed to be passed on, nudged and shared. He mentioned the biblical verse about the the Widow of Zarephath, whose stock of food and oil was constantly replenished in recognition of fulfilling her duties. Similarly, Robert Louis Stevenson tells us, "Keep your fears to yourelf, but share your courage with others."

General Sam exhibited physical fitness in enduring the hardships of combat in the jungles of Burma. Dick Winters, of *Band of Brothers* TV series fame, specifically said that combat leadership is impossible without being in good shape.

Taking orders is also a core military value, defined in the years between the Civil War and World War I when it became, according to sociologist Samuel P. Huntington in *The Soldier and the State*, "the highest glory of the soldier."

But a new idea surfaced around the same time, sociologist Morris Janowitz said in *The Professional Soldier*. Military discipline and authority shifted from top-down direction to a more follower-focused reliance on persuasion and consensus. In these contrasting notions lies a dilemma both for obedience and for courage.

Today, the ideal of courage clashes with the idea of equality. No one is greater than anyone else. Individual courage is under assault, according to Todd Lindberg in his recent book, *The Heroic Heart*. Yet the hero, defined as "someone who is willing to risk death out of fidelity to an inner sense of greatness," survives. Even a senior military officer joined in saying,

> … It would be a serious mistake to imagine that personal performance is what matters in combat. Combat is not a contest between individuals, like poker or tennis; it is a team event whose success depends on group cooperation and morale. So the behavior that concerns us is not individual achievement but the social dynamics of relationships and groups.

T. E. Lawrence may have pinned down such a philosophy in characterizing modern armies of his day, explaining that it:

> … meant the hunt, not of an average but of an absolute; the hundred percent standard in which the ninety-nine were played down to the level of the weakest man on parade. The aim was to render the unit a unit, the man a type; in order that their effort might be calculable, and the collective output even in grain and bulk. The deeper the discipline, the lower was the individual excellence; also the more sure the performance."

Decide for yourself as you read of men and women of courage in this book, some of whom Lawrence might call "the kingfisher flashing across the pool." Their individual actions or performance often had momentous impacts on combat and wars.

In *Parade* magazine, Elizabeth Svoboda, author of *What Makes a Hero*, listed four characteristics common to real-life heroes: 1) They abide by a moral code. 2) They've been trained to take action. 3) They're highly compassionate. 4) They perform ordinary acts of kindness.

It all sounds like "Golden Deeds" performed by trained military men and women, who have fidelity to their duty and care for their fellows, especially in combat. They also do good things for their country and local communities while on active duty or retired. Read on to meet such people.

OF HEROES AND COMBAT

It is remarkable how many people exert themselves and go through contortions to prove that battles and wars are won by any means except by … fighting.

Cyril Falls

HEROISM

Karl Marlantes

The heroic journey can be taken consciously or unconsciously. There's a time in one's life when the unconscious heroic journey is understandable, when one is young and in positions of little authority. The young warriors of the future will still largely perform their heroic tasks unconsciously. It is a part of development, eventually to be outgrown.

As warriors grow older, however, and move into positions of power and authority, far more is at stake because their actions affect a far wider field. Because there is more to lose, they will have to perform their heroic acts with full consciousness of the often painful consequences for everyone, including themselves. Many heroic acts of this kind will go unnoticed by society—if not actively denigrated. There will be no medals. This makes such acts far more difficult to do, and therefore even more heroic.

A wise man once said to be careful of what you wish for, because you may get it. I wanted to be a hero.

Our company had been pulled out of the bush to act as a reaction force. On the one hand it meant a rest. We got to be in tents set up next to a small airfield in the center of a narrow valley about 20 kilometers east of Khe Sanh. There were showers heated by diesel fuel, hot food, and a portable electricity generator so that in the evenings we could sit outside, rain or mist, and see a movie. Then there was the other hand. We were in combat readiness at all times, waiting. We sat there, most of the lower ranks unfairly having to fill sandbags, all of us whittling, writing letters, bullshitting, but always listening in on the battalion and regimental nets, trying to determine which firefight was going to turn into the mess that would send in the Marines.

So whether in the outdoor shower or at the movie watching Clint Eastwood, we were constantly aware that within minutes we could be running for our rifles and packs, the skipper shouting for the platoon commanders, maps out, hearts racing, while the thumping of rotor blades echoed off the green walls of the valley as the choppers peeled off one by one to take us to where some of us surely were going to die.

I remember that particular dying day. The soft gray of the sky was slowly going dull as the sun began its afternoon slide into Laos. I watched two squads, who'd been filling sandbags for some one-star general at a place called Task Force Hotel, run full bore the long half mile to their gear, which waited neatly stacked by the runway. Marines were in trouble. Semper Fi.

I remember the stomach-turning lurch of the chopper as it came out of a deep spiral just north of the Rock Pile, about 10 kilometers south of the DMZ. I was trying to get my bearings on the revolving hilltops and rivers, my map out, my hands trembling. My neck snapped backward, whipping my helmet against the bulkhead, as the chopper jolted into the ground. I remember the crew chief screaming at us to get out of the chopper because we were taking fire standing in the landing zone. Several kids on the helo team had to jump for it because the pilot lost his nerve and gunned the chopper out of the zone too soon. The last one dropped around ten feet with ninety pounds on his back. He broke his leg. We temporarily lost his squad because they had to stay on the LZ to protect him, weakening the company, and then another chopper crew had to risk their lives to get him out. Combat magnifies small acts terribly.

The shooting was all over before I knew what was going on.

A company from another battalion had been in a fight somewhere to our east with an NVA unit of unknown size but big enough to cause some heartburn when they started chewing on each other. We were launched to take the NVA unit from behind, simultaneously blocking their exit in this narrow valley. They'd taken us under fire as we came in, but, seeing they would soon be between the hammer and the anvil, they had quickly disengaged. Now they were moving toward an ominous-looking ridgeline that stretched across our northern horizon, dark and gray-green in the somber light, sheathed in clouds and fog.

Through our field glasses, whenever the swirling fog would thin a little, we could see movement and fresh diggings of a sizable unit already on top. And now reinforcements were climbing to join them. The order came to exploit the situation. The other company and our company would assault at first light. To do this meant we had to sneak up on them that night. We stripped down to essentials, leaving our gear in a neat pile on the jungle floor, and started climbing at around 0130 that night.

In war you need to be lucky. Be at war long enough and you'll have some bad days. Just before dawn, about 500 meters from the NVA position, we started running into booby traps, trip wires leading to mines lashed in the trees at chest level. Our point men were terrified. We rotated them every five minutes, pushed ahead. Then we stumbled into a listening post and a brief firefight erupted. So much for surprise.

The other company, working up another finger to our right, took a couple of nasty hits. I heard someone screaming after the dull crump of an explosion. The screaming went on for a full minute, a lone voice, piercing through the fog and jungle from a couple of kilometers away from us until abruptly cut off. I found out later it was a friend of mine from the Basic School. I was told that his lower jaw, his entire face, and a leg had been blown off by a DH-10 directional mine, normally used against tanks. His platoon sergeant had run up to see what the screaming was all about and had cut it off by placing his hand against the hole where the voice box was still intact. Eventually, I understand, he pinched off the carotid artery and my friend died, still fully aware.

The other company commander lost his nerve and stopped. It happens, even in the Marine Corps. Our company made the assault alone.

The next day we took a second hill just to our west but couldn't hold both for lack of Marines. We regrouped on the first hill and were assaulted that night by NVA sappers and ground troops. Another friend who'd gone with me through Platoon Leaders Class[1] was in the company that stopped. He took his platoon, on his own authority, and worked his way up to join us. He reached us when we were much in need defending the hill against counterattacks. The greater part of our ammunition had been spent in the assault and we were now two full nights without sleep. I remember him and his platoon sergeant making the rounds of the holes under fire just after they'd arrived, eager to make amends for not joining the assault, eager to prove themselves always faithful—which they did.

Instead of going with them to help familiarize them with the perimeter, I just watched, telling myself that I'd already risked my neck enough. I'm still ashamed of it.

In the midst of all this chaos and carnage, cowardice and honor, I won my first medal, a Bronze Star. It was during the initial assault. The platoon commander who replaced me when I was moved up to XO was green. He had been in only one real fight, not counting the hot landing. I couldn't stand to have my old platoon make the assault without me. My actual post, as number two, was with the command group on a small knoll just down the ridgeline from the hill we were assaulting. My job was to help the skipper direct the artillery and the supporting fire from the weapons platoon and be there to take over if he got killed or wounded. I couldn't stand it. I told the skipper I was joining the assault and didn't wait to hear an answer.

The small knoll and the larger hill where the NVA were dug in were connected by a blasted barren neck, the top of the ridge. I ran alone down this neck between the command post and the assaulting Marines. The assault group was already at the FLD² draped across the ridgeline, one end of the string hanging down the south slope and the other end hanging down the north slope. I knew that one very critical tactical task would be to keep the assault together, as the tendency is for the squads to slide down their respective sides of the ridge, opening a gap in the assault and weakening the force to be applied against the NVA bunkers. In any assault the defenders are usually considered to have at least a three-to-one advantage, mainly because they are dug in and have prepared defensive fires on all the easy ways up. *Up* is the other operative word. Assaulting a hill slows and exhausts the attackers enormously, making them very vulnerable to fire. To succeed, an assault depends on all-out fury focused at the smallest possible point.

Artillery shells were piling into the hill above us. Pieces of nearly spent shrapnel were falling beside me as I ran toward the FLD. While I was running toward my old platoon and the coming assault, I felt an overwhelming sense of excitement, almost joy. I was rejoining *my* unit. I was nearly crazy with adrenaline. The screaming and earth-shattering artillery rounds filled the air around me with vibrant shaking noise that I felt pounding right up through the soles of my jungle boots and smashing into my face and ears from the shivering air. I've jumped out of airplanes, climbed up cliff sides, raced cars, done drugs. I've never found anything comparable. Combat is the crack cocaine of all excitement highs—with crack cocaine costs.

The artillery stopped, smoke grenades were popped, and we stood up and walked up the hill in an eerie silence, waiting for the first bullets. Then, all across our front, unseen machine guns and small arms opened up. Bullets cracked past our ears, kicked dirt, and killed. We surged forward. Everything was blood in the throat, shouting, running, furious thinking, noise, and chaos.

I kept screaming at the troops to try to keep the gap from opening. They responded admirably. We hit the slope of the hill as one. Then began the extremely hard job of climbing it under fire. The new platoon commander immediately had his hands full trying to force through, or around, a concentration of bunkers and holes on our right flank, about midway up the hillside. I went tearing around a small bump of dirt to the left of where the ridgeline joined the steeper hill, working my way sideways on the hillside, trying to link two squads that had drifted apart while at the same time spreading people to our left trying to keep them from bunching up.[3] There I saw Utter, a tall awkward kid of eighteen, leaning with his back against the steep hill, frantically trying to clear his M-16. I remember his Adam's apple pumping up and down. He was near panic.

I threw myself against the hillside, so steep here that both of us were actually standing, leaning our backs against it, looking out over the valley below us. Bullets, exceeding the sound barrier, made loud sonic snaps over our heads, but we were safe in this little cup that protected us. Utter's magazine hadn't been properly seated, causing the bolt to hang up on its forward edge, a common problem with the M-16. I cleared it for him, fired a short burst, and handed the rifle back to him. I asked him where his squad leader was. He didn't know exactly. Over there someplace.

I looked up over the lip of the cup and could see that the brush had been carefully cleared away from the ground up to about knee level. By this time I'd been around long enough to know this meant a machine-gun emplacement. They'd shoot the legs first. When the attacker fell, the bullets would finish him off as the body fell through the kill zone.

I grabbed Utter by the shirt and forced his head above the lip to show him the trap, shouting at him not to go up that way, to try to find some way around. He stared at the cut brush. I yanked him down and then told him to stay put. I'd find his squad leader and we'd get a team together and get the gun by flanking it from the left side. Don't go up there. He nodded, still dazed with fear. I made him shoot a couple of rounds. He nodded; he was all right.

I took off to organize an attack on the machine gun. As I left the protection of the cup I saw Utter take off, straight up the hill. I'll never know why. Perhaps he too wanted to be a hero. Maybe he just wanted to show me he was a good Marine.

My former platoon sergeant, Staff Sergeant Bell, came running around from the opposite side. His radioman, Lance Corporal Putnam, piled into the hillside right after him. Bell, a terrific platoon sergeant, was doing the same thing I was, trying to get the two squads back together, but from the other direction. So the gap was getting closed.

I shouted at him, "Utter's just gone up the hill toward that machine gun. Where in hell's Second Squad?"

He just pointed over his shoulder and leaned his back against the side of the hill, his chest heaving. I saw movement in the brush and heard the sound of an M-16, so knew that Bell and the second squad leader had closed the gap.

Then we all heard the enemy machine gun open up. You can definitely tell this machine gun by its heavy popping sound, methodical and hammerlike, unlike the heavy slapping sound of the AK-47 or the tense, high-pitched scream of our own M-16s.

I heard Utter cry out, "I'm hit."

The machine gun kept firing.

I looked at Bell and he looked at me. He shook his head, lips pressed tight. I finally said, "I don't have anything else to do. I'll go get him."

Bell looked directly at me and said, "Don't go up there, Lieutenant."

I was split three ways. I'd known Utter for months. He was my guy, even though I'd just been replaced. He was hit. I simply wanted to get him before he bled to death. Another part of me was screaming to listen to Bell and stay safe. Then there was the third part. I wanted a medal.

I'd always wanted a medal, ever since I looked at my father's medals from World War II, ever since I'd seen Audie Murphy in *To Hell and Back*, ever since I was never chosen first when we chose up sides. All that. It wasn't enough to do heroic things. I had to be recognized for it. That meant putting the ribbon on my chest so that when I went home other Marines would know not only that I'd been there but that I'd done something extraordinary. I would be extra ordinary. I'd be special among a special group.

I have heard Napoleon quoted to the effect that an army runs on its stomach and ribbons. This man understood the desire to feel special and how it motivates. This man, who could have been the savior of the French revolution and all its ideals, as much revered as George Washington, also blew it by making himself emperor. He too wanted to be special.

When I first got back from Vietnam I hadn't yet received any medals except my two Purple Hearts and Combat Action Ribbon,[4] paperwork being paperwork. I felt proud. They showed that I'd been there, that I was one of the group. But while I was at the Pentagon the paperwork started catching up with me and it seemed as if every few weeks I was in front of some general getting another medal. It became a sort of office joke. And I, Mr. Hotshot, got more and more special.

Wanting to be a society-certified hero is a specialness issue. I see people killing themselves at work and at home to pay for mortgages that are too much for them, or taking vacations they can't afford in the right spots, all to be special. Wanting a medal in war is just killing yourself at a faster pace, for all the same wrong reasons.

With every ribbon that I added to my chest I could be more special than someone who didn't have it. Even better, I quickly learned that most people who outranked me, who couldn't top my rows of ribbons, didn't feel right chewing me out for minor infractions.[5] I pushed this to the limit. I read the regulations on hair. I grew mine to the absolute limit allowed, getting it cut weekly to keep it there on the margin of acceptability. I found out mustaches were permitted. I grew a scraggly little thing that made me look like a corn-fed Ho Chi Minh.

It all came to an abrupt halt when a major from another department with whom I occasionally had to work asked me into his office. He had nowhere near my rows of medals, but he had been in Vietnam. I remember him sitting on his desk, looking out of the window while I stood there, quite at ease. Then he turned to me and said, "Marlantes, I don't give a fuck how many medals you've got on your chest. You look like shit. You're a fucking disgrace to your uniform and it's a uniform I'm proud of. Now get out of here and clean up your goddamned act."

I can't remember the man's name. If I could, I'd thank him personally. He called my shit.

I walked away feeling terrible. Too many of my friends had died wearing a Marine uniform. I cleaned up my act. It also started me thinking about why I was behaving so badly.

We all want to be special, to stand out; there's nothing wrong with this. The irony is that every human being is special to start with, because we're unique to start with. But we then go through some sort of boot camp from the age of zero to about eighteen where we learn everything we can about how not to be unique. This spawns an unconscious desire to prove yourself special, but now it's special in the eyes of your peers and it comes out in the form of being better than or having power over someone else. In the military I could exercise the power of being automatically respected because of the medals on my chest, not because I had done anything right at the moment to earn that respect. This is pretty nice. It's also a psychological trap that can stop one's growth and allow one to get away with just plain bad behavior.

To a large extent my behavior could be explained as a result of experiencing the dreadful time of return that so many Vietnam veterans experienced. I desperately wanted to be accepted by my other peer group, college-age kids in civilian society. So to prove my loyalty to the college kid crowd and try to gain their respect and admiration by being the "war-protesting rebel Marine" I started to put down military values such as pride in one's uniform. Some protest.

Looking even deeper, I realize now that I also had very mixed feelings about some of the medals on my chest. I knew many Marines had done brave deeds that no one saw and for which they got no medals at all. I was having a very hard time carrying those medals and didn't have the insight or maturity to know what to do with my combination of guilt and pride. So I attacked my image. Some solution.

The truth is there were important aspects about the medals that weren't in the write-ups. That day on the assault I felt like someone in a movie. I remember thinking, "This is like a movie. I'm the hero, and the dumb kid has just gotten in trouble with the enemy machine gun, and now the hero will go rescue him." The movies are America's mythological matrix. I also remember thinking, "This is your chance. You throw this one away and you'll never get your medal."

I turned to Bell and made a wise-guy sort of joke out of it. I was aware that I was talking as if I were reading a script. I had become a character, come out of myself somehow. "Is it worth a medal if I go get him? You write me up for one?" I laughed to make sure he knew I was joking.

"Don't go. You'll get killed," was all he said. Bell, around age twenty-seven, with a couple of kids at home, was far more mature than me.

"He's going to die if someone doesn't go get him," I said. I actually think I was bargaining with Bell. I'll go get him *if* I can get a medal.

If Bell hadn't said what he did say I'd probably still have gone because I'd already been taken over by this inner (or maybe outer) force. But he said, "I'll write you up, but you'll be fucking dead."

That was all the hero needed. You see, heroes don't die. They're immortal. They return from the land of the dead and bring back the boon.

The land of the dead was that thin zone of cleared brush, just over a foot high, through which the bullets were tearing with a methodical deadly intensity. The boon to bring back was Utter. I was going. There was no stopping me.

I told Bell to pass the word for Doc Southern and seated a fresh magazine in my rifle. "I'll be firing as I go up. You and Putnam try and keep the gunners' heads down." Bell shouted at the fire team to our immediate left, telling them I was going after Utter and not to shoot my ass and help try to force the gunners down with rifle fire. Putnam was shouting, "Corpsman! Corpsman!"

I threw myself up over the protecting lip of the hillside, rolled quickly sideways, and opened up on full automatic, straight up the cleared zone. I crawled on my elbows and knees as fast as I could, firing my rifle with one hand, trying desperately to keep the heads of the NVA machine gunners down while I moved up toward Utter, not knowing where he was, just going by the fix I'd gotten when he'd cried out.

I found him staring up at the sky, feet uphill toward the machine gun, head toward me, rifle flung back downhill.

I tried to tug him back down, actually sheltering behind his body. The machine gun had opened up and the bullets were impacting all around me. I couldn't drag him: too much friction.

I turned him sideways to the hill and flung myself forward on top of him. I wrapped my arms and legs around him and our rifles and started rolling with him, embracing him as the machinegun bullets went slamming into the dirt all around us. Me on top. Utter on top. Over and over, down the hill together, me on top, Utter on top, bullets thudding into the wet clay around us, sounding like someone clapping his hands next to my ears as they passed overhead.

I remember desperately hoping that if the bullets hit us Utter would be on top when they did. This was the same part of me that had wanted to stay with Bell in the first place. Now that the deed was nearly over, the hero in me was departing, and the other parts of me were coming back to the fore.

We reached the steep lip and thudded to the ground. Doc Southern was just arriving. Bell and Putnam took off. They had other jobs to do. I covered for Doc Southern as he bent over Utter, giving him mouth-to-mouth resuscitation. Utter was spitting up vomit and blood and Southern kept spitting it out of his mouth and onto the ground next to Utter, sometimes right on Utter's shirt. He kept pushing and pounding Utter's chest, now sticky with vomit and blood, trying to keep his heart going. He'd suck in a lungful of air while doing this and press his mouth to Utter's over and over again.

Suddenly he looked up at me and sighed, slowly shaking his head back and forth. He cradled Utter's head in one hand and pulling back bloody matted hair exposed a neat hole in the top of Utter's skull. "I just saw this, sir. He ain't going to make it." He laid Utter's head on the wet red clay and scrambled off to attend the constant chorus of "Corpsman! Corpsman!"

One night, alone on watch, I began to think. How could Utter have cried out "I'm hit" with a bullet in his brain? The bullet must have gone in after he'd cried out. He had been lying head down toward me. The bullet went into the top of his head. I could have put it there myself when I was trying to keep the machine-gun fire down as I crawled up to get him. I'll never know.

The best words I've ever heard on the subject of medals come from a fellow lieutenant who'd been my company XO when I first arrived in Vietnam. The company came under mortar attack. Tom, then a platoon commander, had found a relatively safe defensive position for himself, but he stood up, exposed to the exploding shells, in order to get a compass bearing on where the shells were being fired from. He then called in and adjusted counterbattery fire, which got the company out of the shit. He was awarded the Bronze Star. When I heard the news and congratulated him, he said, "A lot of people have done a lot more and gotten a lot less, and a lot of people have done a lot less and gotten a lot more."

Medals are all mixed up with hierarchy, politics, and even job descriptions. What is considered normal activity for a grunt, and therefore not worthy of a medal, is likely to be viewed as extraordinary for someone who does the same thing but isn't a grunt, so he gets a medal and maybe an article in *Stars and Stripes*. Your common garden-variety grunt is only doing his job, and is usually someplace too dangerous to be interviewed by a reporter anyway. Rank counts for the same reasons. Major Smith grabs a grenade and overruns a bunker and it's at least good for a Bronze Star. If Lance Corporal Smithers does it, it's likely to go unnoticed, because Smithers did it yesterday and two weeks earlier as well. If the colonel and his favorite haven't gotten quite enough stuff on their record to ensure their next promotion, well, remember that night when they had to leave the Combat Operations Center to piss because they'd had too much beer and the north end of the perimeter had a rocket come in? Well, that certainly showed bravery under fire … It was ever thus.

I got my medals, in part, because I did brave acts, but also, in part, because the kids liked me and they spent time writing better eyewitness accounts than they would have written if they hadn't liked me. Had I been an unpopular officer and done exactly the same thing, few would have bothered, if any. The accounts would have been laconic, at best, and the medals probably of a lower order. The only people who will ever know the value of the ribbons on their chests are the people wearing them—and even they can fool themselves, in both directions.

After the experience with Utter I was no longer so anxious to get a medal of any kind. But the same phenomenon of being taken over by something, or someone, still seemed to operate. What is extraordinarily hard for me to comprehend is that I won my next medal during the same assault where I lost myself to the bloodlust and lost my radioman Isle.

We had moved up in the dark and waited in the jungle, strung out on line as the jets roared in to bomb the enemy defenses at first light. But because of a screwup the jets dropped their bombs on the wrong hill. I screamed bloody murder over the battalion FAC[6] net but was told I was out of line and to get off because I couldn't possibly see what was going on.

Going up against bunkers is hard enough, but doing it without any air prep was decidedly unnerving. A huge value of the air prep is the boost to the morale of the attacking infantry. We came out of the jungle onto the exposed earth below the bunkers and were instantly under fire from the untouched machine-gun positions. Everyone dived for logs and holes. The whole assault ground to a halt, except for one kid named Niemi, who had sprinted forward when we came under the intense fire and disappeared up in front of us somewhere. We figured he was down and dead.

I actually don't know how long we all lay there getting pulverized out in the open like that. I knew it would be only a few minutes before the NVA rockets and mortars found us.

Again, I seemed to step aside. I remember surveying the whole scene from someplace in the air above it. I saw the napalm smoke burning uselessly on the wrong hill. The machine guns had us pinned down with well-planned interlocking fire. The NVA were pros. Everyone was strung out in a ragged line hiding behind downed trees and in shell holes, even me, tiny and small, huddled down there below me with the rest. I distinctly remember recalling the words of an instructor at the Basic School, a particularly colorful and popular redheaded major who taught tactics, talking to a group of us about when it was a platoon leader earned his pay. I knew, floating above that mess, that now that time had come. If I didn't get up and lead, we'd get wiped.

I reentered my body as the hero platoon leader, leaving the rest of everyday me up there in the clouds. It was at this point I started screaming at the wounded machine gunner to crawl up to my log and start that machine-gun duel, which would keep the crew of one of the interlocking machine guns busy. I then got an M-79 man to move up next to me and had him start lobbing shells at the observation slit of an adjacent bunker that was also giving us fits, directly up the hill from us. Then I stood up.

I did a lot of things that day, many of which got written into the commendation, but the one I'm most proud of is that I simply stood up, in the middle of all that flying metal, and started up the hill all by myself.

I'm proud of that act because I did it for the right reasons. I once watched a televised exchange on the hero's journey between Bill Moyers and Joseph Campbell. The camera had cut to a boot camp scene with Campbell saying, "There are some heroic journeys into which you are thrown and pitched." The camera then cut to scenes from Vietnam, helicopters, a young black man limping forward in agony. Then, it cut to war protesters, and Moyers then asked Campbell, "Doesn't heroism have a moral objective?"

Campbell replied, "The moral objective is that of saving a people, or person, or idea. He is sacrificing himself for something. That is the morality of it. Now, you, from another position, might say that 'something' wasn't worth it, or was downright wrong. That's a judgment from another side. But it doesn't destroy the heroism of what was done. Absolutely not."

I was no more heroic this time than when I went after Utter. Both times I faced a lot of fire. In fact, both times my actions were an effort to save a person, Utter, or a people, my little tribe exposed and dying on that scourged hillside. But my motives had changed. And because my motives had changed, I feel a lot better about what I did.

I made no heroic gestures or wisecracks this time. I simply ran forward up the steep hill, zigzagging for the bunker, all by myself, hoping the M-79 man wouldn't hit me in the back. It's hard to zigzag while running uphill loaded down with ammunition and grenades. Every bit of my consciousness was focused on just two things, the bunker above me and whether I could keep running and zigzagging with everything I had. Another 400-meter sprint with Death. A long desperate weekend. A time out of time.

I was running in a long arc to get between the machine-gun bunker and the one I was heading for, and to avoid the M-79 shell snow exploding against the observation slit, which I hoped were blinding the occupants. As I made that arc I was turned sideways to the hill and I caught movement in my peripheral vision. I hit the deck turning and rolling, coming up in a position to fire. It was a Marine! He was about 15 meters below me, zigzagging, falling, up and running again. Immediately behind him a long ragged line of Marines came moving and weaving up the hill behind me. Behind the line were spots of crumpled bodies, lying where they'd been hit.

They'd all come with me. I was actually alone only for a matter of seconds.[7]

We took the bunker, and the next, and together with Second Platoon joining up with us on our right flank broke through the first line of bunkers, only to come under fire from a second, interior line of fighting holes higher on the hill. At this point I saw the missing kid, Niemi, pop his head up. He sprinted across the open top of the hill, all alone. The NVA turned in their positions to fire on him. I watched him climb on top of a bunker and chuck two grenades inside. When they went off I saw him fall to the ground. I assumed that this time he'd been killed for sure.

Being hit from behind by Niemi both unnerved the NVA and encouraged us to hurry to reach him. All semblance of platoon and squad order were gone by now. Everyone was intermingled, weaving, rushing and covering, taking on each hole and bunker one at a time in individual groups.

It was just about that time I got knocked out and blinded by a hand grenade. I came to, groggy. I could hear my radioman, who seemed very far away, telling the skipper I was down and that he didn't know if I was dead or not. I grunted something to let him know I wasn't dead and tried to sit up, but then went back down. I felt as though I couldn't get my breath. Then I panicked, because I knew I'd been hit in the eyes. I started rubbing them, desperate to get them open, but they seemed glued shut. My radioman poured Kool-Aid from his canteen onto my face and into my eyes, and I managed to get one eye to clear. The other eye was a bloody dirt-clogged mess and I thought I'd lost it.[8]

We kept scrambling for the top, trying to reach Niemi, trying to win, trying to get it all over with. I got held up by two enemy soldiers in a hole and was attempting to get a shot or two off at them and quickly ducking back down when a kid I knew from Second Platoon, mainly because of his bad reputation, threw himself down beside me, half his clothes blown away. He was begging people for a rifle. His had been blown out of his hands.

He was a black kid, all tangled up in black power politics, almost always angry and sullen. A troublemaker. Yet here he was, most of his body naked with only flapping rags left of his jungle utilities, begging for a rifle when he had a perfect excuse to just bury his head in the clay and quit. I gave him mine. I still had a pistol. He grabbed the rifle, stood up to his full height, fully exposing himself to all the fire, and simply blasted an entire magazine at the two soldiers in front of us, killing both of them. He then went charging into the fight, leaving me stunned for a moment.

Why? Who was he doing this for? What is this thing in young men? We were beyond ourselves, beyond politics, beyond good and evil. This was transcendence.

Many of us had by now worked our way almost to the top of the hill. Fighting was no longer them above and us below. Marines and NVA intermingled. Crashing out of the clouds into this confusion came a flaming, smoking twin-rotor CH-46 helicopter. It was making a much-needed ammunition run to the company waiting in reserve and firing support for us from the hill we'd taken several days before. We think that the bird got hit by a mortar round as it was coming in and, in the confusion and scudding cloud cover, the pilot picked the wrong hill or he did it because he had no choice. The result was the same. Down it came, right where we were assaulting, and the NVA just tore that bird to pieces. Spinning out of control, it smashed right on the very top of the hill, breaking its rotor blades.

I saw Niemi pop into sight again. He sprinted to the downed chopper. Later we found out he'd spent his time crawling behind holes and bunkers, shooting people from behind. He'd watched aghast as the chopper came screaming out of the sky nearly hitting him. Later he told me that it looked as if the thing simply started sprouting holes as the NVA turned their weapons on it. When he saw the crew bail out and crawl for cover underneath the chopper,[9] the only thing he could think to do was sprint across the open hilltop to see if he could find a place from which he could lay down fire to protect them. He didn't debate this. He just did it. It was an unconscious, generous, and potentially sacrificial act.

Many of us coming up the hill saw Niemi sprint into the open. Knowing now that he was still alive and that he and the chopper crew were dead for sure if we didn't break through to them, we all simply rushed forward to reach them before the NVA killed them. No one gave an order. *We*, the group, just rushed forward all at once. *We* couldn't be stopped. Just individuals among us were stopped. Many forever. But *we* couldn't be. This too is a form of transcendence. I was we, no longer me.

Lance Corporal Steel, nineteen, who'd been acting platoon commander until I reorganized things and was now acting platoon sergeant, got there first. The crewmen were so grateful and happy they gave their pistols away. I got the pilot's .38 Smith and Wesson.

Niemi got a Navy Cross.

I got a Navy Cross.

The helicopter pilot got a front-page story in *Stars and Stripes* with the headline, "Copter 'Crashes' Enemy Party, Takes Hill."[10]

The kid who borrowed my rifle didn't get anything.

This is a chapter from What It Is Like To Go To War, *by Karl Marlantes, Navy Cross. A version of this piece also appeared in the* Wall Street Journal. *Karl is also author of the highly acclaimed* New York Times *bestseller Vietnam War novel* Matterhorn.

Notes

1   Platoon Leaders Class, a U.S. Marines officer candidate school.

2   The final line of departure, the preplanned line on the ground that is the last stop before committing everything to the assault and the control point for managing artillery, naval gunfire, and air support just prior to the assault.

3   Controlling an assault—and the word *control* is used loosely—treads a fine line between not having any gaps, which weakens the attack, and not bunching up, which makes it too easy for the defense to kill you.

4   The Purple Heart is a medal given for wounds received in combat. The Combat Action Ribbon is awarded to people who have experienced combat, although this is a tougher one to judge on the surface. A person could be at an air base, where one rocket hit the base half a mile from the person, and still be awarded a CAR the same as an infantryman who spent months fighting in the jungle.

5   Medals have a hierarchy. In the Marine Corps the order of medals for valor in combat, from top to bottom, is Congressional Medal of Honor, Navy Cross, Distinguished Flying Cross, Silver Star, Bronze Star, Single Mission Air Medal, Navy Commendation Medal. Once you're in the service, you can read a person's ribbons and quickly know where you fall in the hierarchy.

6   Forward Air Control.

7   The official commendation makes it sound as if I took a bunch of bunkers all alone. I did lead the charge, but I often remind people that none of those kids who wrote the eyewitness accounts could have done so if they hadn't been right there with me.

8   I stayed with the company until we were relieved, I must say feeling very sorry for myself. Luckily, the blindness was temporary. The surgeon on the hospital ship, the *Repose*, later told me that several metal slivers were just microns from the optic nerve.

9   Aircrews are armed only with pistols, virtually useless in a fight like this. They may as well have been unarmed.

10 To be clear, I know the stupid headline was completely out of the control of the pilot and crew, who, like all aircrews, were risking their lives to help us.

HEROES OF THE VIETNAM GENERATION

James Webb

The rapidly disappearing cohort of Americans that endured the Great Depression and then fought World War II is receiving quite a send-off from the leading lights of the so-called '60s generation. Tom Brokaw has published two oral histories of "The Greatest Generation" that feature ordinary people doing their duty and suggest that such conduct was historically unique.

Chris Matthews of "Hardball" is fond of writing columns praising the Navy service of his father while castigating his own baby boomer generation for its alleged softness and lack of struggle. William Bennett gave a startlingly condescending speech at the Naval Academy a few years ago comparing the heroism of the "D-Day Generation" to the drugs-and-sex nihilism of the "Woodstock Generation." And Steven Spielberg, in promoting his film *Saving Private Ryan*, was careful to justify his portrayals of soldiers in action based on the supposedly unique nature of World War II.

An irony is at work here. Lest we forget, the World War II generation now being lionized also brought us the Vietnam War, a conflict which today's most conspicuous voices by and large opposed, and in which few of them served. The "best and brightest" of the Vietnam age group once made headlines by castigating their parents for bringing about the war in which they would not fight, which has become the war they refuse to remember.

Pundits back then invented a term for this animus: the "generation gap." Long, plaintive articles and even books were written examining its manifestations. Campus leaders, who claimed precocious wisdom through the magical process of reading a few controversial books, urged fellow baby boomers not to trust anyone over 30. Their elders who had survived the Depression and fought the largest war in history were looked down upon as shallow, materialistic, and out of touch.

Those of us who grew up on the other side of the picket line from that era's counter-culture can't help but feel a little leery of this sudden gush of appreciation for our elders from the leading lights of the old counter-culture. Then and now, the national conversation has proceeded from the dubious assumption that those who came of age during Vietnam are a unified generation in the same sense as their parents were, and thus are capable of being spoken for through these fickle elites.

In truth, the "Vietnam generation" is a misnomer. Those who came of age during that war are permanently divided by different reactions to a whole range of counter-cultural agendas, and nothing divides them more deeply than the personal ramifications of the war itself. The sizable portion of the Vietnam age group who declined to support the counter-cultural agenda, and especially the men and women who opted to serve in the military during the Vietnam War, are quite different from their peers who for decades have claimed to speak for them. In fact, they are much like the World War II generation itself. For them, Woodstock was a side show, college protestors were spoiled brats who would have benefited from having to work a few jobs in order to pay their tuition, and Vietnam represented not an intellectual exercise in draft avoidance or protest marches but a battlefield that was just as brutal as those their fathers faced in World War II and Korea.

Few who served during Vietnam ever complained of a generation gap. The men who fought World War II were their heroes and role models. They honored their fathers' service by emulating it, and largely agreed with their fathers' wisdom in attempting to stop Communism's reach in Southeast Asia. The most accurate poll of their attitudes (Harris, 1980) showed that 91 percent were glad they'd served their country, 74 percent enjoyed their time in the service, and 89 percent agreed with the statement that "our troops were asked to fight in a war which our political leaders in Washington would not let them win." And most importantly, the castigation they received upon returning home was not from the World War II generation, but from the very elites in their age group who supposedly spoke for them.

Nine million men served in the military during the Vietnam War, three million of whom went to the Vietnam theater. Contrary to popular mythology, two-thirds of these were volunteers, and 73 percent of those who died were volunteers. While some attention has been paid recently to the plight of our prisoners of war, most of whom were pilots, there has been little recognition of how brutal the war was for those who fought it on the ground. Dropped onto the enemy's terrain 12,000 miles away from home, America's citizen-soldiers performed with a tenacity and quality that may never be truly understood. Those who believe the war was fought incompetently on a tactical level should consider Hanoi's recent admission that 1.4 million of its soldiers died on the battlefield, compared to 58,000 total U.S. dead. Those who believe that it was a "dirty little war" where the bombs did all the work might contemplate that it was the most costly war the U.S. Marine Corps has ever fought— five times as many dead as World War I, three times as many dead as in Korea, and more total killed and wounded than in all of World War II.

Significantly, these sacrifices were being made at a time the United States was deeply divided over our effort in Vietnam. The baby-boom generation had cracked apart along class lines as America's young men were making difficult, life-or-death choices about serving. The better academic institutions became focal points for vitriolic protest against the war, with few of their graduates going into the military. Harvard College, which had lost 691 alumni in World War II, lost a total of 12 men in Vietnam from the classes of 1962 through 1972 combined. Those classes at Princeton lost six, at MIT two. The media turned ever-more hostile. And frequently the reward for a young man's having gone through the trauma of combat was to be greeted by his peers with studied indifference or outright hostility.

What is a hero? My heroes are the young men who faced the issues of war and possible death, and then weighed those concerns against obligations to their country. Citizen-soldiers who interrupted their personal and professional lives at their most formative stage, in the timeless phrase of the Confederate Memorial in Arlington National Cemetery, "not for fame or reward, not for place or for rank, but in simple obedience to duty, as they understood it." Who suffered loneliness, disease, and wounds with an often contagious élan. And who deserve a far better place in history than that now offered them by the so-called spokesmen of our so-called generation.

Mr. Brokaw, Mr. Matthews, Mr. Bennett, Mr. Spielberg, meet my Marines.

1969 was an odd year to be in Vietnam. Second only to 1968 in terms of American casualties, it was the year made famous by Hamburger Hill, as well as the gut-wrenching *Life* cover story showing the pictures of 242 Americans who had been killed in one average week of fighting. Back home, it was the year of Woodstock, and of numerous anti-war rallies that culminated in the Moratorium march on Washington. The My Lai massacre hit the papers and was seized upon by the anti-war movement as the emblematic moment of the war. Lyndon Johnson left Washington in utter humiliation. Richard Nixon entered the scene, destined for an even worse fate.

In the An Hoa Basin southwest of DaNang, the Fifth Marine Regiment was in its third year of continuous combat operations. Combat is an unpredictable and inexact environment, but we were well-led. As a rifle platoon and company commander, I served under a succession of three regimental commanders who had cut their teeth in World War II, and four different battalion commanders, three of whom had seen combat in Korea. The company commanders were typically captains on their second combat tour in Vietnam, or young first lieutenants like myself who were given companies after many months of "bush time" as platoon commanders in the Basin's tough and unforgiving environs.

The Basin was one of the most heavily contested areas in Vietnam, its torn, cratered earth offering every sort of wartime possibility. In the mountains just to the west, not far from the Ho Chi Minh Trail, the North Vietnamese Army operated an infantry division from an area called Base Area 112. In the valleys of the Basin, main-force Viet Cong battalions whose ranks were 80 percent North Vietnamese Army regulars moved against the Americans every day. Local Viet Cong units sniped and harassed. Ridge lines and paddy dikes were laced with sophisticated booby traps of every size, from a hand grenade to a 250-pound bomb. The villages sat in the rice paddies and tree lines like individual fortresses, criss-crossed with trenches and spider holes, their homes sporting bunkers capable of surviving direct hits from large-caliber artillery shells. The Viet Cong infrastructure was intricate and permeating. Except for the old and the very young, villagers who did not side with the Communists had either been killed or driven out to the government-controlled enclaves near DaNang.

In the rifle companies we spent the endless months patrolling ridge lines and villages and mountains, far away from any notion of tents, barbed wire, hot food, or electricity. Luxuries were limited to what would fit inside one's pack, which after a few "humps" usually boiled down to letter-writing material, towel, soap, toothbrush, poncho liner, and a small transistor radio.

We moved through the boiling heat with 60 pounds of weapons and gear, causing a typical Marine to drop 20 percent of his body weight while in the bush. When we stopped we dug chest-deep fighting holes and slit trenches for toilets. We slept on the ground under makeshift poncho hootches, and when it rained we usually took our hootches down because wet ponchos shined under illumination flares, making great targets. Sleep itself was fitful, never more than an hour or two at a stretch for months at a time as we mixed daytime patrolling with night-time ambushes, listening posts, foxhole duty, and radio watches. Ringworm, hookworm, malaria, and dysentery were common, as was trench foot when the monsoons came. Respite was rotating back to the mud-filled regimental combat base at An Hoa for four or five days, where rocket and mortar attacks were frequent and our troops manned defensive bunkers at night.

Which makes it kind of hard to get excited about tales of Woodstock, or camping at the Vineyard during summer break.

We had been told while in training that Marine officers in the rifle companies had an 85 percent probability of being killed or wounded, and the experience of "Dying Delta," as our company was known, bore that out. Of the officers in the bush when I arrived, our company commander was wounded, the weapons platoon commander was wounded, the first platoon commander was killed, the second platoon commander was wounded twice, and I, commanding the third platoon, was wounded twice. The enlisted troops in the rifle platoons fared no better. Two of my original three squad leaders were killed, the third shot in the stomach. My platoon sergeant was severely wounded, as was my right guide. By the time I left my platoon I had gone through six radio operators, five of them casualties.

These figures were hardly unique; in fact, they were typical. Many other units—for instance, those who fought the hill battles around Khe Sanh, or were with the famed Walking Dead of the Ninth Marine Regiment, or were in the battle for Hue City or at Dai Do—had it far worse. When I remember those days and the very young men who spent them with me, I am continually amazed, for these were mostly recent civilians barely out of high school, called up from the cities and the farms to do their year in Hell and then return. Visions haunt me every day, not of the nightmares of war but of the steady consistency with which my Marines faced their responsibilities, and of how uncomplaining most of them were in the face of constant danger. The salty, battle-hardened 20-year-olds teaching green 19-year-olds the intricate lessons of that hostile battlefield. The unerring skill of the young squad leaders as we moved through unfamiliar villages and weed-choked trails in the black of night. The quick certainty with which they moved when coming under enemy fire. Their sudden tenderness when a fellow Marine was wounded and needed help. Their willingness to risk their lives to save other Marines in peril. To this day it stuns me that their own countrymen have so completely missed the story of their service, lost in the bitter confusion of the war itself.

Like every military unit throughout history we had occasional laggards, cowards, and complainers. But in the aggregate these Marines were the finest people I have ever been around. It has been my privilege to keep up with many of them over the years since we all came home. One finds in them very little bitterness about the war in which they fought. The most common regret, almost to a man, is that they were not able to do more—for each other and for the people they came to help.

It would be redundant to say that I would trust my life to these men. Because I already have, in more ways than I can ever recount. I am alive today because of their quiet, unaffected heroism. Such valor epitomizes the conduct of Americans at war from the first days of our existence. That the boomer elites can canonize this sort of conduct in our fathers' generation while ignoring it in our own is more than simple oversight. It is a conscious, continuing travesty.

This piece first appeared in American Enterprise Institute (July/August 2000).

With so many of its living members veterans of the Vietnam War, the Legion of Valor is a partner in the commemoration of the 50th Anniversary of the Vietnam War. President Obama proclaimed this commemoration. And here's what the President said at the kickoff ceremony at The Vietnam Memorial Wall on May 25, 2012:

"And one of the most painful chapters in our history was Vietnam—most particularly, how we treated our troops who served there. You were often blamed for a war you didn't start, when you should have been commended for serving your country with valor. [Applause.] You were sometimes blamed for misdeeds of a few, when the honorable service of the many should have been praised. You came home and sometimes were denigrated, when you should have been celebrated. It was a national shame, a disgrace that should have never happened. And that's why here today we resolve that it will not happen again."

It seems more than appropriate then to highlight one of our distinguished members of the Legion of Valor and a Vietnam veteran by including his revised profile from our General Orders.

Born in St. Joseph, Missouri, James H. Webb, Jr., is a descendent of the Scots-Irish settlers who came to this country in the 18th century and became pioneers in the mountains of Southwest Virginia. He graduated from the Naval Academy in 1968, receiving the Superintendent's Award for outstanding leadership and a commission in the Marine Corps. First in his class of 243 at the Marine Corps Officers' Basic School in Quantico, Webb served with the Fifth Marine Regiment in Vietnam where, as a platoon and company commander in the infamous An Hoa basin, he was awarded the Navy Cross, the Silver Star, two Bronze Stars, and two Purple Hearts. He later served as a platoon commander and as an instructor in tactics and weapons at the Marine Corps Officer Candidates School and as a member of the Secretary of the Navy's immediate staff before leaving the Marine Corps in 1972.

Webb received his J.D. at Georgetown University in 1975. He served in the U.S. Congress as counsel to the House Committee on Veterans Affairs from 1977 to 1981. In 1982, he proposed and led the fight for including an African American soldier in the memorial statue that now graces the Vietnam Veterans Memorial on the National Mall. In 1984, he was appointed the inaugural Assistant Secretary of Defense for Reserve Affairs. In 1987, he became the first Naval Academy graduate to serve in the military and then become Secretary of the Navy.

In addition to his public service, Webb enjoyed a long career as a writer. He has authored ten books, including six best-selling novels, and has worked extensively as a screenwriter and producer in Hollywood. He taught literature at the Naval Academy as their first visiting writer, has traveled worldwide as a journalist, and earned an Emmy Award from the National Academy of Television Arts and Sciences for his PBS coverage of the U.S. Marines in Beirut. In 2004, Webb went into Afghanistan as a journalist, embedded with the U.S. military. He speaks Vietnamese and has done extensive pro bono work with the Vietnamese community dating from the late 1970s.

Jim Webb also served as the junior Senator from Virginia, launching his career there by introducing a GI Bill designed to provide veterans who have served since 9/11 a level of educational benefits identical to those received by the veterans of World War II. He is also an original co-sponsor of bills pertaining to new ethics rules, prescription drug pricing, the recommendations of the 9/11 Commission, stem cell research, energy/global warming, college affordability, and rebuilding the military.

Webb served on the following Committees: Foreign Relations, Joint Economic, Armed Services, and Veterans Affairs. In his first year in office, Webb's legislative priorities were guided by three themes on which he campaigned for the U.S. Senate: re-orienting America's national security posture, promoting economic fairness, and increasing government accountability.

He is the proud father of Amy, Jimmy, Sarah, Julia, Georgia and step-daughter Emily. He lives in Arlington, VA with his wife Hong Le Webb. He is also a proud Vietnam veteran and his contribution to this anthology shows how fervent he is about them.

THE CONTEXT OF COURAGE FOR INFANTRY IN VIETNAM

Lieutenant Colonel Barry D. Gasdek, USA Ret.,
Distinguished Service Cross

The "grunts," as they were affectionately called, not only reflected their closeness to mother earth as "ground pounders," the infantryman, but also the noises they made as they donned their 80-pound packs and walked for endless miles through the plains, jungles and highlands of Vietnam.

As I reflect back upon my experiences in Vietnam from 1967 to 1969 I think of the strong bonds and camaraderie that existed in my infantry outfit during that war. In a combat situation your survival depended on your or your fellow soldiers' reactions to situations as they present themselves, doing what they were trained to do. In many instances, actions went beyond what was expected, because in a firefight you either did what you were trained to do, or you probably didn't survive. Unfortunately, you were not usually given a second chance during an ambush or meeting engagement to ponder your options! Luck also had to be on your side.

Vietnam was unique from other wars in that there were actually no real defined friendly lines. The firebase you were in or your unit perimeter defense was usually the only secure or safe area you had. The rest of the real estate belonged to the enemy or "Charlie" (Viet Cong). This was especially true in I Corps between Chu Lai and Da Nang, north to the DMZ and east/west from the South China Sea to the Laotian border.

I was an Infantry Company Commander, D Company, and we operated as an independent unit throughout this area of operation (AO). We were part of the 4th Battalion, 21st Infantry, 11th Brigade, Americal Division, in the north of South Vietnam. It was imperative that infantry company personnel knew how to call in artillery fire, close air support, medical evacuations, and read a map with precision. Knowing where you were was obviously necessary to accomplish the above. Any of those skills at one time or another, could and probably did save your life or that of your men.

A typical day in combat consisted of some of the following prior to a tactical operation. You normally got briefed by the battalion operation and intelligence officer. The missions varied from searching all area or village to trying to make contact with either the local Viet Cong (VC) or North Vietnamese Army (NV A). We normally would break our company down into platoon-size elements and saturate an area looking for the enemy. We would move in a "cloverleaf" fashion with the company headquarters in the middle. This made for good control and was easily reinforced in case of contact with the enemy. We could easily consolidate if contact was made, and their force was much larger than ours.

These "search and destroy" operations many times were dry wells with little or no contact. War in Vietnam usually consisted of long periods of boredom occasionally overlaid by short or brief periods of extreme violence. You had to guard against complacency, because when you made contact with the enemy, you'd better be prepared. If not, your company/men would pay the price, usually in lives lost.

As one might imagine, with the thick vegetation, and many times, triple canopy jungle, you had to almost move in single file, with limited flank security.

Vietnam was a Company Commander's war because this size unit was large enough to sustain itself, yet small enough to operate in this type of environment. We would operate from a firebase and extend outward, sometimes on 35–45-day operations or missions. We would get resupplied by air, normally helicopters, every two or three days and get periodic intelligence updates either at our field location or get evacuated back to the headquarters firebase, get briefed and then back to the field positions. This way the company could continue the operations from day to day, remaining in the bush for longer periods of time.

The "point" or lead man was rotated every so often, as this was one of the most dangerous/tedious positions in the company. He was basically the "eyes and ears" of the lead element of the company. His survival and that of the unit often depended upon his skills, reaction, instincts and training. "Kill or be killed" was understood, and one's finger was never very far from the trigger. The same principle applied to "tunnel rats," soldiers who had to go into tunnels to search for the enemy. The 45 cal. pistol was the weapon of choice for this dangerous task. Usually a highly skilled and fearless soldier who enjoyed that kind of "rush," volunteered for this dangerous and potentially life-shortening duty.

Personal hygiene was important, not only for sanitary reasons, but to instill discipline in your unit. When you were engaged in a firefight, the more disciplined and trained you were, the less casualties you took. "Sweat in training saved lives on the battlefield!" How true that was!

General George Patton had it right when he said, "The idea of warfare was to have that poor SOB die for his country rather than you for yours." Unfortunately, it did not always work or turn out that way. Often aggressiveness paid dividends by surprising the enemy as to your intentions. In other cases it might bring on an ambush. The less the enemy knew about your tactics, the more successful you were in accomplishing your mission.

We would "dig in" every evening, call in artillery defensive fires, close to our position, in case we needed to adjust it, or got attacked. Shrapnel coming near your perimeter was not only an incentive for your unit to dig in, but also a deterrent to enemy attack at night. Ambush patrols were sent out nightly to guard routes into your location—an early warning system you could not afford to be without. This was not normally a popular duty, but necessary for security of the company perimeter. Ambushes using claymore mines, which shot out hundreds of ball bearings, proved to be very effective. One night when the company perimeter was about to be attacked, an North Vietnamese Army soldier was just about to pick up one of the claymores when it was detonated. All that was left of this individual was two hands in front of where the mine was located. All of my men carried at least one claymore mine.

Our infantry company seldom got attacked, unless in a chance meeting, as we were mobile and seldom in the same spot for more than one day.

Fixed installations/fire bases took the brunt of both Tet and counter-Tet operations. We watched many firebases under attack from miles away at our field locations. Units would ask where the rocket/mortar fire was coming from, and it was usually "sappers" (specially trained infiltration outfits of VC/NVA who got inside firebase perimeters to raise havoc). This was usually confirmed by enemy bodies in the area the next day. One morning we found 19 enemy bodies still in the wire. Ten motor pool vehicles had Chicom grenades in them, but none went off—it must have been a bad lot of grenades.

It became hard to establish strong friendships after having a few close friends killed. It was easier emotionally and psychologically to do your job to the best of your ability, be friendly, but not get too personally involved, other than taking care of the needs of your men. This may have been a mild form of Post-Traumatic Stress that enabled one to tolerate some of the rigors of combat. Leadership decisions you made many times were potential life and death decisions for you and your men. As a leader, you had to live with that decision and its outcome. Again, quality training enabled one to make the best decision possible.

River or stream crossings were great in that one could do their laundry, bathe, shave and be ready to go for a few more days on the other side or the river. This was of course, after you set up proper security. Uniform changes were made every 30–45 days whether you needed it or not! Underwear was seldom worn; and the thought of using a "flush toilet" again was only dreamed about! Basic survival needs ruled most of the time as an infantryman needed just food, water, and ammunition to survive. Maslow's hierarchy of needs was experienced in its most rudimentary form. Priority in your pack and what you carried was ammunition. Water and food last. Malaria pills (both the large and small ones) were taken daily, plus water purification pills (iodine tablets) were always used. Kool aid sent in "care packages" from the U.S.A., helped flavor the water masking the "nasty" iodine taste. Mosquito and leach repellent also helped make life in the jungle more bearable. Cigarette butts were also effective in removing leaches.

"Flak jackets" were available, but seldom used except for fire base duties. Extra weight carried in the jungle heat was not worth the effort unless it was ammunition. Nobody complained about carrying ammunition! New recruits were normally given a week or two to adapt to the extreme heat and humidity, before being "farmed out" to infantry units in the field. Sometimes this was not enough. One day, we had five new recruits sent to our company field location, and all five were medically evacuated out that evening for heat exhaustion. We were operating in 14-foot-high elephant grass and 119 degrees Fahrenheit. A tough environment to adapt to! I normally carried 28–20 round magazines of M-16 ammo, four clips of 45 caliber ammo, an M-16, a 45 caliber pistol, eight fragmentation grenades, five smoke grenades, compass, maps, poncho and poncho liner. Creature comfort items such as sleeping bags, air mattresses, and ground pads were not used because of weight and environment.

After "humping" (walking) all day, and each evening digging in, it was not too hard to fall asleep. You never fell in a "deep sleep," awakening at the least strange battlefield noise. I've slept, or "cat napped" on a pile of rocks, and in fox holes filled with water during the monsoons. During one three-week period of continuous monsoon rain, the war almost came to a halt, as neither we nor they could operate. Islands of land "jutted out" in a sea of water. It was an undeclared temporary truce! Resupply and "med-evacs" were also hampered by the monsoons. If the ceiling was too low, aircraft couldn't fly, nor could you get close tactical air support.

Well, what lessons were learned from this Vietnam infantryman's combat experience? First, effective training can save you or your men's lives—pure and simple. Respect, confidence, support and dependability on your fellow man could help save your life. Luck could even save your life. However, being at the wrong spot at the wrong time could prove to be very detrimental to your health and well-being. Lucky charms were not uncommon, and were often worn or carried. The belief that you would not be a casualty sometimes helped. Once your men had confidence in you as a leader, they would follow you anywhere. You became a key part of their extended family. Never expect your men to do something that you would not do yourself.

Be an assertive and proactive leader. Lead by example. This is the style of leadership I used and it served me well. Others used different styles that served them well.

A True Wyoming Hero

Barry was honored on June 21, 2012 in the United States Senate by the Honorable John Barrasso, Wyoming Senator, who entered the following words in the Congressional Record.

As Walter Lippmann once said, "The final test of a leader is that he leaves behind him in other men the conviction and the will to carry on." In his 49 years of service to our country, Barry's proven dedication and loyalty have touched hundreds of lives. From his extensive active duty service in the U.S. Army to his quest to aid the veterans of Wyoming, Mr. Gasdek is a true Wyoming hero.

Barry's path to Wyoming is similar to the historic trails that cross Wyoming's terrain. He started out in the east and eventually headed west. Barry showed the strong will and discipline of a natural-born leader. Growing up in Pennsylvania, he excelled as an athlete and a scholar. He earned the rank of Eagle Scout in high school. At the Indiana University of Pennsylvania, where he graduated with a B.S. in Education, he earned letters in three sports. All of these honors prepared him for a lifetime of service to his country.

He started his career serving in Germany, fresh from the ROTC program. Later, he was called to serve in Vietnam as the conflict there worsened. Barry proved himself in Vietnam. He flew observation missions and eventually returned for a second tour of duty. One of his commanders joked that he was like a magnet for drawing fire. Despite the adversity he faced, Barry met his challenges head-on and with fortitude. He continued his military service well after Vietnam by training to become a Ranger and a Pathfinder. He is a qualified leader, and his military achievements reflect his success. He was awarded the Distinguished Service Cross, Silver Star, five Bronze Stars, two Purple Hearts, and the Soldier's Medal in addition to other military awards.

He retired from the Army after serving a tour as a professor of military science at the University of Wyoming but Barry knew his mission in Wyoming had not been completed. This time, he took up the banner to fight for veterans' issues serving as the veterans service officer for the Wyoming Veterans Commission for twelve years. His goal was to support the state's current veterans while teaching the next generation about the important sacrifices our Armed Forces make each and every day. He also serves on the UW Veterans Task Force, and as an Army Reserve Ambassador.

Barry Gasdek has devoted his entire life to serving his country, his brothers in arms, and the people of Wyoming. He is a fighter, a mentor, a teacher, and a good man. He embodies the cowboy ethics and what it means to be a citizen of Wyoming. It is certain that the legacy of his leadership will inspire new generations of brave soldiers. On behalf of the State of Wyoming and the United States of America, I thank Barry for his service. His boots will be hard to fill.

This piece appeared in the Legion of Valor General Orders.

BATTLE AT CAMP A SHAU 1966

Bennie G. Adkins, USA, Medal of Honor

Command Sergeant Major Bennie G. Adkins distinguished himself during 38 hours of close-combat fighting against enemy forces, March 9–12, 1966. At that time, then-Sergeant First Class Adkins was serving as an Intelligence Sergeant with Detachment A-102, 5th Special Forces Group, 1st Special Forces at Camp A Shau, in the Republic of Vietnam.

At the time of action, Sergeant Adkins and nine other U.S. Army Special Forces Soldiers were based at Camp A Shau, a Special Forces camp positioned to observe and interdict enemy infiltration into South Vietnam from the north. Camp A Shau was located in the northern part of the country, in the isolated A Shau Valley, which bordered Laos and was separated from the nearest friendly forces by approximately fifty kilometers of dense jungle-covered mountains. The triangular camp was fortified with barbed wire defenses, with an airstrip located just outside its perimeter.

In addition to the 10 U.S. Army Special Forces Soldiers manning Camp A Shau, there were six Vietnamese Special Forces, (LLDB) and 210 Vietnamese Civilian Irregular Defense Group (CIDG). In the days leading up to the attack on March 9, two North Vietnamese defectors warned Adkins' camp of an imminent assault by enemy forces. And so in preparation, Camp A Shau was reinforced with seven additional U.S. Special Forces personnel, 149 additional CIDG (Nung) troops, and nine interpreters.

At 3:50 a.m., on the morning of March 9, Special Forces Detachment A-102 at Camp A Shau was subjected to a full-scale assault by an estimated two reinforced North Vietnamese regular Army regiments equipped with mortars, rifles, antiaircraft guns and machine guns. The battle opened with a mortar barrage and small-arms fire, which continued throughout the night, until 4 a.m., March 10, when the enemy forces assaulted the camp in waves.

On the onset of the first day's attack, Adkins awoke and ran through intense enemy fire to man the American mortar position, which was adjacent to the team house. Adkins continued to man the position despite the position taking direct mortar hits that wounded him and killed several other defenders at his position.

Upon learning that two Americans were killed, and several Americans and Vietnamese were injured in the initial volley, Adkins temporarily turned the mortar over to another soldier and ran through a hail of exploding mortar rounds to a trench in the center of camp, where the wounded and dying were pinned down. Through the morning of March 9, Adkins would provide aid, drag the seriously injured to safety, and recover the remains of dead American and Vietnamese personnel. With disregard for his own safety, Adkins repeatedly exposed himself to sniper and mortar fire, while moving casualties to the camp dispensary, and to a casualty collection point by the main gate, on the east wall.

Late in the morning of March 9, Adkins assembled a group to provide cover at the camp's airstrip, so that a severely wounded Master Sergeant Gibson could be evacuated. Ignoring any personal risk, Adkins assisted in loading Gibson onto the evacuation aircraft, while under fire, and then provided covering fire support during take-off.

During the evacuation, Adkins was again wounded.

Later that day, two helicopters attempted to land in the center of camp to evacuate the approximately 40 wounded defenders. The first helicopter was shot down and crashed. When the second helicopter landed, Adkins stood fully exposed to enemy fire, and loaded the wounded soldiers onto the helicopter, despite the enemy directing heavy machine gun and small-arms fire on the helicopter and evacuees.

Later that day, when a resupply air drop landed outside the camp perimeter, Adkins successfully maneuvered outside the camp walls to retrieve the much-needed supplies.

At approximately 4 a.m., March 10, the enemy launched their main attack against the south and east walls. When the assault began, Adkins was in the American mortar pit, and began firing illumination and high-explosive shells. During this action, Adkins' position took a direct hit that killed one, wounded two, knocked down the mortar and wounded him, yet again. With no regard for his injuries, Adkins restored the mortar and continued to fire.

Adkins drew more enemy fire to his position when covering a rescue mission on Camp A Shau's airstrip. U.S. Air Force A-1E pilot Major Dafford Myers, along with Major Fisher and one other A-1E flight, had been engaged in strafing the enemy at the south and east walls, when Myers' plane caught fire. Myers was forced to make a crash landing on the airstrip. At this time, Adkins increased his volume of fire onto the enemy, drawing their attention onto his own position so that Fisher could safely land and pull the wounded Myers from the runway. Twice, enemy fire struck the American mortar pit and literally blew Adkins into the air, killing and wounded several others at his position. However, the rescue was successfully completed, and Fisher later received the Medal of Honor for his daring action.

Since the start of the March 10 assault, Adkins' position had been hit a total five times—killing four and wounding several others, including Adkins. By 6:30 a.m., Adkins was the only soldier left firing in the camp.

When all the mortar rounds were expended, Adkins manned a recoilless rifle and turned his attention to a break in the south camp wall, only 30 meters from his position, where enemy was infilling to assault the American mortar position. From his position facing the wall break, Adkins inflicted heavy casualties on the enemy and stalled their attempts to overrun the camp. At this time, Adkins was again wounded, when his recoilless rifle took a direct hit.

The enemy had broken into the camp in strength, and the remaining defenders were forced to withdraw to the north wall. During the withdrawal, some joined Adkins in the mortar pit. The defenders in the pit continued to take fire until they exhausted their supply of hand grenades. In time, almost all the defenders in the pit were dead or wounded, with no relent in the enemy assault.

Out of ammunition and with only an M-16 rifle to resist the enemy, Adkins led the remaining defenders to an American communications bunker, in which several Americans were attempting to fight off a company-sized assault through the south gate, and over the wall. Twice, Adkins and his fellow defenders in the bunker succeeded in repulsing the enemy assault on their position. Throughout, Adkins provided medical care to the survivors and coordinated for air support with aircraft overhead.

By about noon, on March 10, the enemy controlled all of the camp except for the American communications bunker, which was held by Adkins and the group at the north wall. The remaining enemy forces launched several unsuccessful counterattacks, but were stopped by Adkins and his team.

His ammunition supply exhausted, Adkins braved intense enemy fire to return to the desolated mortar pit, gathering vital ammunition and evading fire, while returning to the bunker. The situation at Camp A Shau grew dire enough that supporting aircraft were instructed to bomb the camp itself, sparing only the portions held by the remaining defenders.

At about 5 p.m., on March 10, the remaining personnel at the communications bunker were ordered to destroy all communications, equipment and signal operating instructions (radio codebook), and to provide cover for an attempted helicopter evacuation of remaining defenders. Crossing the camp to reach the north wall exposed Adkins and his team to additional enemy fire once more.

Once at the north wall, Adkins and several remaining defenders braved enemy fire in a 350-meter rush to the landing zone, carrying other wounded men. They arrived at the landing zone only to find that the last helicopter had departed moments earlier.

Adkins began to organize and rally the remaining Vietnamese into a patrol, and began an escape by foot through the jungle. The patrol evaded pursuit and continued their escape throughout the night, stopping only for a two-hour rest. Late in the afternoon on March 11, Adkins and his patrol were able to make radio contact with rescue helicopters for another attempted evacuation. Although the group was able to board a rescue helicopter, it was destroyed by enemy machine-gun fire before takeoff. The group replenished their supplies and continued to flee through the jungle. They successfully evaded the enemy until they were rescued by helicopter, on the morning of March 12.

Camp A Shau was abandoned only after near-continuous close combat for 38 hours, without reinforcements, with limited resupply, and with limited air support, with the surviving defenders engaged in escape and evasion, for an additional 48 hours. Approximately 200 of the camp defenders were killed in action, with 100 wounded. The enemy suffered an estimated 500 to 800 casualties. It is estimated that Adkins killed between 135 and 175 of the enemy, while suffering 18 different wounds. His contribution to the defense of the camp and recovery of the survivors, at great risk to his own life, represents extraordinary heroism and selflessness, above and beyond the call of duty, and are in keeping with the highest traditions of the military service, and reflect great credit upon himself, Detachment A-102, 5th Special Forces Group, 1st Special Forces and the United States Army.

This account comes from official Army records.

Command Sergeant Major Bennie Adkins was drafted into the Army in 1956, at the age of 22, from Waurika, Oklahoma. He served with the Special Forces for more than 13 years deploying to the Republic of Vietnam for three non-consecutive tours between 1963 and December 1971.

His awards and decorations include the Medal of Honor, Distinguished Service Cross, Silver Star, Bronze Star Medal with one Bronze Oak Leaf Cluster and "V" Device, the Purple Heart with two Bronze Oak Leaf Clusters, the Republic of Vietnam Bravery Medal with Brass Star, and the Republic of Vietnam Gallantry Cross with Bronze Star.

He retired from the Army in 1978, earning both undergraduate and graduate degrees from Troy State University. He established Adkins Accounting Service, Inc., in Auburn, Alabama, serving as its CEO for 22 years. Adkins has been married to his wife, Mary, for 60 years, and together they have raised five children.

Bennie Adkins served as Commander, Legion of Valor of the United States of America, Inc., 2012–2013.

TAMING THE WILD WEST

William Frederick Cody, "Buffalo Bill," Medal of Honor

William Cody's Medal of Honor citation simply reads "Gallantry in Action." His heroism took place during the Indian War on April 26, 1872 while serving as a civilian scout for the 3rd Cavalry, U.S. Army at Platte River Nebraska. In 1917, an Army review board rescinded the award since Cody was not officially enlisted in the military service. An additional 910 personnel were also purged from the medal's rolls by this review board. Cody's award was reinstated in 1989 by Congress.

Cody was born in 1846 at Le Claire, Iowa and died in Denver, Colorado. He was buried on June 3, 1917 at Lookout Mountain, Golden, Colorado. His initial service to the military took place during the Civil War when he served as a scout for the Union 7th Kansas Cavalry. In 1868, he became chief of scouts for the 5th Cavalry and took part in 16 battles including Cheyenne's defeat at Summit Springs, Colorado in 1869. He later became famous as "Buffalo Bill" in his Wild West Show that toured the United States and Europe for many years.

He recounted some of his scouting and fighting in the West in his autobiography:

> Upon reaching Fort McPherson, I found that the Third Cavalry, commanded by General Reynolds, had arrived from Arizona, in which Territory they had been on duty for some time, and where they had acquired quite a reputation on account of their Indian fighting qualities. Shortly after my return, a small

party of Indians made a dash on McPherson station, about five miles from the fort, killing two or three men and running off quite a large number of horses. Captain Meinhold and Lieutenant Lawson with their company were ordered out to pursue and punish the Indians if possible.

I was the guide of the expedition and had an assistant, T. B. Omohundro, better known as "Texas Jack," and who was a scout at the post. Finding the trail, I followed it for two days, although it was difficult trailing because the red-skins had taken every possible precaution to conceal their tracks. On the second day Captain Meinhold went into camp on the South fork of the Loupe, at a point where the trail was badly scattered. Six men were detailed to accompany me on a scout in search of the camp of the fugitives.

We had gone but a short distance when we discovered Indians camped, not more than a mile away, with horses grazing nearby. They were only a small party, and I determined to charge upon them with my six men, rather than return to the command, because I feared they would see us as we went back and then they would get away from us entirely. I asked the men if they were willing to attempt it, and they replied that they would follow me wherever I would lead them. That was the kind of spirit that pleased me, and we immediately moved forward on the enemy, getting as close to them as possible without being I finally gave the signal to charge, and we dashed into the little camp with a yell. Five Indians sprang out of a willow tepee, and greeted us with a volley, and we returned the fire. I was riding Buckskin Joe, who with a few jumps brought me up to the tepee, followed by my men. We nearly ran over the Indians who were endeavoring to reach their horses on the opposite side of the creek.

Just as one was jumping the narrow stream a bullet from my old " Lucretia" overtook him. He never reached the other bank, but dropped dead in the water. Those of the Indians who were guarding the horses, seeing what was going on at the camp, came rushing to the rescue of their friends. I now counted thirteen braves, but as we had already disposed of two, we had only eleven to take care of. The odds were nearly two to one against us.

While the Indian re-enforcements were approaching the camp I jumped the creek with Buckskin Joe to meet them, expecting our party would follow me; but as they could not induce their horses to make the leap, I was the only one who got over. I ordered the sergeant to dismount his men, leaving one to hold the horses, and come over with the rest and help me drive the Indians off. Before they could do this, two mounted warriors closed in on me and were shooting at short range. I returned their fire and had the satisfaction of seeing one of them fall from his horse. At this moment I felt blood trickling down my forehead, and hastily running my hand through my hair I discovered that I had received a scalp wound. The Indian, who had shot me, was not more than ten yards away, and when he saw his partner tumble from his saddle he turned to run. By this time the soldiers had crossed the creek to assist me, and were blazing away at the other Indians. Urging Buckskin Joe forward, I was soon alongside of the chap who had wounded me, when raising myself in the stirrups I shot him through the head. The reports of our guns had been heard by Captain Meinhold, who at once started with his company up the creek to our aid, and when the remaining Indians, whom we were still fighting, saw these re-enforcements coming, they whirled their horses and fled; as their speeds were quite fresh they made their escape. However, we killed six out of the thirteen Indians, and captured most of their stolen stock.[1]

Notes

1   Buffalo Bill and William Lightfoot Visscher, *Buffalo Bill's Own Story of His Life and Deeds* (Homewood Press, c1917). Hathi Trust Digital Library.

HIT, HIT, AND HIT AGAIN

S. Donald Singelstad, Distinguished Service Cross

Don Singlestad, from Waseca, Minnesota, joined the National Guard in 1939 and was called to active duty at the start of WWII. Training took place at Fort Benning and Fort Dix prior to participating in the first U.S. invasion in Africa where he was captured by the Germans. He was placed in a French POW camp, where his sustenance was bread and wine. He was released when the French joined the Allied Forces in Europe.

Following this action in Africa, he was shipped to the British Isles where he trained the elite Army "American Rangers." Although it was a principle of the Rangers not to accept married men, they made an exception since Don previously worked with them in Africa. He was attached to the 34th "Red Bull" Division in General Patton's Fifth Army. "I met General Patton a couple of times," he recalled. "Patton had a lot of guts. You didn't see other generals on the front lines like he was."

While in Africa he was involved with taking "Hill 609," a German stronghold. Climbing the hill with hooks and ropes amid enemy grenades being tossed at him, he was wounded and later received the Purple Heart. He and his platoon were declared missing in action during this mission, but actually were on a 200-mile, 15-day trek around the mountains to finally reach American lines.

Don then participated in the first invasion of Italy at Salerno. He remembers, "Of 45 guys in my platoon, 11 were killed." He was among three divisions of about 45,000 troops heading for Naples. "The Germans put up a strong defense. We pushed through one foot at a time, including fighting through minefields." "For 45 to 50 days it was hit, hit, and hit again," he said, "but we kept going." For actions in Italy, he was awarded the Distinguished Service Cross, the Silver Star and the Gold Cross from Italy, one of only 67 awarded during WWII.

Don's Distinguished Service Cross award was for action on February 4, 1944 near Cairo Montenotte, Italy. After being attacked and cut off from his company by a large German force, Don fought his way free by moving toward and through the enemy, throwing hand grenades as he advanced. He killed at least six and wounded several others. When he used up his ammunition, he used his rifle as a club, knocking two Germans with his rifle butt. He then dove over a rock wall, seized another rifle and continued fighting until he reached his company command post.

His Silver Star was for action on July 17, 1944 in Italy when his company was forced to withdraw so that artillery fire could be laid on some enemy positions. Don remained behind, even with artillery shells landing within 50 yards of him, to prevent the Germans from enveloping their left flank. Don observed a five-man enemy demolition squad moving up to blow up the bridge where he was located. He, with only his carbine, wounded three of them and held them off until his company returned to assist him in saving the bridge and defeating the enemy.

According to a Minnesota National Guard article, Singlestad received "the Italian Military Medal of Valor Gold Cross, a citation equivalent to the Congressional Medal of Honor for his role in operating with partisans behind enemy lines. He is one of five persons and one of three Americans to be recognized with this honor during World War II."

After the war he spent a year getting his mind and body back in shape as a patient in the veteran hospital network. Once fully recovered, he and his wife purchased a restaurant in Litchfield, Minnesota and then a clothing store in Bloomington, Minnesota. On retirement he kept active in veteran and Legion of Valor activities. He died on November 18, 2010.

DAYS OF VALOR: AN INSIDE ACCOUNT OF THE BLOODIEST SIX MONTHS OF THE VIETNAM WAR

Robert L. Tonsetic

A Battle Joined

Ho Nai Village—0420–0530 Hours, January 31, 1968

Nick Schneider's squad was in the lead of 3rd Platoon as the Charlie Company grunts moved north from Ho Nai Village, Suddenly, Schneider signaled his men to halt. Schneider spotted three figures crossing the road from east to west in the darkness about fifty meters to his front. Unable to make out whether the men were members of the LRP team or villagers, Schneider and his men held their fire. The lead ACAV, Track 12, moving north along the road spotted the figures at the same time. Suddenly, someone popped a handheld flare, illuminating the area. Schneider's point man, Specialist Ken Barber, sized up the situation immediately. He saw three VC running toward a 12.75 machine gun positioned on the west side of the road. The men were carrying belts of 12.75 ammunition. Schneider yelled for Barber to take cover just as the alert 20-year-old Virginian blasted the trio with his 12-gauge pump-action shotgun, killing all three before they reached the gun. Dozens of AK-47 assault rifles and light machine guns opened fire on the Americans. The battle for Ho Nai village began in earnest.

Platoon Sergeant Wyers saw that Schneider's men were pinned down, and shouted to his other squad leaders to bring their men on line and lay down a base of fire. The lead ACAV also rolled forward to support

Schneider's embattled squad. Platoon Sergeant Jayne's 4th Platoon pressed forward on the east side of the road trying to stay on line with the column of ACAVs.

From the cupola of the lead ACAV, Sergeant Payne, the track commander, spotted a group of some 30 to 40 VC crossing the stream on the west side of the road, trying to flank Wyer's 3rd Platoon. He turned his .50 caliber machine gun on the group, mowing down a number of the enemy soldiers. The survivors rushed forward until they ran into an unexpected obstacle. Months earlier, Army engineers had dug a large gravel pit while constructing the road. The VC ran right into it until they reached a steep embankment about ten feet high. The lead ACAV turned all of its firepower on the trapped VC. Schneider and a couple of his men took advantage of the covering fire and rushed to the ACAVs to retrieve their rucksacks that contained more ammunition and grenades.

An enemy RPG team moved to a firing position next to a house on the east side of the road. The VC took aim at the lead ACAV as Sergeant Payne fired the vehicle's .50 caliber machine gun at their comrades trapped in the gravel pit. Nick Schneider had just retrieved his rucksack from the ACAV and was rushing back to his squad when the RPG struck the vehicle's right front side. The shaped charge burned into the engine compartment, setting the engine on fire and blowing the engine access panel into the side of the driver, Jim Choquette, the ACAV's M79 gunner, was standing in the rear of the troop compartment when the RPG struck the vehicle. Miraculously, shrapnel from the blast blew over Choquette's upper torso and head, missing him completely. He knew immediately, however, that the track was immobilized and that the fire in the engine compartment would soon reach the fuel lines and eventually the gas tank. He moved forward to assist the injured driver and other crewmembers off the vehicle.

Hobbling along on his sprained ankle, Specialist Bob Archibald took cover in a ditch that paralleled the road once the firing began. He and two other grunts who were in the ditch made their way to the burning ACAV to assist the cavalrymen off the vehicle. George Hauer, a medic attached to Charlie Company, patched up the injured men and sent them to the rear. John Payne, Jim Coquette, and Private First Class Jerry Byers, crewmembers on the disabled ACAV, elected to stay in the fight.

Under heavy fire, they ran to the second ACAV in the column and climbed aboard. Seconds later, two more RPGs slammed into the road, slightly damaging two ACAVs behind the lead track. The near misses caused only minor damage to the vehicles. A piece of shrapnel from the blasts nicked Nick Schneider as he ran back to his squad's position. The Cav platoon leader, Lieutenant Ehler, gave the order for the ACAVs to withdraw. Since the road was too narrow for the vehicles to turn around and it had ditches on both sides, the ACAV began to move in reverse.

Platoon Sergeant Cliff Jaynes and most of 4th Platoon took cover in the drainage ditch on the east side of the road. Jaynes spotted the hideout of the RPG team in the abandoned house and yelled to his M79 gunners to fire their 40mm grenades at it. Two of the grenades dropped on the thatched roof of the house, setting it ablaze, while the riflemen took aim and poured a heavy fire into the windows and doors.

Captain Tonsetic and his CP group were moving a few meters behind Wyer's 3rd Platoon when the fight broke out. His immediate concern was that his men were about to be flanked on the west side of the road. After spotting a group of VC dart behind a house to his left, Tonsetic and his senior RTO, Cliff Kaylor, fired a couple of shots at the men. Then the captain pulled two grenades from his web gear and lobbed them over the roof of the house. The grenades landed behind the house and exploded. The captain then turned his attention to the house across the road. Tonsetic saw members of his 4th Platoon firing at the house that was now ablaze, and he shouted to the gunner on the recoilless rifle track to finish the job with a 106mm round. The ACAV was in the process of backing up the road, and Tonsetic couldn't get the track commander's attention over the noise of the battle. It didn't matter. Seconds later, the burning house, containing a cache of enemy ammunition including a stockpile of B40 rockets, exploded in a fiery blast that sent shock waves in all directions.

LRP Team 37 was still concealed in their position about a kilometer to the north of the battle. Lieutenant Colonel Maus was unable to land in the area to extract his team. Enemy soldiers were still arriving in the area. AT 0445, the LRP team leader, Specialist Vincent, radioed to his CO to report a huge explosion to his south. The team saw smoke rising 200 to 300 feet in the air. He reported that several houses in the village had blown up. In fact, it was the house that Tonsetic's men had just destroyed. The patrol also spotted the flames and thick black smoke that engulfed the burning ACAV. Ammunition stored on the ACAV was cooking off, showering the surrounding area with sparks and shrapnel. It was like an awesome fireworks display. Orbiting overhead in his C&C ship, Lieutenant Colonel Maus radioed his patrol leader, Specialist Vincent, and told him to sit tight, telling him, "We will pull you out when you link up with the infantry." There was one problem. Vincent knew that the better part of a VC battalion was between his team and the embattled Charlie Company.

South of the LRP team's position, the battle continued to rage. Captain Tonsetic radioed for gunship support and was told a gunship team was en route. The heavy volume of enemy small arms, machine-gun, and 61mm mortar fire was taking its toll. The enemy held the high ground to his north, and continued to place accurate fire on Tonsetic's two platoons. Lieutenant Ehler's ACAVs had backed up the road out of RPG range, and were no longer able to provide covering fire for the infantrymen.

Platoon Sergeant Wyers' 3rd Platoon held the most exposed position. Wyers had been wounded and knew he could not hold his position for long. Sizing up the situation, he ordered Specialists Nick Schneider, Alonzo Shelton, Ken Barber, and Private First Class Dale Reidenga to lay down a base of fire to cover the platoon's withdrawal. The remainder of the platoon began to pull back with their wounded. In addition to Platoon Sergeant Wyers, Specialists Lester Brown, James Hayward, Terrance Miller, and Jerold Partch were all wounded, as were Privates First Class Ronald Bills and Mattlaw.

Fourth Platoon was in better shape than 3rd Platoon, but Jayne's unit had casualties as well. Sergeant Ronny Simons was wounded, and so were Specialists Frank Tesler and Michael Tuszl. Jaynes told his wounded sergeant to take the platoon's casualties back to the rear, while the remainder of 4th Platoon continued to protect the company's right flank with rifle and grenade fire. Most of Jaynes' men were firing from the drainage ditch that paralleled the road.

Captain Tonsetic and his CP group took cover in one of the houses, along with an M60 machine gunner from 3rd Platoon. He directed the machine gunner to cover the rear of the house from a window, while

Archibald covered a side window with M16. Archibald recalled that after squeezing off a few rounds, "My M16 jammed up tighter than a sealed drum … if my CO hadn't been there, I might have just smashed it." Specialist Cliff Kaylor and the captain worked the radios as enemy fire was directed at the house.

Sergeant Wyers radioed that his platoon was falling back and Tonsetic told Kaylor to call for artillery fire to cover the withdrawal. He had no idea of the whereabouts of his FO. While Kaylor radioed for artillery support, Tonsetic radioed the Warrior battalion TOC requesting gunship support and reinforcements. Lieutenant Colonel Mastoris informed Tonsetic that a gunship team was en route, and that a company from 2/3d Infantry was conducting a forced night march to reinforce Charlie Company. The Old Guard Company was reportedly five kilometers to the north and moving south to link up. Charlie Company's request for artillery support was denied. According to the artillery FDC (fire direction center), the impact area was too close to the village, and the rules of engagement did not allow for collateral damage.

Fighting On All Sides

Camp Frenzell-Jones—0500 Hours

As dawn broke on the first full day of the Tet Offensive, both the west and east perimeters of Camp Frenzell-Jones (the 199th Light Infantry Brigade's main base) were under heavy fire. UH-1C gunships from A Troop, 3/17th Air Cavalry, nicknamed the "Silver Spurs," engaged the VC positions. Streams of green tracer rounds arched skyward as the VC antiaircraft gunners tried to bring down the gunships. The gunships took multiple hits but managed to stay airborne, pounding the VC positions with rockets and machine-gun fire. Under murderous fire from the Silver Spur gunships, the VC were unable to mass their troops for a ground attack.

A 12.75mm machine gun firing from the hospital tower in Ho Nai village was scoring most of the hits on the gunships. The pilots radioed for assistance to silence the antiaircraft gun. Two howitzers from A Battery, 2/40th Artillery were moved to firing positions on the northeast side of the perimeter where they could engage the tower with direct fire. Lieutenant

Colonel Myer, the 2/40th commander, shouted directions to the gun crews manning the guns. The crews lowered the tubes to the direct-fire level, and began slamming 105mm rounds into the tower. The gun section scored six direct hits on the tower, silencing the enemy antiaircraft fire.

After knocking out the antiaircraft position, Lieutenant Colonel Myer was informed that the 195th Assault Helicopter Company pad and the II Field Force Headquarters area were taking heavy fire from a densely overgrown area east of their perimeter. The artillery commander responded, displacing a howitzer section to that threatened area. The howitzer was towed by truck to a firing position near the 12th Aviation Group helipad, where it was soon in action. The howitzer crew zeroed in on the target area with three white phosphorus rounds. The gunners then followed up with 20 HE rounds, and a beehive round for good measure. The enemy fire ceased. Days later, an engineer unit that was clearing away the brush from the area found 18 mangled enemy bodies.

While Lieutenant Colonel Meyer's howitzers blasted away at the VC, Colonel Davison contacted the II Field Force Commander requesting reinforcements for his embattled brigade. At 0500 hours, the 199th LIB was given operational control of a task force consisting of a portion of the battalion headquarters and Companies A and C of the 2/47th Infantry. Colonel Davison directed the force to link up with the brigade's embattled Ready Reaction Force north of Ho Nai village. A 2/47th mechanized task force under the command of Major Bill Jones was more than 12 kilometers away when it received the order to reinforce the 4/12th company. The enemy, not the distance, was the problem. In order to link up with Captain Tonsetic's force at Ho Nai village, Major Jones' task force had to move west of Highway 15 to an intersection with Highway 316, and then turn northeast and fight its way to the intersection with Highway 1. The mech infantry column then had to move east through Ho Nai village until it reached Charlie Company position on the north–south engineer road. There were enemy snipers and likely ambush sites all along the route.

Ho Hai Village—0530–0630 Hours

First Sergeant George Holmes began moving Charlie Company's wounded back toward the center of Ho Nai village. When he reached a schoolyard that was large enough to land a medevac chopper, he set up a perimeter using the walking wounded, and called Long Binh dust-off control. Holmes had two things on his mind. First, he wanted to medevac the most serious of the wounded. He was also concerned that his CO, Captain Tonsetic, his RTOs (radio telephone operators), and a few grunts were cut off from the remainder of the company. Holmes knew from the radio traffic that the "Old Man" was in a forward position directing gunship strikes on the enemy battalion. When the gunships had to leave station to rearm and refuel, Holmes knew that the captain's position would likely be overrun.

Dust-off 19 arrived on station over Ho Nai village at 0538 hours. A VC antiaircraft machine gun opened up on the helicopter with 12.75mm fire. Braving the heavy machine-gun fire, the pilot tried to land at the LZ in the schoolyard, but was driven off on its first two attempts after sustaining several hits. Undaunted, the WO pilot landed on the small LZ on his third attempt. Amid a whirlwind of dust and smoke kicked up by the chopper's rotor blades, three wounded Charlie Company grunts and four Cav troopers were loaded onto the UH-1H. At 0605, the dust-off ship lifted off and flew toward the 93d Evacuation Hospital at Long Binh. Four wounded grunts from Charlie Company opted to stay and fight it out with the company.

From his forward position, Captain Tonsetic continued to direct the gunships on the enemy battalion less than 100 meters to his north. The burning ACAV illuminated the area, and Tonsetic could clearly see the VC as they were cut down by machine-gun and rocket fire from the gunships. A few 3rd Platoon grunts dashed by the door of the house where the captain stood directing the strikes. Figuring that none of his men were forward of his position, Tonsetic began to direct the strikes closer to his own position. He told the gunship team leader to plaster the area around the burning ACAV that was about thirty meters away from the house where his CP group had taken cover. The Captain was not aware that Platoon Sergeant Jaynes and few men from 4th Platoon were still providing covering fire for the command group from a drainage ditch across the road. Jaynes' men spotted several VC rushing toward the house where Tonsetic and his RTOs were holed up, and cut them down with M16 fire.

When First Sergeant Holmes saw the dust-off ship lift off, he grabbed a squad from 3rd Platoon and headed north through the village to find his CO. Holmes and his squad crept forwar to a position about twenty meters from the house where the CP group was set up. He shouted to his CO to withdraw toward his position: "You've got to fall back. The rest of the Company is back up the road. We'll provide covering fire."

Since the gunships were running low on ammunition, Tonsetic decided his CP group had better make a break for it. One by one, the RTOs, machine gunner, and the captain sprinted out the doorway toward Holmes' position, while the rifle squad accompanying the First Sergeant laid down a base of covering fire. Once Jaynes saw that Captain Tonsetic and his men had made it out of the house, he began pulling back toward the company position at the juncture of the engineer road and Highway 1 in the village. Dawn began to break over the smoke-covered battlefield.

When Captain Tonsetic and his RTOs arrived at the road junction where his men had set up a perimeter, he assessed the situation. Of the original eight ACAVs, one was destroyed and two were damaged. The 106mm ACAV was positioned to cover the engineer road leading north out of the village, while the undamaged tracks were positioned in a herringbone pattern along Highway 1. The Captain asked his First Sergeant how many men were still able to fight. Holmes replied that there were 30 men in the two platoons, including four who were slightly wounded. The Captain knew that there was a Company from the 2/3d Infantry somewhere to his north, and that a 9th Division mech outfit was on the road headed for his location, but he didn't know how long it would take for either of the reinforcing units to arrive. He knew that the VC battalion to his north was not going to sit and wait. He had to keep the pressure on, or the enemy would regain the initiative.

Captain Tonsetic decided to attack the enemy dug in on the high ground to his north. With gunship support, he hoped to gain a foothold on the high ground. Then he would hopefully be reinforced. The Captain ordered the Cav platoon leader to secure the road junction with his ACAVs. The 106mm recoilless rifle track was positioned facing north on the engineer road to support the attack. The signal for Charlie Company's infantrymen to move out was a blast from the

106mm Recoilless rifle aimed straight down the road. Third Platoon again took the west side of the road while 4th Platoon moved out on the east side. Resistance was light until the grunts arrived in the vicinity of the destroyed ACAV.

As the Charlie Company grunts approached the burned-out ACAV, enemy 61mm mortars opened fire from the high ground to the north. Some rounds fell short into the stream bed, but one detonated in the branches of a tall tree that grew next to the road, showering the area with shrapnel. Scanning the ridgeline, Captain Tonsetic spotted the enemy mortar crews dropping rounds into their tubes, and shouted to Platoon Sergeant Jaynes to take them out with M79 fire. Jaynes' grenadiers, all experts with high-trajectory fire, lobbed round after round of 40mm grenades at the enemy mortars, destroying the position.

Platoon Sergeant Wyers' 3rd Platoon made good progress on the west side of the road until an enemy squad concealed in a patch of brush south of the streambed opened fire with light machine gun and AK-47s. Wyers men hit the dirt and returned fire, Private First Class Alfred Lewis, a 21-year-old from Detroit, and 20-year-old Mike Raugh, a native New Yorker and new replacement, jumped into the ditch that paralleled the road. Standing upright in the ditch, Lewis fired several 40mm grenades from his M79 toward the enemy position. From the ditch, Lewis couldn't tell if his grenades hit their target. After telling Mike Raugh to stay put, Lewis crawled forward several feet, then crept out of the ditch. He made his way up a gentle slope until he was silhouetted against the skyline. The VC machine gun opened up with a long burst that was answered by a volley of M16 fire from a group of 3rd Platoon riflemen. Lewis, who was caught in the crossfire between his own men and the VC, was shot.

Several members of 3rd Platoon crawled forward to pull Lewis to safety but he died before they reached him. Continuing on, the 3rd Platoon grunts engaged the enemy squad with hand grenades and M16 fire, killing eight and capturing a light machine gun and several AK-47 rifles. The 3rd Platoon was then taken under fire from the enemy-held ridgeline north of the stream. Specialist Byrd took a round through the cheek that shattered his jaw and knocked out several teeth. Bleeding profusely, he stumbled to the rear, assisted by the platoon medic, George Hauer. The 3rd Platoon's advance was stalled by the heavy volume of enemy fire.

Captain Tonsetic was standing beside the burned-out ACAV hulk directing a gunship team when an enemy soldier armed with a machine pistol jumped out of the brush fifteen meters away, and fired a burst at the captain and his RTOs. Sharp pings of bullets against the armored hull of the ACAV sent Tonsetic, his commo Sergeant Larry Abel, and his RTO Cliff Kaylor diving for cover. The intrepid VC then dashed for the cover of a culvert that ran beneath the road. Several Charlie Company grunts fired at the fleeing VC, but missed as he dove into the culvert opening. The artillery FO, Lieutenant Tillotson, and his recon sergeant were closest to the culvert. The pair moved forward and the FO pulled the pin from a hand grenade and tossed it toward the culvert opening before hitting the dirt. The grenade bounced off the rim of the culvert into some weeds. The artillery lieutenant thought that the grenade was a dud. As he moved his body to the push-up position to have a look, the grenade exploded. A small piece of shrapnel tore into his right shoulder.

Moments later, the trapped VC emerged from the culvert on the west side of the road and sprinted for a vine-covered embankment, firing his machine pistol as he ran. Two men from 3rd Platoon blasted the VC's hiding place with their M16s and followed up with hand grenades. The first grenade detonated and blew the upper half of the man's torso out of the brush. Then a second grenade exploded and the remainder of the body was blown out of the brush.

The close combat continued as the Charlie Company grunts tried to cross the streambed. Their advance was stalled by the heavy fire coming from the high ground to their north. As his gunship support departed to rearm and refuel, Captain Tonsetic realized that his out-numbered and outgunned platoons could not seize the high ground by themselves. He decided to pull back toward the village and await the arrival of reinforcements.

Ho Nai Village—0800–1400 Hours

After fighting their way up Highway 316 past the main gate of Camp Frenzell-Jones, Major Jones' 2/47th task force turned east on Highway 1 and rumbled through Ho Nai village. The improvised unit, dubbed Task Force (TF) Panther, included Alpha Company and elements of the battalion headquarters company.

As TF Panther sped through the village, enemy snipers took aim at the M113A1s and their crews. Specialist Russ Vibberts from the 2/47th Scout Platoon was driving the lead vehicle, taking his orders from Major Jones, who rode in the commander's cupola. Eleven M113A1s carrying Alpha Company's infantrymen followed behind the command track in column formation. When Major Jones learned that the rear of this column was taking heavy sniper fire, he ordered Vibberts to pick up speed. As Vibberts pressed the accelerator to the floor, he saw a tall first sergeant on the road waving for him to stop. A platoon of ACAVs were parked along the road in a herringbone pattern.

Major Jones' command track sped past First Sergeant Holmes, who had to jump out of its path to avoid being run over. The column rolled on for another kilometer before the Commander realized that the First Sergeant had been trying to direct him to Charlie Company's location.

The 2/47th column then rolled to a halt and reversed direction, speeding back to Holmes' position at the road junction. First Sergeant Holmes told the major that Charlie Company was in heavy contact some three hundred meters north on the engineer road. Major Jones ordered his infantrymen to dismount and follow First Sergeant Holmes up the road followed by the M113s. The odds were now turning in the Americans' favor.

The battalion of the VC 275th Regiment had been stopped in its tracks by Captain Tonsetic's Charlie Company. The enemy battalion had been badly battered by almost constant gunship strikes and small-arms fire. Its lead elements that engaged Charlie Company during the night were for the most part destroyed or taken prisoner. The bodies of more than 50 VC were strewn around the gravel pit and streambed. The ridgeline to the north was also strewn with enemy dead and wounded. Some VC took advantage of the opportunity to flee into the surrounding jungle when the gunship teams departed to rearm and refuel, but the diehards remained.

A number of the fleeing enemy soldiers ran right into Specialist Vincent's LRP team. The LRPs killed eleven, but three members of Vincent's team were wounded in the clashes. Lieutenant Colonel Maus decided to distract the team. He knew their situation was precarious; they were running low on ammo. In full view of the enemy, he ordered his C&C ship to land and pick up the team. Amid a hail of gunfire, the

LRPs rushed toward the helicopter with their wounded. Seconds later the pilot pulled pitch and took off as the door gunners opened up on the VC below. Lieutenant Colonel Maus was awarded the Distinguished Service Cross for his role in the battle, and Specialist Vincent was awarded the Silver Star. The LRP team had provided critical early warning of the 275th Regimental attack on Long Binh, and triggered the US response.

The remainder of the enemy battalion, many of who were wounded, still held the ridgeline that ran northwest to northeast some 1,500 meters north of the village. A US rifle company from 2/3d Infantry had established a blocking position 1,200 meters to the north astride the engineer road, closing that escape route. The enemy were left with two choices: fight to the death or surrender. The majority chose the former option.

Major Jones, the TF Panther commander, briefed Captain Tonsetic and his Alpha Company commander on a plan of attack. He instructed Captain Tonsetic to attack northward with his two platoons of light infantry on the west side of the road while Alpha Company's mechanized infantrymen would attack on the east side. During the first phase of the attack, infantrymen from both units had to cross the streambed and seize the high ground to the north. They would then continue the attack up a gentler slope to rout the dug-in enemy from their positions. Major Jones would then lead the M113A1s across the culvert and up onto the high ground to assist in the final phase of the attack.

The attack jumped off around 0830 hours. Alpha Company drew the tougher assignment. The enemy strongpoint on the ridgeline was in a small cemetery east of the road. It was not well maintained. Knee-high bushes and weeds grew between the graves and positions dug by the enemy during the night. West of the road, the enemy positions were spread farther apart, and several had sustained direct hits during the gunship strikes. However, the diehard defenders were still capable of putting out a heavy volume of automatic weapons fire.

The Charlie Company grunts maintained a steady pace as they crossed the stream, climbed its bank and began to move uphill. Enemy positons were taken out using fire and movement, usually ending with a hand grenade tossed into the enemy foxhole. Alpha Company also crossed the stream quickly and began to sweep northward into the cemetery, killing 13 VC and capturing a number of others. However, the mech infantrymen missed several well-concealed enemy positions. As the attack continue, the VC who were bypassed began to pop up from their holes and fire into Alpha Company's ranks from the rear. Three Alpha soldiers were killed before a lone infantryman from Charlie Company saw what was happening.

Specialist Bob Archibald, still limping badly on a sprained ankle, hobbled across the road to the Alpha Company sector where he engaged the enemy positions with hand grenades and blasts from his 12-gauge shotgun. Archibald was credited with killing 12 diehard VC. It wasn't until after the battle that Archibald realized he'd sustained a minor flesh wound to his leg. Commenting on his role in the battle, Archibald wrote, "I was really pumped then. Later, I thought I might just get a Bronze Star … then I forgot about it." The 21-year-old Californian knew his friend Al Lewis had been killed an hour earlier, but he had no thoughts about retributions when he attacked the enemy positions. He said, "I did what I thought I was supposed to do."

As mopping-up actions continued, Major Jones led his tracked vehicles forward. After the tracks crossed the culvert they left the road and assisted the dismounted infantrymen in eliminating additional enemy positions. It was slow and dangerous work. As the light infantry and mech infantry companies swept northward for another 1,500 meters, they continued to flush the VC from their hiding places. Gunships from A Troop, 3/17th Cav cut the fleeing VC down in their tracks before they could reach the surrounding jungle. Thirteen prisoners were taken during the attack. Battlefield interrogation of these prisoners revealed that they were NVA fillers assigned to the 275th VC Regiment. North Vietnamese documents and currency found on their persons substantiated their identities. The POWs also told their interrogators that there were two additional VC battalions of the 275th Regiment in and around the Long Binh area.

As the 4/12th and 2/47th soldiers pushed closer toward the blocking position held by Bravo Company 2/3d Infantry, the few remaining enemy soldiers were caught in a deadly crossfire. As the attackers neared the blocking position, a Bravo Company soldier was shot and killed by a fleeing VC. At approximately 1400 hours, the troops from Charlie Company 4/12th and Alpha Company 2/47th Infantry reached the 2/3d Infantry blocking positions.

The enemy battalion was all but destroyed as a fighting force with its men either killed, captured or fleeing into the surrounding jungle. A captured sketch map found on a dead VC officer indicated that the main objective of their attack had been Camp Frenzell-Jones. The enemy battalion never got to launch its attack due to the early warning given by Specialist Vincent's LRP team, and the subsequent deployment of the 199th LIB's Ready Reaction Force.

Charlie Company had fought the VC battalion to a standstill, and the timely arrival of the 2/47th Infantry's TF Panther insured its total defeat.

Excerpts from Robert L. Tonsetic, Days of Valor: An Inside Account of the Bloodiest Six Months of the Vietnam War *(Philadelphia, PA: Casemate Publishers, 2007).*

Robert Tonsetic was born and raised in western Pennsylvania. After graduating from the University of Pittsburgh in 1964, he entered the Army as an infantry lieutenant. After completing Special Forces training, he deployed to Thailand as an advisor to Royal Thai Army Special Forces. During the Vietnam War, he served as a light infantry company commander and as an advisor to Vietnamese Ranger and Airborne units. He was awarded the Army Distinguished Service Cross and Silver Star for extraordinary heroism during the 1968 Tet and May Offensives. In 1970, he returned to Vietnam, and served as a senior advisor to South Vietnamese Ranger and Airborne battalions earning the Vietnamese Cross of Gallantry and the U.S. Bronze Star for Valor. He retired from the Army at the rank of Colonel after 27 years of service as an infantry and Special Forces officer. After completing his Doctorate in 1996, he taught at the graduate level at the University of Central Florida. In 2014, Colonel Tonsetic was inducted into the US Army Ranger Hall of Fame. He resided on Maryland's eastern shore where he continued to write until his death in June 2016.

TO SERVE, AND TO SACRIFICE

Jared C. Monti, USA, Medal of Honor

Remarks by President Obama at the Presentation of the Medal of Honor to Sergeant First Class Jared C. Monti, September 17, 2009.

Duty. Honor. Country. Service. Sacrifice. Heroism. These are words of weight. But as people—as a people and as a culture, we often invoke them lightly. We toss them around freely. But do we really grasp the meaning of these values? Do we truly understand the nature of these virtues? To serve, and to sacrifice. Jared Monti knew. The Monti family knows. And they know that the actions we honor today were not a passing moment of courage. They were the culmination of a life of character and commitment.

There was Jared's compassion. He was the kid at school who, upon seeing a student eating lunch alone, would walk over and befriend him. He was the teenager who cut down a spruce tree in his yard so a single mom in town would have a Christmas tree for her children. He even bought the ornaments and the presents. He was the soldier in Afghanistan who received care packages, including fresh clothes, and gave them away to Afghan children who needed them more.

There was Jared's perseverance. Cut from the high school basketball team, he came back the next year, and the next year, and the next year—three times—finally making varsity and outscoring some of the top players. Told he was too young for the military, he joined the National Guard's delayed entry program as a junior in high school.

And that summer, while other kids were at the beach, Jared was doing drills.

There was Jared's strength and skill—the championship wrestler and tri-athlete who went off to basic training, just 18 years old, and then served with distinction as a forward observer, with the heavy responsibility of calling in air strikes. He returned from his first tour in Afghanistan highly decorated, including a Bronze Star and Army Commendation Medal for valor.

And there was Jared's deep and abiding love for his fellow soldiers. Maybe it came from his mom, who was a nurse. Maybe it came from his dad, a teacher. Guided by the lessons he learned at home, Jared became the consummate NCO—the noncommissioned officer caring for his soldiers and teaching his troops. He called them his "boys." And although obviously he was still young himself, some of them called him "grandpa." (Laughter.)

Compassion. Perseverance. Strength. A love for his fellow soldiers. Those are the values that defined Jared Monti's life—and the values he displayed in the actions that we recognize here today.

It was June 21, 2006, in the remotest northeast of Afghanistan, near the border with Pakistan. Sergeant Monti was a team leader on a 16-man patrol. They'd been on the move for three days down dirt roads; sloshing through rivers; hiking up steep mountain trails, their heavy gear on their backs; moving at night and in the early morning to avoid the scorching 100-degree heat. Their mission: to keep watch on the valley down below in advance of an operation to clear the area of militants.

Those who were there remember that evening on the mountain—a rocky ridge, not much bigger than this room. Some were standing guard, knowing they had been spotted by a man in the valley. Some were passing out MREs and water. There was talk of home and plans for leave. Jared was overheard remembering his time serving in Korea. Then, just before dark, there was a shuffle of feet in the woods. And that's when the treeline exploded in a wall of fire.

One member of the patrol said it was "like thousands of rifles crack-ling." Bullets and heavy machine gunfire ricocheting across the rocks. Rocket-propelled grenades raining down. Fire so intense that weapons were shot right out of their hands. Within minutes, one soldier was killed; another was wounded. Everyone dove for cover. Behind a tree. A rock. A stone wall. This patrol of 16 men was facing a force of some

50 fighters. Outnumbered, the risk was real. They might be overrun. They might not make it out alive.

That's when Jared Monti did what he was trained to do. With the enemy advancing—so close they could hear their voices—he got on his radio and started calling in artillery. When the enemy tried to flank them, he grabbed a gun and drove them back. And when they came back again, he tossed a grenade and drove them back again. And when these American soldiers saw one of their own wounded, lying in the open, some 20 yards away, exposed to the approaching enemy—Jared Monti did something no amount of training can instill. His patrol leader said he'd go, but Jared said, "No, he is my soldier, I'm going to get him."

It was written long ago that "the bravest are surely those who have the clearest vision of what is before them, glory and danger alike, and yet, notwithstanding, go out to meet it." Jared Monti saw the danger before him. And he went out to meet it.

He handed off his radio. He tightened his chin strap. And with his men providing cover, Jared rose and started to run. Into all those incoming bullets. Into all those rockets. Upon seeing Jared, the enemy in the woods unleashed a firestorm. He moved low and fast, yard after yard, then dove behind a stone wall.

A moment later, he rose again. And again they fired everything they had at him, forcing him back. Faced with overwhelming enemy fire, Jared could have stayed where he was, behind that wall. But that was not the kind of soldier Jared Monti was. He embodied that creed all soldiers strive to meet: "I will always place the mission first. I will never accept defeat. I will never quit. I will never leave a fallen comrade." And so, for a third time, he rose. For a third time, he ran toward his fallen comrade. Said his patrol leader, it "was the bravest thing I had ever seen a soldier do."

They say it was a rocket-propelled grenade; that Jared made it within a few yards of his wounded soldier. They say that his final words, there on that ridge far from home, were of his faith and his family: "I've made peace with God. Tell my family that I love them."

And then, as the artillery that Jared had called in came down, the enemy fire slowed, then stopped. The patrol had defeated the attack. They had held on—but not without a price. By the end of the night, Jared and three others, including the soldier he died trying to save, had given their lives.

I'm told that Jared was a very humble guy; that he would have been uncomfortable with all this attention; that he'd say he was just doing his job; and that he'd want to share this moment with others who were there that day. And so, as Jared would have wanted, we also pay tribute to those who fell alongside him: Staff Sergeant Patrick Lybert. Private First Class Brian Bradbury. Staff Sergeant Heathe Craig.

And we honor all the soldiers he loved and who loved him back—among them noncommissioned officers who remind us why the Army has designated this "The Year of the NCO" in honor of all those sergeants who are the backbone of America's Army. They are Jared's friends and fellow soldiers watching this ceremony today in Afghanistan. They are the soldiers who this morning held their own ceremony on an Afghan mountain at the post that now bears his name—Combat Outpost Monti. And they are his "boys"—surviving members of Jared's patrol, from the 10th Mountain Division—who are here with us today. And I would ask them all to please stand. (Applause.)

Like Jared, these soldiers know the meaning of duty, and of honor, of country. Like Jared, they remind us all that the price of freedom is great. And by their deeds they challenge every American to ask this question: What we can do to be better citizens? What can we do to be worthy of such service and such sacrifice?

Sergeant First Class Jared C. Monti. In his proud hometown of Raynham, his name graces streets and scholarships. Across a grateful nation, it graces parks and military posts. From this day forward, it will grace the memorials to our Medal of Honor heroes. And this week, when Jared Monti would have celebrated his 34th birthday, we know that his name and legacy will live forever, and shine brightest, in the hearts of his family and friends who will love him always.

May God bless Jared Monti, and may He comfort the entire Monti family. And may God bless the United States of America. (Applause.)

The Official Narrative of the action for which Jared earned his award in Afghanistan may be found at http://www.army.mil/medalofhonor/monti/narrative.html

VIETNAM LETTERS

Daniel P. Garcia and General Barry R. McCaffrey, USA Ret., Distinguished Service Cross

Dear General McCaffrey

For many years I labored under the delusion that you had been killed in Vietnam after I returned. The one letter I received to this effect was obviously exaggerated and the discovery of your survival, let alone your achievements, induced a nearly metaphysical reaction within the darkest corners of my soul. When Joe Galloway finally pieced together the fact that we had known each other and as I fully grasped that after all these years I might actually speak to you again, I suddenly realized that to do so I would need to walk amid the wreckage in my own memory to clarify my thoughts and tell you what it meant to know that you are alive and well. Upon reflection, I further realized that to effectively communicate my thoughts to you, without being overcome or distracted by the rush of excitement or reawakened pain and confusion, I would need to write to you first. This then is my meager effort to relate back to you some of what we lived through together; what it meant to me—all told to you in a way that I would never have told you as a mere enlisted man in your company.

Speak Memory.

(Thank you, Mr. Nabakov.)

I remember that the 2–7th Cavalry left I Corps at the end of October and took up residence at a base camp 300 miles south in the flat, forested area on the Cambodian border. As President Johnson stopped the bombing of Cambodia on November 1, 1968, we were there to await the anticipated movement of NVA [North Vietnamese Army] troops from their now safe havens across the border. And they did come. I remember clearly the pitched battles and firefights the first week of November. I remember your predecessor, shot through the head and hauled by us back to our base camp. On that gray day as I was returning from the hospital to rejoin the outfit, we had lost 30 men without having encountered a single enemy soldier.

It was in this state that you came to us, our new "Amber Outlaw 6." I do not remember the exact date, but I can see the place and feel the silent mixture of apprehension and resentment masked by an outward apathy borne of fear and hardship upon our first meeting with you. You told us that at the first signs of danger you would call in artillery fire or gunships and that we would proceed with caution, not with recklessness. You made a point of coordinating our movements with support fire. We heard, we listened, but along with the rest of our innocence, faith in the words and promises of another commander had long since perished. But even among those of us in whom the beasts of death and survival were most ferocious, a spark of a single human frailty called hope was rekindled by your words.

As fate would have it, within a day or two you had a chance to prove that you were true to your word. And you were. Not long after you joined us, I remember talking to one of the platoon leaders. Those of us responsible for our platoons acknowledged that you were different from our previous leaders, that you seemed genuine. After we left the border we had a few skirmishes, or so it seems to me now, but after the intense fighting in early November we were okay until that day in December—the 16th or so. I remember very clearly that one or two platoons were scouting on recon. My platoon was in the lead and you were not far behind. I recall one of my machine gunners saw movement and blasted away, managing to scare away two chickens! We found a bunker; no one would go in. I went down and found the rotting corpses of two NVA soldiers, whom I shot, because I caught a flicker of rat movement from the corner of my eye. My shots burst the corrupt flesh. I recall that I was sick and disgusted and that I was in such a hurry to blow the bunker up that I barely gave anyone, including myself, time to scatter as I dropped the fragmentation grenade onto the bunker floor and fled. It was as though I could seal away the memory and disgust of that putrid bunker by burying its physical evidence.

One of my squad leaders rushed up and told me in the gravest tone that I needed to go ASAP to headquarters as something was up. I scrambled back and found you on two handsets talking to battalion command and someone else. You were dead serious. My RTO was in the cluster around you and he motioned to me. Over his frequency I heard the screams of the dying in Delta Company, and I knew at once you were ordering choppers for us to fly to their relief. They came shortly thereafter. I could see in their jerky, erratic flight movements that the pilots were scared, and it told me that we were headed to a place of death.

Alpha Company had gotten there first and, as I recall, the firing was sparse, but by the time we got there most of us knew that Delta Company had ceased to exist as a unit, that many had died and most of the others were wounded. As we moved to broaden their perimeter, we passed their remains: broken, bullet-hole-riddled equipment, a smashed helmet here, body parts there. We saw where the NVA had burned the tall grass and shot the men at close range. It was very hard. Some of my own men recognized a handkerchief or some other belonging from one of their friends and knew that he was alive no more. But we did not speak a single word to one another. I remember the fighting that followed over the next five days as we tried time and again to break out of the more or less surrounded position we were in. I remember an NVA charge at Alpha Company as I, and others from Bravo, came to their relief. I remember the bomb strikes sailing directly over our heads, exploding in front of our perimeter. Maybe I'm dreaming, but I recall your anger at the battalion commander who had failed to coordinate the artillery prep with the air assault so that the NVA had hours to set up their .50-caliber machine guns and mow down doomed and unsuspecting Delta Company. At least that is what I thought all these years.

I remember how on the third day or so of this engagement, the battalion commander showed up for an award ceremony in the middle of the perimeter. In fact, I think I received one—only to have it broken up by enemy rockets and mortars. It was folly and so we finally withdrew. I was the last one to leave the perimeter that last day near Christmas 1968, and as I left for the only time during my combat experience, I fired from the chopper as it left the ground a sort of signal of defiance mingled with respect for a grim, determined enemy who had taken much and given little.

During those five or six days, our casualties were comparatively light. Other units with us were not so lucky. I recall several wounded and a few men (ours or Alpha's?) lying on ponchos in a row while the snipers fired at them. I recall my rage at seeing them exposed and so I returned the fire above the heads of our own mortar crews, who were angry at me. But the sniper stopped and a chopper came. That chopper pilot was scared out of his wits. He left so hastily he whacked a tree branch while taking off. We watched as the chopper lurched downward, but his main rotor held and he was able to limp away noisily back to base. We heard he made it and we were relieved, for nothing seemed worse to us than dying on a medevac chopper after being hit. In the main, however, as danger lurked behind every tree, every rock, you protected us. By the end of that week, those of us who had any powers of observation left believed in you.

We fled to mud and elephant country and some place I recall with the bizarre name of LZ Odessa. Somehow an R&R allocation came down for me and I left for six or seven days in Manila. But no matter what I drank or what woman I was with, the sounds of gunfire and the screams of the wounded and dying were, by now, as with all of us, permanently locked inside my mind and heart.

When I came back, I remember a few slow days. Then we encountered "the complex." January 18, 1969. This day was the turning point in my life, and you played a key role in it. I have played out these events through the lens of my mind's eye many times. As I write this, I can feel the celluloid strip of memory protect each image on the screen of my consciousness.

It was late morning. It was hot, and the humidity was its normal low 90s. The second platoon was on point; my third platoon was next in line. The gunfire between Delta Company (again cursed with ill fortune) and the NVA, who apparently surrounded them, rumbled somewhere in the distance, vaguely in front of us. Our advance to relieve Delta had been slowed because of the growing sounds of machine-gun and automatic weapons fire. We could hear the flutter of gunships running sorties somewhere above the jungle's triple canopy.

Suddenly, machine-gun fire erupted in front of me. As I was third man in my column, I could see a few flashes and soldiers scrambling for cover. The second platoon leader had pulled his men up on a crude line, and I brought my platoon up alongside. Firing was heavy. Some of my men disappeared, hiding at the first sound of contact. The second platoon's men were firing weakly, as were mine. A period of perhaps 10 minutes ensued, although it seemed like hours, while both sides exchanged intense fire to little effect. I could not find all of my platoon as I tried vainly to direct fire toward several bunkers ahead of us which were pouring hundreds of rounds into our ranks.

After much arduous screaming, one grunt pointed to a bunker we had passed perhaps 25 yards behind, saying that some of my men were hiding there. I realized that without my missing soldiers, I was immobile and unable to direct any movement or fire. The second platoon had three or four men shot already, and they seemed desperate as they were receiving the sharpest fire and were closely pinned down. I took a chance and stood up, running to the rear, hoping to find my troops. As I ran, I could see bullets felling vines and perforating jungle leaves immediately next to and ahead of me. One bullet passed directly under my arm, slightly ripping my loose fatigue shirt.

The ground sloped slightly from the area where the main action was taking place. I reached the bunker and could see one figure in the half shadow below. I called twice but received no answer. Finally, I went down the steps and threatened to kill anyone who didn't come out. I didn't know if I meant it, for anger, adrenaline and desperation had driven me to the brink. Either way, I must have been convincing because five of my men quickly emerged, their faces filled with shame and fear. My own deep anger and contempt raged inside of me until I saw my best friend, whom I loved as a brother, come out. When I saw him, I thought my heart would break.

Our eyes met, but only for a moment as he hung his head. As he ran back to the line I could see his tears, and the anger that had built up inside me, its own separate force, suddenly burst. I ran back to the center of the line. Once again the firing was thick and my body was tiring. Machine-gun bullets were now close on me and I threw myself behind a large anthill. I can still see the brass-colored machine-gun slugs slamming into the anthill I lay behind, spinning over my head, their lead sparkling in the pockets of deep azure shining through the gaps in the layered trees. These slugs began to form a pile between my feet as I lay on my back.

Eventually, the bunker in front of me and I exchanged many rounds until I think I killed the gunner and his ammo bearer. After that, I was able to find my RTO. Thus, you, I, and the others were able to communicate. At your direction, the second platoon leader popped smoke on the far right of his side of the line, my men on the far left of ours. We were so close in contact we did not throw the smoke to mark our positions in front, but rather a bit behind our positions. The gunships you had called were near and they streaked in quickly. Their first burst of cannons and rockets crossed into our lines and two of my men were hit, including a private who lay next to me, his cheeks and face riddled with shrapnel. I hollered to you over the net and you helped redirect the fire almost at once, saving our lives. Some time passed and under the cover of gunships and bunker support, you rallied us to an immense old bomb crater to the left rear of our ragged line.

By this time, I had seven casualties, none fatal. One of my squad leaders had been shot in the thigh. You had told us that napalm was coming soon—to be dropped on our vacated positions. When it came, we were to flank the contact area and circle around to link up with Delta Company. As I had the squad leaders report to me the presence of each of their men, we suddenly realized that two were missing.

From my vantage point I could see two men alone and 50 yards away—a machine gunner and his ammo bearer. I knew that if they stayed there, they were doomed. Time was fleeting and I wasn't sure what to do, so I resigned myself to retrieving them. I remember crossing myself as I got up to go back. One of my squad leaders saw me leaving and pulled at me, begging me not to. But I was cold inside now. In a detached way, I figured I wouldn't make it, but I was so determined not to leave two of my men abandoned that I shrugged him off and ran back to the contact area.

As I got within 10 yards of their position, I stopped, screaming for them to move out while I gave them covering fire. I stood up and began shooting at the trees and bunkers in front of us. As they began to scramble out of their frozen supine positions, I could see a flicker of enemy movement. It was an RPG crew, and we shot at each other simultaneously. I'm certain I got them, and their rocket exploded into the soft earth almost directly between my legs. The explosion blew me straight up, twisted my rifle like a pretzel and lacerated my pistol belt with shrapnel. When I landed I knew I was hurt, but I didn't know how badly as, I suppose, I was in shock.

I reached out and begged for help from the machine-gun crew as they were running right at me. But I could see they were terrified. One soldier brushed my hand aside. They both glanced at me but continued running to the rally point in the bomb crater. I was now alone with no weapon. I pulled a piece of the rocket's tail fin out of my thigh with my fingers. I remember it was still hot, but it had not penetrated deep. Forty yards or so away I could see men from my own platoon watching me. I called out for help, but no one budged. By now the NVA had seen me move, so they began to open fire on me. Because the ground sloped a little where I was, their bullets seemed high. I was afraid, and felt more alone than I had ever felt in my whole life; more alone than I would ever feel again. I began to crawl back to the bomb crater.

I could see and feel the enemy's bullets whizzing over me and chewing up earth and foliage all around me. I could hear men screaming. But I did not know what or who they were screaming at. I have no idea how long it took me to crawl back; it could have been three minutes, maybe 10. It was a dark, pitiless eternity to me.

When I was a few yards away from the crater, I could hear our own machine guns firing to cover me. Finally my medic—the same one I had evicted from his hiding place in the bunker earlier—risked his life as he ran upright and dragged me in the rest of the way. As he quickly examined me, he shoved some ammonia up my nose and told me that I had shrapnel in my legs and hip and some superficial facial wounds but nothing serious. This woke me from my stupor and I found I could walk. Within the crater you were clearly in charge, your grim determination steadied me and gave me faith. Events moved quickly. We got set to move out. I distributed the remainder of my gear to my other men. Since I was walking fine and had no equipment other than bandoleers of M16 ammo, I agreed to be a human crutch for a sergeant, whose thigh was severely wounded by a machine-gun bullet.

Our exodus then started. Two lieutenants from other platoons (and maybe you, too) stood firing machine guns as we began to stream out, single file, on the far side of the crater. Small arms fire rattled everywhere. The din was incredible. As we exited the crater on our way to Delta Company, I could hear the jets overhead waiting to drop their deadly bombs. I was near the end of the column and could see and hear the "woosh-woosh" of the first napalm canisters as they began to fall toward the initial contact area. At the first explosion, we could feel the heat from the burst and the air seemed to be sucked out of us for a moment. We could see panic-stricken NVA soldiers vacate bunkers and start to parallel our movements maybe 15 to 20 feet away from us. We began a steady exchange of gunfire, but now we seemed to have the upper hand. We shot down several NVA soldiers during this retreat.

Finally, as dusk was settling in, you agreed to let me come in on the last chopper with some of the other ambulatory wounded. Only one chopper could land in the tiny LZ we had hacked out of the forest and it was a near-vertical descent and ascent for the choppers, making them a great target. I was unsure of whether I should leave, but I was very tired. As my chopper lifted upward, I saw another sight still seared in my mind. There, on a scarred sloping hillside littered with fallen timber, debris and a few enemy corpses, 150 or so American infantrymen had set up a perimeter awaiting the next contact. The smell of cordite and gunpowder choked the humid air, and a cloud of white and black gunpowder smoke seemed to linger over the whole area. The earth, denuded now of foliage from the intense combat, was a pocket of brown surrounded by a forest wall of green. No animal or insect noises were apparent. Every minute a tracer round or two was shot aimlessly at our perimeter by hidden NVA snipers. As the chopper I boarded moved higher, the small circle of men, their dirty faces and sweat-matted fatigues became less visible, then smaller and smaller while the impenetrable jungle and forest around them grew. The scene reminded me of something ... one of Bosch's visions of hell. That picture in the An Loc forest became the embodiment of hell to me.

We finally reached our base camp and went to the MASH ward, I and six others from B Company, 2–7th. We waited a long time while the doctors were feverishly operating on what looked like an NVA soldier. Later we were treated, released and sent, all seven of us, to a tent with a wood floor and canvas cots—luxury! It was apparently next to the officers' tent. Even in my enervated state, my sleep was racked with tormented images. I could hear conspiratorial whispering somewhere in my dream. Some animal instinct shook me awake. I bellowed with all my might for the men in my tent to get out, and pushed the last two down the steps and into the dirt outside just as the grenade exploded inside, ripping the tent apart. I found I had landed near the open urine pits and I vomited hard. It was as if by vomiting, I could purge my body and soul from the nightmare this had become.

By morning I had resolved to return to the unit even though my wounds were not healed. I figured I'd rather die fighting the NVA than stay behind and be fragged.

I came back to our company sometime that afternoon. By then our unit had discovered that the NVA had been protecting the evacuation of a huge underground hospital complex that we had inadvertently stumbled upon. The enemy had withdrawn; the crises had quietly evaporated. You and I spoke that evening. You told me that I was being put in for a Silver Star. It was then or perhaps a little later—but I think then—that you asked me to stay, offering me a battlefield commission. Could you possibly remember this conversation? I do because it created an immense conflict within me. I had long since ceased caring about my physical safety. In my own rough way I was dedicated to my men, and I was, for the first time in my life, being told by an adult male, whom I admired that I was needed. Someone needed me.

But the events of the day before had taken away from me the last vestiges of strength. I feared what I would become if I stayed. I assumed I would die if I stayed. But it was not fear of anything that caused me to say no to you. Rather, it was that for the first time in months I suddenly found a will to live. The physical and emotional pain from my gunshot wounds in July 1968 no longer obscured my desire to live. And so I declined, and in doing so I did not tell you "no." I said, "I can't." You said you understood. During that conversation I remember looking at you closely and seeing your pain, your isolation, the humanity in your eyes and in the expression on your face. It was a powerful turning point in my life. I realized suddenly that our leader; a man we all respected, had simply become a human being to me, with all the strength and weaknesses of other human beings. It was there, in this moment, and through our other experiences, that great truths were revealed to me about the nature of leadership.

After this my memory becomes confused. I was wounded one more time in a small firefight and left shortly thereafter in early March 1969. Between the January 18th action and my departure, however, I remember that the other young platoon sergeants and I became increasingly worried about you. You seemed to be taking more personal risks. You were pushing yourself and, sometimes, us harder. It seemed to all of us that something had happened inside of you. We noticed because, you see, we cared very much about what happened to you.

One episode stands out—maybe it's distorted, maybe by now it's confused. We were in a dry creek bed. A small, flat clearing lay in front of us. On its far side, up near the treeline 25 yards away or so, was an enemy bunker, a high one that was clearly visible.

The memory is jumbled now. The second platoon leader is hit in the neck. We pour fire into the bunker; it falls silent. You begin to order some of us to move on the bunker. You change your mind. All of a sudden, you get up and charge the bunker holding only a pistol. We are all dumbfounded. I crawl out of the creek bed and stand ready to kill anything if you are shot. You reach the bunker. No one has fired. You throw a smoke grenade in the bunker. You go inside! Four or five others and I start running toward the bunker. We are all afraid for you. You emerge from the smoke. Your face is red. You are coughing. There is a baby in your arms. In a few seconds, an old woman also emerges. We are all silent. We have never seen a child on the battlefield.

Later a chopper comes to pick up the wounded sergeant and maybe me (why?). They put him in first on a stretcher. I hop in the other side. I have a pistol on me (why?). Someone gives the infant to the wounded sergeant. The door gunner nudges me and waves his head toward the sergeant, who is holding the child in his hands, arms outstretched. Is he mad? The medic outside the chopper is shouting something at the sergeant, and I start to panic, afraid that something terrible may occur. I reach for the pistol, realizing I may have to shoot. I pull it out of my holster. My heart is sinking. The sergeant then lowers the child to his chest, embracing it. He is crying softly. The crisis passes. We begin to rev up for takeoff. Someone plops a nine-year-old girl in my lap. I'm sitting in the doorway as usual, my legs dangling out, and now so is she. She is scared. I can feel her tiny frame shaking. We begin to take off. She bites me, not hard, but firm. All I can think is that she is scared and believes that I'll throw her out of the chopper. Finally I stroke her and find a voice in me I've never had before, and it says, "I won't hurt you." We leave. I know not any longer if all of this happened. I think it did, at least most of it. Maybe the little girl wasn't real. Maybe she's a symbol of my guilt, our collective guilt. Either way, for years she visited my dreams. She is with me still.

This ends my story. The windup is tortured and long because these memories are so. But I tell you this in detail so that despite the differences of time and space and rank, and all of the later experiences of our lives, you will know what happened there, at least in my eyes. One of us has lived to tell you now directly, on paper how important you were to us. You were the first company commander who cared about us. I think we would have done anything for you. It was not lost on any of us that despite the combat in these months and the awesome losses in our sister companies, our own losses were light. But more than that, we came to trust you and believe in who you were. In that way you allowed us to believe in ourselves, and in doing so you saved some part of each of us. This may have been your greatest achievement in that theater.

And now the essence of my message. From you I learned that leadership, particularly in times of great crisis, is a demanding and isolating experience. I learned that understanding and compassion must be combined with technical competence and strength to lead, and that selflessness, not selfishness, is required. I learned that through one leader the lives of many can be changed, and thus every human being has the ability to influence the behavior of the world in some small way. I learned that calm in the center of a storm is crucial, and that whatever the distractions, one must focus on the big picture. You taught me all this from your example.

War had caused me to watch everything in life with discernment. You removed much of the mystery of the human experience. In many ways, you taught me more about the world than anyone, including my own father. Yet we were not close. You were Amber Outlaw 6 and I, a simple platoon sergeant, was Amber Outlaw 3–5. Nonetheless, you were, and always have been, a powerful force in my life.

My experience in the military shaped the rest of my life. Having survived, I felt a special sense of obligation to live, in effect, for many who did not return. I dedicated and drove myself and my career in a way that I hoped would make some small contribution to the world beyond my own petty existence. While my personal life has been uneven and filled with mistakes in relationships, I've certainly wandered an eventful and diverse professional trail. If I have contributed anything to this world, much of it is attributable to your influence on a hardened, watchful 21-year-old platoon sergeant who once served, proudly, under your command.

Dan Garcia
Once "Amber Outlaw 3–5"

Dear Dan,

Your letter of Vietnam memories was a treasure—a capsule of time that reappeared from 29 years past. The power and clarity of your letter make it one of the most profound pieces of writing on our war I have ever read. Dan—it seems like just yesterday to me, even now. I can see your face with film clarity—such a young man of integrity, courage and leadership under such enormous pressure—responsible for the lives of other even younger soldiers who were barely beyond being boys. You and the others were my family, my brothers, and my constant burden of worry during the eight months I commanded B Company, 2–7th Cavalry.

All that you have achieved with your life is a source of great pride to me. The discipline, sheer talent and energy you showed as a 21-year-old rifle platoon sergeant in combat has followed you. You did all that was asked of you and more. You were wounded three times. You took care of your soldiers. You were an example to all of us.

Your letter awakened some terrible sleeping memories. I have shared your letter with my family and some close friends—particularly the Vietnam vets who have stayed close throughout the years. I can see your memories as an out of body experience from your stark images. My recollections capture the same pictures from different angles and with other hazy, distorted and bloody perspectives.

A handful of soldiers—and particularly you—have stayed in my thoughts and prayers throughout the decades. I really loved all of you and desperately wanted you to live and go home intact in spirit. Our country did not treat any of you with the respect, support and compassion you deserved. It was a shameful blot on our history to send the country's young men off to this terrible conflict and then use our soldiers as objects of blame for the divisive political struggle that ripped the nation apart for a decade.

Dan, you are a superb example of a Vietnam veteran with life-long dedication to America when you returned to civilian life.

When I met you as I took command of B Company, 2–7th Cavalry in November 1968, I was five years older than you. I was also on my third combat tour; had been wounded twice; had a wife, son and baby daughter whom I adored; was a West Point and Ranger School graduate; and was an old man. All my youthful spirit for adventure, for what for glory was gone—ground out of me in the mud and artillery fire of the DMZ fighting as part of the Vietnamese Airborne Division.

Fresh out of West Point, I had volunteered for the 82nd Airborne Division, as a new 2nd lieutenant in 1964 because I believed the division would go to Vietnam. We ended up instead in the Organization of American States intervention in the Dominican Republic. Our combat experience was minimal, but I got the shock of seeing American soldiers lying dead on canvas stretchers. Now I knew.

From the Dominican Republic, I immediately volunteered for Vietnam. After extensive language and advisor training, I ended up based in Saigon with the Vietnamese 2nd Parachute Infantry Battalion.

Those were the days of wine and roses: air-conditioned BOQs, jeeps, nightclubs, older airborne NCOs, and the cool beauty of the surf on the beaches at Vung Tau. The other reality was midnight alerts: the roar of C4Is and C-130s lifting us from Tan Son Nhut Air Base and heading out to some savage firefight on the frontier or a besieged provincial capital. Within days of leaving city lights, milk shakes and PXs, we might be involved in a massive battle with hundreds killed or wounded. In many cases the NVA would outnumber us and have overmatching rocket, mortar and artillery firepower.

After coming home, I went directly from Vietnam to Panama to be a general's aide. My poor West Point Spanish got me a wonderful year-long interlude of peace. My beautiful young wife and children shut the door on Vietnam. I worked for a wonderful old general who was a Bataan Death March survivor. He treated me like his son. He wanted me to follow in his footsteps as an instructor in political science at West Point. I was to go to graduate school at Harvard and then join the faculty. In your letter you mentioned your feelings of abandonment as you left your friends upon departing Vietnam after your third Purple Heart. It is a common feeling among American soldiers who have survived combat.

In my case, I was still in Panama when the Tet Offensive started on Christmas 1968. The graphic news media coverage was on our Armed Forces Network television each night—ferocious scenes of combat.

Our soldiers, our soldiers, were dying in great numbers. I was one of three infantry captains with a Combat Infantryman Badge serving among the 15,000 troops in Panama. My sense of guilt at seeing our Army fighting for its life while I prepared to head off to graduate school broke me within a few days. Without telling the general, I called the infantry assignment officer in Washington and volunteered for immediate return. I told my wife, Jill, who understood. She was scared, but she always understood. The general was scared, sad and regretful. He wanted me to be a general; he wanted my friendship. He let go reluctantly.

When I left Jill with her parents in Corona Del Mar, Calif., I had a powerful sense of letting go. This was what I was supposed to do. My friends were dying and being maimed in massive numbers. There was simply no option but duty.

When you saw me take command of B Company at LZ Billie on the Cambodian border in III Corps, I had been the 2–7th Cavalry assistant battalion operations officer (S-3) for two months. The 1st Cavalry Division conducted an emergency deployment from I Corps to Quan Loi in III Corps in response to intelligence of a planned 100,000-soldier NVA offensive. The enemy's intention was to sweep out of Cambodia down the Surgess Jungle Highway to capture the huge American logistics complex at Long Binh. Long Binh was the biggest military installation in the world—destruction of its millions of tons of supplies, ammunition and fuel was to be a war-winning knockout blow. The garrison of 40,000 REMFs would be easy pickings. The emergency mission of our 1st Cavalry Division was to put a reconnaissance-in-force on the Cambodian border and then fall back in a fighting covering force to bring about the attrition of the enemy offensive. In the largest sense we succeeded admirably—Tet '69 was eventually stillborn. Only one NVA battalion ultimately survived the 100-kilometer meat grinder campaign offensive and stumbled out of the jungle a few kilometers from Long Binh. This one NVA battalion was then killed almost to the last man by the 11th Armored Cavalry Regiment.

We had done our job. But what a trail of tears the 1st Cavalry Division left behind during our bloody full-court press with the attacking NVA divisions and logistics troops. So many Garry Owen soldiers in green bags, so much suffering, so much blood, confusion, despair, courage, sacrifice and love. So many memories brought back by your powerful letter: Dan Garcia—handsome, poised, serious, intelligent. Your fellow platoon leader—one of the most gifted natural leaders I have ever met. The lieutenant who loved his soldiers and controlled his fear with enormous combat courage. The endless memories of the faces of teenage soldiers with their energy, respect, affection for each other and enduring courage. Our first sergeant was a rock to me. He helped shoulder the moral burden. He was also on his third combat tour and would earn his third Purple Heart with B Company. He had first served in 2nd Battalion, 7th Cavalry, in the Korean War and had been badly wounded as a young private. For most of my command tenure, the first sergeant was the only other soldier in our company who was both Regular Army and more than 25 years old.

Our company ranged in strength from 73 to 125 men. We were essentially all draftees, ages 18 to 22—the officers, the NCOs, the soldiers. The first sergeant and I absolutely loved and respected all of you young men. We knew in our hearts that many of you would be wounded or killed while serving in the company. We also believed that if we could do our job properly—coordinate air and artillery; maintain tactical coordination with other battalion elements; ruthlessly enforce security, digging-in, helmets, noise/light discipline and use helicopter reconnaissance—most of you would go home alive. That was our abiding passion and purpose month after month.

I took command of B Company from a captain who was killed in action on LZ Billie after the company had been badly chewed up in our first III Corps firefight. One of the rifle platoon leaders had gotten aggressive, stupid and lost. (He survived to die of a tragic self-inflicted accidental gunshot wound 18 months later.) All of our brigade fire bases came under heavy NVA attack. An ARVN [Army of the Republic of Vietnam] firebase off to our east was overrun. Delta Company from our battalion attacked out from the firebase toward the frontier to try to push back the 107-mm rocket, 122-mm artillery and mortars that were pounding us. They promptly got stuck in close combat. The company commander (an old friend) and the company head medic were both killed and their bodies left. Alpha Company, which was commanded by another friend, then attacked out to link up with D Company and was also promptly caught in a buzz saw. Charlie Company was then in turn committed to the attack and barely got into the jungle line before the NVA machine guns opened up. Their company commander was also killed.

All day, as your brand-new B Company commander, I listened with growing dread on the radio to the sounds of D Company disintegrating and the mounting tragedy of casualties in A and C Companies. The battalion commander was a wonderful and brave man (later to be replaced by an honorable but incompetent lieutenant colonel who did indeed play a role in the later destruction of the same D Company during the Christmas fighting). In the very late afternoon, I heard the battalion commander give the orders to launch our B Company at dusk by helicopter to land directly on the remnants of Delta. When I received the order, the 18 helicopters were already inbound and were to land within 45 minutes. Dan—I did not know any of you. I assembled the B Company command group and platoon leader and gave a simple five-paragraph combat order. My hands were shaking but my head was clear. I then explained the attack order in Vietnamese to the "Kit Carson" NVA scout (turncoat) and the two Viet interpreters who served with us. (All three promptly deserted on an outgoing medevac chopper.)

The company XO was a shaken young man. He listened in anguish to my attack order and then said quite clearly to the entire command group, "Captain, these soldiers aren't going to go. They're scared and won't get on the choppers." I told him to get out of the company and report to the battalion headquarters. We also left behind one more of the platoon leaders—a young, frightened, stupid officer who should not have survived OCS. Finally I told the first sergeant, "I'll go out on the first aircraft. You come in on the last helicopter and give me a closing report." Looking around the circle of officers and NCOs, I laid it on the line, "Our friends are dying—we need to help."

There was an immense choking swirl of dry season dirt from 18 landing helicopters. I jumped aboard the lead "Huey" with my CP element (whose names I barely knew). My RTO was holding on to my web gear as I hung out the side of the Huey, desperately trying to visualize the terrain as we roared across the jungle treetops. The sun plunged below the horizon as the choppers turned short on final approach. Heavy enemy gunfire erupted from the ground. A gigantic blow hit our Huey as a round tore through the floor behind the RTO; his eyes widened and he laughed and gave me a thumbs up. Then the LZ came into sight. Thirty or so D Company survivors lay flattened as enemy mortar rounds smacked into the ground. They were wraiths in the gathering dusk as they clawed their way onto our departing choppers and left. (They had been told to stay with us, but were leaderless, disorganized and scared.)

My CP group and I headed in the 12 o'clock direction on the LZ and set up our CP on a large recognizable mound in the deepening darkness. (It turned out to be an occupied NVA bunker.) The last of our B Company helicopters could be heard as they lifted off in a burst of suppressive gunfire.

Then the first sergeant emerged from the darkness. "Captain," he said, "they all came. We have 123 soldiers on the ground." Dan, I had spent all of my 25 years getting ready for that night. I had buried my brother-in-law, who had been killed in action in August of 1964. I knew my dad, an Army lieutenant general, would honor me in death. I dearly wanted to live to see my wife and children. But, Dan, that night three kilometers north of LZ Billie—with automatic weapons gunfire whip-cracking across the LZ, with the ferocious roar of bamboo burning and exploding from the artillery strikes, with the stench and fear of death around us—I said a prayer that I could live up to the demands of commanding a company of brave young soldiers like you, soldiers who would fly into a savage night firefight because other unknown teenage soldiers from 2–7th Cavalry were dying and needed help. That night I was home in B Company.

The following months of combat are distorted now. I was so very proud to command such a group of soldiers. The memories of unending vigilance; ripped hands from constant digging; the shock of making contact as firing built up quickly in a crescendo; the acrid smell of grenades, cordite, C4 explosives, trip flares; the incredible stench of filthy soldiers, the sight of torn uniforms, the constant pain from bites, destroyed feet, pulled muscles from carrying 80 pounds of water, ammunition, weapons, packs; and the agony of seeing screaming, wounded soldiers and dragging the dead to helicopters. Thank God for our extremely low B Company casualties. Much of it was due to the incredible diligence of young NCOs like you. Much of it was due to the experience and cunning that the first sergeant and I had gained from surviving many years of combat between us. Some of it was luck and the hand of God.

I do remember offering to nominate you for a combat field direct commission. You were such a superb leader. I did understand that you could not do it. You were way beyond the limit and had to go. Death was waiting to harvest you.

So, Dan Garcia, here we sit after all these years—alive with our memories and grateful that we both survived to write these letters on Vietnam. We have bridged this chasm of time and opened a door on the courage and pain we shared in combat. I'm proud of your enormous accomplishments: the law degree, the partnership in a famous firm, the high corporate office in an international company and your splendid record of public service in city government.

Mostly, though, I'm proud of the vivid image I have of the courage in ferocious combat of a 21-year-old rifle platoon sergeant in B Company, 2nd Battalion, 7th Cavalry. You were a superb soldier. You took care of your men. You led by example. I'm glad my prayers have been answered, with one more Garry Owen soldier home at last.

Barry McCaffrey
Captain, Infantry 1968–69
Once "Outlaw 6"

These letters appeared in ARMY Magazine (Vol. 47, No. 11, November 1997), with an introduction by General Jack N. Merritt, USA Ret. Copyright 2014 by the Association of the U.S. Army and reprinted by permission of ARMY Magazine.

Daniel P. Garcia is a senior vice-president of real-estate planning and public affairs for Warner Bros. in Burbank, California. He has served on the boards of directors of the Kaiser Foundation, the Los Angeles Chamber of Commerce and the Rockefeller Foundation. He served with distinction in Vietnam, where he earned three Purple Hearts, the Silver Star, two Bronze Stars, and an Air Medal. A graduate of Loyola University, he holds an MBA from the University of Southern California and a Juris Doctorate from UCLA School of Law.

General Barry R McCaffrey, USA Ret., served as commander-in-chief, U.S. Southern Command, before being appointed by President Clinton in 1996 as director of the White House Office of National Drug Control Policy. In addition to his combat tours in the Dominican Republic and Vietnam, he commanded the 24th Infantry Division (Mechanized) in Iraq during Operation Desert Storm. General McCaffrey was the most highly decorated and youngest Army four-star general at retirement. He earned three awards of the Purple Heart, the Distinguished Service Cross with Oak Leaf Cluster (second award) and two Silver Stars. He has served on the National Security Council and the President's Drug Policy Council. A graduate of the United States Military Academy, he holds a master's degree from American University.

MEMORIES OF DAI DO

Brigadier General William Weise, USMC Ret., Navy Cross

The battle of Dai Do was a fierce and bloody struggle between an understrength Marine battalion landing team, 2nd Battalion, 4th Marines (BLT 2/4), and major elements of the 320th North Vietnamese Army (NVA) Division during three hot, humid spring days in 1968 (April 30–May 3). I was privileged to command those magnificent Marines and sailors who stopped the well-equipped 320th in its tracks on the north bank of the Bo Dieu River and drove it back toward the Demilitarized Zone (DMZ). I believe that we conducted a successful spoiling attack that prevented the much larger NVA unit from launching a ground assault on the Marine combat/combat service support base at Dong Ha, headquarters of the 3rd Marine Division (Forward).

I would like to say that our success was part of a carefully orchestrated plan. It was not. We reacted first to hasty orders from higher headquarters, then to targets of opportunity, and finally to one desperate situation after another. That we succeeded was more a tribute to the extraordinary performance of individual Marines and Sailors and their small unit leaders than to brilliance or insight by higher echelons. Bravery, competence, initiative, toughness, and selflessness carried the day. Oddly enough, except in the memories of those who took part, little is known and even less is written of this battle. To help rectify this shortfall, I offer the following account of the battle of Dai Do as I remember it.

Enemy Closes the Cua Viet and Bo Dieu Rivers

Dai Do, and the hamlets of An Loc, Dong Huan, Dinh To, and Thoung Do lie on the north bank of the Bo Dieu River, 2½ kilometers northwest of Dong Ha, 13 kilometers south of the DMZ, and 13 kilometers west of the Golf of Tonkin. In 1968, most of the supplies for U.S. and South Vietnamese forces in the northernmost part of South Vietnam were ferried from cargo ships in the Gulf of Tonkin up the Cua Viet and Bo Dieu Rivers to Dong Ha by U.S. Navy landing craft. About 4:00 a.m. on April 30, 1968, a U.S. Navy utility boat (LCU) was struck by rocket rounds and small arms fired from An Loc, a heavily wooded hamlet on the north bank of the Bo Dieu River. One sailor was killed and several wounded. The damaged LCU returned fire and limped to Dong Ha loading ramp. The 3rd Marine Division then closed the river to friendly traffic until the enemy ambush could be investigated and eliminated—a normally simple task that, this time, proved to be not so simple.

The problem area of Dai Do and the surrounding hamlets lay in the 1st Army of Vietnam (ARVN) Division's tactical area of responsibility (TAOR). On that morning, however, there were no ARVN units available to investigate and clear the ambush site. The task was given to BLT 2/4, which had been operating northeast of Dai Do, north of the Cua Viet River for the past two months. For two days prior to the Dai Do battle, enemy movement had been detected along Highway 1 north of Dong Ha, and ARVN units reported heavy enemy contact. To help the 2nd ARVN Regiment, Echo Company, BLT 2/4, commanded by Captain James Livingston, was sent to defend a key bridge on Highway 1 about six kilometers north of Dong Ha. Echo Company operated directly under 3rd Marine Division while at the bridge.

At BLT 2/4's command post (CP), we learned of the LCU ambush within minutes of the event. We monitored the Navy River Assault Force tactical net and heard the initial report. Almost simultaneously, we received a report from Hotel Company, BLT 2/4, which had a patrol not far from the incident. We relayed the report to Colonel Milton Hull, commanding officer (CO) of the 3rd Marines, at his CP near the mouth of the Cua Viet River.

I felt uneasy. Something big was happening. Major George F. "Fritz" Warren, BLT 2/4 operations officer, felt the same way. Things had been too quiet. So we told all subordinate units to be prepared for anything and assessed our situation.

Although under strength, BLT 2/4 was a tough, battle-tested unit. We had proved ourselves in heavy combat against NVA units in the DMZ area during the enemy 1968 Tet and post-Tet offensives. In addition, we trained continuously in military basics appropriate to our area: assaults on fortified positions, small arms marksmanship, patrolling, stream crossing, crew-served weapons, ambushes, calls for supporting arms, camouflage, etc. When not in actual combat, the reserve company followed a formal training schedule. In a less formal fashion, rifle companies in patrol bases also conducted prescribed training, one platoon or squad at a time. Whenever possible, we operated during darkness and became quite effective in night operations. During April 1968, our night patrols and ambushes were particularly productive. Most of our kills were at night with very few friendly casualties. We even conducted a successful battalion night attack. We literally took the night away from the enemy. I firmly believe the enemy began to avoid our area because he was consistently beaten and wouldn't bear the cost.

On April 30, 1968, when the battle of Dai Do began, the four rifle companies of BLT 2/4 were widely dispersed: Echo was guarding the bridge on Highway 1; Golf occupied a patrol base to the north in Lam Xuan (west) and Nhi Ha; Foxtrot, designated as BLT 2/4 reserve, had two platoons at Mai Xa Chanh and one platoon at My Loc to the east; while Hotel had a patrol base in the southwestern sector. The BLT 2/4 CP, 81mm mortar platoon, 4.2-inch mortar battery (W/2/12), and Headquarters and Service Company were located at Mai Xa Chanh (Mai Xa Thi on some maps) in the south center of BLT 2/4 TAOR. Also at Mai Xa Chanh were the reconnaissance platoon, engineer platoon, the tank platoon (with only two tanks), the amphibian tractor platoon(-), and various headquarters elements. The BLT's normal 105mm howitzer battery (H/3/12) and Ontos platoon had been pulled away and were under operational control of other 3rd Marine Division units. Off the coast, aboard ships of Amphibious Ready Group Alpha were Maj

Charles W. Knapp, BLT 2/4 executive officer (XO), and the remaining BLT attachments. The effective strength of the four rifle companies was about 125 Marines each, about 75 less than the prescribed table of organization strength.

I did not have authority to move Golf Company or Foxtrot Company without the approval of 3rd Marine Regiment since Echo Company was out of my area under control of 3rd Marine Division, the only maneuver unit immediately available when the Dai Do battle began was Hotel Company, itself widely dispersed. Fortunately, Hotel Company was commanded by Captain James L. "Jim" Williams, a superb combat leader, who set the pace for an extraordinary three-day display of small-unit combat leadership.

Attacks by Hotel and Foxtrot Companies

About two hours after the LCU was struck by enemy rocket and small-arms fire, BLT 2/4 was ordered to investigate and eliminate the enemy ambush site. Since An Loc was in the ARVN area, we requested that our boundary be shifted westward to include An Loc and its surrounding terrain. We wanted to be able to fire and maneuver with a free hand. The boundary shift was not approved for several hours. In the interim, we continued preparations. I ordered Captain Williams to assemble Hotel Company in Bac Vong, 1½ kilometers north of An Loc, and prepare to eliminate any enemy still at the An Loc ambush site. Small enemy units and individuals often fired at the river boats and "disappeared" before we could react. This time I had a feeling that the enemy would not run.

Captain Williams and one platoon moved immediately toward Bac Vong. Upon reaching the southwestern corner of that hamlet, the platoon received heavy enemy fire from Dong Huan, about 200 meters south. Enemy machine guns in Dai Do, 800 meters southwest, also fired on Hotel Company. We obviously had to eliminate the enemy in Dong Huan before we could take An Loc. I modified Hotel Company's order: attack and seize Dong Huan.

I requested the return of Echo Company and permission to move Foxtrot and Golf Companies. Permission was granted to move two

Foxtrot platoons and company headquarters moved out immediately from Mai Xa Chanh toward Bac Vong aboard amtracs (amphibian tractors). Golf Company would not return for 36 hours.

To be closer to the action, my forward CP group and I boarded an armored LCM-6 "Monitor" of the River Assault Group and moved along the Cua Viet River to the vicinity of Bac Vong. My group consisted of Sergeant Major John M. "Big John" Malnar,[1] First Lieutenant Judson D. "Judd" Hilton, Jr., the forward air controller (FAC), four radio operators, and a runner (messenger). The "Monitor" proved an ideal command post with good communications and significant firepower—a breech-loaded 81mm mortar, two 20mm cannons, plus .50 and .30 caliber machine guns—to support our attacks and engage targets of opportunity. Marines of our group, including me, got a chance to fire these weapons—a little direct involvement in the early stages of the battle. We used a skimmer boat (a 14-foot fiberglass boat with a 35-horsepower outboard motor) to move ashore when required. From the "Monitor" I had an excellent view of the early assaults as they occurred close to the river banks.

Before Hotel Company could attack Dong Huan, Captain Williams had to reconnoiter the creek that separated him from his objective, locate a ford, issue orders, and otherwise prepare his Marines for a daylight attack.

Everything about the situation favored the enemy defenders. The approaches to Dong Huan offered no cover and very little concealment. Surrounded by open rice paddies, and separated from Bac Vong by an unfordable stream, Dong Hun itself, was hidden by dense hedgerow. (Vietnamese civilians had moved from the area some time earlier.) The heavy volume of fire received by the Hotel Company patrol—mortars, rockets, and automatic weapons—told us that the enemy occupied Dong Huan in strength and intended to stay there. I sensed that a major fight was brewing. I made my first urgent request for Ontos, "How Sixes" (105mm howitzers mounted on amphibian tractor chassis), and more tanks to support my meager force, but they never appeared.

Terrain and available resources dictated the plan for the assault on Dong Huan. The reconnaissance platoon, led by First Lieutenant C. William "Bill" Muter, an inspiring and fearless officer under fire, and two M48 tanks would remain in Bac Vong to support the attack by Hotel Company. Using the limited concealment afforded by the stream bank, Hotel Company would move north about 700 meters to a fording point, cross the stream and turn south to Dong Huan. Foxtrot Company, mounted on amtracs, would then cross the stream, move to the cemetery east of Dai Do, pour fire into Dai Do to silence enemy weapons there, create a diversion for Hotel Company as it moved into its assault. Foxtrot Company (reinforced by Golf when it arrived by helicopter) would also be prepared to assault Dai Do.

As Hotel Company started its move north to the fording point, fixed-wing aircraft delivered bombs and napalm on Dong Huan. After the company forded the stream and turned south, it had to negotiate 700 meters of open rice paddy in broad daylight to reach its assault position. To obscure this movement, Captain Williams used white phosphorous and smoke. Artillery, naval gunfire, tank, and machine-gun fire helped keep enemy heads down, as Hotel Company literally crawled the last 700 meters of open rice paddy. Other enemy positions were pounded with naval gunfire. Miraculously, Hotel Company sustained few casualties during this daring move. Foxtrot Company, mounted on amtracs, moved into the cemetery and opened fire on Dai Do as planned. The two tanks and the reconnaissance platoon in Bac Vong increased their rate of fire on Dong Huan. Then, within a few meters of the enemy forward positions, Captain Williams lifted supporting fires and Hotel Company assaulted Dong Huan. Considering the large number of bunkers, trenches, and spider holes, not to mention the doggedness of the enemy, Hotel Company moved quickly. Well-trained assault teams destroyed one fortified position after another. In about two hours, Dong Huan was secured. Unfortunately, Captain Williams was seriously wounded by an enemy hand grenade during the assault, but he lived to tell the tale. With his 45 caliber pistol, he killed the enemy soldier who wounded him. First Lieutenant Alexander "Scotty" Prescott assumed command, consolidated the position, and reorganized Hotel Company into a hasty defense.

Once I felt that the Hotel assault would carry through Dong Huan, I ordered Foxtrot Company to assault Dai Do. Attached to Foxtrot were two 106mm recoilless rifles mounted on top of amtracs, secured with sandbags (a field improvisation to provide mobility for these heavy weapons). One of the two Foxtrot platoons gained a toehold in the village, but the assault was stopped by heavy artillery and small arms fire. Two amtracs were disabled. Foxtrot Company needed assistance. I ordered it to hold, hoping to reinforce with Golf Company.

But Golf Company, under the able command of Captain Jay R. Vargas, was having problems of its own withdrawing from Lam Xuan (west) and Nhi Ha to the northwest. Intense enemy supporting arms fire and a ground attack forced cancellation of the helilift after the 81mm mortar section and some supplies were lifted out. Golf Company was forced to conduct a night retrograde movement by foot under heavy fire to Mai Xe Chanh. Captain Vargas and several others were wounded during the move. (This was Vargas' third wound in three months.) But they all made it to Mai Xa Chanh to board LCM-8s the next day. At first glance, Golf Company's activities on April 30 do not seem extraordinary, considering everything else going on. But think about it. After a full night of patrolling, Golf Company was alerted, prepared for a heliborne assault, underwent enemy supporting arms and ground attacks, canceled the helicopter lift, beat off the enemy attack, conducted a night retrograde under fire, and successfully moved on foot to a new assembly point for further movement—all without sleep for 36 hours, but very much full of fight as we shall see later.

Meanwhile, Hotel Company evacuated its casualties and consolidated its hard-won positions in Dong Huan. Foxtrot was hanging by the skin of its teeth in the eastern edge of Dai Do, and we were pounding enemy positions with artillery, naval gunfire, and organic weapons.

About 3:30 p.m., the CO of the 3rd Marines, his operations officer, Maj Dennis J. Murphy (now Major General), and his sergeant major, Ted McClintock, arrived at my forward CP aboard the Navy "Monitor." They had traveled the 11 kilometers from their CP at the mouth of the Cua Viet River by unarmed "skimmer boat." This was done at considerable risk because the enemy had been firing at everything that moved on the water, including our armored LCM-6, all afternoon. Colonel Hull, a proven combat leader in World War II and Korea, holder of the

Navy Cross and Silver Star, seemed unimpressed by his own daring dash up the river or by the artillery and mortar rounds exploding around us. He had already been ashore to visit Hotel Company. We discussed the situation, and Colonel Hull ordered me to continue attacking in our area and to keep the pressure on the enemy. He placed Bravo Company, 1st Battalion, 3rd Marines and another platoon of amtracs under my operational control, so we could attack the enemy at An Lac.

Late Afternoon Attack by Bravo Company, 1st Battalion, 3d Marines

We had worked with Bravo Company before, and I was happy to get that fine company under the able command of First Lieutenant Norris. Bravo Company had been operating south of the Bo Dieu River not far from the Dai Do area. First Lieutenant Norris reported in by radio. After a quick briefing, I ordered his company to mount the amtracs, cross the river, attack and seize An Loc, the hamlet from which the enemy had attacked the Navy utility boat.

Covered by a heavy bombardment of artillery and naval gunfire, Bravo Company, atop amtracs,[2] crossed the river in a classic amphibious assault wave. As the assault wave neared the northern river bank, the enemy opened up with heavy small arms, mortars, rockets, and artillery. The scene reminded me of films of the Iwo Jima assault in World War II. The direct-fire weapons of the River Assault Group boats gave excellent support as Bravo Company dismounted and fought its way over the river banks and into the fortified positions. The fighting was close and very heavy. Rockets destroyed two amtracs and damaged several others. Hotel Company spotted and cut down a group of enemy in the open moving south, apparently trying to reinforce An Loc. In An Loc, casualties were heavy on both sides. One of those killed early in the fight was First Lieutenant Norris.

As the assault continued, it became obvious that the waning strength of Bravo Company was insufficient to sweep all the way through the hamlet. About an hour before darkness, I ordered the company (now confused, disorganized, and with only one officer left) to halt, reorganize, form a defensive perimeter in the western half of the hamlet, evacuate casualties, and carry out resupply.

I also ordered Foxtrot Company to withdraw from the southeastern edge of Dai Do under the cover of the darkness and join Hotel Company in Dong Huan. I did not want to have three separate perimeters that night. Foxtrot Company had difficulty in withdrawing from Dai Do and reorganizing. During the withdrawal, the company commander reported only 26 men left. (Actually, the figure was twice that number, as I learned later.) I was concerned about Foxtrot Company, but there were more pressing problems to deal with that night.

After digging in and being resupplied, both Bravo and Hotel Companies registered close artillery and mortar concentrations, which proved fortuitous. They later received several probes, which were beaten back. As the night wore on, enemy activity around the two companies' perimeters quietened down. I ordered Bravo Company to send a reconnaissance patrol into the eastern half of An Loc. The patrol reported that the enemy had withdrawn. On order, the company quietly occupied the remainder of the hamlet under the cover of darkness.

Assessing the situation at the end of the first day, April 30, I felt we had done well with what we had. But I was frustrated because we did not have enough power to continue the attack on Dai Do after Hotel Company successfully assaulted Dong Huan.

I was also disappointed that we did not have our Ontos platoon and more tanks with their potent 106mm and 90mm direct fire weapons, and we did not get enough air or heavy (8-inch) artillery support. The heavy artillery shells and bombs with delayed fuses might have cracked some of the enemy's fortifications. If the bombs and heavy artillery were followed by napalm, the destruction of the enemy positions would have been much greater. I especially wanted, but did not get, a radar-controlled 2,000-pound bomb strike by Marine A-6 Intruder aircraft. Throughout April 30, we received only one air strike and no 8-inch artillery support despite numerous emergency requests.

At first light on May 1, Hotel Company spotted a large group of enemy in open fields north and west of its positions and immediately took them under fire. After the bitter fighting of the previous day and night, being able to see and shoot enemy in the open from covered positions proved quite a morale booster. We were not sure if they were stragglers who had withdrawn from An Loc during the night. This was not the last time. Large numbers of enemy troops would be spotted in the open in daylight during this battle.

Attack by Golf Company, May 1, 1968

Golf Company, meanwhile, had completed its night move to the BLT 2/4 CP at Mai Xa Chang. The company was resupplied and briefed on the current situation by Maj Warren. I originally hoped to move Golf Company to An Loc by Navy LCM-8 landing craft during darkness, to land at night behind Bravo Company, and launch a predawn attack on Dai Do. The two LCM-8s did not become available until much later, and it was 9:00 a.m. before Golf Company and our two tanks were aboard and ready to move west. I boarded a skimmer boat and met Captain Vargas in the lead LCM-8 about 9:45 a.m. My orders were simple: land south of An Loc, pass around the right flank of Bravo Company, attack northwest, seize and hold the village of Dai Do. That's exactly what happened. We had been shelling Dai Do heavily with delayed-fuse high-explosive and white phosphorous shells for more than two hours before Golf began its attack. We had also intermittently run the amtrac engines and moved them short distances to disguise the sound of our tanks when they landed with Golf Company at about 10:40 a.m. Two A-4 Skyhawks delivered bombs and napalm on Dai Do prior to the assault, then made dummy attacks as Golf Company moved forward. Hotel Company and several Navy patrol boats provided Golf Company with a base of fire.

Golf Company crossed the rice paddies leaning into supporting fires with two platoons in the assault and one in reserve. The tanks were located between the assault platoons. Two hundred meters south of Dai Do heavy enemy fire slowed and then halted the left assault elements, but Captain Vargas personally led the remaining assault units forward, penetrating the first line of enemy bunkers. The fighting was close and furious. The assault lost and regained momentum several times. On one occasion Captain Vargas personally assaulted a bunker and killed seven enemy defenders. Finally, Golf Company Marines reached the northern edge of Dai Do. Fighting continued to eliminate the enemy in cleverly concealed, bypassed positions, especially in the southwest portions of the village where the assault had bogged down. During these mopping-up operations, the enemy counterattacked Golf Company from the north and the west. Enemy also fired from bypassed positions in the rear (east). Golf Company was by now weakened by heavy casualties and desperately needed resupply. I ordered Vargas to fall back and establish a defensive perimeter in the eastern part of Dai Do. He did, receiving his fourth wound in the process.

Golf Company reorganized, evacuated casualties (which were heavy), set up a hasty defense, and called for supporting fires and resupply. During reorganization, Golf Company reported large numbers of enemy in the open north of Dai Do moving south from the vicinity of Truc Kinh. They were taken under fire by machine-gun, artillery, and naval gunfire. An aerial observer also reported enemy movement in and around Truc Kinh and called in fixed-wing aircraft and armed helicopter strikes. On our air net we could hear the excited pilots as they strafed, bombed, and rocketed the enemy in the open daylight—a rare sight.

By now, the afternoon of the second day of our fight, our heavily engaged BLT was given priority for close air support (CAS). We were happy to get it, but wished it had arrived earlier. Even with the higher priority we didn't get all the CAS we requested, nor as quickly as we needed it. Our fixed-wing support had not been responsive during the early months of 1968. Even preplanned strikes were usually late, and sometimes canceled without notice. During March and April, including the first day and a half of the Dai Do battle, CAS was not adequate. We learned to operate without relying on CAS, the king of Marine Corps supporting arms.

Instead, we depended on our own mortars, artillery, and naval gunfire. Destroyers equipped with five-inch guns were usually on station and within range in the Cau Viet area. Sometimes, powerful eight-inch gun cruisers provided support. Whenever a new Navy gunship came on line, our naval gunfire officer, Lieutenant (jg) Joe Carroll, USNR was aware of it. He and his naval gunfire support team spent many hours registering the guns of each "new" ship and establishing and operating camaraderie with the shipboard gunners and operating personnel. There were always more targets than bullets in the Cua Viet area. We were happy to get the support, and the ships loved to shoot, especially when we reported the destruction of targets (which was often). We found naval gunfire support to be accurate, reliable, and, best of all, available when needed.

Golf Company had barely reorganized on the eastern edge of Dai Do when the enemy attacked. The attack was beaten back, as was another an hour later. I was really worried about Golf Company, down to about 60 foxhole strength after several tough fights and without sleep for 48 hours. I ordered Foxtrot Company (still minus one platoon) to move northwest from Doug Huan to link up with and support Golf Company in Dai Do. But as soon as Foxtrot Company moved into the rice paddies leading into Dai Do, it was pinned down by heavy enemy fire. Vargas boxed in his position with artillery, naval gunfire, and 4.2-inch and 81mm mortar fires. He also called in CAS. But something more was needed to take the pressure off Vargas and give the enemy something else to worry about.

Return of Echo Company and Assault by Bravo Company, May 1, 1968

My morale went up several notches when I learned that Echo Company had been released by 3rd Marine Division and was en route to my position, now located ashore in An Loc. But Echo Company would not arrive in time to help Golf Company that second night. I would have to use one of the companies already nearby. I had tried using Foxtrot Company, but it failed. Hotel Company was too weak for a major effort. I decided to use Bravo Company, which had received a new CO, XO, and several experienced staff noncommissioned officers from its parent battalion.

I hoped that Bravo Company would be able to slip into Dai Do while we kept the enemy pinned down with fire. But luck was not with us. Bravo Company was unable to penetrate Dai Do. As darkness fell, things looked grim indeed. Then Echo Company arrived and the picture brightened.

Captain Jim Livingston knew that he was badly needed at Dai Do. A natural fighter, he overcame his inclination to stomp on the enemy positions that harassed him and tried to delay him. He returned fire only when absolutely necessary, skirted enemy strongpoints, and moved to An Loc as quickly as possible. His last obstacle was a "nearly unfordable," fairly swift stream about 5½ feet deep. Captain Jim solved that problem in typical Livingston fashion. He had a half dozen of his tallest Marines strip down, plant themselves in the deepest part of the stream, and pass the shorter, heavily laden Marines hand-to-hand to the shallow water. Not very fancy and not found in any field manual, but "Livingston stream-crossing expedient" worked. (I recommend it to anyone in a similar situation.) Second Lieutenant Jack E. Deichman, Golf Company's XO, described Livingston on his arrival at An Loc:

> I was impressed at his anxiousness for combat, and he sort of had a smile on his face, like the combat he had been waiting for had at long last arrived, and he wasn't going to miss it for the world. He was itching for a fight and he got it.

My first concern was helping Bravo Company out of its predicament. (Its second company commander and most of its key personnel were wounded during the late afternoon attack to relieve pressure on Golf Company.) I looked to Captain Livingston and my ubiquitous reconnaissance officer, First Lieutenant Bill Muter. Those two combat leaders never let me or their fellow Marines down. Always on top of the situation, they personally led a number of small expeditions during darkness, across the fire-swept rice paddies, and helped Bravo Company successfully withdraw back to An Loc with all its wounded.

Captain Vargas of Golf Company also played an important role in Bravo Company's withdrawal. When Bravo's second company commander and key leaders were wounded, a young, inexperienced Marine assumed command. The young leader, overwhelmed by the chaos around him, was close to panic. Speaking to him over the radio, Vargas's calm confident voice settled the excited Marine down, enabling him to gain control of the situation.

The Night of May 1/2; Predawn Attack by Echo Company on Dai Do Followed by Hotel Company Attack on Dinh To, 2 May

No one slept that night as we prepared for our next action. Colonel Hull's orders to continue the attack and keep the pressure on the enemy meant that we had to retake the portion of Dai Do vacated by Golf and continue to attack north through the hamlets of Dinh To and Thoug Do.

My concern about Golf Company, isolated 500 meters from the rest of the BLT, increased greatly as it started to receive enemy probes. To take the pressure off Golf, I decided to launch Echo Company in a predawn attack on Dai Do. I ordered Hotel Company to be prepared to follow Echo Company. Echo's attack would be northwest from An Loc. We had to move quickly because Golf Company's situation grew worse by the hour. Two large enemy night attacks and several small probes were beaten back. Captain Vargas ringed his position with supporting fires and exhausted his supply of small-arms ammunition. A daring resupply was made by Captain Lorraine Forehand, BLT 2/4 logistics officer, and his people. Golf Company held, but just barely, thanks in no small part to some miraculous logistics support.

The thunder of Golf's defensive fires muffled the movement of Echo Company as it crossed the line of departure and moved into the rice paddies toward assault positions just south of Dai Do village. Before Echo Company reached its assault positions, the enemy opened up with heavy volumes of small-arms and mortar fire. The two forward (assault) platoons received heavy casualties and lost forward momentum. But Captain Livingston immediately committed his reserve platoon, personally leading it forward to penetrate the forward enemy defenses and moved well into Dai Do. Livingston then widened the penetration by attacking to the right and left. He brought forward the two platoons previously pinned down in the rice paddies and continued to attack. The fighting was furious. Although twice wounded by grenade fragments Livingston continued to move wherever required to encourage his men and to maintain the momentum of the assault. Each enemy position had to be located, pinned down by accurate fire, blinded with white phosphorous, and destroyed by grenades, flame-throwers, satchel charges, and LAAWs (light assault antitank weapons).

Several times Echo Marines gained the flank of trench lines and placed killing, enfilade fire on large numbers of NVA soldiers who remained to die in their positions. One young machinegunner killed more than 30 enemy soldiers in this manner and later received the Silver Star.

Casualties were heavy as the assault continued for several hours. Golf Company broke out of its perimeter to assist Echo Company clear Dai Do. Finally, after several hours of heavy fighting and heavy casualties, Dai Do was secured.

Early on the second day, I put Captain Richard J. Murphy, our intelligence officer, in charge of the position at An Loc, now manned by survivors of Bravo Company, the 81mm mortar platoon, amtrac platoon, plus various supply, reconnaissance, medical, and communications personnel. Medical personnel performed initial triage at An Loc before evacuating wounded by skimmer boat to Mai Xa Chanh for further treatment and helilift to USS *Iwo Jima* or the hospital ship *Repose*. An Loc received too much enemy artillery fire to risk landing medevac helicopters, and we wanted to avoid lifting supporting fires while evacuation helicopters were in the battle area.

Our forward supply point was also located at An Loc. Captain Forehand again performed miracles with his Otter drivers and supply personnel, assisted by the reconnaissance platoon and other BLT units. These unsung heroes kept our assault units resupplied and evacuated the wounded, often exposing themselves to direct enemy fire and becoming casualties themselves.

About 10:00 a.m. on May 2, Colonel Hull arrived at An Loc. Echo and Golf Companies had just about completed the recapture of Dai Do. (While we were talking, an enemy soldier carrying a machinegun popped up in the rice paddy about 50 yards north of our position. Sergeant Major Malnar spotted him first. My radio operator, Sergeant Charles W. Bollinger, and runner, Corporal Greg R. Kraus, polished him off in short order.) We had just about run out of steam.

I called upon Hotel Company, ordering Lieutenant Prescott to pass through Dai Do and Echo Company, attack north, guide on the stream to the left, and seize Dinh To. Hotel crossed the line of departure on the northwest of Dai Do and entered Dinh To, receiving light enemy small arms in the process. As the advance continued, enemy fire increased, reinforced with mortars, rockets, and artillery, About one third through Dinh To, the enemy fire became so great that it halted Hotel's assault. Shortly thereafter, the enemy counterattacked. Hotel Company repulsed the counterattack, but was in desperate straits. Lieutenant Prescott asked for help. He thought his company would be overrun by the next enemy counterattack, which he believed was coming very soon.

Four hundred meters to the south, Captain Jim Livingston had been listening to Hotel Company's reports. He quickly assembled what was left of Echo Company after the morning attack (about 30 Marines) and moved to the aid of Hotel Company. It's hard to describe the electrifying effect Captain Livingston's action had on Hotel Company, which was about to be overrun. Lieutenant Prescott explained it this way:

> We were really desperate. Than my radio operator told me, Captain Livingston is coming. I knew then that we would be okay. I yelled, "Echo is coming. The cry was repeated by others. Echo is coming... Echo is coming." Everyone felt like I did.

Such was Livingston's reputation. Even the riflemen in other companies knew him as a skilled, effective combat leader—a master craftsman at closing with and destroying the enemy.

Captain Livingston's arrival inspired Lieutenant Prescott and Hotel Company to rally. Unfortunately, Lieutenant Prescott suffered a serious wound and had to be evacuated. Second Lieutenant Baynard V. "Vic" Taylor[3] assumed command of Hotel Company (the third company commander in three days). Captain Livingston and Lieutenant Taylor resumed the attack north with remnants of Echo and Hotel Companies. After fighting through a series of defended trench lines, they were halted by a large volume of heavy (12.7mm) machine-gun fire and a counter-attack. The ferocity of the fighting by Echo and Hotel Companies is described by Lieutenant Taylor in a letter to me years later:

> The enemy counterattack dwarfed the fighting that had gone before in intensity and volume. I recall seeing banana trees and the masonry walls of a hooch cut down by (enemy) automatic weapons fire. The bushes to our front seemed to be alive with heavily camouflaged NVA soldiers. The Marines of Hotel and Echo held their ground and threw every available round back at them. PFC Scafiti, a

lean, tough machinegunner from New York City, standing in the open, mowed down a column of charging NVA. Having run out of oil long before, his M60 was lubricated with the greasy juice of C-ration beans and franks.... Another Marine, armed only with a pistol and a sandbag full of hand grenades, was pitching them at groups of enemy as fast as he could pull the pins. They were all superb, they never gave the counterattack an inch—but it was apparent that the odds were not in our favor. We began to take fire from our left flank again, RPGs (shoulder-launched rockets) and rifles. (A large group of) NVA were coming down the shallow stream (on the left) using the bank for cover... We (also) discovered enemy on our right flank and a few to our rear.

Echo Company's 2nd Platoon, led by Lieutenant David R. Jones, intercepted the enemy company moving south along the streambank. In a brief, savage clash the enemy was thrown back. Lieutenant Jones was badly wounded and Sergeant James W. Rogers became 3rd Platoon commander. In a letter to me, Sergeant Rogers recalled the bitter fighting in Dinh To:

> ....We began the assault into Dinh To and (at first) the resistance seemed to ease up. I could see NVA getting up and running away.... A Marine on my flank opened up with an M60 machinegun.... He tore them (NVA soldiers) up... Some NVA stated returning fire. I was hit in the cartridge belt and knocked to the ground. The round was deflected and went through my canteen... It seemed like the NVA were regrouping and attacking.... NVA soldiers were all over ... as soon as you shot one, another would pop up in his place. We were receiving a lot of machine-gun fire. Lieutenant Livingston seemed to be everywhere at once. His coolness and calmness ... kept us from panicking....

Realizing Echo and Hotel could not hold their position in Dinh To, I told both company commanders to pull back to Dai Do. At this point, Captain Livingston was hit in both legs by machine-gun fire. Unable to move, he would not permit himself to be dragged to the rear until he was certain that all the other wounded were evacuated. He then ordered the able-bodied Marines in his immediate vicinity to pull back, fearing that they would be overrun protecting him. But the Marines refused to leave their leader and pulled him to safety.

During the Echo/Hotel withdrawal, Lance Corporal James L. O'Neil, a sniper attached to Hotel Company, and his partner, Private First Class Robert Griese, had finished helping two wounded Marines back to a temporary aid station in the northern part of Dai Do. A corpsmen pointed out some enemy in the open about 700 meters to the northwest. Upon checking the area with his telescope, O'Neil saw three 12.7 mm machine-gun positions cleverly concealed to look like graves. Whenever an aerial observer would appear, the guns and crews would remain hidden. When the plane left, the gun crews would remove the overhead cover and deliver murderous fire into Echo and Hotel Companies.

O'Neil and Griese zeroed in on the enemy machine guns and fired at the gunners with deadly accuracy. As O'Neil described to me in an audio tape:

> … I would … shoot the machine gunners and they would fall over their guns. The A (assistant) gunner would just pick up the gunner, move him off (to) the side, and the A gunner would keep shooting … somebody else would become the A gunner. Then I would shoot the gunner again … It was a turkey shoot… Pretty soon I counted 24 kills…

O'Neil's amazing feat was observed by a sergeant from the interrogator-translator team who couldn't believe his own eyes. O'Neil also observed and fired on large numbers of enemy moving along trails in the open northeast of Dai Do. He reported them to our FAC, Lieutenant Hilton, who had already seen them and had ordered airstrikes.

Echo and Hotel Company brought all their wounded and withdrew to Dai Do where they formed a perimeter under the leadership of Maj Warren. Warren had earlier brought the main CP Group forward to the southern edge of Dai Do. Wounded were evacuated. Echo and Hotel Companies were resupplied and reorganized.

Major Warren had been doing a tremendous job running things at the CP at Mai Xa Chanh, especially hounding regiment and division for more air and artillery support. He also stripped headquarters units of personnel to replace casualties in the rifle companies. A number of these Marines came from aboard ship; BLT 2/4 was the ground combat element of Special Lading Force Alpha, the equivalent of a present day Marine amphibious unit, which remained off the coast only 15 minutes away by helicopter from Dai Do. They were truck drivers, cooks, clerks, supply people, and others. They fit right in and did an admirable job.

Combined Attack by BLT 2/4 and ARVN Mechanized Battalion, Afternoon May 2

I was ordered to conduct a combined attack with an ARVN mechanized battalion that reportedly had occupied Dong Lai, about 500 meters west of Dai Do. We worked out a tentative plan, which was simple. The ARVN mechanized battalion and BLT 2/4 would start out abreast at 3:00 p.m., and attack northwest. The ARVN battalion was to seize Thuong Nghia. BLT 2/4 was to seize Dinh To and Thuong Do. The boundary line between the two units was a shallow stream that drained into the Bo Dieu River.

Coordination and communication with ARVN units was difficult at best. This day was no exception. Normally, we placed one of our own liaison officers and a radio operator with the ARVN commander and his U.S. Army advisor. This time, because of insufficient time and the shortage of officers, we didn't do it. Major Warren and I both talked to the U.S. Army advisor by radio. He seemed to understand the plan and said that the ARVN commander agreed to it. I was disappointed about not coordinating face-to-face with the ARVN commander and not having my own liaison officer present in his command group. But that's the way it was—unfortunately.

By the afternoon on May 2, BLT 2/4 was weakened by heavy casualties, loss of key leaders, and fatigue from more than two days of heavy fighting. Equipment casualties were also high. Our last two tanks had to be dragged off the battlefield, and less than half of our amtracs were operating, Many machine guns and mortars had to be replaced. Worst of all, most of the M16 rifles in the rifle companies had malfunctioned and were discarded in favor of captured AK-47 assault rifles.[4] In fact, when I visited Golf Company I saw only one M16 rifle. It was carried by Captain Vargas, the company commander. The only other functioning M16 I saw that afternoon was carried by me. Clearly, Marines felt their rifles had let them down. Personnel and equipment problems notwithstanding, we had a job to do, and we did it.

I did not have much choice in selecting the companies for the afternoon attack of May 2. Echo, Hotel, and Bravo Companies were decimated and unsuitable for offensive action. Golf Company, although down to about 40 effectives, including 4 officers, was still a viable, spirited fighting outfit, despite its 2-day ordeal. Captain Vargas knew his men well, and they knew and respected him for his outstanding competence as a combat leader and his compassion. I knew that I could depend on him and Golf Company.

The only other company was Foxtrot, the strongest with about 80 effectives, including three officers. (Foxtrot's 3rd Platoon had finally been relieved of duty at My Loc and returned to my control about noon on May 2.) I had misgivings about Foxtrot's company commander, but the troops and small unit leaders were capable. I hoped to keep a close watch on the company commander during the forthcoming attack.

As I briefed Captain Vargas and Foxtrot's company commander on the northern edge of Dai Do, we saw another rare sight—large numbers of enemy troops in the open fields northwest of Dai Do. We called in air, artillery, and mortar fire. Pilots in the attacking aircraft were ecstatic at being able to strafe and bomb enemy troops in the open. We listened to their excited chatter on our air net. Some of the enemy were within small-arms range. Marines had the morale-boosting experience of squeezing off carefully aimed shots and watching the enemy drop. A Marine sniper, impatient with the slow rate of fire of his bolt action sniper rifle, borrowed an M14 semiautomatic rifle from our S-2 scout so that he could "kill 'em faster." I wondered if the enemy commander had gone berserk, allowing us another daylight turkey shoot. I bet the reenlistment rate in the 320th Division dropped after Dai Do.

I ordered Golf Company to lead the attack, followed closely in trace by Foxtrot.

The attack jumped off from Dai Do at 3:00 p.m., as planned. Golf Company moved into Dinh To. Except for occasional small-arms fire, there was little enemy opposition. Enemy fighting holes and bunkers were checked out as assault elements moved cautiously forward. Crossing the open area northwest of Dinh To, Golf Company came under heavy enemy fire from the front and right flank as it entered Thoung Do. Enemy mortars, rockets, and artillery added to the tempo. I told Captain Vargas to hold up and ordered Foxtrot Company forward. But Foxtrot could not move. After some delay, I learned Foxtrot Company was pinned down in the rice paddies east of Dinh To and Thuong Do. It was the first I knew that Foxtrot had not followed directly behind Golf Company as ordered. Golf Company's rear was hanging in the air, unprotected.

About the same time, approximately 5:00 p.m., we began receiving heavy automatic weapons fire from the west (our left flank) where the ARVN battalion was supposed to be. Than we saw troops moving toward us from across the stream to our left. They were clearly North Vietnamese soldiers. We tried, unsuccessfully, to contact the ARVN battalion. Later we learned that the ARVN battalion had simply withdrawn without telling us. We began to receive light small-arms fire from our rear and realized that some enemy had slipped in behind us. Things were not looking good at all. Then a large group of enemy assaulted from our front. Simultaneously, heavy automatic weapons fire hit us from our right (east) flank. Things were getting worse.

Desperate circumstances require desperate measures. Vargas called his two assault units back and attempted to draw his company into a tight perimeter. We called in artillery so close that shrapnel landed among us. We called for naval gunfire to plaster our front and asked for emergency air support. Several helicopter gunships responded. The fighting was close and violent. Everyone in the Golf Company and battalion command groups fired his weapon. There were plenty of targets, and we dropped enemy assault troops within a few yards of our positions. Sergeant Major Malnar blasted away with his 12-gauge shotgun. Even the radio operators fought between transmissions. The enemy frontal attack finally stopped, but our losses were great. Big John Malnar was killed by a rocket round. Both my radio operators and I were wounded. All of Golf Company radio operators were either killed or wounded. Captain Vargas was painfully wounded (his third in three days and fifth in three months) but managed to stay on his feet and control things—in fact, he helped move me part of the way to the rear. I ordered Vargas to withdraw. He did, bringing all the wounded, and occasionally firing his rifle. His presence, inspirational leadership, personal actions, and total disregard for his own safety averted complete disaster and turned an impossible situation into an orderly withdrawal.

First Lieutenant Hilton, our FAC, also played a key role in the successful withdrawal. He organized a pickup squad of eight Marines, which laid down a withering hail of fire to the flanks and front as we pulled back. He fired an M79 grenade launcher until he ran out of ammunition. Then he fired various enemy weapons picked up along the way. He also "talked in" several helicopter gunships that fired their rockets right into the midst of attacking enemy only 20 yards from his position. And he helped move wounded. Judd Hilton, our duty aviator, fought as well as any infantryman on the battlefield. Many Marines owe their lives to that courageous officer.

Major Fritz Warren, leading a provisional platoon of Marines and several amtracs, moved northwest from Dai Do and met us in Dinh To. We were indeed happy to see him. The wounded were loaded aboard amtracs, moved to the banks of the Bo Dieu River, transferred to Mai Xa Chanh by skimmer boat, and then flown to medical facilities. I passed command to Major Warren, who strengthened the perimeter of Dai Do and remained in command of BLT 2/4 until relieved by the battalion executive officer (Major Charles W. Knapp) that evening. The reorganized BLT 2/4 spent an active night on May 2–3. They received some light probes and a few dozen enemy rounds. But heavy fighting was over. The next day, 1st Battalion, 3rd Marines arrived and moved through BLT 2/4 into Dinh To and Thuong Do. The enemy had withdrawn.

Dai Do in Retrospect

Some officers, not aware of the ferocity of the fighting, have asked why BLT 2/4 suffered so many casualties. Here is my answer:

• First, we were attacking a well-trained, well-equipped, well-supported enemy in excellent fortified positions. Attacking such an enemy is always costly. Just think of the casualties suffered in World War II assaults on Tarawa, Peleiu, Iwo Jima, and Sugar Loaf Hill on Okinawa.

- Second, BLT 2/4 was piecemealed into the battle. When the battle began, the rifle companies were spread out over a wide area (one, Echo Company, was not even under my operational control). It took too long to gain the required authority to move even those units under my direct control (Golf Company and 3rd Platoon, Foxtrot Company). Higher authority than me had to give approval. Had I been able to assemble and deploy my entire battalion the first day, we could have exerted greater pressure on the enemy, when his positions in Dai Do were not fully occupied. With all four rifle companies readily available, we could have seized Dai Do immediately after Hotel Company seized Dong Huan. To take Dai Do, the enemy would have had to attack two or three well-dug-in rifle companies rather than the pitifully understrength companies we had to use on May 2.
- Third, BLT 2/4 was not reinforced during the battle, but the enemy continued to reinforce his units and to replace his casualties. Thus, the enemy became stronger while BLT 2/4 became weaker from casualties and exhaustion.
- Fourth, about half of our casualties occurred during the afternoon attack of May 2. During that attack, the ARVN battalion on our left flank withdrew without notice, allowing the enemy to move in on that flank. Also, during the same afternoon attack, Foxtrot Company failed to follow closely behind Golf company and was not available to reinforce Golf Company as I had planned. Some enemy, therefore, were able to move in behind Golf Company.
- Fifth, if we had more fixed-wing air support, especially during the first 36 hours, assaulting enemy fortified positions would have been less costly. Large bombs with delay fuses followed by napalm would have caused breaks in the enemy's mutually supporting fires. There would have been more dead spaces to crawl through and fewer enemy to shoot at our Marines.
- Sixth, we should have been reinforced with at least 10 tanks (we had only 2) and an equal number of Ontos (we had none). The heavy firepower, greater mobility, and the shock of these weapons systems would have made our assaults more rapid and much more potent.

But despite numerous problems and possible treason, BLT 2/4 accomplished its mission. A superior enemy force was driven from the river banks, and the vital Cua Viet and Bo Dieu Rivers were open to traffic.

How badly was the 320th NVA Division hurt at Dai Do? I'm not sure, but much of its fighting effectiveness was destroyed. Major General Raymond Davis, who became commanding general, 3rd Marine Division, after the battle of Dai Do, stated that the defeat of the 320th Division during August through September 1968 was hastened by the punishment it took during April and May. Other U.S. and ARVN units fought against the 320th prior to and after Dai Do, but I'm certain that BLT 2/4 played a major role in its defeat.

Brigadier General Weise earned the Navy Cross for his actions at Dai Do. He served on active duty from 1951 to 1982 including combat tours in Korea and Vietnam. He commanded the "Magnificent Bastards" of the 2nd Battalion, 4th Marines during the heaviest fighting of 1967–68. In addition to the Navy Cross, his combat decorations include the Silver Star, two Legions of Merit (one with combat "V"), three Purple Hearts, and the Vietnamese Cross of Gallantry (with Gold Palm). His Battalion Landing Team 2/4 was awarded a Navy Unit Citation "for outstanding heroism in action against insurgent communist forces." He is a graduate of the Naval War College, and has a B.S. from Temple University and a MBA from Arizona State University. He co-chaired the Marine Corps Heritage Center committee and led the group, which furnished the vision for the National Museum of the Marine Corps. A book about him, One Magnificent Bastard: BGEN William Weise, USMC (Ret.), *by Mark Huffman was published in 2013.*

Notes

1   Sergeant Major John Malnar played and important role in the forward CP group. He was the "tactical commander," responsible for assigning individual positions on the march, during breaks, and whenever we halted. He could, and sometimes did, brief senior commanders on the situation when I was busy fighting the battle, He trained the CP radio operators and runners to a high state of proficiency and

individual initiative. For example, Sergeant Charles W. Bollinger, the battalion tactical radio net operator, a very capable Marine, was so well informed and competent that he kept our rear CP fully informed of what was happening during fast-moving situations. He also answered many questions asked by the companies, without referring to me. He relayed messages clearly and in short order. Corporal Greg R. Kraus, our messenger, was another all-around, capable team member who could do almost anything. All of our group were good in a firefight. The contributions of Big John Malnar and our well-trained forward CP group were critical to our success.

2   We usually avoided riding inside the LVPP5 amtracs because of their highly volatile gasoline fuel tanks located beneath the troop compartment. We feared there would be little chance of escape if the amtrac struck a land mine. Land mines were plentiful in our area.

3   Taylor was aboard the USS *Iwo Jima* collecting money to pay Hotel Company troops when the battle began on April 30, he had not fully recovered from a wound suffered several weeks earlier. He learned of the battle as wounded were being delivered to the *Iwo* by helicopters. He grabbed a rifle and jumped aboard a returning helicopter, rejoining Hotel Company at Dong Huan after the assault.

4   Problems with M16 rifles in Vietnam in 1967–68 were many. First, the M16. 5.56mm rifle was placed in the hands of troops who were not thoroughly trained in its use. Those troops had trained with the older, heavier, reliable M14, 7.62mm rifle. They were not familiar with the idiosyncrasies of the lighter, less rugged, rapid-firing M16. Every new rifle takes time to get used to. The M16 was introduced to troops in a combat zone with inadequate familiarization. Second, cleaning materials were in short supply, and the M16 had to be kept clean to function properly. Third, several of the early lots of M16 ammunition experienced large numbers of ruptured cartridges and other malfunctions. Fourth, early versions of the M16 rifles did not have corrosive-resistant bores, and the damp climate and salt air in RVN caused rapid bore deterioration. Fifth, the early M16 rifles would not function with dirt or grit in the receiver, unlike the highly reliable, "troop proof" AK-47 rifle carried by the enemy. In heavy, continuous combat, such as we experienced at Dai Do, keeping a rifle clean was nearly impossible for most troops. Sixth, the irresistible tendency by many Marines to use full automatic fire also contributed to jams and wasted ammunition. A related problem arose when Marines fired captured AK-47 and SKS rifles, which sounded distinctly different from M16s. Other Marines sometimes mistook friendly troops firing enemy rifles for the enemy, especially during darkness. On the night of May 1–2, Bravo Company engaged in a Marine vs. Marine firefight with enemy weapons. Fortunately, no casualties occurred.

COMBAT

Lieutenant Colonel Richard J. Rinaldo, USA Ret.,
Distinguished Service Cross

Despite 24-hour news coverage of Operation *Iraqi Freedom*, the American public is only getting a glimpse of what combat is really like, especially ground combat. Even the best coverage of any war can hardly fully capture its essence. There are military veterans, like retired Army Generals Wesley Clark and Barry McCaffrey among the TV commentators. Their war wounds and medals for valor received for actions during the Vietnam Conflict attest to their ability to tell some of this story. But they are a small and shrinking minority in and out of uniform, and we all pray that the current conflict will add only small numbers to their ranks. Few will talk a lot anyway. When they do, as did McCaffrey in "Vietnam Letters," published with his former platoon sergeant Daniel P. Garcia in *ARMY* (November 1997) 30 years after their service together, the results have been rightly called, "a distillation of close combat."

McCaffrey wrote of "memories of unending vigilance; ripped hands from constant digging; the shock of making contact as firing built up quickly in a crescendo; the acrid smell of grenades, cordite, C4 explosives, trip flares; the incredible stench of filthy soldiers, the sight of torn uniforms, the constant pain from bites, destroyed feet, pulled muscles from carrying 80 pounds of water, ammunition, weapons, packs; and the agony of seeing screaming, wounded soldiers and dragging the dead to helicopters."

To gain more than a glimmer of what combat is like and to better understand the sacrifice of our soldiers, sailor, airmen, and Marines in

Operation *Iraqi Freedom*, we might ponder works of history along with some fiction and good movies. I believe that these give us texture, provide context, and with the passage of time, offer a broader perspective about combat than can be found in the immediacy of current events.

What do such sources tell us?

"Nobody Dies." If you are a military movie buff, you will recognize John Ireland's ironic phrase from the epic World War II film, *A Walk in the Sun*. Somebody dies all the time in war, but few really believe they will be the ones to fall—at least until the bullets come close. Death, however, is just one peril of the battlefield. There is also dizzying confusion bordering on havoc, immobilizing fear and terror, gruesome maiming, nerve-wracking noise and cruelty.

Thirty years ago the distinguished British historian John Keegan, in *The Face of Battle*, described a war like the one in progress today. Continuous operations last for days with little respite at night; combat involves lethal weapons and fratricide and accidents occur. According to Keegan such a war would be intolerable. Modern man, he claims, would not be able to cope with the level of stress generated by its grand scale. Such misgivings are not new. As early as the 1860s military thinkers like Colonel Ardant DuPicq in his *Battle Studies*, decried the terrible effect modern weapons would exact on a war's military participants. Still the British fought for five months at Ypres during World War I to capture 45 square miles of territory. They lost 370,000 men, or 8,222 troops per square mile. In one 19-day artillery bombardment they used 321 trainloads of shells—one year's production for 55,000 workers. According to one historian, "Never had so many men been so long under such fire." Nevertheless, that war continued, and 25 years later the human ability to endure such grand-scale horrors would again prove itself during World War II. About Vietnam, Daniel Garcia would recall ferocious "beasts of death and survival," but also hope.

Part of the staying power of such phenomena is a perverse "fox-hunt syndrome" of battle. Keegan mentions: "the excitements of the chase, the exhilarations of surprise, deception and the *ruse de guerre*, the exaltations of success, the sheer fun of prankish irresponsibility."

In *The Warriors*, philosopher J. Glenn Gray lists "the delight in seeing, the delight in comradeship, the delight in destruction." In the movie

Patton, the great war leader tells us: "I love it. God help me, I do love it so, more than my life!" Patton was expressing an aspect of the soldier's thrill of flirting with danger and of testing one's mettle. In the movie *Apocalypse Now*, a 1979 blockbuster about the Vietnam conflict, Director Francis Ford Coppola staged a breathtaking attack of a Viet Cong village by an air cavalry unit. F-5 jets engulfed a tree line in flames. Helicopter gunships raked and shook the ground with rockets. Door gunners blazed away at the VC. All this took place while the tune of Wagner's *Ride of the Valkyries* wailed over the loudspeakers of the command and control ship. If you saw this movie on the spectacular 70 mm-wide screen and heard the Dolby stereo effects you would have felt the riveting, compelling and enthralling embrace of the excitement it depicts. Is there any wonder that even today so many folks are glued to CNN or other coverage? Or that media are eager to be there for the opening shots?

As potent as these lures of battle may be, they are also transitory. A more permanent consideration is self-preservation. Paul, Erich Maria Remarque's protagonist in the World War I classic, *All Quiet On The Western Front*, put it this way: "We defend ourselves against annihilation. Death with hands and helmets is hunting us down. If your own father came, you would fling a bomb into him."

If self-preservation is so strong on the battlefield, what accounts for its many famed deeds of self-sacrifice?

Ernest Hemingway used Clausewitz's categories to divide his anthology of war stories, *Men at War*. The first of these was courage—the kind that conquers what Remarque called, "the deadly tension that scrapes along one's spine like a gapped knife." Clausewitz believed it could be influenced. The ancients knew this too, and some 2,400 years ago, in *The Anabasis*, Zenophon called for leaders to set the example. Julius Caesar, in his famous *Commentaries*, stressed the importance of battle cries and trumpets. Both ancients and moderns, Xenophon and Gray, as examples, realized that the repetition and drill of military training will serve to create a reflex reaction during battle.

Similarly, T. E. Lawrence, of Arabian fame, also talks about preparation for combat in *Seven Pillars of Wisdom*. To him an "adjustment of the spirit" was necessary to prepare the psyche in order of battle, just as strategy and tactics would array the forces physically. Even more critical was what he called a "felt" element of troops which finds its crisis at the breaking points of life and death, or wear and tear. On the second day of the Battle of Gettysburg, a lone northern regiment defended the Little Round Top. Outnumbered, with ammunition running low, one-third of his troops killed or wounded, the colonel of the regiment ordered the bayonet charge, thus changing the outcome of the Civil War. The U.S. Army uses the story in its textbook on leadership. A novel about the battle, *The Killer Angels*, by Michael Shaara, earned a Pulitzer Prize and became grist for the epic movie, *Gettysburg*.

Still, courage can be fleeting. In Stephen Crane's classic *The Red Badge of Courage* the youth "recalls with a thrill of joy the respectful comments of his fellows upon his conduct. Nevertheless, the ghost of his flight from the first engagement appeared to him and danced." In 1730 French military theorist Marshal de Saxe observed that "the courage of the troops must be reborn daily. There is nothing that is so variable." A hundred years later DuPicq is equally sure of our fickleness. He said, "What is too true is that bravery often does not at all exclude cowardice."

Faint hearts grow stronger in groups, and most of us want good repute. A study of human behavior in combat during World War II, *The American Soldier*, affirms that personal survival will take a back seat to group norms about cowardice. S. L. A. Marshall's study about battle dynamics in the Korean War, *Men Against Fire*, finds few soldiers aspiring to heroics, but even less willing to be branded cowards.

Pericles' famous funeral oration, reported in the *History of the Peloponnesian Wars*, characterizes the humiliation of one who lets up in battle as "more painful to bear than death." DuPicq describes four brave men who did not know one another and therefore would not attack a lion. Four others, who knew one another well, would attack "resolutely." Even relative strangers could become courageous fighters. In the Battle of the Bulge in 1944, cooks, clerks, and mechanics from different units joined together to fight well and stave off the German counteroffensive.

In the long run though, there is another important dynamic. Charlton Ogburn, Jr., finds the key to the incredible feats of arms and survival of Merrill's Marauders of World War II fame in Pericles: "The secret of happiness is freedom, and the secret of freedom is a brave heart." Again, General McCaffrey is instructive as he voluntarily leaves home to head to Vietnam. "This is what I was supposed to do. My friends were dying and being maimed in massive numbers. There was simply no option but duty," he tells us.

Combat then will involve noble causes, duty, danger, fear, perverse fun, leadership, and bravery. But, who could ignore luck? Some, like the Humanist Petricius, even claim that, "although intelligence, courage, and knowledge of military science may help, Goddess Fortuna remains the decisive factor."

Paul, in Remarque's classic, resigned himself morosely to the idea that "no soldier outlives a thousand chances. But every soldier believes in chance and trusts his luck."

Somehow warriors know intimately that in combat, like life, fate takes its cue from the random strike, the sleight misstep, the accidental turn, despite all our plans and efforts. In this, media got it right in showing soldiers and others getting ready for recent combat—checking their gear, writing home, and making sure they had their rosaries, crosses, crescents, or Stars of David and maybe a rabbit's foot too.

Too often it will not help. Colonel Frank Haskell, a participant at Gettysburg summed up its finale: "The fight done, the sudden revulsions of sense and feeling follow.... The whole air roared with the conflict but a moment since—now all is silent, men, some composed, with upturned faces sleeping the last sleep, some mutilated and frightful, some wretched, fallen, bathed in blood."

And probably, like Captain Murray in *Saving Private Ryan*, their commanders would cry for them.

This piece appeared in ARMY Magazine (Vol. 53, No. 7, July 2003). Copyright 2014 by the Association of the U.S. Army and reprinted by permission of ARMY Magazine.

REVENGE

William E. Davis III, USNR, Navy Cross

According to a local news report on his death, "William E. Davis, III, was a senior in college when the Japanese bombed Pearl Harbor, and he vowed to get revenge." Judging from the results of his military career, he did just that.

Bill Davis came to understand the threat of war during his first-ever combat mission over Guam during World War II.

"We started our dives, and immediately the antiaircraft fire increased," he later wrote in his book about his war experience, *Sinking the Rising Sun: Dog Fighting & Dive Bombing in World War II*. The Japanese were throwing everything they had at us. I glanced over at Duke, my roommate and close friend. One moment he was there, the next there was a tremendous explosion, then nothing."

That first combat mission took place after two years of training. Until then, Bill knew flying was dangerous but he was having too much fun to really contemplate the finality of death at the hands of an enemy. Training deaths happened once in a while but now the probability of death was a daily occurrence as he settled into flying one strike mission a day in addition to a four-hour combat air patrol over the fleet while being assigned to Torpedo Squadron 19 on the USS *Lexington*.

After Guam, Bill went on to Palau for more close air support. Next came strikes at Iwo Jima, Haha Jima, and Cebu Island in the Philippines where Bill downed his first Zero. After several days around Cebu, the fleet headed north to Luzon where the fleet was able to seriously disrupt the Japanese ground defense.

Flying combat every day became a way of life; a routine of getting up in the morning, flying to work, doing the job, and then flying back to the ship. But it was a different way of life than Bill thought he would be doing when he was offered a position with the Radio Corporation of America upon graduating with an engineering degree from the University of Pennsylvania in 1942. The attack on Pearl Harbor changed that and instead of a desk it was now an aircraft.

The routine of combat however took a back seat when a typhoon hit the Fleet. Winds over 100 miles an hour and waves the size of mountains become the norm. By the second night, the carrier was climbing the side of these mountains. As she neared the top, the bow would climb out into space and would continue until the center of gravity passed the point of balance, then the bow would dive and the screws would come out of the water at the stern. As the carrier burrowed into each wave, the flight deck would go under water as much as twenty feet. Would the ship survive? Most of the flight crews thought it wouldn't. Then, when the winds reached 150 miles an hour the ship rendered frightening sounds of metal on metal and Bill thought the ship was breaking up but word finally came over the loudspeaker stating all was well and the *Lexington* would live to fight another day.

As soon as the storm blew itself out Bill's unit headed straight for the main harbor at Naha where they sunk two cruisers and then went around the island looking for targets of opportunity. A lone destroyer was spotted but the flight was out of bombs so they used the next best thing. All eight aircraft made two runs each and fired their .50 Caliber Browning machine guns aiming at the waterline hoping to set off an explosion, but no luck. Preparing for a third run, Bill noticed that the ship was riding lower so they circled and watched the ship sink as a result of some two thousand half-inch holes drilled through the light skin of the destroyer.

The next mission took the USS *Lexington* to Formosa, where they engaged the Japanese in their largest dog fight to date. It was fifty Zeros against eighteen F6Fs but Uncle Sam was victorious, with Bill receiving credit for downing three Zeros. Then, after several days of constant air battles, the *Lexington* retired to refuel and head back to Luzon where Bill received credit for two probables and two confirmed enemy bombers.

The following days consisted of finding and attacking the Japanese fleet of four carriers (one was the *Zuikaku* which took part in the attack at Pearl Harbor), two battleships, two cruisers, and ten destroyers. After flying for two hours the enemy was sighted and Bill waited until he was directly over the *Zuikaku* at thirteen thousand feet before starting his attack. He flew through deadly clouds of 40mm bursts at ten thousand and 20mm at four thousand feet. When it seemed he was going to hit the ship, he released his bombs and pulled out. Unfortunately the G forces blanked him out and when he came to he was on the deck heading directly for the Oyodo, a Japanese heavy cruiser. Only through great airmanship was he able to clear the ship by flying between the cruiser's second gun turret and the bridge. He received the Navy Cross for his part in sinking the *Zuikaku* carrier.

The following mission took them back to the waters off Leyte searching for a Japanese heavy cruiser that had been damaged and was unaccounted for. They found and sunk it but Bill's luck finally ran out and he was forced to crash at sea some sixty miles from land as another typhoon materialized. Fortunately a destroyer rescued him but he was then forced to spend several days in waves up to 100 feet and winds of 170 miles an hour.

After being transferred back to the carrier his unit was relieved from their first combat tour and he was able to spend Christmas at home prior to being scheduled for a second combat deployment. Fortunately for him the Navy had other ideas. He was sent to California Institute of Technology for two years to earn his master's degree in aeronautical engineering. The war was over when he completed his studies so he was released from active duty. He then accepted a job with Bell Aircraft Company as a design engineer and test pilot and was selected to pilot the X-1, the first plane to break the sound barrier. Unfortunately, the Army Air Corps was in charge of the program and they selected an Army pilot by the name of Chuck Yeager.

After several years working for Bell, Bill started a successful aviation-related sales company. He died in 2012 at age 91.

Adapted from a piece in Legion of Valor General Orders.

MILLETT'S CHARGE

J. C. Bean

Most of the men of Company E, 2nd Battalion, 27th Infantry Division, probably knew how to play the game "King of the Hill." A popular childhood game back in the fifties, most who grew up during that era, at one time or another during their lives, had mimicked war. From the bottom of a real or make-believe hill, they would try to dethrone a friend turned imaginary enemy king. Assaulting the Hill's top, each sought to drag the imposter king to the bottom in victory. But not always in success. Sometimes, the attacker would find himself "Heels up at Hill's bottom."

Several years later, on an early bitter-cold February morning in 1951, soldiers of Company E found themselves in a real-life analogy as they approached AB Hill 180 near Osan and close to Pyongtaek, Korea. In late 1950, Chinese communists had pushed United Nations Forces from the Chinese and North Korean borders to the south of Seoul. Numerous Communist forces were entrenched throughout the territory that now includes Osan and Suwon Air Bases.

About 30 miles away, members of Company E moved toward 180 in an open-box formation. Two platoons formed the left and right sides of the box while a third formed its base as they approached a range of hills head on. The hills dog-legged right a mile or so to the rear. An open rice paddy stretched out in front of the hills for about

1,000 yards. Realizing this was no game, the intensity increased as the soldiers clutched their rifles and prepared to fix bayonets, if necessary, before meeting the enemy.

One of the bayonets belonged to then-Captain, now retired, Army Colonel Lewis L. Millett. "I knew the enemy at the top of the hill carried orders to kill, just as I did," he said. "As company leader, I divided the group of 100 men into three platoons. 'Operation Ripper' was designed to destroy the Communist troops holed up on 180. I also knew I was smarter than they. Because they were at the very top, the enemy faced a strategic problem."

Unlike the child's game, when it comes to real war, real weapons with real bullets, one's location on the hill top poses a distinct disadvantage. Because of the degree of the hill's incline, bullets fired from there travel in a straight line and above the heads of ascenders. Once the attacker gets above a certain level and within a zone of about 40 feet from the crest of the hill, he becomes most vulnerable. Millett had found himself in that position, and that knowledge was foremost on his mind.

Another thought preyed on him. Millett said that word had come down that an enemy document put out and circulated by the Chinese was accusing American GIs of fearing cold steel and close combat. "Knowing that," Millett said, "we trained hour after hour, day after day, in the use of bayonets." Fierce determination melded their spirits

That determination proved a major factor to members of Company E just a short while after they had reached the base of Hill 180. The enemy's fire popped all around them.

Once in that crucial 40-foot zone, Millett decided to proceed with the assault.

"You know, nowadays guys with raised arms and clenched fists join to glean victory all the time. Back then, though, it was uncommon for a group of soldiers to stand together and cheer themselves for victorious efforts. But we did. We went to the top of that hill, raised our arms, shouted out loud, jumped up and down in excitement—and some even hugged each other for their efforts."

According to Millett, an operations analyst for battle studies from a famous university in the United States had conducted interviews to find out what happened on Hill 180. "As the soldiers repeated accounts of the battle," Millett said, "I was shocked to find out that I had actually swung my bayonet like a baseball bat." With each swing, Millett and his comrades came closer and closer to victory. Some blows that didn't cause death, caused wounds. Regardless of death or wounds, the enemy scattered. "We stripped those dead lying on the ground to validate the cause of death. We discovered quite a few had multiple wounds."

Of the nearly 400 or so enemy fighters, 167 died and more than 200 were wounded. Millett killed 9 of 18 victims by bayonet alone. "One enemy soldier," he recalled, "held his gun so low in his foxhole that he couldn't respond to my thrusting bayonet quickly enough."

Later that year, Millett traveled to Washington and the White House. There, President Harry S. Truman presented him with the Medal of Honor. Millett said that during the ceremony, Truman told him he'd "rather have this (the medal) than be President."

"I'm proud I won the Medal of Honor," Millett said, "but it all boiled down to team effort. I told my men that we had come to Korea to fight, and fight we did. At the same time," he concluded, "I never asked them to do anything I wouldn't do. I know you've probably heard it before, but I'll say it again. I think that's the way it should be."

Lewis Millett died at age 88 in Loma Linda, California after serving for more than 15 years as the honorary colonel of the 27th Infantry Regiment Association. In the 1960s he ran the 101st Airborne Division Recondo School, for reconnaissance-commando training, at Fort Campbell, Kentucky. Then he served in a number of special operations advisory assignments in Southeast Asia during the Vietnam War. He founded the Royal Thai Army Ranger School with help of the 46th Special Forces Company. This unit is reportedly the only one in the U.S. Army to ever simultaneously be designated as both Ranger and Special Forces.

Millett was born in Maine and first enlisted in 1940 in the Army Air Corps and served as a gunner. Soon after, when it appeared that the U.S. would not enter World War II, he left and joined the Canadian Army

In 1942, while Millett was serving in London, the United States entered the war. Millett turned himself into the U.S. Embassy there.

He was eventually assigned to the 1st Armored Division. As an antitank gunner in Tunisia, Millett earned the Silver Star after he jumped into a burning halftrack filled with ammunition, drove it away from Allied soldiers and jumped to safety just before the vehicle exploded. He later shot down a German fighter plane with a vehicle-mounted machine gun.

As a sergeant serving in Italy during the war, his desertion to join the Canadian forces caught up to him. He was court-martialed, fined $52 and denied leave. A few weeks later he was awarded a battlefield commission. After the war, he joined the 103rd Infantry of the Maine National Guard, and attended college, until he was called back to active duty in 1949.

In addition to the Medal of Honor, Millett earned the Distinguished Service Cross, the Silver Star, two Legions of Merit and four Purple Hearts during his 35-year military career. After his retirement, he remained active in both national and local veterans' groups from his Idyllwild, California home.

This piece appeared as "From Metal to Medal: Retired Army Colonel led Army's Last Bayonet Charge" Arnews Sidebar (October 29, 2010).

GEORGE S. PATTON AS WE KNEW HIM

Brigadier General John C. "Doc" Bahnsen USA Ret.,
Distinguished Service Cross

This takes place in early Jan or Feb 1969. While I was commanding Air Cav Troop, 11th ACR, during an operation in War Zone D my Aero-Rifle Platoon had made ground contact with an enemy force in bunkers. I was not sure of the size of the enemy force, but proceeded to pound the area with air strikes and artillery fire. I had pulled the rifle platoon back and asked for ground reinforcements. M Company of 3rd Squadron, 11th ACR, was given opcon (operational control) to me. It consisted of eight or nine M-48 tanks.

When they arrived in the contact area I lined them up with the company commander's tank in the middle of the line. I then placed my rifle platoon behind the tanks. While this was going on I had Cobra gunships and Scout helicopters circling the area to make sure no enemy leaked out of the bunker area. I continued to pound the bunker complex with artillery fire while I briefed the tank company commander on my plan of action.

About this time I got a radio call from Colonel Patton wanting a situation report. He was in a helicopter and had just flown into the area. I quickly briefed him and told him I was getting ready to make an attack into the bunker complex. He asked me to pop smoke and then his helicopter landed behind the line of tanks. He joined me behind the company commander's tank with some new colonel in tow. He told me that this was his good friend Colonel Bev Reid, a VMI graduate who was visiting from the Pentagon, and was a DSC holder from the Korean War. I quickly told them my plan of attack and gave them a quick update on what the enemy situation looked like.

My air strikes and artillery fire had leveled a large part of the trees where the bunkers were located. Patton asked me what he could do to help. I told him that I did not need anything, but if he wanted to join the attack he could join my squad leader on the right and help us overrun the bunkers and clear them. He said, "Okay—what about Colonel Reid?" I told him he could join the rifle squad leader on the left and help in the attack. Reid was carrying a pistol and I gave him some grenades that I was carrying. I shifted the artillery fire another 200 meters to our front and I then got on the tank telephone and told the tank company commander to move out slowly.

The attack moved out as planned and we very shortly got into the bunkers, running over knocked-down trees. My riflemen proceeded to put grenades in bunkers, and the tanks blasted the area with canister rounds. A few of the enemy broke and ran and were cut down by the tanks. We moved about 150 to 200 meters and the tanks stopped. I had shifted the artillery fire another 200 meters and had got my gunships flying on the flanks, cutting down escapees. The attack was over and my riflemen were policing up the dead and checking for papers and weapons. Colonels Patton and Reid were there with us and Patton was at a high emotional level. Final body count was over 30 enemy dead, no POWs. Patton used his revolver to shoot some enemy dishes found in the bunkers. He was charged up and enjoying the moment.

My soldiers in particular loved George Patton—and he loved them. He told Colonel Reid that this was a typical day of combat in the 11th Armored Cavalry Regiment—which was a small stretch, but close. Prior to this time, in late 1968 Colonel Patton had been recommended for two Distinguished Service Crosses. He had been counseled by his bosses to quit taking risks and to cease leading ground attacks. He told me to keep this action under my hat, especially the fact that he had exposed Colonel Reid to enemy fire. On any number of occasions he would join me on the ground to talk, but this was the only time I asked him to join me in an attack of an enemy force.

He was a brave man and for me, the perfect combat commander. I knew for a fact he would never ask me to do anything he was not willing to do. We had a very special relationship that was hard to define. He used to say I was a Fighting Son of a Bitch, but I was *his* Fighting Son of a Bitch.

US Army retired Brigadier General John C. "Doc" Bahnsen is a '56 graduate of West Point. He commanded a platoon, a troop and a squadron during two combat tours in Vietnam and a tank platoon, tank company and tank battalion in Germany during two tours. He is a fixed-wing and rotary-wing aviator with 1,600 hours of combat flying time. Among his over 70 decorations he has a Distinguished Service Cross, five Silver Stars, four Legions of Merit, three Distinguished Flying Crosses, four Bronze Stars (three for Valor) 51 Air Medals (three for Valor) and two Purple Hearts. He commanded an Aviation Brigade and was the Assistant Division Commander of the 2nd Armored Division. He was selected to the Army Aviation Hall of Fame in 2007 and the Georgia Aviation Hall of Fame in 2015. He is the co-author of the book American Warrior—A Combat Memoir of Vietnam *(2007).*

THE UNKNOWN LEGEND

Colonel Peter J. Ortiz, USMC, Navy Cross With Gold Star

Lance Corporal Benjamin Harris

Dan Daly. Smedley Butler. John Basilone. Lewis "Chesty" Puller. These names and their stories are drilled into the heads of every Marine while in initial training. The name and story of Colonel Peter J. Ortiz, however, isn't as recognizable.

Colonel Ortiz, lost the only battle of the many he fought on May 16, 1988, when he died of cancer. He was buried with full military honors in Arlington National Cemetery in Arlington, Virginia.

Ortiz fought in Europe during World War II. While his exploits may seem the stuff of legend, his story is real and exemplifies a Marine tradition of adapting and overcoming tremendous odds to complete the mission.

Born July 5, 1913, in New York City, Ortiz spent much of his youth in his father's native country of France. Looking for fun and adventure, he joined the famed French Foreign Legion at the age of 19. Starting as a private, he attained the rank of "acting lieutenant," with the promise of being commissioned as a second lieutenant if he reenlisted and became a French citizen. Ortiz turned down the offer, and returned to the United States in 1937.

However, Ortiz was not out of the military for long. In 1939, with World War II underway, Ortiz returned to the French Legion. The following year, he conducted a daring demolition raid on a fuel dump his fellow Legionnaires had failed to secure before evacuating the area. Ortiz succeeded, but a gunshot wound temporarily paralyzed him and he was captured by the Germans.

For 15 months, Ortiz repeatedly tried to escape from prisoner-of-war camps in Germany, Poland, and Austria. In 1941, he finally succeeded and escaped to the United States. Ortiz then made his way to Marine Corps Recruit Depot Parris Island, S.C., to start his enlistment in the Corps.

Ortiz stood out from the moment he arrived at the depot. He was allowed to wear the ribbons he had earned as a Legionnaire, and made an impression on everyone who saw them, including Colonel Louis R. Jones, who at the time was the chief of staff at MCRD Parris Island. Jones contacted the commandant of the Marine Corps about commissioning Ortiz immediately into the Marine Corps Reserve, citing his numerous awards and military bearing and character.

By August 1, just 40 days after starting his enlistment in the Marine Corps, Ortiz was a second lieutenant, and was promoted again to captain in December.

Headquarters Marine Corps immediately took an interest in Ortiz's file, and came up with a plan that utilized his experience with the Legion, his ability to speak ten languages and his uncommon resolve to complete any mission given to him. In July 1943, Ortiz reported to England to prepare for a guerilla operation in France. In January, he arrived with two other officers. They become the first uniformed Allied officers to appear in France in four years.

Ortiz quickly acquired a reputation as a fearless leader and a faithful Marine. He often wore the service "alpha" uniform, even while on reconnaissance in German-controlled towns.

The Gestapo quickly took notice of Ortiz's actions and considered capturing him to be a high priority. German officers grew to dislike him so much that they would curse his name and the Marine Corps as a toast. One unlucky group of officers did this when Ortiz was in attendance. Accounts vary, but the consensus is that Ortiz opened his jacket, revealing his uniform underneath, shot the offending officer, and then escaped into the night.

The mission was recalled in May, due to the impending Normandy invasion on D-Day.

In August, Ortiz returned to France with a larger team, including five fellow Marines. After a surprise encounter with a German convoy, Ortiz and two of his Marines tried to escape through a nearby town but instead turned themselves in to save the lives of the local villagers.

The guards were warned of Ortiz and his past exploits as a POW, and kept a close eye on him, although this didn't stop his efforts to flee. Facing an Allied assault, the Germans had to move the prisoners and Ortiz managed to escape again. He met up with members of the British armed forces in April 1945 and returned to England where he received his second Navy Cross.

After the war, Ortiz returned to California and remained in the Marine Corps Reserve.... In 1955, Ortiz retired and was promoted to the rank of colonel in recognition of his service, which included two Navy Crosses, the Legion of Merit, two Purple Hearts, and five Croix de Guerre. On May 16, 1988, Ortiz passed away, and America lost one of her finest heroes.

This piece first appeared in CORPS LORE *(March 24, 2010).*

Upon return to civilian life, Ortiz became involved in the film industry. He worked with director John Ford, a former member of the OSS himself. Two movies were produced depicting Ortiz's exploits: 13 Rue Madelein, *with James Cagney, etc., and* Operation Secret *with Cornel Wilde. Ortiz also had small parts in such films as* The Outcast, Wings of Eagles, *and* Rio Grande. *He played the part of Major Knott in the film* Retreat Hell, *a movie about the Marines at the Chosin Reservoir in 1950.*

FIGHTING ON THE LONG, HARD ROAD

James Megellas, Distinguished Service Cross

Known as "Maggie" to his fellow paratroopers in the U.S. Army's 82d Airborne Division, Jim was born in Fond du Lac, Wisconsin in 1917. He entered the Army as a second lieutenant in the spring of 1942 after graduating from Ripon College in Wisconsin. One year later after going through various schools he received his parachute badge at Fort Benning and was finally on his way to fulfill his destiny as the most decorated officer in the history of the 82d Airborne Division.

The World War II Foundation, a 501 (c) (3) organization produced an outstanding leadership documentary film covering Jim's war experiences starting with his first combat in the rugged Apennine Mountains near Naples, Italy.

> After being wounded and hospitalized at Anzio he returned to his unit and never missed another day of combat until May 8, 1945, the end of the war.
>
> Soon Maggie's outfit was tapped to run one of the most star-crossed missions of World War II. From the fiasco on the beach of Anzio to Field Marshal Montgomery's vainglorious Operation *Market-Garden* in Holland, months of hard combat were followed by the Battle of the Bulge—and the long hard cross road across Germany to Berlin.

Jim's Distinguished Service Cross was awarded for his action in Holland in 1944. Arriving at an enemy observation post, he crawled forward alone and killed two outpost guards and the crew of a machine-gun nest.

He then brought forward his patrol, attacked the main enemy defenses and singlehandedly secured three prisoners and killed two more. Two blockhouses were then attacked and destroyed. His mission complete, he led his men back through enemy lines while under mortar fire. He personally carried a wounded man while firing his Thompson with one hand. After the war, Jim served for 18 years with the U.S. Agency for International Development, including work in Yeman, Panama, Vietnam and Columbia. Now in his nineties, he spent a Christmas in Afghanistan with his old military outfit, the 504th Parachute Infantry Regiment, along the Pakistani border.

OPERATION *RED WINGS*

Michael P. Murphy, USN, Medal of Honor

On June 28, 2005, deep behind enemy lines east of Asadabad in the Hindu Kush of Afghanistan, a committed four-man Navy SEAL team was conducting a reconnaissance mission at the unforgiving altitude of approximately 10,000 feet. The SEALs—Lieutenant Michael Murphy, Gunner's Mate 2nd Class (SEAL) Danny Dietz, Sonar Technician 2nd Class (SEAL) Matthew Axelson and Hospital Corpsman 2nd Class (SEAL) Marcus Luttrell—had a vital task. They were scouting Ahmad Shah, a terrorist in his mid-30s who grew up in the adjacent mountains just to the south.

Under the assumed name Muhammad Ismail, Shah led a guerrilla group known to locals as the "Mountain Tigers" that had aligned with the Taliban and other militant groups close to the Pakistani border. The SEAL mission was compromised when the team was spotted by local nationals, who presumably reported its presence and location to the Taliban.

A fierce firefight erupted between the four SEALs and a much larger enemy force of more than 50 anti-coalition militia. The enemy had the SEALs outnumbered. They also had terrain advantage. They launched a well-organized, three-sided attack on the SEALs. The firefight continued relentlessly as the overwhelming militia forced the team deeper into a ravine.

Trying to reach safety, the four men, now each wounded, began bounding down the mountain's steep sides, making leaps of 20 to 30 feet. Approximately 45 minutes into the fight, pinned down by overwhelming forces, Dietz, the communications petty officer, sought open air to place a distress call back to the base. But before he could, he was shot in the hand, the blast shattering his thumb.

Despite the intensity of the firefight and suffering grave gunshot wounds himself, Murphy is credited with risking his own life to save the lives of his teammates. Murphy, intent on making contact with headquarters, but realizing this would be impossible in the extreme terrain where they were fighting, unhesitatingly and with complete disregard for his own life moved into the open, where he could gain a better position to transmit a call to get help for his men.

Moving away from the protective mountain rocks, he knowingly exposed himself to increased enemy gunfire. This deliberate and heroic act deprived him of cover and made him a target for the enemy. While continuing to be fired upon, Murphy made contact with the SOF Quick Reaction Force at Bagram Air Base and requested assistance. He calmly provided his unit's location and the size of the enemy force while requesting immediate support for his team. At one point he was shot in the back, causing him to drop the transmitter. Murphy picked it back up, completed the call and continued firing at the enemy who was closing in. Severely wounded, Lieutenant Murphy returned to his cover position with his men and continued the battle.

An MH-47 Chinook helicopter, with eight additional SEALs and eight Army Night Stalkers aboard, was sent in as part of an extraction mission to pull out the four embattled SEALs. The MH-47 was escorted by heavily-armored, Army attack helicopters. Entering a hot combat zone, attack helicopters are used initially to neutralize the enemy and make it safer for the lightly-armored, personnel-transport helicopter to insert.

The heavy weight of the attack helicopters slowed the formation's advance prompting the MH-47 to outrun their armored escort. They knew the tremendous risk going into an active enemy area in daylight, without their attack support, and without the cover of night. Risk would, of course, be minimized if they put the helicopter down in a safe zone. But knowing that their warrior brothers were shot, surrounded and severely wounded, the rescue team opted to directly enter the oncoming battle in hopes of landing on brutally hazardous terrain.

As the Chinook raced to the battle, a rocket-propelled grenade struck the helicopter, killing all 16 men aboard.

On the ground and nearly out of ammunition, the four SEALs, Murphy, Luttrell, Dietz and Axelson, continued the fight. By the end of the two-hour gunfight that careened through the hills and over cliffs, Murphy, Axelson and Dietz had been killed. An estimated 35 Taliban were also dead.

By his undaunted courage, intrepid fighting spirit and inspirational devotion to his men in the face of certain death, Lieutenant Murphy was able to relay the position of his unit, an act that ultimately led to the rescue of Luttrell and the recovery of the remains of the three who were killed in the battle.

This was the worst single-day U.S. Forces death toll since Operation *Enduring Freedom* began. It was the single largest loss of life for Naval Special Warfare since World War II.

This piece is taken from official Navy records.

KEEP YOUR BOOTS ON

Jill Jorden Spitz

The 101st Airborne had an ironclad rule: Keep your boots on.

Sergeant James D. Spitz bent that rule ever so slightly by loosening his tight boots just a bit before bedding down on March 26, 1969 in a remote region of Vietnam known as Fire Base Jack. But that didn't stop him from taking on two charging battalions of suicide squad sappers, Vietnamese soldiers who wore satchels of grenades they intended to set off in a crowd of Americans.

At 3 a.m. on March 27, Spitz' base was rocked by mortar fire followed by five charging enemy battalions—including two battalions of sappers. Instead of taking cover, he charged toward them and took out three of four approaching enemy soldiers.

After that initial attack, Sergeant Spitz—then 39 years old, given the nickname "Gramps"—ran in and out of a tent that was ablaze, pulling four wounded men to safety. Then he charged again, taking out a group of seven sappers who were rushing the perimeter of the American base. At one point he was literally knocked out of those slightly loose boots when a rocket-propelled grenade landed near him.

The fighting that day lasted for several hours and ultimately earned Spitz the Distinguished Service Cross for his "exceptionally valorous actions." From the citation:

> When a heavy concentration of hostile mortar fire began to pound the base, Sergeant Spitz dashed to his mortar section and began supervising the firing of

high-explosive and illumination rounds. As the incoming barrage slacked and the enemy initiated a ground assault, he moved along the perimeter bunker line to direct the defense. While making his way through the fusillade of enemy rocket grenades, he encountered four communists storming the berm. Sergeant Spitz immediately charged the four enemy soldiers and drove them back. Before the hostile force could obtain reinforcements and attempt another assault, Sergeant Spitz regrouped the men along that section of the perimeter. Six of the enemy returned with satchel charges and rocket-propelled grenades, but Sergeant Spitz' intrepid counterattack drove them back once more. While gunships riddled the area outside the berm, Sergeant Spitz directed his attention to the M-42 self-propelled gun crew's tent, which had been struck by enemy fire. He rushed to help remove the wounded and then assisted in firing the M-42 gun at the charging enemy.

Spitz enlisted in the Army in 1949 at age 17 (he had to lie about his age to get in) in Hutchinson, Kansas. He completed basic training at Fort Riley, Kansas and was first stationed at Fort Breckenridge, Kentucky. He chose jump school because it paid a $50-a-month premium over the base pay of $59 a month. He broke his toe and couldn't finish jump school, so he was sent to Sagamo War Criminal Prison in Tokyo as a guard.

Spitz was sent to Korea in the infantry in 1950. He arrived on July 19, his 19th birthday, and stayed until November 1951. After Korea, he went to Chicago as a communications specialist with the artillery until he was discharged in 1952. He went home to Hutchinson, where he joined the National Guard. He went back to high school, which he hadn't completed, and became the first veteran at his school on a GI bill. He didn't finish until 1959, when he was stationed at Fort Ord and learned that in order to get promoted, he had to have a high school diploma. He earned his GED on September 22, a year after he married Tokie Hagita of Tokyo, a week before the birth of their son Tom and three years before the birth of their daughter Bonny.

Spitz served again in Korea in 1962 and was stationed in Hawaii in 1964–1965. He first deployed to Vietnam in 1966 with the Security and Assault platoon, and again in 1968–1969 as an infantry platoon leader with the 101st Airborne. In 1967 and 1968 he was a drill instructor at Fort Ord. In July 1969, the helicopter he was riding in was shot down, breaking Spitz's back. After six months in the hospital, he returned to duty at Fort Ord as a drill sergeant. He received orders to return to

Vietnam in February 1971, but instead decided to retire, which he did that May.

Spitz was National Commander of the Legion of Valor in 1982–1983. He also is a founder of "Col. Maggie's" All Services Airborne Drop-In, held each Labor Day weekend in Marina, California. The event is held in the name of Martha Raye, a Vaudeville and early movie star who spent much of her career entertaining troops overseas. Colonel Maggie was dedicated to the group and attended their gatherings until she died in 1994.

Spitz's other medals and decorations include a Silver Star earned in Korea, a Bronze Star with oak leaf cluster, three Purple Hearts, the Army Commendation Medal, Meritorious Service Medal, Combat Infantryman's Badge 2nd Award, and a Senior Paratrooper Badge.

Jill Jorden Spitz is the proud daughter-in-law of Jim Spitz.

VALOR AT OAHU

Tim Frank

On December 7, 1941, America was thrust into war when air units of the Japanese navy attacked U.S. Pacific Fleet ships and military installations at and around Pearl Harbor, Hawaii. The strike caught the American soldiers, sailors and airmen off guard and inflicted severe damage throughout the island. Chief Aviation Ordnanceman John W. Finn had been asleep in his quarters at Naval Air Station, Kaneohe Bay, when the attack started, but soon found himself in the midst of the chaos. Undaunted by numerous wounds, Finn met the enemy head on, becoming one of the first Medal of Honor recipients of WWII.

Finn was born on July 24, 1909 in Los Angeles, Calif. When he was 15, he heard his uncle tell his cousin about an opportunity to enlist in the Navy and even try for the Naval Academy. Finn recalls, "We were poor people and this was a good chance to go to college, but the Naval Academy didn't interest me."

A few weeks before he turned 17, Finn went to the recruiting station, where a chief gave him a few tests and told him to come back after his birthday. Finn ran home to tell his parents he was a Navy man, even though he still had two weeks to go. When he returned after his birthday, the chief asked Finn if he was absolutely sure he wanted to join the Navy. He didn't have to ask, because Finn couldn't wait to "see the world." On July 29, 1926, Finn was sworn in.

Trained as a gunner's mate, he found his calling in mid-1934 when he successfully completed the exam for aviation ordnanceman. Following an assignment with Patrol Squadron 14 at NAS North Island, Calif., he was transferred to Kaneohe Bay in 1941.

Finn remembers December 7 in great detail. Since it was Sunday, he and his wife were asleep at their quarters one mile from the air station when the attack started. "The first thing I heard was machine-gun fire. I thought, 'I'm the chief ordnance officer, who the hell is firing machine guns today? Hey, it's Sunday!'"

When a plane flew past his window, he first thought the Navy was staging a mock attack, as it sometimes did. Then he thought his men might be testing a malfunctioning machine gun. Still unaware of the attack, he put his whites on and walked out to the car. His neighbor joined him for the ride to the base.

"We didn't even say 'Good morning'—just got in the car, drove the base speed limit, even stopping to give a kid a ride." About halfway to the base, Finn heard a "terrible roaring" and saw a plane streak by with a red dot on its underside. "I threw that old Ford into second gear and tore down to the corner, almost running over some sailors," he recalled.

Just as he turned the first corner into the station, the first hangar was starting to flicker and blaze. Some of the planes on the ground were also starting to burn. Before the car stopped, he said, "I ran like a deer to the armory. I immediately got one of the guns and moved way out on the ramp so I could see the planes." Meanwhile, all 33 patrol planes and their hangars had caught fire. Finn ordered his men to retrieve any usable machine guns, but most were burned beyond use. The sailors used whatever was salvageable to fire on the attacking Japanese planes, even though they had no mounts for the machine guns.

Throughout the attack, the Japanese were shooting and dropping bombs all around Finn. "Pretty soon, I picked up quite a few hits—18 to 21, some of them just scratches," he recalled.

Despite his wounds, he continued to man the gun and return fire. When the attack was finally over, Finn refused medical attention and supervised the repair and installation of machine-gun pits around the station. Although most of the weapons were designed for aircraft, Finn said, "if the Japanese had come back, they would have had one hot reception from all those machine guns. Somebody would have hit them."

After making sure they were prepared for another attack, he finally agreed to go to the aid station about 0200 the next morning. Finn said, "I needed rest and sleep. I was hurting all over." He went to sick bay and found the doctors were taking care of the seriously wounded, so he decided to wait. He went home to check on his wife and reported to sick bay a few hours later.

He entered the hospital on the 8th and stayed until the 24th. After he was released, he went on with his duties until September 15, 1942, when his commanding officer called him in. He informed Finn that he was to receive the Medal of Honor. That same day Finn was designated an ensign for temporary service, ranking from June 15.

About a week later, Finn and his wife were brought to *Enterprise* (CV 6), which was undergoing repairs at Pearl Harbor. "Just before the ceremony started, they shut off all the noise. Right off the bat, Admiral Nimitz stepped up to the little lectern and he gave a nice talk, one that made me really happy." Finn remembered Nimitz commenting: "Do not think for an instant that we have the enemy on the run. He is a tough, aggressive, seditious and determined enemy. However, we are making progress."

There was a war going on and little time to spare. "The minute the ceremony was over, all those jackhammers and everything started back up banging and crashing, and the flight deck looked like a mess." Some photos were taken of Finn, and he went on with his duties.

Finn's WWII service continued with several shore assignments, followed by duty aboard *Hancock* (CV 19) from April 1945 to December 1946. He retired as a lieutenant on September 1, 1956.

Today, Finn is still proud of his days in the Navy, but does not consider himself a hero; to him, the Medal of Honor is but one aspect of his years of naval service. But his actions above and beyond the call of duty during the attack on Pearl Harbor embody the spirit of valor and sacrifice that the Medal of Honor represents.

This piece first appeared in Naval Aviation News *(May–June 1998).*

Mr. Frank is the Historian of Arlington National Cemetery.

THE SILVER CROSS FOR VALOR

The Legion of Valor established the Silver Cross for Valor in 1957. It is reserved for recognition of a recipient's valorous actions involving lifesaving activities at great personal peril. Few medals have been awarded because, by its very nature, the Silver Cross is given sparingly and only after a thorough review by members of the Legion of Valor Board of Directors. Here are some stories about this prestigious award.

Father Edmond Carmody

Father Carmody Camody of San Antonio, Texas, was attending a picnic on July 4, 1972 at Canyon Lake, Texas, when a violent storm swept the area. He noticed two boats attempting to reach land when one over-turned. Carmody immediately went to their rescue. As he approached, waves drove the prow into his leg (subsequent medical exams revealed that both bones were broken.) Disregarding the injury, he succeeded in bringing the occupants to shore. The second vessel, containing nuns, faltered 60 feet from shore and began to sink. Despite his wound, Father Carmody swam to the boat which just capsized spilling its occupants into the turbulent lake. He assisted the nearest nun, who was floundering helplessly, toward the shore. As he neared land, waves tossed him onto some rocks, tearing ligaments in his other leg. Despite extreme difficulty, he returned a third time to the raging waters. As he approached the boat this time, a large wave overturned it, trapping one of the nuns who had been clinging to the gunwhale underneath. A bystander swam out to help, dove underneath and pushed the unconscious nun out to Father Carmody. Keeping the nun's chin above water, he succeeded in reaching shore saving the nun from death.

Ulrike Derickson

On June 15, 1985, Ulrike was Chief Stewardess for TWA Flight 847 when the plane was hijacked and one person killed. Disregarding her own safety and exposing herself to possible danger, she stepped between the assailant and passenger informing the hijacker "That's enough," saving the passenger's life and thwarting the possibility of other assassinations.

Nancie Santiago

In April 1996, in Gainesville, Florida, twelve-year-old Nancie leaped from a four-foot-high streambank into Sweetwater Branch and dove under water to pull her unconscious and severely bleeding friend, Tyee Hammons, from in front of a 10-foot alligator. Nancie held Tyee under his arms to keep his head above water and got him to the bank where she handed him to an adult, who began to administer first aid. Nancie then jumped from the water and quickly ran one and a half miles through the woods and up a hill to a pay phone where she dialed 911 for emergency help.

Cadet Deon Peterson

In 1997 near Stony Creek, Virginia, a tour bus left the road and careened down a 150-foot embankment crashing through trees and landing on its side in the water. One chaperone was killed, and all the passengers were injured. Cadet Peterson and another passenger managed to open the window of the side of the bus not submerged in the water. Cadet Peterson swam to the closest shore and determined the water en route to be approximately five feet deep. She returned to the bus and organized the passengers into a human chain from the bus to the shore. All of the passengers who were non-swimmers were passed along the chain to the shore of the river and to safety. Cadet Peterson was the primary reason the passengers remained calm and focused on the task of getting all able-bodied passengers to safety.

Sergeant Mark Alan Todd, Sr. and Sergeant Kimberly Denise Munley

On November 5, 2009, Sergeants Munley and Todd were members of the Fort Hood Civilian Security Force. A 911 call alerted them to shootings at a building on the base. They immediately responded. Arriving at the building, Todd approached it from one side and Munley from the other. Seeing Todd, the gunman made a break for the side of the building covered by Munley. She came face-to-face with him and fired her weapon, until she was hit by a bullet. As she began to reposition herself, he ran at her firing two rounds that hit her in the leg, severing her femoral artery. As he stood over her, preparing to fire more rounds, Todd was able to wound him severely, bringing an end to the incident.

AWARDS AND DECORATIONS

The best words I've ever heard on the subject of medals were from a fellow lieutenant who'd been my company XO when I first arrived in Vietnam.... He was awarded the Bronze Star. When I congratulated him he said, "A lot of people have done a lot more and gotten a lot less, and a lot of people have done a lot less and gotten a lot more."

Karl Marlantes

"GALLANTRY AND INTREPIDITY"

Valor Decorations in Current and Past Conflicts

Eileen Chollet

The battle of Chosin Reservoir lasted 17 bitterly cold days in late November and early December 1950. Thirty thousand United Nations (UN) troops were surrounded by 120,000 Chinese troops, and they fought as a Siberian cold front brought the temperature down to -30°F. Back in the United States, the country had been enjoying the peace dividend following the end of World War II, and soldiers and Marines were sent to Korea with equipment that was not designed for the environment. By the time the UN forces broke the encirclement and fought their way to evacuation at Hungnam, 3,000 U.S. Servicemembers had been killed, another 6,000 had been wounded, and 12,000 had suffered frostbite injuries. Fourteen Marines, two soldiers, and a Navy pilot were awarded the Medal of Honor for heroic actions during the battle of Chosin Reservoir.

The scorching deserts of Iraq and Afghanistan are a long way from frozen Chosin, and 60 years have elapsed since the Korean War. The nature of warfare has changed, from a brutal force-on-force engagement to a high-tech counterinsurgency operation. During 11 years of war, nearly 2.5 million U.S. troops have served in Iraq and Afghanistan, more than 5,000 have been killed, and nearly 50,000 have been wounded due to hostile action. However, only 13 Medals of Honor have been awarded for actions in those 11 years, compared with 17 awarded for those 17 days in Korea. Servicemembers and civilians alike wonder why.

Valor Decorations Then and Now

Official criteria for the three highest U.S. decorations for valor—the Medal of Honor, the service crosses, and the Silver Star—were established shortly after World War II, so reliable comparisons can be made for these awards through the Korean War, the Vietnam War, and in Iraq and Afghanistan. The Medal of Honor is presented to service members for gallantry and intrepidity in risking their lives above and beyond the call of duty. A service cross (the Navy Cross, Distinguished Service Cross, or Air Force Cross) is presented for heroism not rising to the level of the Medal of Honor. The Silver Star is presented for heroism not rising to the level of a service cross.

Although records on military decorations are public information (subject to the Freedom of Information Act), no complete database exists, with the Pentagon citing privacy concerns and incompleteness of records following a 1973 fire in an Army records building in St. Louis. Following the recent Supreme Court overturning of the Stolen Valor Act, which upholds the right to lie about receiving a valor decoration, the Department of Defense (DOD) has begun to compile a database, initially intended to include only Medal of Honor winners going back to September 11, 2001, and recently expanded to include service cross and Silver Star recipients. A complete database of Medal of Honor winners is maintained by the Congressional Medal of Honor Society, but the only mostly complete database of service crosses and Silver Star awards is the Military Times Hall of Valor, which is maintained by military historian Doug Sterner.

Although the incompleteness of the data complicates the analysis, a comparison of award rates for current and past conflicts shows that 20 times fewer valor decorations have been awarded during the Iraq and Afghanistan wars than during Vietnam and Korea. The Medal of Honor is the most talked about example.

Explaining the Decrease

Lawmakers, journalists, and military historians have speculated on what might be causing the 20-fold decrease in award rates. In a 2009 *Army Times* article, former Marine Joseph Kinney argued that being killed in combat had become a de facto criterion for winning a valor decoration, charging that DOD has an "inordinate fear that somebody is going to get the Medal of Honor and be an embarrassment." Of the 11 medals awarded for the current conflicts, only four went to living recipients, and the first was not presented until 2010. The cases of Captain Charles Liteky, USE (a Vietnam-era chaplain who later renounced his medal in protest of U.S. policies in Central America), and Major General Smedley Butler, USMC (who later wrote a book denouncing war as a government "racket" to protect the interests of corporations), argue for caution in presenting the high-profile Medal of Honor to living recipients. However, the award rates for the service crosses and Silver Star have dropped by the same factor of 20, suggesting that something common to all three decorations that is, something beyond the widespread publicity unique to the Medal of Honor, is causing the decrease.

In a report accompanying the National Defense Authorization Act for fiscal year 2010, the House Committee on Armed Services requested that DOD study the Medal of Honor award process to determine whether commanders in the field had inadvertently raised the criteria for valor, leading to the low numbers of awards. DOD reported that it was confident that the process had not changed and cited two reasons for the decrease in award rates: the current use of "stand-off" technology (unmanned aerial vehicles, or "drones") by U.S. forces, and the use of improvised explosive devices (IEDs) by the enemy. However, a closer look at the data shows that these changes in the nature of warfare are only part of the answer, accounting only for a factor of about 6 from the factor of 20.

The DOD Answer: Drones and IEDs

In current conflicts, drones have played a prominent role in surveillance and targeted killing, replacing some service members who would otherwise be put in harm's way. Since risk of one's life is required for valor decorations, the use of drones does indeed partially explain fewer valor decorations, but not the entire factor of 20. Though the exact number of missed combat actions is difficult to estimate, casualties can be used as a proxy for combat actions since each casualty due to hostile action probably represents a chance for valorous action. Only 1 in

50 service members in the Iraq and Afghanistan theaters have been killed or wounded due to hostile action, compared with about 1 in 15 in the Korean and Vietnam wars. Since the casualty rate between the past and current conflicts has dropped by a factor of three, lack of opportunities for valor due to remote warfare probably accounts for a factor of 3 out of the factor-of-20 decrease in awards.

Among those who do experience combat and are wounded or killed as a result, the number of valor decorations is still lower than it was in the past. Since personnel who do experience combat are receiving five times fewer decorations, the lack of personal combat actions cannot entirely explain the missing factor of 20.

IEDs have been called the "signature weapon of the 9/11 era," accounting for two out of three casualties in Iraq and Afghanistan. Given the unpredictable nature of these weapons, Service members probably have fewer opportunities to demonstrate "gallantry and intrepidity … above and beyond the call of duty." However, three factors argue against IEDs playing a large role in the drop of award rates.

First, explosives were extensively used in Korea and Vietnam, and they historically account for more casualties than small-arms fire. Even the Vietnam War, known for its close fighting in the jungle rather than distant shelling, had more casualties due to explosives such as artillery, land mines, and grenades than to small-arms fire according to the Office of the Secretary of Defense, Southeast Asia Combat Casualties Current File. While it might be "hard to be a hero against an IED," as one military historian put it, it is just as hard to be a hero against artillery fire, which can have an effective range of more than 10 miles.

Second, all the Medals of Honor awarded for combat in Afghanistan were for incidents that occurred in 2005 or later, when IEDs were most heavily used. If IEDs were causing the drop in award rates, we would expect the awards to be clustered at the beginning of the war when IED use was minimal.

Finally, reading through citations makes it clear that involvement in a close-combat firefight is not the only (or even the most common) way to be decorated for valor. Numerous awards have been presented to service members who jump on grenades or other explosives to shield their comrades. Rescue of one's comrades from danger even while not under direct hostile fire fits the criteria for a valor decoration. For example, Sergeant First Class Rodney Yano, USA, was a helicopter crew chief during the Vietnam War, and he was marking enemy positions with white phosphorous grenades. One exploded prematurely, partially blinding him and covering his body with severe burns while igniting other ammunition in the helicopter. He began shoving the burning ammunition out of the helicopter to protect his comrades, suffering additional burns that eventually took his life. He was awarded the Medal of Honor. By comparison, Sergeant First Class Alwyn C. Cashe, USA, was decorated posthumously only with a Silver Star following his heroic rescue effort in Iraq. After his vehicle hit an IED, fuel from the vehicle spewed everywhere and ignited. Sergeant Cashe repeatedly returned to the vehicle to pull his fellow soldiers to safety all while his own uniform was on fire.

If casualties are again used as a proxy for combat actions, and one-third of casualties are due to hostile action that does not include IEDs, then IEDs can account for at most another factor of 3 in the factor-of-20 decrease in valor decorations. Once IEDs do not completely prevent valorous actions, these weapons probably cause a decrease by a factor of about 2. Between the factor of 3 due to fewer combat actions and the factor of 2 from IEDs, the official DOD explanations do explain a factor-of-6 decrease in awards, but not the observed factor-of-20 decrease. Something else must be contributing.

Times Are Changing

While the official criteria for the three highest valor decorations have not changed, the broader military culture has, and these changes may be causing the rest of the observed decrease in award rates. Following Vietnam, several decorations received authorizations to include the Valor devices for combat service, and commanders may nominate service members for these awards instead of decorations specifically for valor. During the 1990s, military officials debated internally whether medals were being awarded haphazardly and too freely, ultimately resulting in a Pentagon review of Bronze Star awards presented for the intervention in Kosovo. Delegations of approval authority for the Iraq and Afghanistan and operations admonish commanders to reserve awards for those "who truly distinguish themselves from among their comrades by exceptional performance in combat or in support of combat operations." It would be unusual for these cultural factors not to affect the number of decorations awarded.

While the award process itself from nomination to award (or not) is understandably kept private, some indirect evidence suggests that something has changed in the award process since the Vietnam War. During the Vietnam era, the median time between a combat action and the presentation of a Medal of Honor was about 20 months. In Iraq and Afghanistan, that processing time has increase to 30 months. In past conflicts, 35 to 40 percent of valor decorations went to officers; in the current conflicts, that percentage has decreased to 25. Meanwhile, the percentage of decorations going to senior enlisted personnel (E7 to E9) more than doubled, from 3 percent to 8 percent. These data do not point to any specific cause, but we could speculate that the changing roles of service members in theater or the transition from a draft force in Vietnam to an all-volunteer force today may be playing significant roles.

The missing pieces of the data, along with the complex and changing nature of warfare and military culture, make the exact causes of the 20-fold decrease in the number of valor decorations in current operations difficult to determine. The prevailing explanation that the nature of warfare has changed is incomplete, explaining at most a factor of 6 out of 20. While the new DOD database makes a good attempt at transparency, it needs to be expanded to include all valor decorations and conflicts. The natures of combat and military culture have changed since the 1970s, and the effects on the award process deserve more careful study to ensure that our soldiers, sailors, Marines, and airmen are awarded the decorations they earn.

This piece first appeared in Joint Forces Quarterly (Issue 72, 1st quarter 2014).

Dr. Eileen Cholett is an Operations Analyst at the Center for Naval Analyst at the Center for Naval Analysis.

RECOGNIZING VALOR

Lieutenant Colonel Richard J. Rinaldo, USA Ret., Distinguished Service Cross

There has been plenty of talk about the apparent lack of high-level awards for valor in Afghanistan and Iraq with facts and statistics. All discussed possible reasons.

Some people have wondered whether an increase in awards may come administratively after the wars. They may be right. In January 2016, the Department of Defense concluded a study of its awards and decorations and ordered a review of selected valor awards for possible upgrades, according to a *Stars and Stripes* report on the subject. But the number of awards forthcoming may not be commensurate with the heroics displayed in our recent battles. As Katherine Zoepf wrote in May 2010 in the *New York Times Magazine* "the military, after its recent experiences with Jessica Lynch and Pat Tillman, is hesitant to publicize or otherwise herald tales of heroism, for fear of later embarrassment."

If public relations is a factor, can we afford to be so careful? What about impact awards for valor, which were common in Vietnam? Their purpose was not only to provide immediate recognition for acts of valor, but also to set inspiring examples—internal public relations, if you will.

Notwithstanding public relations, Zoepf posits a better explanation. She cited Defense Department spokeswoman, Eileen M. Lainez, who credited the trend to "changes in the nature of warfare, noting that the enemy forces of Vietnam and earlier wars typically engaged in 'close conflict' with U.S. forces, whereas today's 'non-uniformed insurgents' rely on 'remotely detonated improvised explosive devices (IEDs), suicide bombers and rocket, mortar and sniper attacks'—all tactics, her statement implied, that create fewer opportunities for U.S. soldiers to demonstrate the traditional valor of close-quarters combat."

Retired chief of military history Brigadier General John S. Brown wondered in an article in *Army Magazine* whether "the American way of war has entered a paradigm that requires less heroism "above and beyond the call of duty." A recurrent piece of battlefield advice is "don't be a hero." In theory, a well-equipped force with solid leadership, rigorous training and polished execution can follow through on a plan without putting anyone at exceptional risk—particularly if it considerably outclasses its adversary."

He posed a provocative question: "If we are awarding fewer medals and burying fewer soldiers, is that not better?"

Pericles, in his famous funeral oration, reported by Thucydides in the *History of the Peloponnesian Wars*, also had something to say about valor:

> He who is a stranger to the matter may be led by envy to suspect exaggeration if he hears anything above his own nature. For men can endure to hear others praised only so long as they can severally persuade themselves of their own ability to equal the actions recounted: when this point is passed, envy comes in and with it incredulity.

The bottom line is that the U.S. military will continue to confront deadly enemies of our nation, and our warriors must be ready and willing, when directed, to seek them out and destroy them. Planning and technology may get better and better. Our warriors will continue to learn marksmanship, first aid, field sanitation, map reading, and similar basic skills. We will always strive to give our troops less risk and more advantage, better training, technology and good plans. However, there is no new paradigm when it comes to valor. America's courageous warriors will continue to stare down the defiance of our enemies before killing or capturing them.

In his classic, *The Hero with a Thousand Faces*, Joseph Campbell wrote that a myth is more than a stereotype, based on a kernel of truth. A myth is a transcending, transfiguring, and transforming reality, and heroism was an example of one such myth.

Campbell also published *Myths to Live By*. He might have titled it, *Myths to Live and Die By*. Carl Marlantes, in his chapter on heroism, highlighted Campbell's insight that heroism often has a moral objective, "saving a people, or person or idea … sacrificing … for something."

By that standard, there are a lot of heroes out there today. And you don't need an award for valor to be one. "Hero" awards sometimes depend on luck and circumstance, sometimes rank and position, and even whether the recipient is well liked by those who write him or her up. This is not to diminish the importance of these awards. But being in a combat zone is solid evidence of heroism. Two soldiers from a transportation unit at Fort Eustis, Virginia were killed in Afghanistan by improvised explosive devices and gunfire. You could argue that being in the wrong place at the wrong time and getting killed or wounded does not make a hero. Another perspective is that it does, even more so for today's warriors and veterans of multiple tours in Iraq or Afghanistan.

In coming to heroism, Marlantes talks about the simple action of standing up when all types of dangerous kinetic objects were in or near his physical space. And those transportation soldiers were in their vehicle with a security (saving) mission in a place where such objects are known to be hidden somewhere and used all too frequently against American soldiers. They did their duty, challenged the dragon, and suffered its hot breath of death. Arguably that makes them heroes.

In *The Marauders*, author Charlton Ogburn, Jr. shared the experiences of Brigadier General Frank Merrill's unit of World War II fame—dysentery, malaria, typhus, "the exhaustion, the drenchings, the disease, the sores, the denial of every comfort and amenity," not to speak of the enemy. Just before disbanding the unit with some 3,000 original members, 130 combat-effectives remained. Ogburn asked one of them, Samuel V. Wilson, who later would become a lieutenant general, how he and the others were able to keep on going, "when they knew sooner or later they were bound to get it, if not around the next bend, then then the one after that." "There was one ability I found I did have," Wilson answered. "You just have to take the next step."

To be on the line, to go forward in duty to your comrades, commanders, and country, to see your friends torn apart by bullets or bombs, to carry on, stand up, or take the next step. That is the stuff of heroism. Those who were there know—and they are heroes too, medals or not.

A MEDAL OF HONOR FOR A VIETNAM-ERA AIR FORCE PILOT?

Fred L. Borch

It is not too late for the Air Force to award a Medal of Honor to retired Air Force Colonel Philip J. Conran. Now 79 years old, "Phil" Conran was awarded the nation's second highest decoration for gallantry in action against the enemy—the Air Force Cross—for his extraordinary valor in combat in October 1969. At the time, Conran had been recommended for the Medal of Honor, but circumstances deprived him of this award.

At 10:45 a.m. on October 6, 1969, five helicopters carrying U.S and friendly troops left for a camp in Laos. Conran was the aircraft commander of the number two helicopter in the formation. After being told that the landing zone or "LZ" was clear, the helicopters started their approach in trail formation. But the LZ was far from safe, and the lead aircraft was shot down while landing. Its crew members and the other troops on board had no choice but to abandon the helicopter and take up defensive positions on the ground.

Phil Conran, still aloft in his helicopter, immediately climbed out of the range of the enemy's small-arms fire, and assumed command of the remaining four helicopters. He then directed fire from two escorting A-1E Skyraiders onto the enemy.

By this time, Major Conran was running low on fuel. He had two choices: return to a safe area and refuel—leaving his fellow Americans on the ground to face almost certain death at the hands of enemy insurgents—or attempt a rescue of the downed crew and reinforce the friendly soldiers on the ground. Concluding that the 26 friendly soldiers would not be able to provide sufficient protection for the downed helicopter crew, Conran decided to land his helicopter.

Although he selected what he thought was the safest approach route, Conran's helicopter was severely damaged by enemy fire while attempting to land. Although he probably could have broken off his approach and returned to a safe area, he elected instead to land and unload the friendly troops—who joined the fight.

Although damaged, Conran's helicopter was still flyable. But, as he began to take the downed crewmembers aboard his helicopter, enemy small-arms fire ripped through the main rotor transmission and cockpit. Take-off was now impossible, and Conran and his crew abandoned the aircraft.

For the rest of the day, Conran repeatedly exposed himself to enemy fire to obtain essential ammunition and food from the downed helicopters. After an HH-3E "Jolly Green Giant" attempting to rescue Conran and the airmen was driven off by an intense barrage of automatic weapons fire, enemy mortar rounds began falling into the friendly positions.

Conran located the enemy mortar crew, and called in an airstrike to destroy it. Later, while trying to strengthen their defenses, Conran was severely wounded in the leg. He did not mention this injury until he had lost all feeling in his leg and felt that, if a rescue helicopter were to arrive to extract them, he might not be able to make it to the aircraft on his own and would need help. In spite of the seriousness of his leg wound, Conran refused to allow anyone to expose themselves to enemy fire to examine his injury.

Just before nightfall, two Jolly Green Giants were able to complete a successful rescue of all 44 personnel. Because Conran was chiefly responsible for the survival of the men on the ground, he was recommended for the Medal of Honor.

When he was subsequently awarded the Air Force Cross—the second highest decoration that an airman may be awarded for combat heroism—Conran said that he was told by then Lieutenant General Lucius D. Clay, the Pacific Air Forces deputy commander, that the Air Force had initially approved the award of the Medal of Honor to him. But his act of heroism had occurred in Laos, where no American military operations were supposed to be taking place. At the time he received his Air Force Cross, Phil Conran was simply grateful to have done his duty and come home in one piece; he did not give the matter of the Medal of Honor much more thought. After all, he had survived a harrowing experience and done more than could have been expected of any man or woman under fire.

Given that Conran was initially recommended for the Medal of Honor, and that it seems a quirk of geography that prevented its award to him in 1969, to now give this airman the nation's highest award is no attempt to re-write history. On the contrary, it is the right thing to do for an airman who showed such caring and concern for his fellow Americans in the jungles of Laos more than 45 years ago.

Fred L. Borch is the Regimental Historian and Archivist for The Judge Advocate General's Corps. He served as an Army lawyer for 25 years before retiring in 2005 and has been a full-time military legal historian since 2006. He wrote For Military Merit: Recipients of the Purple Heart *(Annapolis, Md.: Naval Institute Press, 2010), and other works listed in Appendix B.*

CHERISHING VALIANT DEEDS

Honorary Member B. G. Burkett

B. G. Burkett, a military researcher, is the co-author *of Stolen Valor: How the Vietnam Generation Was Robbed of its Heroes and its History*. The Legion of Valor Board of Directors granted Burkett honorary membership in appreciation of his outstanding support in cherishing the memories of the valiant deeds for which the Medal of Honor, Distinguished Service Cross, Navy Cross, and Air Force Cross are insignia.

Stolen Valor won the coveted William E. Colby Award for an outstanding military book. Burkett also served as the Co-Chairman of the Texas Vietnam Memorial with former President Bush as Honorary Chairman. His work has been the subject of two *Reader's Digest* stories, as well as award-winning pieces on ABC's *20/20* and other national programs. He is a graduate of Vanderbilt University and the University of Tennessee. Burkett served in Vietnam with the 199th Light Infantry and was awarded the Bronze Star, Vietnamese Honor Medal and the Vietnamese Cross of Gallantry with Palm. In July 2005, he was inducted as an honorary member in the U.S. Army Ranger Hall of Fame at Fort Benning, Georgia. He also introduced the Stolen Valor Act of 2005 on Capitol Hill with Congressman Salazar of Colorado.

This piece first appeared in the Legion of Valor General Orders.

INTRODUCTION TO THE ARMY AND NAVY LEGION OF VALOR OF THE UNITED STATES OF AMERICA

Frank La Fayette Anders, Medal of Honor

This piece appeared in the 1926–27 Army & Navy Legion of Valor Memorial to the Intrepidity of the American Soldier, Sailor and Marine. Part of the history of the Legion, it describes well our legacy of a thoughtful and humble approach to awards and decorations and forms a fitting finale to this part.

The people of the United States inherited a peculiar feeling in relation to titles and decorations for service that seems to be at variance with the history of the human race as we know it. This feeling must have been very acute in the early history of the Republic, for we find it reflected in the constitution of our country and in many early papers of our statesmen. That attitude of mind is not hard to understand by those who have given close and intensive study of the times when decorations and titles were synonymous with power and oppression of the masses by the classes, and that was to a certain extent so fostered by the bestowal of titles and decorations.

However, the decorations that our government has seen fit to bestow through the acts of its legislative bodies do not create a titled class nor one endowed with power to wield. These decorations have been bestowed by a grateful Republic to those who valued the liberty of all the people greater than life itself, and through their acts have given proof that they were willing to make the supreme sacrifice that the Republic might not "Perish from the earth."

It must not be understood that those who have been so decorated have been the only ones who have performed deeds of valor. The names of thousands of men, yes more than that, are written on the rolls of the Army and Navy who have performed similar deeds, but unfortunately their acts have been unobserved and we know of them only through the final results achieved. Only those have been decorated whose deeds were observed by impartial and disinterested witnesses who saw the deed performed.

This organization stands uncovered and in respectful silence before the unseen monuments and the unwritten archives that commemorate the deeds of those who have, with no one but God as their witness performed those deeds that have insured the continued existence of our noble inheritance.

Frank La Fayette Anders received the Medal of Honor for actions in the Philippines in 1906. Without waiting for the supporting battalion to aid them, he and eleven other scouts charged around 150 yards and completely routed about 300 enemy soldiers. He went on to become an engineer, businessman, military historian and politician. He was National Historian, 1926–1927, and senior vice commander of the Legion of Valor.

FIDELITY

Fidelity is the derivative of personal decision. It is the jewel within reach of every man who has the will to possess it.

S. L. A. Marshall

HISTORY OF THE AMERICAN GOLD STAR MOTHERS, INC.

Judy C. Campbell

During World War I, a Blue Star was used to represent individuals serving in the military of the United States of America. Upon the death of military personnel a Gold Star was substituted and superimposed upon the Blue Star. This act was to pay honor to the person for his/her supreme sacrifice in offering their life for our country.

Gold Star Mothers whose sons and daughters made the supreme sacrifice while serving in the armed forces of the United States of America, along with immediate family members, are issued a Gold Star pin by the Department of Defense. The recipients include: widow, widower, mother, father, stepmother, stepfather, mother through adoption, father through adoption, foster mother in loco parentis, foster father in loco parentis, son, daughter, stepson, stepdaughter, son by adoption, daughter by adoption, brother, sister, half-brother and half-sister.

In 1928 a group of twenty-five Gold Star Mothers residing in Washington, D.C. decided to organize a national organization to be known as American Gold Star Mothers, Inc. On January 5, 1929, the organization was incorporated under the laws of the District of Columbia. The original copy of the Federal Charter granted to them was placed in the Archives of Congress.

The organization's purpose includes, but is not limited to, inculcating patriotism, assisting veterans, perpetuating the memory of those who sacrificed so we may treasure the freedoms we hold so dear and extend assistance to all Gold Star Mothers and their descendants whenever possible. The organization works closely with all veterans' organizations.

In 1940, the late President Franklin D. Roosevelt issued a proclamation designating the last Sunday in September as Gold Star Mother's Day and the American Gold Star Mothers annually conduct a moving service on the last Sunday in September in Arlington National Cemetery to pay honor to all Gold Star Mothers for the loss of their child. All are welcome to attend. You may learn more about the American Gold Star Mothers by visiting their web site: www.goldstarmoms.com.

This article about the Gold Star Mothers first appeared in the Legion of Valor General Orders. *Judy is the sister of Keith Campbell, Distinguished Service Cross, who gave his life in Vietnam while serving as an Army combat medic. Judy is an associate life member of the Legion of Valor.*

A Gold Star Mothers' postage stamp was issued on September 21, 1948. The last Sunday in September is American Gold Star Mothers and Families Day. The President annually issues a proclamation, which honors not only our Gold Star Mothers, but fathers, spouses, children and siblings. Judy C. Campbell has worked in her home state of Delaware to have a similar proclamation, and it has become one of the few states to do so.

REPATRIATION OF A HERO FROM KOREA

LIEUTENANT COLONEL DONALD C. FAITH, MEDAL OF HONOR

David Vergun

This story is one of the heroism and repatriation from Korea of Donald C. Faith, Jr, a posthumous Medal of Honor recipient. It epitomizes not only the valor of Don Faith, but also the fidelity of his daughter Bobbie and the United States to recovering and repatriating the remains of those killed in its conflicts.

Lieutenant Colonel Don C. Faith Jr., a World War II and Korean War veteran and Medal of Honor recipient, was buried in Arlington National Cemetery, Virginia, today. Faith, who commanded 1st Battalion, 32nd Infantry Regiment, 7th Infantry Division, was killed December 2, 1950, by Communist forces. But it would take decades and a lot of help from other soldiers and Defense civilians before his remains were finally recovered in North Korea and identified. Only then could his family finally have the closure they so desperately wanted.

Happy Memories

Barbara Broyles, or "Bobbie," as she likes to be called, was only four years old when Faith left for Korea. She was young but still remembers. It would be the last time she would see her father alive.

"What I recall most about my father was that he was happy. I still can hear him laughing. He enjoyed life. And above all, he enjoyed the Army," she said.

Bobbie said her father used to read to her from his own childhood books, a collection of six volumes titled *My Book House*. She said when he left for Korea, her mother, also named Barbara, read those books to her. She still has them.

Later, President Harry S. Truman presented the Medal of Honor, posthumously, to Bobbie.

Faith was born in 1918 and grew up in China, the Philippines, Fort Benning, Ga., and Washington, D.C., since his father was in the Army. After the December 7, 1941 attack on Pearl Harbor, many Americans flocked to recruiting stations. However, Faith had decided to join the Army months before, while a student at Georgetown University.

In February 1942, he received his commission and was assigned to the 82nd Airborne Division, where he served with great distinction in the North Africa campaign and later in Europe. He was awarded two Bronze Star medals.

Following the war, Faith served in China and then Japan. He was in Japan when the war in Korea started in the summer of 1950.

A lieutenant colonel at that time, he was given command of 1st Battalion, 32nd Infantry, a unit that would soon be in the thick of the fighting.

Medal of Honor

Some of the fiercest fighting of the war took place in the vicinity of a place called Chosin Reservoir in North Korea in November and December 1950. That's where Faith and his battalion were when the Chinese decided to enter the war. The Chinese sent thousands of troops south across the Yalu River into Korea.

The entry of China into the war and their drive south into Korea surprised the Americans who were quickly outnumbered and outgunned.

Faith's Medal of Honor citation describes the action he took during this attack, noting that he "personally led counterattacks to restore (the battalion's) position" and link up with other units, as they'd been disbursed by the enemy's "fanatical attack":

> … although physically exhausted in the bitter cold, [he] organized and launched an attack which was soon stopped by enemy fire. He ran forward under enemy small-arms and automatic weapons fire, got his men on their feet and personally led the fire attack as it blasted its way through the enemy ring. As they came to a hairpin curve, enemy fire from a roadblock again pinned the column down. Lt. Col. Faith organized a group of men and directed their attack on the enemy positions on the right flank. He then placed himself at the head of another group of men and in the face of direct enemy fire led an attack on the enemy roadblock, firing his pistol and throwing grenades. When he had reached a position approximately 30 yards from the roadblock, he was mortally wounded, but continued to direct the attack until the roadblock was overrun. Throughout the five days of action Lt. Col. Faith gave no thought to his safety and did not spare himself. His presence each time in the position of greatest danger was an inspiration to his men. Also, the damage he personally inflicted firing from his position at the head of his men was of material assistance on several occasions.

Faith's Repatriation

Faith was killed December 2, 1950, in the vicinity of Hagaru-ri, North Korea. He was 32 years old at the time.

What follows is an account of his repatriation, the process of returning his remains to the United States. Leading the effort was Faith's daughter, Bobbie. She was helped by a lot of dedicated men and women of the Department of Defense.

In the decades that followed the Korean War, thousands of remains of service members missing in action in Korea were recovered and returned home. In September 2004, some remains were excavated in the vicinity of Chosin Reservoir by the Joint Prisoners of War/Missing in Action Accounting Command, or JPAC.

Among the remains were those of Faith, according to Michael J. Mee, chief, Identifications Past Conflict Repatriations Branch, Human Resources Command. "Most Americans don't realize that there are 87,000 unaccounted-for service members who never came home from

America's 20th-century wars," Mee said. That number includes around 83,000 from World War II, Korea and Southeast Asia, primarily Vietnam, the conflicts "mandated by Congress."

Over the years, Bobbie has been in close contact with the accounting community, which includes the Defense Prisoner of War/Missing Personnel Office, JPAC, AFDIL and other organizations.

Mee, who has been with the program since 2009, said he had the honor of calling Bobbie with the good news that the remains of her father were positively identified. He said she had been in contact with the accounting community for years, hoping they could locate the remains of her father and return them to the United States.

Within just days of telling Bobbie the good news, Mee scheduled a meeting with her in October 2012 in her home in Baton Rouge, La.

Accompanying Mee at the visit was a casualty assistance officer from nearby Fort Polk.

The meeting with Bobbie "was a big deal for her and her family," Mee said. "We've known for years that she was looking forward to this day."

Bobbie said she hopes others who are waiting for the return of their loved ones will find a measure of peace and closure, like she has.

And for his part, Mee said he hopes to help make that happen.

"Repatriation is one of the most rewarding and honorable missions I've ever performed," he said.

This piece is extracted from Army News Service, *April 17, 2013.*

AMERICA NEEDS THE LEGION
OF VALOR

Vice Admiral J. Paul Reason

This address was delivered at the Legion of Valor Banquet in Williamsburg, Virginia, in 1996.

I agree completely with Captain Stephan, your National Commander, that Colonial Williamsburg is a most fitting place for you to assemble, for this is an area hallowed by the first American patriots.

I cannot help but imagine that the Founding Fathers smile with paternal approval and pride on the gathering here of those of their fellow Americans who have been recognized as the bravest in the Home of the Brave.

I hope they and you do not think it frivolous of me to begin my thoughts with a reference to a recent product of a town completely unlike Williamsburg—namely, Hollywood. In a powerful scene in the movie *Braveheart*, the hero, William Wallace (a commoner), confronts Robert the Bruce, (the highest-ranking Scottish noble), and exhorts him to lead the Scots in battle against the English.

Wallace says something to the Bruce which is striking because it seems self-evidently true: "Men don't follow titles; they follow courage."

Indeed, men follow courage. The Romans knew it for a fact, and their language reflected it. The very Roman name of your association links you to them: Legion of Valor, Just by uttering "legion" you hark back to Caesar, Cicero, and the tramp of the sandaled legionary with his shield and short sword.

"Valor," a word which in English connotes the highest degree of courage, is derived from the Latin verb meaning "to be strong." Julius Caesar could step into this room right now and understand what your association is about.

Please indulge my professorial bent for just a moment longer and consider one more word, one that is tossed about today in our current cultural convulsions about values, ethics, morals, and character. I mean the word "virtue." Its Latin ancestor, "virtus" does also mean "goodness," "high character," "moral perfection," and "virtue," but its primary meanings are "strength," "bravery," "courage," and—as you might guess—"valor."

The Romans instinctively linked courage and character. Their highest ideals of civic virtue were inseparable from notions of courage. They understood, even in the very fiber of their language, that men follow courage, and, correlatively, that the most courageous should lead.

Americans generally recognize and admire those who display exceptional bravery in combat. They sense, at the deepest level, that those who wear the highest decorations of their nation's armed services exemplify the loftiest standards of citizenship, and that those citizens should lead.

In the Home of the Brave, the bravest should lead. What better, easier way to know such citizens than by symbols—devices of metal and ribbon—which conspicuously confirm that they are the bravest!

In many sectors of society, "men follow courage" is becoming "men *ought* to follow courage." That is, it is becoming less a statement of fact, and more of a social and moral imperative. There is not the least question that America's greatness will continue, but there is also not the least question that we must work, tirelessly, to ensure such continuity.

America needs the Legion of Valor. The liberty we now cherish must be guarded, and our young men and women must be inspired to protect it. To this end we have dedicated ourselves in whatever capacity we can—whether at the scale of the home, the church, the playing field, the school, the city, the state, or the nation. You must teach, and inspire, those future generations, who will keep the land of the free, truly, the Home of the Brave.

Knowing that men follow courage, you, the courageous, have recognized your duty to lead. You have my most sincere wishes and most heartfelt prayers for the success of your mission.

This address is excerpted from Legion of Valor General Orders.

Warriors of 4/12 Infantry await helicopters to land on pick-up zone near Fire Support Base Stephanie, June 1968. (Photo courtesy of Specialist Depuis, 40th Public Information Detachment [P.I.D.], 199th Infantry Brigade)

Medal of Honor winner, 199th Infantry Brigade Catholic Chaplin Angelo Liteky (left), and Major Ed Kelley, 4/12 Infantry, talk with a Warrior infantryman. *(Photo courtesy of 40th P.I.D., 199th Infantry Brigade)*

Troops of Alpha Company 2/1 Inf at Catholic Mass, March 1969 in Vietnam following a very bloody engagement. *(Photo courtesy of Donald Smith)*

Robert L. Tonsetic and his wife Polly at the Infantry School, Fort Benning, Georgia in front of the famed "Follow Me" statue following his induction into the Ranger Hall of Fame on July 16, 2014. *(Photo courtesy of Polly Tonsetic)*

Jesus Oleta, a rifleman of Alpha 2-1 Inf navigates a stream on March 18, 1969. He was killed in action the next day in a fierce meeting engagement with entrenched North Vietnamese Army regulars. *(Photo courtesy of James Kaiser)*

Colonel George S. Patton (left) and Major Doc Bahnsen. *(11th Armored Cavalry Regiment PIO, US Army)*

Specialist 4th Class Thomas J. McMahon (left), age 20, company medic, Alpha 2/1 Inf, received the Medal of Honor posthumously for actions in Vietnam in March 1969. *(Photo courtesy of Donn Westfall)*

General Westmoreland presenting DSC to Captain William Mullen, Phu Loi, Vietnam, November 1966. *(Photo courtesy of William Mullen)*

Officers of C Company, First Battalion, 2nd Infantry Regiment, 1st Infantry Division, Vietnam, July 1966. Captain Mullen, company commander, is seated at left. *(Photo courtesy of William Mullen)*

Captain Barry Gasdek aiding South Vietnamese civilians fleeing the fighting in Vietnam, 1968. *(Photo courtesy of Barry Gasdek)*

Captain Barry Gasdek calling for artillery in support of Operation Wheeler/Wallowa, 1968, Vietnam. *(Americal IO)*

Medal of Honor recipient Specialist First Class Jared C. Monti in Afghanistan in 2006. *(Personal photo via Army.mil)*

Right: Brigadier General William Weise, NC, while commanding 2/4 Marines in Vietnam. *(Photo courtesy of Leatherneck magazine)*

Below, left: Retired United States Army Colonel Lewis Millett, a Korean War Medal of Honor recipient for his bayonet charge up a hill in 1951. *(U.S. Army)*

Below, right: Medal of Honor recipient and Catholic candidate for sainthood Father Emil Kapaun celebrating Mass using the hood of a Jeep as an altar, October 7, 1950. *(Public domain photo by Army Colonel Raymond Skeehan)*

The iconic photo of Teddy Roosevelt and his Rough Riders on top of San Juan Hill, Cuba, during the Spanish–American War, 1898. *(Library of Congress, photographer William Dimwiddie)*

Mary Edwards Walker, the only woman awarded the Medal of Honor. It was awarded for actions during the Civil War. *(Library of Congress, photograph by C. M. Bell)*

Admiral Chester W. Nimitz, USN, Commander-in-Chief, Pacific Fleet, pins the Navy Cross on Doris Miller, Steward's Mate 1/c, USN, at a ceremony on board a U.S. Navy warship in Pearl Harbor, May 27, 1942. *(Library of Congress)*

Illustration of Doris Miller defending the fleet at Pearl Harbor. *(Charles Alston, Office of War Information and Public Relations)*

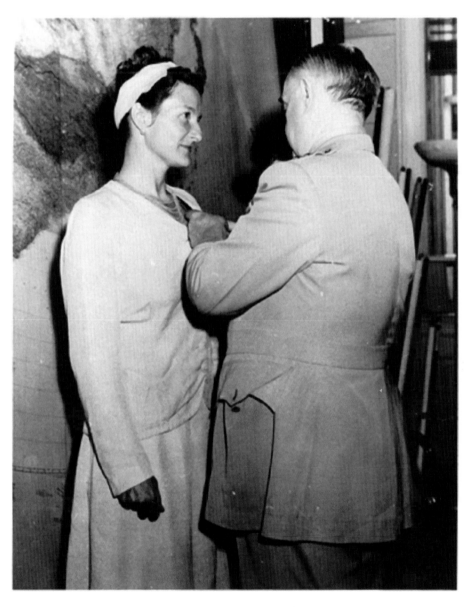

OSS operative Virginia Hall receiving the DSC from General William J. "Wild Bill" Donovan in 1945. *(Public domain)*

Joe M. Jackson, MOH. *(AF photo by Tech Sgt Adrian Cadiz)*

"The Grunt Padre" Chaplain Vincent R. Capodanno. MOH and Catholic candidate for sainthood, KIA while supporting 3/5 Marines, Vietnam, 1967. *(Public domain)*

Left: James B. Morehead, DSC. *(US Army Air Force)*

Bronze relief of Army Combat Medic Specialist 4th Class Keith A. Campbell, DSC recipient, donated to the Keith A. Campbell Memorial Library at Joint Base San Antonio, Fort Sam Houston. *(Image courtesy of Judy C. Campbell)*

To Betsy and Bill Raposa
With best wishes,

World War II Naval aviator William C. Raposa, who earned two Navy Crosses torpedo bombing Japanese ships. *(Photo courtesy of Caren Williams)*

Buffalo Bill, c. 1880.

PRESERVING THE HISTORY OF VALOR AWARDS

Honorary Member C. Douglas Sterner

Bob Hope once said, "As a patriot, speaker, writer and historian you are among the best. The fact that Doug laughed at my jokes in Da Nang (Vietnam) in 1971 has nothing to do with the praise I give him. Okay, It helped a little."

Don Marx, AFC, during the Legion of Valor Convention banquet in Norfolk, VA, in 2012 presented Doug with a certificate awarding him an honorary life membership in the Legion of Valor. Don stated:

> Doug Sterner is the curator of the Military Times Hall of Valor. The HALL OF VALOR now contains 104,246 valor award citations of heroes from the U.S. armed services. If it were not for Doug's tenacious and extraordinary efforts many of these stories would have simply drifted quietly into the past and the nation would have lost this important heritage. Doug has been a friend of the Legion for many years. He has been the pre-eminent champion for protecting the very concept of valor that would otherwise die in the face of modern political correctness. And so it is appropriate that the Legion of Valor award Mr. Doug Sterner with Honorary Membership.

Doug enlisted in the Army in 1969 and trained at Fort Leonard Wood, MO before completing the Non-Commissioned Officers' Candidate Course. He began his two tours of Vietnam duty in August 1970, as a squad leader in Company A, 65th Engineer Battalion (Combat), 25th Infantry Division at Dau Tieng. Less than two months later, on a mission near the Cambodian border he received the first of two

Bronze Star Medals. The following February he received the Army Commendation Medal for Valor as a squad leader for the engineer unit that led the combat air assault to re-open the Khe Sanh Valley in Operation *Lam Son 719.*

Following release from active duty he remains active in several veteran organizations, and is considered the most knowledgeable historian of America's highest award for valor, the Medal of Honor. He has made numerous television appearances on Fox News, as well as ABC's *Good Morning America* and other national network broadcasts.

He is best known for his work in support of the Stolen Valor Act of 2005 which was authored by his wife, Pam Sterner. He also compiled the most comprehensive database for military valor awards. His work can be reviewed online at homeofheroes.com. He championed HR 666: the Military Valor Roll of Honor Act, which mandated a federally administered database of military valor award citations. He stated this legislation was not only a Stolen Valor issue, but a critical measure that would ensure all veterans and their families are able to secure the benefits to which they are entitled.

Doug's HomeOfHeroes website is one of the largest and most popular military sites on the Internet, receiving 15 million hits each month. It has been featured on Fox News, in *The New York Times, The Reader's Digest, The Chicago Herald, Focus on the Family* radio broadcasts, CNN, and much more. He has been published in numerous magazines, newspapers and is a contributor to the popular book, *Chicken Soup for the Veteran's Soul.*

Doug was advisor and a key figure in the production of the acclaimed 2004 documentary *Beyond the Medal of Honor,* a 5-DVD set that aired on PBS and was subsequently placed, with curriculum, in every high school in America. Doug has further authored more than 100 major books on U.S. military history, many of which are available through his website.

Doug and his wife Pam have four children and make their home in Pueblo, Colorado where their civic and patriotic activities have become a family effort. Their then-12-year-old son testified before the Colorado State Legislature in a successful effort to enact legislation authorizing distinctive vehicle license plates for Medal of Honor recipients.

Their son-in-law is an officer in the U.S. Air Force, and is a veteran of Operation *Iraqi Freedom*.

They have received numerous awards including the Boy Scouts of America's "District Award of Merit" and the Distinguished Citizen's Award from the Congressional Medal of Honor Society. Their driving goal is to make sure our nation properly preserves an accurate history of veterans' service, sacrifice and heroism.

From Legion of Valor General Orders *and other sources.*

MAKING D-DAY WORK

Leonard G. "Bud" Lomell, Distinguished Service Cross

Historian Stephen Ambrose credited Lomell, our Legion of Valor National Commander in 1964, as the single individual, other than Eisenhower, most responsible for the success of D-Day. Although wounded when he first landed on D-Day, he climbed the 100-foot cliffs of Pointe de Hoc, France and led a 12-man patrol through the heaviest kind of automatic weapons fire to destroy an enemy machine-gun nest. He, with another man, then penetrated the enemy lines and discovered five 155mm coastal artillery guns with a range of 12 miles capable of being aimed at the beach or the invasion fleet. Leonard, using thermite incendiary grenades rendered the traversing, elevation and breech blocks of all five guns inoperable. He also smashed all the gun sights with his gun butt. After accomplishing this miraculous mission in the midst of the enemy gun crews all before 8:30 a.m. on D-Day, he rejoined his D Company and set up a roadblock to successfully prevent the passage of any German troops until he was relieved on D+2.

Leonard, born on January 22, 1920 in Brooklyn, New York, graduated from Tennessee Wesleyan College in 1941 and entered the Army in 1942. After receiving the Distinguished Service Cross for his heroic action on D-Day, he received a battlefield commission as a second lieutenant. He was also awarded a Silver Star for his actions in the Hurtgen Forest on December 7, 1944. He was medically discharged on December

30, 1945. Other medals he earned for gallantry in combat included the Bronze Star, Purple Heart with two clusters, the British Military Medal, the Croix de Guerre with Silver Lining, and the Chevalier of the French Legion of Honor. He was also inducted into the Ranger Hall of Fame and received honorary doctorates from Tennessee Wesleyan Collage, Monmouth University, and Ocean County College.

After returning to civilian life, he studied law under the GI Bill, was admitted to the New Jersey Bar in 1951 and established his own law firm in 1957. His many civilian accomplishments include co-founding the Garden State Philharmonic Symphony, serving as President of the Ranger Battalion Association of WWII and Director and Vice President of Statewide Bancorp. He died March 1, 2011.

AMERICA'S GREATEST FEMALE
SPY OF WORLD WAR II

VIRGINIA HALL, DISTINGUISHED SERVICE CROSS

Virginia Hall was born in Baltimore, Maryland in 1906. As a young woman, she acquired the language skills and displayed the intrepidness that would lead her to the front lines of intelligence gathering during World War II. After studying at Barnard and Radcliffe, she headed to Paris and Vienna in 1926 to finish her studies. She stayed on in Europe, intending to pursue a career in foreign affairs. However, Hall became ineligible for the Foreign Service when a hunting accident led to the amputation of her lower left leg in 1933 and for the rest of her life she used a wooden prosthetic leg, earning her the sobriquet "The Limping Lady." Until 1939, she worked in clerical positions for the State Department in Turkey, Italy, and Estonia. In Paris when war broke out in 1940, she volunteered as an ambulance driver until the French surrender. She moved on to London, where she secured a clerical job in the American Embassy.

In London, Hall came to the attention of the British Special Operations Executive (SOE). The SOE was in search of agents to work with the French resistance in training, logistics, and sabotage. Hall arrived in Lyon in August 1941, posing as a correspondent for the *New York Post*. Over the next 14 months, she helped downed fliers escape, provided courier services, and obtained supplies for clandestine presses and forgers, while filing articles for the *Post* to maintain her cover. During this time, German officials became aware of her presence and published her likeness on a wanted poster.

When the Germans seized all of France in November 1942, Hall barely escaped to Spain by walking across the snow-covered Pyrenees. She spent the next year working for SOE in Madrid because the British believed it was too risky for her to return to France.

In 1944, Hall joined the US Office of Strategic Services (OSS), the predecessor of the CIA, in order to return to France. Disguised as an elderly female farmhand, Hall organized sabotage operations, supported resistance groups as a radio operator and courier, mapped drop zones, and helped sabotage German military movements. She helped train three battalions of resistance forces to wage guerrilla warfare against German forces and kept up a stream of valuable reporting. Her work during this period is depicted in the painting, *Les Marguerits Fleriront ce Soir*, which hangs in the CIA's Intelligence Art Gallery.

For her efforts, General Donovan in September 1945 personally awarded her a Distinguished Service Cross—the only one awarded to a woman in WWII. She becomes the second women to be a member of the Legion of Valor. The only other female recipient was Helen McClelland, a nurse in WWI. Virginia Hall died in 1982. Her medal and citation is on permanent display at the CIA Exhibit Center, Langley, Va.

Details of Hall's career remained unknown to the public for many years. With the release of British and American World War II records in the 1980s and 1990s, historians have begun to bring her remarkable story to light. To learn more about her, see Hayden B. Peake's book review in *Studies in Intelligence*, Vol. 49, No. 4 as well as Judith L. Pearson's *The Wolves at the Door: The True Story of America's Greatest Female Spy*.

This piece first appeared in the Legion of Valor General Orders *with acknowledgment to the Central Intelligence Agency for material about her. The OSS Society also helped.*

THE ADMIRAL'S LEGACY

Jeremiah Denton's life and work

Commander Joseph McInerney

On October 25, 1967, U.S. Navy pilot Jeremiah A. Denton Jr. found himself in a new home. A prisoner of war since his A-6 Intruder was shot down in North Vietnam two years earlier, then-Cmdr. Denton was brought to a windowless three-by-nine-foot cell, ventilated by a few small holes and lit by a 10-watt light bulb. Affectionately known to its residents as "Alcatraz," this detention center was reserved for prisoners that the North Vietnamese had identified as the "diehard" leaders of American POWs.

A choking feeling welled up in Cmdr. Denton's throat as the heavy wooden door closed behind him and its bolt slid into place. "Alcatraz" would mean solitude, torture and desolation for the next two years of his captivity.

During his seven year and seven month odyssey in the prison camps of North Vietnam, Denton distinguished himself as a leader of many heroic men serving their country in horrific conditions. Upon his return to the United States in 1973, he continued to serve his nation as a civic and political leader, with a special concern for the poor and defenseless.

When Admiral Denton died March 28 at age 89, he left behind the legacy of an extraordinary life. As a committed Catholic and Knight of Columbus, Admiral Denton's many accomplishments—together with his hope amid the direst of circumstances—were grounded in the firm foundation of his faith.

Life in Prison

It was a hot and sunny day in July 1965 when Cmdr. Denton led his A-6 squadron on an attack of Tan Hoa bridge, about 75 miles south of Hanoi. The 41-year-old father of seven had deployed just a month earlier. According to his 1976 memoir, *When Hell Was in Session*, he was diving toward his targets when his plane was hit twice, forcing him and his navigator, Lieutenant Bill Tschudy, to eject over enemy territory. During their slow descent toward the Ma River, Denton devised an escape plan: to swim underwater, away from his equipment and away from the soldiers watching him drift down to the water. Yet, a tendon in his leg had been torn during the attack, and his swim instead became a desperate fight for survival. He struggled to the surface of the river's brown water and soon found himself captured by North Vietnamese soldiers.

Fifteen years earlier, the Korean War had demonstrated that Communist prisoner-of-war camps did not merely sit on the sidelines of a conflict. The North Vietnamese, like the North Koreans, were intent on manipulating prisoners to further their goals, and torture was the means of influencing U.S. prisoners into providing propaganda that might turn the tide of American popular opinion, thereby taking the war from the jungles of Vietnam to the streets of the United States.

Mistreatment in the form of humiliation, malnutrition and lack of adequate medical care accompanied Denton and his fellow prisoners from day one of their captivity, and the brutality of physical torture followed shortly thereafter.

"They beat you with fists and fan belts," Denton later recalled in an interview with the *Los Angeles Times*. "They warmed you up and threatened you with death."

The men were further subjected to exposure to the cold, the use of ropes to cut off circulation and cause intense muscle spasms, and other torture devices.

Despite the suffering they endured, Denton and his companions resisted the torture to such a great extent that when they finally broke and agreed to provide information, they physically could not write or speak in a way that was useful to their captors. Once they had adequately recovered, their will had recovered as well, and their resistance to the torture would begin once again.

Even among this group of heroes, Denton stood out among his peers. As one of the most senior officers in captivity, he often had the obligation of leading his fellow prisoners in resistance. In circumstances that were anything but encouraging, he earned the nickname "president of the optimist club."

Due to what his captors saw as a "negative" influence over his fellow prisoners, the North Vietnamese subjected Denton to solitary confinement for more than four years of his captivity, two years of which were spent in the claustrophobic confines of the "Alcatraz" cell.

But Denton's most prominent act of leadership came in May 1966 when he was forced to participate in a propaganda interview that was subsequently aired on U.S. television. During the interview, Denton repeatedly blinked the word T-O-R-T-U-R-E in Morse code, which gave U.S. intelligence officials their first confirmation that the North Vietnamese were in fact torturing American prisoners of war. Admiral Denton later wrote that what took more courage than his blinking during the interview was the answer he gave to one of the questions. When asked what he thought of U.S. policy in Vietnam, he answered, "I don't know what's going on in the war now … but whatever the position of my government is, I agree with it, I support it, and I will support it as long as I live."

Denton's leadership, courage and optimism, so impressed President Lyndon Johnson that he wrote to Denton's wife, Jane, on May 12: "I wish to share with you and your seven children sincere pride in the courageous statement made by Commander Denton of support for the United States and for our policy in Vietnam. It has given me renewed strength."

"One Nation Under God"

In the days following the Paris Peace Accords on January 27, 1973, nearly 600 American prisoners of war left Hanoi, beginning with those who had been imprisoned the longest. Denton had been promoted to captain while in captivity, and as the senior officer in the first group of 40, he stepped off the plane at Clark Air Force Base in the Philippines and said, "We are honored to have had the opportunity to serve our country under difficult circumstances. We are profoundly grateful to our commander-in-chief and to our nation for this day. God bless America."

Denton soon attained the rank of rear admiral and in 1977 retired from the Navy, returning to his home town of Mobile, Alabama. Three years later, he was elected to the U.S. Senate, becoming the first Catholic ever to hold statewide office in Alabama and the first Republican to represent the state since post-Civil War Reconstruction.

Admiral Denton's post-military career also focused on humanitarian relief abroad. As a senator, he established what became known as the Denton Program, which allowed private donors to ship humanitarian aid cost-free to countries in need by using extra space on U.S. military aircraft. Since it began, the program has helped to transport more than 20 million pounds of supplies.

In order to continue his own international humanitarian relief efforts after his six-year term as senator, Denton founded the National Forum Foundation. He also formed a partnership with IMEC America, an organization that seeks to support impoverished communities throughout the world. Now known as the Admiral Denton Legacy Initiatives and operated by IMEC, the humanitarian programs that Admiral Denton established more than 25 years ago continue today.

A celebrated war hero, a respected national politician and a humanitarian with international impact, Jeremiah Denton's life was filled with remarkable accomplishments. Yet, Admiral Denton would assert that at the foundation of his extraordinary achievements was something very ordinary: his love of Christ and the Church.

"We were drawn closer to God by much suffering and deprivation," he wrote in his 1975 *Columbia* essay, reflecting on his and the other prisoners' experience.

During one of his most difficult torture sessions, Denton uttered a simple, desperate prayer: "God, I'm putting it all in your hands now. I've taken all I can take."

According to his account, God's response was instantaneous and powerful. "Never before have I had a prayer answered so spectacularly. From the instant I phrased it, it was answered. I never before have experienced such physical comfort and serenity of mind."

Such is the example that Admiral Denton offers to those who remember his legacy. Human greatness is to be found above all in humble witness and is accessible to anyone who calls on the name of Christ in faith.

This full version of this piece originally appeared in the November 2014 issue of Columbia *magazine.*

Commander Joseph McInerney is permanent military professor of applied ethics in the leadership, ethics and law department at the United States Naval Academy in Annapolis, Md. He is a member of Annapolis Council 1384.

LEADING AND INSPIRING PRISONERS OF WAR

ADMIRAL JAMES B. STOCKDALE, MEDAL OF HONOR

Admiral Stockdale was born on December 23, 1923 in Abingdon, Illinois. After graduating from the Naval Academy in 1946, he attended flight training in Pensacola, Florida and in 1954, was accepted to the Navy Test Pilot School where he quickly became a standout and served as an instructor for a brief time.

Stockdale's flying career took him west, and in 1962, he earned a Master's Degree in International Relations from Stanford University. He was the first to amass more than one thousand hours in the F-8U Crusader, then the Navy's hottest fighter, and by the early 1960s, Stockdale was at the very pinnacle of his profession when he commanded a Navy fighter squadron.

In August 1964, Stockdale played a key role in the Gulf of Tonkin incident, which the Johnson Administration used to justify large-scale military action in Vietnam. Stockdale always maintained that he had not seen enemy vessels during the event, but the next morning, August 6, 1964, he was ordered to lead the first raid of the war on North Vietnamese oil refineries.

On September 9, 1965, at the age of 40, Stockdale, who was the Commanding Officer, VF51 and Carrier Air Group Commander (CAG-16), was catapulted from the deck of the USS *Oriskany* for what would be the final mission. While returning from the target area, his A-4 Skyhawk was hit by antiaircraft fire. Stockdale ejected, breaking a bone in his back. Upon landing in a small village, he badly dislocated his knee, which subsequently went untreated and eventually left him with a fused knee joint and a very distinctive gait.

Stockdale wound up in Hoa Lo prison, the infamous "Hanoi Hilton," where he spent the next seven years as the highest-ranking naval officer and leader of American resistance against Vietnamese attempts to use prisoners for propaganda purposes. Despite being kept in solitary confinement for four years, in leg irons for two years, physically tortured more than 15 times, denied medical care and malnourished, Stockdale organized a system of communication and developed a cohesive set of rules governing prisoner behavior. Codified in the acronym BACK U.S. (Unity over Self), these rules gave prisoners a sense of hope and empowerment. Many of the prisoners credited these rules as giving them the strength to endure their lengthy ordeal. Drawing largely from principles of stoic philosophy, notably Epictetus' *The Enchiridion*, Stockdale's courage and decisive leadership was an inspiration to POWs.

The climax of the struggle of wills between American POWs and their captors came in the spring of 1969. Told he was to be taken "downtown" and paraded in front of foreign journalists, Stockdale slashed his scalp with a razor and beat himself in the face with a wooden stool, knowing that his captors would not display a prisoner who was disfigured. Later, after discovering that some prisoners had died during torture, he slashed his wrists to demonstrate to his captors that he preferred death to submission. This act so convinced the Vietnamese of his determination to die rather than to cooperate that the Communists ceased the torture of American prisoners and gradually improved their treatment of POWs. Upon his release from prison in 1973, Stockdale's extraordinary heroism became widely known, and he was awarded the Medal of Honor by President Gerald Ford in 1976.

He was one of the most highly decorated officers in the history of the Navy, wearing 26 personal combat decorations, including two Distinguished Flying Crosses, three Distinguished Service Medals, two Purple Hearts, and four Silver Star medals in addition to the Medal of Honor. He was the only three-star admiral in the history of the Navy to wear both aviator wings and the Medal of Honor.

When asked what experiences he thought were essential to his survival and ultimate success in the prison, Admiral Stockdale referred to events early in his life: his childhood experiences in his mother's local drama productions, which encouraged spontaneity, humor, and theatrical timing; the lessons of how to endure physical pain as a football player in high school and college; and his determination to live up to the promise he made to his father upon entering the Naval Academy that he would be the best midshipmen he could be. It was the uniquely American ability to improvise in tight situations, Stockdale believed, which gave him the confidence that the POWs could outwit their captors and return home with honor despite their dire situation.

In 1984, Admiral Stockdale and his wife Sybil co-authored *In Love and War*, detailing his experiences in Vietnam as well as her experiences founding the League of American Families of POWs and MIAs at the same time that she was raising their four sons. After serving as the President of the Naval War College, Stockdale retired from the Navy in 1978 and embarked on a distinguished academic career.

He served 15 years as a Senior Research Fellow at the Hoover Institute of War, Revolution, and Peace where he wrote numerous articles; published both *A Vietnam Experience: Ten Years of Reflection* and *Thoughts of a Philosophical Fighter Pilot*; was awarded 11 honorary doctoral degrees; and lectured extensively on the stoicism of Epictetus and on those character traits which serve one best when faced with adversity. In 1992, he graciously agreed to the request from his old friend H. Ross Perot to stand in as the vice-presidential candidate of the Reform Party. Stockdale disliked the glare of publicity and partisan politics, but throughout the campaign, he comported himself with the same integrity and dignity that marked his entire career.

Upon his retirement in 1979, the Secretary of the Navy established the Vice Admiral Stockdale Award for Inspirational Leadership, presented annually in both the Pacific and Atlantic fleet. Admiral Stockdale was a member of the Navy's Carrier Hall of Fame and the National Aviation Hall of Fame, and he was an Honorary Fellow in the Society of Experimental Test Pilots.

This biography is from the Stockdale Center of Ethical leadership, United States Naval Academy.

Editor: James B. Stockdale died on July 5, 2005 at his home in Coronado, California.

ROCKY THE REACTIONARY

Captain Humbert R. Versace, Medal of Honor

C. Douglas Sterner

"As long as I am true to God and true to myself, what is waiting for me after this life is far better than anything that can happen now. You might as well kill me here and now if the price of my life is more than giving you my name, rank and serial number."

Army Captain Jack Nicholson listened time and again to the reports of the local villagers. It was late in 1963, and Captain Nicholson made frequent patrols in the Mekong Delta region of South Vietnam. The reports spoke of a large American who had been captured by the Viet Cong.

What got to Captain Nicholson were the reports of a tall American who had been repeatedly yanked from village to village. He was rail thin, had no shoes, his skin was yellowed by jaundice, his head swollen, and his hair completely white.

This particular prisoner seemed to stand out, not so much for his appearance, but for his resistance to the enemy. It was said that he was constantly arguing with his captors, rebutting their propaganda in their own language. "He had a funny expression about him, a smile, a flashing of teeth, that got their attention," Nicholson later recalled. As he was forced to walk among the local populations in what the enemy hoped was a humiliating display, he spoke out in fluent Vietnamese and French, words of resistance that began to impress the very people the VC had hoped themselves to impress. "When they (villagers) heard him speak, they listened, because they couldn't help it."

Throughout the Delta, the story of the defiant American prisoner became something of a legend. This was a man like no ordinary man … a man with a will beyond the strength of his captivity, his failing health, or his captors. Captain Nicholson knew the man had to be Captain Rocky Versace, and knew that a man like Captain Versace needed to be rescued. Three times, based upon intelligence reports, rescue missions were mounted. Each time, they failed. Rocky Versace remained in the hands of those who hated him, but could not help but admire his strength of character.

November 1963

Lieutenant Nick Rowe shifted uncomfortably in the 4x6 foot bamboo cage that had been his prison cell now for nearly two months. In that time he had seen or heard little of his two friends, but he knew that like himself, all of them had suffered unbelievable torture and treatment at the hands of their enemies.

After their capture the previous October, the men had been stripped of their boots and socks, blindfolded with their hands bound behind them, and moved under cover of darkness to a small grass hut. In the early hours of that first long night, they could hear the nearby cries of the badly wounded Captain Versace: "Bac si! Bac si! … (doctor)."

A few hours later the Americans had been placed in a sampan and transported to a makeshift camp within the forest, surrounded by knee-deep mud and heavy vegetation. There, the three men were placed together into a small cage made of mangrove logs nailed and tied together with barbed wire. Just large enough to contain the three of them, it was a cramped and uncomfortable prison for three men, all of whom were wounded. Captain Versace's leg left him groaning in great pain. One of the BAR rounds appeared to have penetrated the bone near the knee. Versace also suffered from two wounds in his back.

As a captain and the ranking prisoner, Versace had assumed responsibility for the small prison population. Held in his own cage out of view of Rowe and Pitzer. Daniel Pitzer later wrote that some of the worst punishment the three men endured was at night. Guards would come to the cages, tell the prisoners "Under the lenient policy of the National Liberation Front, we're going to wash your mosquito net … and we want your pajamas too."

With a wicked smile, the enemy would thus leave their prisoners naked and totally exposed to the elements. "I've seen mosquitoes so thick on my ankles that I thought I had black socks on," Pitzer later noted in the book *To Bear Any Burden* by Al Santoli.

During those horrible nights, Captain Versace often sang messages to the other prisoners, interlaced in popular songs of the day. When not using his voice thus to communicate with his fellow Green Berets, he could often be heard arguing loudly with the enemy. "Rocky stood toe to toe with them. He told them to go to hell in Vietnamese, French and English," Pitzer continued in Santoli's book.

Three weeks after the fateful battle outside Le Coeur, Rocky Versace made his first escape attempt. Still recovering in the makeshift field hospital, he dragged himself outside and crawled into the dense jungle of the U Minh Forest. Still suffering from his wounds, even crawling was almost impossible, but crawl he did. At the slow pace, dragging his body through the jungle, it didn't take the Viet Cong long to recapture him. Rocky was returned to the camp, placed in leg irons, and received no further treatment for his festering leg wounds. Placed on a starvation diet of rice and salt, he was beaten and tortured but refused to break. His Viet Cong jailors told the other American POWs that Versace remained unbroken, even when on at least one occasion, his tormentors had attempted to coerce him into cooperation by twisting his wounded and infected leg.

Because they could not break Versace, the Viet Cong labeled him "reactionary" and "unrepentant" (for his war crimes against the Vietnamese people). They isolated him from the other prisoners, shackling him on his back in irons. He was confined to a hot isolation box measuring 6 feet long, 2 feet wide, and 3 feet high. To quiet him, many nights his mouth was gagged. When the gag was removed, Rocky Versace would again defy his tormentors in all three languages he spoke.

The Defense Prisoner and Missing Personnel Office (DPMO) reported:

> CPT Versace demonstrated exceptional leadership by communicating positively to his fellow prisoners. He lifted morale when he passed messages by singing them into the popular songs of the day. When he used his Vietnamese language skills to protest improper treatment to the guards, CPT Versace was again put into leg irons and gagged. Unyielding, he steadfastly continued to berate the

guards for their inhuman treatment. The communist guards simply elected harsher treatment by placing him in an isolation box, to put him out of earshot and to keep him away from the other US POWs for the remainder of his stay in camp. However CPT Versace continued to leave notes in the latrine for his fellow inmates, and continued to sing even louder.

His escape attempt shortly after his capture, despite its futility, also would not deter him. The unbreakable Rocky Versace is known to have attempted escape at least three times more, each again with futility, and every attempt followed by beatings and torture. Still, he never gave up, and never quit trying.

February 19, 1964

As two months stretched into four months, all four American prisoners had wasted away, suffering from a meager diet, disease, and their mistreatment at the hands of the enemy. Captain Versace seemed to suffer the worst. Whatever the Viet Cong tried to do to him, he resisted. Rocky lived the Code of Conduct, refusing to tell the enemy more than his name, rank, serial number and date of birth. He lived valiantly and heroically by the West Point motto: Duty, Honor, Country.

Shortly after the capture of the three men, Lieutenant Rowe had concocted a cover story that appeared to be working in his favor. Realizing that if the Viet Cong recognized him as a Special Forces officer they would do everything in their power, including torture, to make him reveal important information about American operations in Vietnam. Rowe had told the enemy that he was NOT a soldier, but a civilian engineer under the employ of the U.S. Army and therefore had little military knowledge. The story had held together, and spared him to this point.

Captain Versace's own resistance became the primary focus of the enemy, shifting attention away from the other prisoners and focusing the efforts and anger of the Viet Cong on himself. It was a cross the young soldier bore with dignity.

More recently, the VC had begun a program of indoctrination for their American POWs, a litany of re-education sessions of Vietnamese history, Communist propaganda, and accusations of American aggression against the people of Vietnam.

Rowe and Pitzer adopted what they called a sit-and-listen attitude to these session, accepting the fact that they were forced to be present for the tirade of enemy propaganda. They quietly tuned it out, knowing to argue or otherwise respond, would be fruitless and would only result in harsher treatment. Not so Rocky Versace.

Promised better food and better treatment if only he would: 1) quit arguing with his indoctrinators, and 2) accept their propaganda, Captain Versace still would not bend. Time and again during the sessions, from a distance, Rowe and Pitzer could hear Rocky arguing with the re-educators, rebutting their philosophies in their own language.

On this night late in February, Lieutenant Rowe could hear the re-educators arguing once again as they tried to break the unbreakable. It had taken TWO guards just to force the intrepid Green Beret to attend the classes. Across the darkness of the camp, he could hear the voice of Captain Humbert R. Versace loudly proclaim: "You can make me come to this class, but I am an officer in the United States Army. You can make me listen, you can force me to sit here, but I don't believe a word of what you are saying."

Writing about that night in his subsequent book, Lieutenant Rowe said of that night while he was sitting alone in the darkness listening to the exchange: "I felt my back straighten and my face grow warm with a feeling of pride."

April 8, 1964

Nick Rowe stirred uncomfortably in his cramped bamboo cage as he heard the commotion in the darkness, coming from the distant vicinity of Rocky Versace's prison cage. Nick was weak, suffering from frequent bouts with dysentery, and wasted away to mere skin and bones. Sergeant Pitzer was in no better shape but, despite their own deplorable condition, neither of the men was as bad off as was Captain Versace.

Rising above the commotion, he could hear the voice of Rocky, still defying his captors. In full resistance, Rocky filled the darkness of the U Minh Forest with a song that echoed the beliefs of his valiant spirit.

The following morning Nick was released from his leg irons and cage long enough to walk to the camp kitchen for his meager ration of rice. As he walked past the area where Captain Versace had been held, all that remained was a twisted piece of aluminum that had been Rocky's cup and pan, and a pile of bloody rags ... what remained of Rocky's gray POW pajamas. The cage itself was wrecked, and Lieutenant Rowe quickly deduced that his comrade must have sustained a horrible beating during the previous night, and was perhaps dead. That night one of the guards came to Lieutenant Rowe's cage and told him that the National Liberation Front had been forced to take drastic action against Captain Versace because he continued to be opposed to the Front.

Indeed, that was the last night Lieutenant Rowe or any other American would ever hear the voice of Captain Rocky Versace. Nick Rowe would never forget the valiant warrior's last words, as he sang *God Bless America* defiantly into the darkness.

The Medal of Honor

On Monday, July 8, 2002 Captain Roger Donlon and other members of the West Point Class of 1959 were invited to the White House to honor the valiant spirit of Rocky Versace. The Friends of Rocky Versace, a group of veterans and civilians determined to see him remembered not as a prisoner but as one of our Nation's greatest heroes refused to let history forget his shining example of Duty, Honor and Country. On that day, President George W. Bush presented Rocky Versace's family with his Medal of Honor.

Sources:

Nick Rowe, *Five Years to Freedom*

Master Sergeant Daniel Pitzer, "The Animal Called POW" *Look Magazine* (February 18, 1969)

Steve Vogel, "Honoring the Defiant One," *The Washington Post* (May 27, 2001)

Pacific Stars and Stripes, VIETNAM Front Pages (1986)

Neil Mishalov's Vietnam War Medal of Honor website

The full version of this article first appeared on HomeofHeroes.com.

DETERMINED ASSAULT ON HILL 329

WILLIS JACKSON, DISTINGUISHED SERVICE CROSS

Willis was born in 1922 on a farm in Christiana, Tennessee. He attended the local elementary school and graduated from Rockvale High School where he played baseball, was president of the senior class, and was selected as Best All Around Boy and Salutarian. In 1942, he enlisted in the Army at Camp Forrest, Tennessee and was sent to an 8-inch howitzer outfit from the Kansas State National Guard. At the urging of his company commander, Willis applied and was accepted for Infantry Officer Candidate School and graduated as a second lieutenant in May 1945. From there, after taking one group of recruits through their 17 weeks of basic training, he was shipped to the Pacific for the coming invasion of Japan. Fortunately, the war ended and he went to Japan as part of the occupation forces.

In September 1950, he was called to active duty as a platoon leader in the 25th Infantry Division. On May 21, 1951 he was engaged in a battle that awarded three Distinguished Service Crosses; Willis, Paul Clawson and Bill McCraney. Unfortunately, Paul was killed in action but Bill and Willis continued to be good friends and all three heroes are members of the Legion of Valor.

Willis was leading one of the assault platoons up Hill 329 near Seoul, Korea when intense and accurate enemy fire halted his men in an exposed area. Although painfully wounded, Willis renewed the attack and fought fiercely for two more hours until the enemy fire became so intense that the unit was pinned down again. In an effort to rally his men into making a final sweeping assault, Willis singlehandedly charged an enemy position and, despite his wound, wrested an enemy soldier's own weapon from him and beat him to death. This courageous action so inspired his men that they charged forward and overran the enemy emplacements. As the enemy fled down the reverse slope, Willis pitched grenades after them and then succeeded in killing three more with his rifle. Despite his painful wound, he organized his men in a defense against a counterattack and only fell back to be treated when his company commander ordered him to do so.

Willis returned to the states and was retired for physical disability He pursued a civilian career in the insurance world and retired at age 63 as Senior Vice President—Individual Insurance for Shenandoah Life Insurance Company of Virginia.

Willis continued to be involved in many civic and military organizations. He served on the Board of Directors for the Life Insurance Marketing and Research Association, President of the Tennessee Association of Underwriters, President of the Knoxville Better Business Bureau, Chairman of the Board of Trustees for his Methodist Church and Chairman of Alum/Insurance Industry Committee to fund the Chair of Insurance at the University of Tennessee. He also served on the Board of the 25th Infantry Division Association and was Legion of Valor National Commander 1975–1976. He also served on the Legion's Finance Committee. He died on June 15, 2014 in the Knoxville area.

This piece first appeared in the Legion of Valor General Orders.

FATHER OF THE DISABLED AMERICAN VETERANS

ROBERT S. MARX, DISTINGUISHED SERVICE CROSS

After World War I came to an end the nation gasped as the disabled came home. Robert S. Marx, Distinguished Service Cross, pulled the veterans together to create the Disabled American Veterans.

He had the distinction of capturing the furthermost point taken by the American Army prior to the Armistice. On November 10, 1918, in the Meuse-Argonne Offensive, just hours before the last shot was fired, a German shell exploded, wounding Captain Marx.

After months in a French hospital, he was finally able to return home to his law practice in Cincinnati, Ohio. In 1919 he was elected to the Ohio Superior Court and, while hosting a Christmas party that year, plans were made to explore the level of interest in an organization for disabled war veterans. In 1920, he presented articles of confederation for the DAV and reported that 741,000 veterans were eligible for membership. On June 27, 1921, the new organization opened its first national convention in Detroit. Over one thousand disabled veterans were in attendance and Robert Marx was elected its first National Commander.

Exerpted from a story in Legion of Valor General Orders.

PIONEER, FIGHTER, TRAINER

KURT CHEW-EEN LEE, NAVY CROSS

Kurt had the distinction of being the first regular officer of Asian ancestry in the U.S. Marine Corps. As such, he had been the de facto pioneer for his race in virtually every command and staff assignment—and the first Chinese-American officer to lead Marines into combat. It was his avowed purpose in joining the Marines to dispel the stereotyping of the Chinese by many as being "meek and bland"—not good soldier material as exemplified by Japanese-Americans in the famed 442nd Regimental Combat Team.

Kurt served 25 years of active duty in the Marine Corps, and is a veteran of World War II, Korea and Vietnam. He said his greatest regret in WWII was not to be with his boot camp buddies who landed on Iwo Jima as part of the 28th Marines (of Mount Suribachi fame) while he was detailed to schooling stateside.

Kurt, who legalized his given name in 1955, was known as Chew-Een Lee in the early years of his Marine career. He was born on January 21, 1926 in San Francisco. At the time, his father was fruit farming in the delta region of the Sacramento River and a political activist in the small Chinese community that settled in the area. Because of the Great Depression, he moved his family to Sacramento to take over a farm produce business that sold bulk produce to restaurants and hotels.

Kurt was the third child and first boy in a family of seven children. They were schooled under the Sacramento public school system and private Chinese schools in the evenings and Saturday mornings. His interest in the military came at age 11 with the outbreak of the Sino-Japanese War in 1937. He seethed with anger over the savagery of Japanese troops depicted in graphic photos in their brutal rape of Nanking. He enrolled in Junior ROTC in senior high school that facilitated his later absorption and personal identification with Marine Corps standards of excellence.

He enlisted in the Marine Corps on April 10, 1944 and after boot camp, to his intense disappointment, he was assigned to learn Japanese while his buddies fought on Iwo Jima. Upon graduation he was made an instructor. The sweetener was accelerated promotion from private to sergeant, the rank he held when the war ended. However, since he was already processed for officer training, he entered the first regular class to convene since 1939 when it was reactivated and moved from Philadelphia to Quantico. His class graduated on April 2, 1946 and Kurt, age 20, was commissioned as the youngest officer in that class. Kurt was adamant that he not be pigeon-holed as another language officer by some superior who was not accustomed to exotic-hued Marine officers. (One actually apologized to his platoon commanders that an "Oriental officer" is joining the unit as its new executive officer.)

When the Korean War broke out in June 1950, Kurt was a guard officer with Marine Barracks, Mare Island Naval Shipyard. But, since he had experience in 1946–48 as a rifle platoon commander with Marine units in Peking and Tsingtao, China, he was able to secure a combat position. He reported to Camp Pendleton in August 1950, and was assigned to Baker Company of the reactivated 1st Battalion, 7th Marines. He organized and trained raw Marine reservists and WWII veterans that he handpicked for his machine-gun platoon.

With only two weeks of training the battalion embarked for war on September 1, 1950. The 7th Marines landed as the Division Reserve in the Inchon-Seoul Campaign. His company was undergoing OJT while engaged in combat against the enemy. This enabled the 7th to assume the major role of spearheading both the Division drive north and its heroic breakout from the trap set by ten Chinese divisions at the Chosin Reservoir. Of the 300 officers and men in Baker Company who fought in Korea, only 27 survivors, with fighting spirit intact, were able to march aboard its evacuating ship at Hungnam on December 12, 1950.

Kurt felt that his most "grueling yet satisfying" time in the Corps was when, upon promotion to major on January 1, 1963, he was selected as the chief of platoon tactics instruction at the Basic School, Quantico. He was retained in this arduous, mentally exhausting assignment for 27 straight months. He and his staff trained a whole generation of new Marine officers as infantry platoon commanders under the adage that "every Marine a rifleman."

In May 1965 he followed his newly qualified lieutenants into combat in Vietnam where he was assigned as the division combat intelligence officer of the 3rd Marine Division. He was gratified to find through observation and combat reports that all his former students performed in superb fashion on the battlefield. While assigned as the operations officer of the Language Branch of the Marine Corps Command and Staff College, Kurt retired after 25 years of active service. He holds the following personal decorations: Navy Cross, Silver Star, two Purple Hearts, and the Navy Commendation Medal with Combat V. But he states that the Presidential Unit Citation (PUC) is more indicative of an officer's performance in combat. He retired with six PUCs (three foreign) and a Navy Unit Citation awarded to units he commanded.

The Smithsonian Institution made a one-hour documentary on the Korean War entitled *Uncommon Courage* that aired on the Smithsonian Channel on Memorial Day, 2010. This film has been endorsed by the Marine Corps as a professional military education training film. It is a good synopsis of the Korean War and the challenges faced by Asian-Americans in America. Using the iconic Chosin Reservoir battle as the backdrop, it showed how Kurt coped with challenges as a lieutenant before the advent of diversity training became policy in the Armed Forces. By any measure, it would appear that he, with resolve and dedication, accomplished this personal mission in the bastion of Marine warrior spirit with flying colors. He died March 3, 2014.

SIX SECONDS

Lieutenant General John F. Kelly, USMC

On November 13, 2010, Lieutenant General Kelly, USMC, gave a speech to the Semper Fi Society of St. Louis, Missouri, ending it with an account of the last six seconds in the lives of two Marines who died with rifles blazing to protect their brother Marines.

I will leave you with a story about the kind of people they are. About the quality of the steel in their backs. About the kind of dedication they bring to our country while they serve in uniform and forever after as veterans.

On April 22, 2008, while I was the Commander of all U.S. and Iraqi forces, two Marine infantry battalions, 1/9 "The Walking Dead," and 2/8 were switching out in Ramadi. One battalion, in the closing days of their deployment, was going home very soon. The other was just starting its seven-month combat tour. Two Marines, Corporal Jonathan Yale and Lance Corporal Jordan Haerter, 22 and 20 years old respectively, one from each battalion, were assuming the watch together at the entrance gate of an outpost that contained a makeshift barracks housing 50 Marines. The same broken-down, ramshackle building was also home to 100 Iraqi police. My men and our Iraqi allies were fighting the terrorists in Ramadi, a city that was, until recently, the most dangerous city on earth and owned by Al Qaeda.

Yale was a dirt poor, mixed-race kid from Virginia with a wife and daughter, and a mother and sister who lived with him and he supported. He did this on a yearly salary of less than $23,000. Haerter, on the other hand, was a middle-class white kid from Long Island. They were from two completely different worlds. Had they not joined the Marines they would never have met each other, or understood that multiple Americas exist simultaneously depending on one's education level, economic status, and where you might have been born.

But they were Marines, combat Marines, forged in the same crucible of Marine training, and because of this bond they were brothers as close, or closer, than if they were born of the same woman. The mission orders they received from the sergeant, I am sure went, something like: "Okay you two clowns, stand this post and let no unauthorized personnel or vehicle pass. You clear?" I am also sure Yale and Haerter then rolled their eyes and said in unison something like: "Yes, Sergeant," with just enough attitude that made the point without saying the words, "No kidding, sweetheart, we know what we're doing." They then relieved two other Marines on watch and took up their post and the entry control point of Joint Security Station Nasser, in the Sophia section of Ramadi, Al Anbar, and Iraq.

A few minutes later a large blue truck turned down the alley—perhaps 60–70 yards in—and sped its way through the serpentine of concrete jersey walls. The truck stopped just short of where the two were posted and detonated, killing them both, tragically. Twenty-four brick masonry houses were damaged or destroyed. A mosque 100 yards away collapsed. The truck's engine came to rest two hundred yards away, knocking most of a house down before it stopped. Our explosive experts reckon the blast was made of 2,000 pounds of explosives. Two died, and because these two young infantrymen didn't have it in their DNA to run from danger, they saved 150 of their Iraqi and American brothers-in-arms.

I traveled to Ramadi the next day and spoke individually to a half-dozen Iraqi police, all of whom told the same story. The blue truck turned down into the alley and immediately sped up as it made its way through the serpentine. They all said, "We knew immediately what was going on as soon as the two Marines began firing." The Iraqi police then related that some of them also fired, and then, to a man, ran for safety prior to the explosion. All survived. Many were injured, some seriously. One of the Iraqis elaborated and with tears welling up said, "They'd run, like any normal man would, to save his life." What he didn't know until then, he said, and what he learned that very instant, was that Marines are not normal. Choking past the emotion he said, "Sir, in the name of God, no sane man would have stood there and done what they did. No sane man. They saved us all."

What we didn't know at the time, and only learned a couple of days later after I wrote a summary and submitted both Yale and Haerter for posthumous Navy Crosses, was that one of our security cameras, damaged initially in the blast, recorded some of the suicide attack. It happened exactly as the Iraqis had described. Exactly six seconds from when the truck entered the alley until it detonated.

You can watch the last six seconds of their young lives. Putting myself in their heads, I supposed it took about a second for the two Marines to separately come to the same conclusion about what was going on once the truck came into their view at the far end of the alley. Exactly no time to talk it over, or call the sergeant to ask what they should do. Only enough time to take half an instant and think about what the sergeant told them to do only a few minutes before: "Let no unauthorized personnel or vehicle pass." The two Marines had about five seconds left to live.

It took maybe another two seconds for them to present their weapons, take aim, and open up. By this time the truck was half-way through the barriers and gaining speed the whole time. Here, the recording shows a number of Iraqi police, some of whom had fired their AKs, now scattering like the normal and rational men they were—some running right past the Marines. They had three seconds left to live.

For about two seconds more, the recording shows the Marines' weapons firing nonstop, the truck's windshield exploding into shards of glass as their rounds take it apart and tore into the body of the SOB who is trying to get past them to kill their brothers—American and Iraqi—bedded down in the barracks, totally unaware that their lives at that moment depended entirely on two Marines standing their ground.

If they had been aware, they would have known they were safe, because two Marines stood between them and a crazed suicide bomber. The recording shows the truck careening to a stop immediately in front of the two Marines. In all of the instantaneous violence, Yale and Haerter never hesitated. By all reports and by the recording, they never stepped back. They never even started to step aside. They never even shifted their weight. With their feet spread shoulder width apart, they leaned into the danger, firing as fast as they could work their weapons. They had only one second left to live.

The truck explodes. The camera goes blank. Two young men go to their God. Six seconds. Not enough time to think about their families, their country, their flag, or about their lives or their deaths, but more than enough time for two very brave young men to do their duty, into eternity. That is the kind of people who are on watch all over the world tonight—for you.

We Marines believe that God gave America the greatest gift He could bestow to man while he lived on this earth—freedom. We also believe He gave us another gift nearly as precious—our soldiers, sailors, airmen, Coast Guardsmen, and Marines—to safeguard that gift and guarantee no force on this earth can ever steal it away. It has been my distinct honor to have been with you here today. Rest assured our America, this experiment in democracy started over two centuries ago, will forever remain in the "land of the free and home of the brave" so long as we never run out of tough young Americans who are willing to look beyond their own self-interest and comfortable lives, and go into the darkest and most dangerous places on earth to hunt down, and kill, those who would do us harm.

God Bless America, and … SEMPER FIDELIS!

This piece first appeared in the Legion of Valor General Orders.

RETURNING FIRE AT PEARL HARBOR

DORIS MILLER, NAVY CROSS

Doris Miller, known as "Dorie" to shipmates and friends, was born in Waco, Texas, on October 12, 1919, to Henrietta and Conery Miller. He had three brothers, one of which served in the Army during World War II. While attending Moore High School in Waco, he was a fullback on the football team. He worked on his father's farm before enlisting in the US Navy as mess attendant, third class, at Dallas, Texas, on September 16, 1939, to travel, and earn money for his family. He later was commended by the Secretary of the Navy, was advanced to mess attendant, second class and first class, and subsequently was promoted to cook, third class.

Following training at the Naval Training Station, Norfolk, Virginia, Miller was eventually assigned to USS *West Virginia* (BB-48), where he became the ship's heavyweight boxing champion and was serving in that battleship when the Japanese attacked Pearl Harbor on December 7, 1941. Miller had arisen at 6 a.m., and was collecting laundry when the alarm for general quarters sounded. He headed for his battle station, the antiaircraft battery magazine amidship, only to discover that torpedo damage had wrecked it, so he went on deck. Because of his physical prowess, he was assigned to carry wounded fellow sailors to places of greater safety. Then an officer ordered him to the bridge to aid the mortally wounded captain of the ship. He subsequently manned a 50-caliber

Browning antiaircraft machine gun until he ran out of ammunition and was ordered to abandon ship.

Miller described firing the machine gun during the battle, a weapon which he had not been trained to operate: "It wasn't hard. I just pulled the trigger and she worked fine. I had watched the others with these guns. I guess I fired her for about fifteen minutes. I think I got one of those Jap planes. They were diving pretty close to us."

For his actions he received the Navy Cross, which Fleet Admiral (then Admiral) Chester W. Nimitz, the Commander in Chief, Pacific Fleet personally presented to Miller on board aircraft carrier USS *Enterprise* (CV-6) for his extraordinary courage in battle.

On December 13, 1941, Miller reported to USS *Indianapolis* (CA-35), and subsequently returned to the west coast of the United States, where he was assigned to the newly constructed USS *Liscome Bay* (CVE-56) While cruising near Butaritari Island, a single torpedo from Japanese submarine *I-175* struck the escort carrier near the stern, sinking the warship. Listed as missing following the loss of that escort carrier, Miller was officially presumed dead November 25, 1944, a year and a day after the loss of *Liscome Bay*. In addition to the Navy Cross, Miller earned the Purple Heart Medal, the American Defense Service Medal, Fleet Clasp, the Asiatic-Pacific Campaign Medal, and the World War II Victory Medal.

Commissioned on June 30, 1973, USS *Miller* (FF-1091), a *Knox*-class frigate, was named in honor of Doris Miller.

On October 11, 1991, Alpha Kappa Alpha Sorority dedicated a bronze commemorative plaque of Miller at the Miller Family Park located on the U.S. Naval Base, Pearl Harbor. Today efforts are in progress to upgrade his award to a Medal of Honor.

This piece is based on Naval History and Heritage Command materials.

THE ROOSEVELT MEDALS OF HONOR

The Roosevelts are the second of only two pairs of fathers and sons to earn the Medal of Honor. The first such recipients were Arthur MacArthur, Jr. and his son Douglas MacArthur. In 2001, Theodore T. Roosevelt was posthumously awarded the Medal of Honor for his action during the charge up San Juan Hill in 1898. He was the only President of the United States to be awarded America's highest military honor, and the only person in history to receive both his nation's highest honor for military valor and the world's foremost prize—the Pulitzer Prize—for Peace. His eldest son, Theodore Roosevelt Jr., also earned a Medal of Honor during World War II for rallying and leading the troops on June 6, 1944 during the Allied invasion at Normandy. He died a month later and the award was presented posthumously in September 1944. Their citations read respectively:

> Theodore T. Roosevelt, United States Army, who distinguished himself by acts of bravery on 1 July, 1898, near Santiago de Cuba, Republic of Cuba, while leading a daring charge up San Juan Hill. Lieutenant Colonel Roosevelt, in total disregard for his personal safety and accompanied by only four or five men, led a desperate and gallant charge up San Juan Hill, encouraging his troops to continue the assault through withering enemy fire over open countryside. Facing the enemy's heavy fire, he displayed extraordinary bravery throughout the charge. He was the first to reach the enemy trenches, where he quickly killed one of the enemy with his pistol, allowing his men to continue the assault. His leadership

and valor turned the tide in the Battle for San Juan Hill. Lieutenant Colonel Roosevelt's extraordinary heroism and devotion to duty are in keeping with the highest traditions of military service and reflect great credit upon himself, his unit, and the United States Army.

Theodore Roosevelt Jr., United States Army: For gallantry and intrepidity at the risk of his life above and beyond the call of duty on 6 June 1944, in France. After two verbal requests to accompany the leading assault elements in the Normandy invasion had been denied, Brig. Gen. Roosevelt's written request for this mission was approved and he landed with the first wave of the forces assaulting the enemy-held beaches. He repeatedly led groups from the beach, over the seawall and established them inland. His valor, courage, and presence in the very front of the attack and his complete unconcern at being under heavy fire inspired the troops to heights of enthusiasm and self-sacrifice. Although the enemy had the beach under constant direct fire, Brig. Gen. Roosevelt moved from one locality to another, rallying men around him, directed and personally led them against the enemy. Under his seasoned, precise, calm, and unfaltering leadership, assault troops reduced the enemy strong points and rapidly moved inland with minimum casualties. He thus contributed substantially to the successful establishment of the beachhead in France.

This first appeared in the Legion of Valor General Orders.

FIGHTER ACE AND PRISONER
OF WAR

ROBINSON RISNER, AIR FORCE CROSS

On April 3 and 4, 1965 Colonel Risner led two successive operations over North Vietnam against vitally important and heavily defended targets. On the initial attack, while exposing himself to heavy ground fire, with complete disregard for his personal safety, Colonel Risner's aircraft sustained a direct hit in the left forward bomb-bay area, filling the cockpit with smoke and fumes. He flew his badly damaged aircraft over heavily fortified hostile territory before successfully landing at a friendly airfield.

On April 4, he again led an attacking force of fighter aircraft on a restrike against the same target. Colonel Risner initiated the attack, directing his aircraft into the target in the face of heavy automatic ground fire. His aerial skill and heroic actions set an example for the others to follow.

In the course of the operation, Colonel Risner's unit encountered the first MIG force committed in aerial combat against the U.S. Forces in Southeast Asia. However, he refused to be diverted from his primary mission of completing the destruction of the assigned targets. Colonel Risner's actions not only deprived the Communist force of its vital supply route and much-needed equipment but further served to emphasize the high degree of U.S. determination in Southeast Asia.

Later Colonel Risner became a prisoner of war in North Vietnam from October 31 to December 15, 1965. After being released from captivity on February 12, 1973, he received a second Air Force Cross for extraordinary heroism. He also earned two Silver Stars, three Distinguished Flying Crosses and two Bronze Stars with "V."

This piece first appeared in the Legion of Valor General Orders.

AF lays to rest an "American hero"

Friends, family members, political leaders, former prisoners of war and service members paid their respects as an Air Force Ace was interred at Arlington National Cemetery January 23.

Brigadier General Robinson "Robbie" Risner, a Korean War fighter ace and Vietnam prisoner of war, died October 22, 2013 at Bridgewater Retirement Community in Bridgewater, Virginia, at the age of 88.

"America has lost one of its greatest heroes," said Ross Perot, a close friend of Risner, during the service at the Memorial Chapel on Fort Myer, Va.

Though Risner's life on earth has ended, his flying legacy lives on, Perot said, speaking about how Risner passed on his aviation wings for both Perot's son and grandson to wear.

"Robbie approved that my son Ross could pin Robbie's wings on my grandson," said Perot. "Can you imagine what that meant?"

Perot went on to share anecdotes from throughout Risner's celebrated career, describing him as an "Oklahoma cowboy" who was hero and a friend, whose "love of God and love of country what was got him through seven and a half years as a prisoner of war."

But for many other POWs, they credited their survival to Risner's leadership.

"When the POWs came home from Vietnam, time and time again, I'd hear them say 'If it hadn't been for Robbie Risner, I wouldn't have made it,'" Perot said, sharing a particular moment that defined Risner's character.

While imprisoned in Vietnam, Risner gathered fellow POWs for a church service—something that was strictly prohibited. While the troops were singing the song *Onward Christian Soldiers*, guards rushed in, taking Risner and two other leaders to what Perot referred to as "the box," a place of solitary confinement.

When this occurred, "more than 40 POWs stood proudly, some of whom are here today, and sang a strictly forbidden song, the *Star Spangled Banner*," Perot recalls. "How's that for guts?"

Upon Risner's return from the POW camp, Perot asked him, "Robbie, what was going on in your mind as they dragged you back to the box?" He looked me in the eye. His eyes were twinkling. He said "Perot, with those guys singing the *Star Spangled Banner*, I was nine feet tall. I could have gone bear hunting with a stick!"

That moment and his words are reflected by a statue, exactly 9 feet high, that now stands at the U.S. Air Force Academy in Colorado Springs, Colorado.

Air Force Chief of Staff General Mark A. Welsh III spoke to the audience about Risner, as someone airmen should look up to.

> What some of you have told me is that he was a leader and a role model at a time in your life when you needed one terribly … a man that somehow maintained his human dignity, his character and his moral strength… They say they saw his conviction that they could survive, would survive … and they believed, because he believed. I'm so sorry that your brother is gone.
>
> To the people of this Nation, he was a noble idea … a comforting thought … the reassuring knowledge that there will always be those willing to answer the bugle's call … to sacrifice more than they have any right to ask, to dare greatly … to risk everything, to fight and die on their behalf.… He's who all of them hope they would be.

Excerpts from a piece that appeared in Air Force News Service by Staff Sergeant David Salanitri, Air Force Public Affair Agency.

TAKING CHARGE OF TOUGH JOBS

Harvey C. Barnum, Jr., Medal of Honor

Barnum, a retired USMC colonel, was the fourth Marine to receive the Medal of Honor during the Vietnam War. He was born in Cheshire, Connecticut on July 21, 1940. He was president of his senior class at Cheshire High, where he played football and baseball. After graduation, he entered St. Anselm College in Manchester, New Hampshire.

While in college, he joined the Marine Corps Platoon Leaders program and was commissioned as a reserve second lieutenant in June 1962 when he graduated with a bachelor's degree in economics.

From December 1965 until February 1966, Barnum served on temporary duty in Vietnam as an artillery forward observer with Company H, 2nd Battalion, 9th Marines, 3rd Marine Division where he was awarded the Medal of Honor.

His citation describes his actions as a forward observer for artillery, on December 18, 1965, while attached to company H, Second Battalion, Ninth Marines, Third Marine Division (Reinforced) at Ky Phu in Quang Tin Province, Republic of Vietnam:

> When the company was suddenly pinned down by a hail of extremely accurate enemy fire and was quickly separated from the remainder of the battalion by over five hundred meters of open and fire-swept ground, and casualties mounted rapidly, Lieutenant Barnum quickly made a hazardous reconnaissance of the area seeking targets for his artillery. Finding the rifle company commander mortally wounded and the radio operator killed, he, with complete disregard for his own

safety, gave aid to the dying commander, then removed the radio from the dead operator and strapped it to himself. He immediately assumed command of the rifle company, and moving at once into the mist of heavy fire, rallying and giving encouragement to all units, reorganized them to replace the loss of key personnel and led their attack on enemy positions from which deadly fire continued to come.

Upon retirement from the Marine Corps, he served as the Principal Director, Drug Enforcement Policy, Office of the Secretary of Defense. He also served as past president of the Congressional Medal of Honor Society.

In addition to the Medal of Honor, his awards include the Bronze Star with Combat V, Navy and Marine Corps Commendation Medal and Achievement Medal with Combat V, and the Purple Heart.

Adapted from a piece in the Legion of Valor General Orders.

RANGER HALL OF FAME

Richard D. "Tex" Wandke, Distinguished Service Cross

Robert L. Tonsetic, Distinguished Service Cross

Tex and his wife Ichiko were given a private tour of the Ranger Hall of Fame at Fort Benning, Georgia on April 26, 2013 during our convention in Auburn, Alabama.

The Ranger Hall of Fame, in which Tex was inducted in 2002, was formed to preserve the spirit and contributions of America's most extraordinary Rangers, including such luminaries as Generals William Darby, Colin Powell, and James Rudder. Each inductee is presented with an engraved bronze Ranger Hall of Fame medallion along with a plaque with his portrait and a summary of his combat service.

Tex was born in San Antonio, Texas in 1937, but his family moved to Maine. While attending prep school there, he was selected to the National Honor Society for excellence in academics. He then applied for and was accepted at the University of Maine, where he graduated in 1963 as a Distinguished Military Graduate. He was then commissioned as a regular Army second lieutenant in the infantry. After completing the Basic Infantry course followed by the Ranger and Airborne Schools he was assigned to an infantry battalion at Fort Lewis, Washington.

Tex served three combat tours in Vietnam. During his first tour in 1965–66 he served as a Ranger advisor to the 43d ARVN Ranger Battalion in the Mekong Delta. During this tour he was awarded a Silver Star for gallantry in action and a Purple Heart. After a tour as an ROTC instructor at the University of Michigan in 1966–68, he returned to Vietnam and served as company commander of A Company, 1st Battalion, 8th Infantry, 4th Infantry Division, where he received another Silver Star and a Purple Heart. Later in his tour, he served as commander of the 3rd Brigade LRRPs (Long Range Reconnaissance Patrols) and commander of C Company, 1st Battalion, 12th Infantry, 4th Infantry Division. He received the Distinguished Service Cross for extraordinary heroism and a third Purple Heart during this tour.

A summary of his Distinguished Service Cross citation follows: On May 27, 1969 his company, while on a search and destroy mission near Landing Zone Mary Lou, came under tremendous enemy fire which resulted in his unit sustaining heavy casualties. After rallying his men to force the enemy to break off their assault, he ordered a withdrawal from the area to establish a landing zone to evacuate the wounded. Although wounded himself, he alone stayed behind to protect the dead and critically wounded. For three harrowing hours he directed artillery fire on the enemy emplacements and with his individual weapon prevented the enemy from overrunning his position.

After being rescued, he was medically evacuated from Vietnam and, upon recovery, attended the Infantry Officer Advanced Course. He then served as an instructor and operations officer at the Mountain Ranger Camp and Ranger Department.

As the United States involvement in Vietnam was coming to an end, Tex was called upon to serve a third combat tour. During 1972–73, he served as the Senior Deputy Staff Advisor for the Republic of Vietnam's Ranger High Command, and earned the distinction of being the last Ranger staff advisor ordered out of Vietnam. In addition to his combat tours, he served in overseas tours in Korea and Japan before his retirement from the Army in 1988 after 25 years of active duty.

During his service he was awarded thirty-two medals for heroism and service including our nation's second and third highest medals for valor, the Distinguished Service Cross and three Silver Stars.

After retirement, Tex served as an Army Junior ROTC senior instructor in California from 1988 to 2006, inspiring hundreds of young men and women to become better citizens and leaders in our great nation.

He was selected as Teacher of the Year at Franklin High School in 1993 and Santiago High School in 2006, and appeared in *Who's Who in American Teachers* seven times. He continues to work to develop leadership in our nation's youth while serving as an American Athletic Union official. In addition, Tex also serves as commander of the Saddleback Valley Chapter of the Military Order of World Wars, as well as maintaining his membership in thirteen other veteran organizations.

Tex served as our Legion of Valor National Commander in 1994–95 and continues to serve on the Legion's Board and as Chaplain and Director of Awards. As chaplain, he organizes and officiates at the Legion's annual Memorial Ceremony. As Director of Awards, he coordinates with the various services for the selection and presentation of the prestigious Legion of Valor Bronze Cross for Achievement to college and high school cadets.

This piece first appeared in the Legion of Valor General Orders.

VOLUNTEERS AT THE "HOME OF THE LEGION OF VALOR"

The Home of the Legion of Valor is at the Veterans Memorial Museum in Fresno, California. The museum grew out of the efforts of several dedicated Legion of Valor members and their wives who worked with the City of Fresno to use the Fresno Veterans Memorial Auditorium. Staffed by volunteers and supported by the City and County of Fresno, the museum houses thousands of items and papers donated by Legion of Valor members as well as others. Numerous framed citations, photographs, and exhibits tell the story of America's wars as seen by individual soldiers, sailors, marines and airmen. Uniforms and equipment of different eras are also on display. Major Charles J. Monges, NC (deceased) was the principal founder and first Director of Veterans Memorial Museum, "Home of the Legion of Valor." While all our museum volunteers deserve recognition, this chapter highlights the spirit of the voluntary accomplishments of a sample of this outstanding group of men.

Bob Specht, Current CEO and Third Director
Honorary Life Member of the Legion of Valor

Bob Specht was born April 29, 1936 in the German section of Fresno, California to parents who were first-generation Americans of Russian-German decent. His father Kris was a brandy maker for the Christian Brothers Wine Company. Bob was born with a pencil in his right hand, drawing pictures at an early age and astounding his mother Edna who often said, "There is no one who is artistic in our family."

By the second grade, Bob had attained a tenth-grade reading level as he spent most of his time either reading books or drawing pictures. In the seventh grade, his parents enrolled him in an art and cartooning course with the Columbia School of Art that he completed by mail as the school was located in San Francisco. In the eighth grade at Roosevelt High School, Bob took a career test that showed he should be a humorist. Cartooning was his first love, but he never pursued it as artists' pay at that time was paltry. But he kept working at his lifelong interest in art.

Bob spent two years at Fresno State College majoring in business. He decided to pursue a sales career with Drake Steel Supply in Fresno, after befriending the company's office manager Al Fox, whose son was an F-86 jet fighter pilot with the Fresno Air National Guard. The Hayward Air Guard in the Bay Area had recently been transferred to Fresno, as the valley was less of a potential target in case of nuclear war. At that time, the Air Guard had an ongoing campaign to enlist badly needed personnel to fill their ranks. In April 1958 Bob enlisted in the California Air National Guard at the Fresno Airport.

His first assignment was to drill 100 other green recruits, like him, in the art of military marching. Bob began ineptly drilling his fellow recruits out in front of the base hanger as he had been ordered by the busy First Sergeant Tafoya. He mistakenly marched the 100 recruits in front of several "Hot Gun" aircraft whose weapons were fully loaded and parked on the tarmac for immediate take off, in case of an emergency attack. All hell broke loose as aircraft technicians came running out of the hangar yelling to get those people out of that dangerous area. Needless to say, Bob was embarrassed but begged off due to his total ignorance of the danger, but the *faux pas* caught everyone's attention. Marching drills were permanently moved to another area, away from the main hangar after that incident.

There were several national crises during Bob's Air Guard career, but the one that was most memorable was the Cuban Missile Crisis during October 1962. The Fresno airbase was placed on 24-hour high alert. But the Russians backed down and shipped their missiles back home.

During his six years in the Air Guard Bob drafted countless amounts of organizational and functional charts, which were used extensively all over the base. He was named FANG Airman of the Month during 1962.

Bob joined the Legion of Valor Museum in April 2000, and began working with Director Chuck Monges as office manager. Upon the passing of Chuck Monges in 2001, Bob became the museum's Deputy Director under Director Art Hill. After a debilitating fall ended Mr. Hill's ability to continue, Bob was elected April 17, 2012 as the Director and CEO of the Veterans Memorial Museum, "Home of the Legion of Valor."

Arthur J. Hill (deceased), Second Director of the Veterans Memorial Museum

Honorary Life Member of the Legion of Valor

Arthur Hill, at age 27, volunteered for the Army Engineers shortly after Pearl Harbor. Because of his construction background, he was sent to Camp Claiborne, Louisiana, early in 1942 to a Special Service Engineer Regiment. On December 23, 1942, Art graduated from Officer Candidate School and the Heavy Equipment School at Fort Belvoir, Virginia, as a second lieutenant. At Camp Swift, Texas, he was assigned to the 146th Engineer (C) Battalion as the Headquarters Company commander with the additional duty of battalion motor officer. He held this command, as a captain, with various additional duties until war's end. While at Saunton Sands, on the north coast of Devon, England, the battalion helped build and operate an assault training center of enemy fortifications duplicated from secret aerial reconnaissance photos of the landing beaches and Siegfried Line defenses. This led to the spearheading of the Omaha Beach D-Day landings across the English Channel on June 6, 1944 at H-hour+3. Five European campaigns followed: Normandy, Northern France, Rhineland, Ardennes-Alsace, and Central Europe.

While the U.S. was still at war with Japan, some men were thinking of home; others with fewer points were thinking of their possible transfer to the other side of the world. Art lacked less than one point of the amount required for discharge and was slated as base commander at one of several embarkation centers for upgrading facilities for pending troop movements. He was at the Biarritz American University (Engineer school) in southern France making preparations when he learned that he had received a foreign award, the Czech Military Medal.

Upon returning home, after his January 8, 1946 discharge, Art worked in the petroleum industry for over 30 years. During his semi-retirement years of 1975–1979, he served as the nine western states representative on the Shell Oil Company National Jobber Council. He retired in 1980 as President of Hill Oil Company. He was the Director of the Veterans Memorial Museum from 2001 to 2010. Art and his wife B. J. (now deceased) were married over fifty years. He died on November 9, 2014.

Floyd Sherwood Hill

Reflections of 85-year-old Floyd Sherwood Hill about his combat experience in Korea were not bitter though it left him with one eye. There was no anger or regret but of hardship during a time of war. To him, nothing could compare to the horror and tragedy faced by the troops in his Army days. The Combat Infantryman's Badge is his most important award that says, "He was there."

Sam, as he likes to be called, enlisted in 1948. After basic training at Fort Ord, California, additional experiences and military schooling qualified him as a tank commander.

In 1950 Sam was assigned to the South Korean theater as part of the cadre to train the South Korean Army. While on the way to Korea, war broke out there. He was reassigned to one of the first combat divisions to fight the Communist North Koreans—the 24th Infantry Division. His unit had no tanks available, so he was tasked as squad leader of C Company of the 19th Infantry Regiment.

His unit fought many battles along the Taejon–Taegu–Pusan corridor. His company survived a hard-fought last-ditch stand to hold the Pusan perimeter, thus allowing additional American forces to join the war. At one point they were cut off from supplies and had to survive on available native food and sustenance.

During the battle of Chinju-Masan Hill was severely wounded and evacuated from a field aid station to the Pusan Army hospital and then transferred to a British hospital ship. He was eventually taken to the Tokyo Army Hospital.

After five weeks of recuperation Sam was sent to Camp Drake Japan, a replacement depot, and assigned as a battalion sergeant major. He got home in June 1952. Sam was released with an honorable discharge as a sergeant first class.

Sam settled in Fresno, California, and began college and subsequently graduated from law school. He spent 42 years in that vocation and became a notable attorney in the area.

He serves as a docent at the Veterans Memorial Museum guiding visitors with a spell-binding tutorial characterizing veterans as the wire that separates the wolves of the world from the sheep. Sam is an example of a good soldier, a community servant, and a valued historian.

Jesse Fabela

A native of Fresno, California, Jesse Fabela was inducted into Army in 1968. He held the tradition of military service close to his heart as all six of his brothers also served in the armed forces.

After completing basic and advanced infantry training, he deployed to Vietnam in 1969, where he was assigned to a rifle company in the 199th Light Infantry Brigade.

His unit's mission was to protect Saigon, which they did by patrolling the nearby countryside. The first three months of his tour found him as point man for his platoon, a job no one cared for. Their designated machine gunner then rotated home and Jess volunteered to take that job carrying the heavy M-60 for the next six months. He mixed that assignment with being a rifleman and carrying the M-79 grenade launcher as well as being a radioman.

In one engagement with the enemy he was wounded by shrapnel from a booby trap. He was walking point through tall elephant grass. He stepped over a mine pressure release device, and his friend behind him stepped on it. Jesse's friend was evacuated. But his helmet was left behind. Jesse picked it up and carried it. Inside the helmet was a picture of his friend's girlfriend and two letters to his parents, leaving Jesse with haunting memories for the rest of his life.

He remembers some of the events he missed during that year of 1969—the moon landing, Woodstock, the Jets beating the Colts in the Super Bowl, the Amazing Mets. To Jesse, after Vietnam, every day of his life seemed more precious.

Jesse was awarded the Combat Infantryman's Badge, the decoration for which he is most proud, the Purple Heart, the Army Commendation Medal and the National Defense Medal. He was reunited with his girl-friend, and they were married. After seven years with the I.R.S. he joined the U.S. Postal Service, where he was employed for 27 years.

Jesse proudly serves as a docent with the Veterans Memorial Museum.

FORTITUDE

Someone who practices fortitude perseveres in his commitment to the good, once he has recognized it, even if in the extreme case he must sacrifice even his own life for it.

The Catholic Catechism

"Hero" isn't the right word, but it's the first word that comes to mind.
Chuck Palahniuk, Choke

MEDICS, MEDEVACS,
AND CHAPLAINS

Lieutenant Colonel Richard J. Rinaldo, USA Ret.,
Distinguished Service Cross

In their book, *Home of the Brave*, Former Secretary of Defense Caspar W. Weinberger and Wynton C. Hall tell us, "To most people the battlefield is a place for killing, a death zone. But Luis Fonseca, Jr, isn't most people. 'I never wanted to harm people, I always wanted to help people,' said Fonseca." He was a Navy hospitalman. In Vietnam alone, four Navy hospital corpsman received the Medal of Honor while 32 of them received the Navy Cross. In the Navy, in fact, the rating of hospital corpsman is the most decorated. Seventeen Army Medical Department soldiers received the Medal of Honor, many posthumously, in Vietnam. Ninety-two of them received the Distinguished Service Cross. In the Air Force air rescue accounted for two Medals of Honor while pararescuemen received 11 Air Force Crosses. Three Catholic chaplains also earned the Medal of Honor, two posthumously, both now candidates for sainthood. Here are stories and tributes to some of our medics, pararescuemen, chaplains, air rescue and medevac pilots, and nurses. No wonder then that LOV member Colonel David Hackworth would extol medics in his bestselling book, *About Face*:

> I didn't know what it was about medics.… Medics didn't wait for a miracle to pull the wounded to a safe shelter—they were the miracle that pulled, slid, dragged, and packed shattered bodies out of danger. And they performed miracles: stopping bleeding, stopping shock, relieving pain with morphine, and getting IVs going to pump life into broken fighters … their job was to save lives, not take them, and they risked their own, again and again, answering calls that took them right into the line of fire—machine-gun, mortar, sniper, mines—without hesitation.

COMBAT MEDIC'S REQUIEM

John J. Duffy

They carried a medical kit.
They braved the enemy fire.
They risked their own lives.
Thus, they could save others.

In the thick of combat–
You always heard the call:
"Corpsman" or "Medic".
It was a call for help.

Combat Medics are heroes.
They are the bravest of the brave.
When others seek shelter,
They seek to help the wounded.

Our combat medic is gone.
He has joined the fallen.
He will be welcomed up there,
For he is a hero come home.

Render you one final salute!
Salute valor, salute the hero,
Salute the man we relied upon.
Say each of you, your goodbye.

Say his name loud one last time. He is no longer amongst the Legion,
He is gone, to join his fallen comrades, Those who died on the field
of battle.
The names ring out from history from where they fought their battles:
Iwo Jima, Normandy, and Chosin, Vietnam, Somalia and Iraq.
Hail the hero, hail the warrior! Hail the lover, and husband true!
Hail the father and granddad too! Hail the hero of this our nation!
Offer you one final salute: Salute the man we call friend,
Salute the comrade we relied upon. Salute valor, let the Legion
mourn.

*This was written in memory of Earl Lincoln Stout, NC and appeared in the
Legion of Valor General Orders.*

*John J. Duffy has published five poetry books and his work has been selected for
two monuments and numerous anthologies.*

INCREDIBLE MEDEVACS IN VIETNAM

MICHAEL J. NOVOSEL, MEDAL OF HONOR

Peter Dorland

It was 4 p.m. on October 2, 1969, and CW4 Mike Novosel had been flying for seven hours. He, W-I Tyrone Chamberlain, Medic/SP4 Herbert Heinold, and Crew Chief/Specialist Joe Horvath were given a new mission. The weather was bad and Novosel had to fly 40 minutes—mostly through thunderstorms—to reach their destination.

At the scene, Captain Harry L. Purdy, an infantry officer, summed up the situation for Novosel. "It was not good by any measure," he said. "First of all, we had no air cover of any kind. We had no gun ships available. We had no Air Force support available. To make matters worse, we had no Americans on the ground."

The men knew that the enemy controlled the area, but they knew little else. "There were an indefinite number of wounded and killed who were down there," Novosel said. "The C&C could see them with his binoculars, I suppose, and he reported the location of a few of these to me. Of course, I naturally asked who I could contact on the ground. I was told, 'no one,' they had no contact with anybody, Vietnamese or American, and that, in fact, there were no Americans there." He later learned that a couple of aircraft had already been shot down in support of this unit and that some Air Force aircraft had been hit.

"I went in to take a look, and brought it to hover in the area where (Purdy) told me to look for this one friendly wounded or suppressed individual. They could not move about because they were totally surrounded and cut off. When I brought it to a hover over this area, I saw no one, absolutely no one, friendly or enemy. But I sure heard a lot of noise. This was all kind of machine guns that were opening up from all around, in front, in back, and off to the side. Why they did not hit me, I don't know. I made an immediate turn to the right and flew out of the area, getting fired at all the time." It turns out Novosel had gone into Cambodia; the main forces of the VC had opened fire on him.

Purdy insisted someone was down there who needed rescue. "We went in a second time, with the same identical results except that rather than turn to the right to go to Cambodia, I turned to the left and did not pick up as much fire," Novosel said.

Again, he saw nothing. But he believed Purdy.

"Well, I know a man that is in the C&C knows what he sees, and, of course, I know I am really pressing and trying to pick up what is down there to get him out of there. I know these people have been there since 8 o'clock in the morning. This is when they were first cut off, they have lost all their weapons, lost the commo equipment, but they are still down there and are being fired at. They are hugging the rice paddies' dikes, such as they are, or the grass or something to keep from being observed and from being hit. Purdy in the C&C can see these people.

"Without any disagreements from the crew, I said, 'Well, we will go again and try.' That was it, we did. It was evident after the second attempt that we were not going to get them from that triangular fort. No way for us to get them there. First of all, we were totally surrounded by enemy bunkers. I think there were about 27 of them surrounding the area. I am not certain that all these were able to fire at us, but enough were able to fire to make us miserable. "

Novosel circled above, hoping the Americans would see him.

"Well, finally, believe it or not, one man had nerve enough to stand up in the grass. This is what he did: stood up and waved his shirt. I knew it could not be the VC, no VC is going to take off his shirt to wave at me. He is going to fire at me.

"So I went, skidded right to him, and we pulled him in. That was our first one. From then on this was the method we used. We just went down there, circled, flew back and forth always moving, and hoping that someone would pop up and with a nerve to say, 'Here I am.' It seemed as if one success brought on another one. At one time we actually had four people standing up and waving at us. We went right to them—some were able to jump in, some were in a bad way. I think when it was finally done, we picked up 29."

All the while, Novosel and his crew were taking heavy fire. Several times they had to make a quick exit, reassemble, regroup, and try again from another direction.

His co-pilot, Tyrone Chamberlain, kept an eye on the instrument panel and gave Novosel regular reports. The medic and crew chief hung out of both sides of the helicopter and, whenever they saw a wounded man, they would help him in. Three times, they picked up a load of men, headed back into Moc Hoa to deliver the wounded to the medical station and refuel, then headed back to the scene.

"When someone says, 'How could so many bunkers fire at you and not hit you?' Well, because the damn bunkers can't turn, and I kept moving. So this one might fire a small burst at me, this one might pick me up later and fire at me, this one might fire at me—see what I am getting at? That was the reason. There was a hell of a lot of fire, don't misunderstand me, but they were also hindered, because I kept moving."

Of course, that's not to say his aircraft didn't sustain damage.

"Oh, yeah, full of holes," he said. "They knocked out my VHF radio, my airspeed indicator. " One bullet struck the sole of his boot. "I think that is what caused me to go out of control because the damn aircraft went like that and for some reason or other, I don't know what happened, but one of my damn feet went in or out.

"This last man we picked up, the maneuver was so violent that he would have gone out of the aircraft, except that Horvath had him by the hand, he had already hauled him in and just as he hauled him in. That's when this bastard opened up—and when I say close, I mean about 30 feet away. He was aiming at me—not at the aircraft, at me personally. When this thing slewed off the side, this man went back out. According to Horvath, we were this time 60 feet in the air by the time we got him back in again."

The aircraft was hit nine or 10 times. "The problem is, they were all in front—that was the bad thing. How this man missed me, I don't know."

After 10 hours of flying, Novosel went back to Moc Hoa and shut down. The crew examined the airplane and found a couple of holes in the rotor in addition to the damage to the front end.

Novosel received a Congressional Medal of Honor for his actions that day and some of the crew members received various medals as well. Novosel had praise for those enlisted men who served as crew members on aeromedical evacuations.

"I could never say anything but give them the highest of accolades. I consider them a part of Medical Service Corps, just the same as I consider the warrant who was assigned to the duty of medical evacuation—Dustoff, if you will. Who trained them, who inspired, them, I don't know. But whoever it was certainly deserves a heck of a lot of credit. I can truthfully say that in two tours, this includes over 2,000 very close and strong combat hours, I never saw one medic or crew chief that ever flinched, that did not do what was asked in all these bad situations.

"Certainly on this particular day, October 2, Specialist Horvath and Heinold, my co-pilot Chamberlain, could have at any of these times said, 'Let's get out here, this is too much,' and they would have been not considered slackers in the least. I am sure it was a tough day. Remember, as I said, I flew 11 hours, and they were with me for all those 11 hours. I certainly was not at the controls for 11 hours—after all, Ty Chamberlain was there to do the flying. We swap off as we do in all these things. I fly one mission, he flies another. This is the way we did it, this is the way we spell ourselves. These enlisted crew members certainly had to be, in my estimation, the best the Army ever produced. I don't think they were ever given enough credit, really and truly, for all the work they have done.

"Remember, we up front have got the ability to make a choice to go in or not to go in. This man in the back, however, has got to sit there and grin and bear it and he rides out the adversity that you create."

Novosel called his two tours in Vietnam "the most rewarding that any individual could imagine." But he saw his role as an odd one. "It is a strange thing to be a part of a war and honestly say you have not killed anyone," he said. "I know that we expect killing."

People who have fought for their county share a common bond, Novosel said. Each one, "if he is honest with himself and honest to God, will say the one thing he hates the most is war—and the one thing he sees the futility of is war."

This account is an edited version of an interview with Congressional Medal of Honor recipient Mike Novosel conducted by Captain Peter Dorland, an Army aviator who researched and wrote a history of Army aeromedical evacuation through the end of the Vietnam conflict. As part of his research, Dorland interviewed and corresponded with many of the leading medevac aviators who had served in Vietnam, including Novosel.

ARMY CHAPLAIN WHO SAVED PRISONERS OF WAR

FATHER EMIL J. KAPUAN, MEDAL OF HONOR

David Vergun

An Army chaplain, Captain Emil J. Kapaun, was posthumously awarded the Medal of Honor for his actions leading up to his capture as a prisoner of war in North Korea.

Kapaun was ordained a priest in 1940, and served under the Roman Catholic Diocese of Wichita in Pilsen, Kansas. In 1944, he began serving as an Army chaplain. In 1993, Kapaun was named a "Servant of God" by the Vatican, and is currently a candidate for sainthood.

During the Medal of Honor ceremony, Obama described Kapaun's acts of courage and compassion.

When commanders ordered an evacuation, he chose to stay and tend to their wounds. When the enemy broke through and there was combat hand-to-hand, he carried on, comforting the injured and the dying, offering them some measure of peace before they left this Earth. When enemy forces bore down, it seemed like the end.

Father Kapaun spotted a wounded Chinese officer. He pleaded with (him) and convinced him to call out to his fellow Chinese. The shooting stopped, and they negotiated a safe surrender, saving those American lives.

Then as Father Kapaun was being led away, he saw another American, wounded, unable to walk, lying in a ditch, defenseless. An enemy soldier was standing over him, rifle aimed at his head ready to shoot. Father Kapaun pushed the enemy soldier aside. And then as the enemy soldier watched, stunned, Father Kapaun carried that wounded American away.

This is the battle we honor today. An American soldier who didn't fire a gun, but who wielded the mightiest weapon of all, the love for his brothers, so pure, that he was willing to die so they might live.

> He carried that wounded soldier for four miles on the death march and when Father Kapaun grew tired, he'd help the wounded soldier hop on one leg. When other prisoners stumbled, he picked them up. When they wanted to quit, knowing stragglers would be shot, he begged them to keep walking.

Among the documents and interviews within the nomination package, one of the narratives reads:

> As Chinese Communist forces encircled (3rd Battalion, 8th Cavalry during the battle of Unsan,) Kapaun moved fearlessly from foxhole to foxhole under enemy direct fire in order to provide comfort and reassurance to the outnumbered soldiers. When the Chinese commandos attacked the battalion command post, Kapaun and other members of the headquarters withdrew 500 meters across a nearby river, but Kapaun returned to help the wounded, gathering approximately 30 injured men into the relative protection of a Korean dugout.

The narrative goes on to describe how the battalion became entirely surrounded by enemy forces. It recounts how Kapaun spent the next day, November 2, repeatedly rescuing the wounded from "no-man's land outside the perimeter."

As the battalion's position became hopeless, "Kapaun rejected several chances to escape, instead volunteering to stay behind and care for the wounded." At dusk, he made his way back to the dugout.

"Among the injured Americans was a wounded Chinese officer," it continues. "As Chinese infantry closed in on their position, Kapaun convinced him to negotiate for the safety of the injured Americans."

The narrative then describes how, after Kapaun's capture, he intervened to save the life of a fellow soldier who was "lying in a nearby ditch with a broken ankle and other injuries. As Chinese soldiers prepared to execute" the soldier, "Kapaun risked his own life by pushing the Chinese soldier aside" thereby saving the soldier's life.

The narrative continues with other acts of bravery and charity, both during the march north and throughout their ordeal at the prisoner-of-war camp. Kapaun died there, May 23, 1951.

Many prisoners of war were inspired by Kapaun, including Mike Dowe, who at the time was a first lieutenant.

He recounted how U.S. soldiers ran out of ammunition in the Anju area in early November 1950, when "wave after wave" of Chinese Communist forces launched a surprise attack across the border into Korea.

Thousands of soldiers were taken prisoner and were forced to march northward in what Dowe termed "death marches." Soldiers who were too weak or injured to keep up were shot, he said. It was then that Dowe, who was a member of the 19th Regiment, 24th Infantry Division, first saw Kapaun carrying the wounded and encouraging others to do the same.

"Kapaun Valley"

The POWs eventually were taken to a valley near Pyoktong, near the Yalu River in northwest North Korea near the Chinese border.

"I don't know the name of that valley, but we called it the 'Kapaun Valley' because that is where Father Kapaun instilled in us a will to live," he said.

Kapaun tended to the wounded and encouraged people to share and help each other, Dowe said. He also snuck out of camp at night and stole food, which he would bring back and share with everyone.

Then, in January 1951, the soldiers were moved to Pyoktong, along the Yalu River. The enlisted were located in a valley and the officers were separated and placed on a hill, Dowe said. Turkish prisoners were co-located with the enlisted.

Conditions in the camps were miserable during winter 1950–1951, which Dowe said was one of the coldest ever in Korea. Temperatures then had dipped to -28F.

Dowe said the soldiers were still wearing their summer uniforms, because they'd been told they would be home by Thanksgiving 1950, not realizing at the time that the Chinese would join the North Koreans in attacking the United Nations forces.

All of the trees in the area had been stripped away, but there was a wood fence around the officers' compound on the hill, Dowe said. Each morning, Kapaun got up before everyone else and went out into the "subzero" weather to collect wood from that fence, he said.

Kapaun would use that wood to heat water for coffee in a pan that he had fashioned from scrap metal. Dowe said he still has vivid recollections of that "little guy with the beard and scraggly hat pulled over his ears, made from the sleeve of a sweater, bringing coffee to everyone. You can't imagine how good that was to start the day off for us."

At night, the men would pass the time telling stories before falling asleep, Dowe said. A favorite topic was describing the food they'd like to order once they got home. "Some of the best stories were told by Father Kapaun, who described his mother's cooking back on the farm," in Kansas, Dowe said. Kapaun was always keeping the men's spirits up, he added.

"Great Thief"

The chaplain continued to make nighttime forays outside the prison camp to the surrounding countryside, with the purpose of stealing food for the soldiers in the camps. Dowe often accompanied him on what he termed "ration runs."

Sometimes they would raid a warehouse where 50-pound bags of millet and cracked corn were stored. Dowe said millet is like bird seed and very hard to digest. The two would first distribute it to the enlisted.

Soon, Kapaun became known as the "Great Thief," Dowe said. He explained that the nickname was given to him, not just because he was so successful at stealing food, but also because it was learned that Kapaun prayed to Saint Dismas, who was the penitent thief crucified alongside Jesus, as described in the Bible.

The Chinese often try to brainwash the POWs by lecturing them on the evils of capitalism and the virtues of a Communist society, Dowe said.

"Father Kapaun would rebut the lectures with intelligent responses that the Chinese found impossible to counter," Dowe recalled. "That would infuriate them. Some who resisted the lectures would be tortured or killed. We thought Father Kapaun would be killed as well."

At one point, the guards took Kapaun away. "We thought that was the end for him," Dowe said. Then, a few days later they brought him back to camp.

"They were absolutely afraid of him," Dowe said, explaining why he was returned. "There was an aura about the guy. He was fearless. He had a way of addressing people that was frank and straightforward. They couldn't understand why he wasn't afraid like others. Threats and intimidation had no effect on him."

More than half of the prisoners died that winter, Dowe said. They often died at night and the soldiers would drag the bodies outside. Every day there were burial details. Soldiers assigned to these details would carry the bodies about half a mile past the enlisted area in the valley and across the Yalu to an island where they would be buried.

"Father Kapaun always volunteered for burial details," Dowe said. "He'd recover the clothing from the dead, wash it, and then provide clean clothing to the enlisted."

Besides providing clothing to the soldiers, Kapaun would dress their wounds, offer words of encouragement and say prayers, Dowe said, adding that he did this despite being warned by the guards not to minister to the soldiers.

Easter Sunrise Service

Despite warnings from the guards, Kapaun got up extra early on Easter Day 1950 to begin a special sunrise service. It would be his last Easter.

"It was a fantastic sermon," Dowe recalled, saying it was the most "momentous event" in his life. He said hymns were sung and the echoes carried. Soon, he said, POWs up and down the valley were joining in. "It was absolutely amazing. There were a few who claimed that Father Kapaun seemed to have a halo around him."

The Chinese quickly arrived, but then became too afraid to stop the service, Dowe said.

The week after the sermon, Kapaun collapsed from a blood clot in his leg, Dowe said. There were some American doctors in the camp who treated it and he was walking and eating again soon after.

Kapaun then contracted pneumonia. The military doctors took care of that as well, Dowe said. After Kapaun recovered, guards became upset that he hadn't died. They prepared to remove him to the "death camp," a place where very sick prisoners were taken to die, and where no food or medical attention was given to them.

When the guards came, "we pushed them away," Dowe said. "They brought in troops with bayonets and threatened everyone if people didn't pick him up and carry him away.

"Father Kapaun told everyone to stop resisting and not to 'fight them on my behalf.' I was in tears," he continued, his voice tinged with emotion. "And then he turned to me and said 'Mike, don't cry. I'm going where I've always wanted to go. And when I get there, I'll be saying a prayer for all of you.'"

After the death of Kapaun, some of the guards who spoke English confided to Dowe that they were afraid of the "unconquerable spirit of a free man loyal only to his God and his country."

After the war, which ended in 1953, Dowe was invited to testify to the committee involved in writing the POW Code of Conduct, which is still in effect today. Dowe said Kapaun had a strong influence on him and he shared that with the committee, which emphasized the "loyalty" and "keeping the faith" aspects of the code.

"Father Kapaun instilled that kind of loyalty in others, enabling them to maintain their honor, self-respect and will to live," Dowe said. "I've seen over and over again that those who did not display that loyalty would invariably give up and die, often within 24 hours."

Dowe said Eisenhower gave him a personal commendation for his contribution to the committee. However, Dowe said the real credit should go to Kapaun, whom he credits with saving the lives of hundreds of POWs, directly or indirectly.

Following the war, Dowe went on to serve in the Army, retiring as a colonel in 1970 and then working as a defense contractor. He currently is a scientist at Raytheon.

He said he prays to Kapaun every night, asking him for help and guidance. And, he said, he knows Kapaun is in Heaven praying for him and his fellow POWs.

Dowe said Kapaun had a positive impact on the many non-Catholics in the prison camp as well. He said the commander of the Turkish POWs told him as they were being liberated, "I will pray to my God Allah for Father Kapaun."

Extracts from Army News Service *(April 11, 2013).*

DARING RESCUE AT KHAM DUC

LIEUTENANT COLONEL JOE M. JACKSON, MEDAL OF HONOR

C. Douglas Sterner

Lieutenant Colonel Jackson would have felt more at home going into combat in a jet fighter than the lumbering C-123 transport identified as No. 542. Enlisting in the Army Air Corps just prior to World War II, his service in that war as a crewmember motivated him to become a pilot. In Korea he had flown 107 combat missions in an Air Force fighter, earning the Distinguished Flying Cross. After that war, he became one of the first Air Force officers to pilot the U-2 reconnaissance planes.

At the controls now of the lumbering, unarmed cargo plane, he was preparing to turn his 296th Vietnam sortie into the most unlikely of routine missions. It was nearing five o'clock in the evening as he raced his twin-engine "mail-plane" over the hills that surrounded Kham Duc, flying at 9,000 feet. He had a pretty good idea what he would find in the valley below, having heard across his own radio reports of what had been happening that afternoon. Eight American aircraft had already gone down, two Army Chinooks, two Marine Corps C-46s, two Air Force C-130s, an O-2 FAC aircraft and and one A-1. Wreckage of three of these, a C-130, the O-2 and one helicopter, was strewn across the badly damaged runway.

Twenty years of experience in the air had taught Jackson that sometimes one has to do the unexpected to accomplish the impossible. Reasoning that the enemy that now controlled the air strip could hear the roar of his engines and were undoubtedly setting up their forces in anticipation of a landing like Lieutenant Colonel Jeanotte had made minutes before, Jackson prepared his own surprise. Banking his cargo plane to line up with the runway, the intrepid pilot cut power and dropped full flaps. The nose of Number 542 dropped and the C-123 was in the kind of dive reserved for fighter planes. Diving in at 4,000 feet per minute, eight times a cargo plane's normal rate of descent, he was pushing his aircraft beyond its capabilities. Later he said, "I was afraid I'd reach the 'blow-up' speed, where the flaps in the full down position, would be blown back up to the neutral position. If that happened, we'd pick up additional speed and not be able to stop."

On the ground the three airmen could hear the whine of the C-123's dive as it broke through the fog. Screaming earthward in an impossible maneuver, the men were filled with a mix of feelings … relief that a rescue craft was on the way … despair at the chances of success. As they watched the cargo plane dropping towards them like a rock, Sergeant Lundie thought, "This guy's crazy. He's not going to make it."

And then No. 542 was on the ground, touching down in the first 100 feet of runway amid a hail of enemy machine-gun and mortar fire. Plummeting down the battered runway at speeds far too high for any safe landing, Jackson fought the controls. Afraid that if he reversed the propellers to slow the C-123 he would blow out the two auxiliary engines needed for escape, he shoved his feet down hard on the brakes to skid past the enemy. Dodging debris, his cargo plane finally came to rest near the drainage ditch.

"There they are," Major Campbell shouted as he spotted three ragged figures rise out of the ditch and break for the waiting rescue plane. Staff Sergeant Grubbs opened the cargo door as the men ran towards the waiting plane, enemy fire erupting all around them. Quickly the haggard men were pulled inside the cargo hold and Jackson was revving the engines and turning his C-123 to take off in the same direction from which they had approached.

As the big cargo plane turned to face down the runway and make its escape, Major Campbell shouted, "Look out." From the edge of the runway the enemy had fired a 122mm rocket to abort the dramatic rescue and destroy No. 542. Both pilot and co-pilot watched in horror as the missile sped towards then, then hit the pavement to bounce and skid within ten meters of their cockpit. As it bounced one final time, the rocket broke in half … then lay there sizzling. Miraculously, it had been a dud.

Sending power to the engines, Joe Jackson raced down the runway and through the gauntlet of enemy fire. All within the cargo plane felt a sense of relief as the wheels lifted off the airstrip, and the C-123 was airborne … racing for home and safety. The plane gained altitude to head for Da Nang, landing shortly after 5:30 in the evening. A haggard Sergeant Jim Lundie walked over to the flight deck to look at Jackson quizzically for a moment, then said, "I wanted to see how you could sit in that little seat with balls as big as you've got." It was the ultimate compliment from a combat controller who for three days had demonstrated his own brand of valor. "We were dead," he later summed up the events of that day, "and all of a sudden we were alive."

Before returning to their billets, Major Campbell and Lieutenant Colonel Jackson checked out their aircraft. Amazingly, despite the withering fire from small arms, 51-caliber heavy machine guns, and the torrential rain of mortars they had braved on the airstrip at Kham Duc, they had not been hit a SINGLE TIME!

A weary Jackson then settled back in his billets to write home. It was Mother's Day, a day of tragedy and terror that had robbed far too many mothers of their sons. Joe's actions that day had spared grief for three mothers. Picking up paper and pen, he began to write a letter to his wife Rose, mother of the couple's two children. "Dear Rosie," he wrote.

"I had an extremely exciting mission today. I can't describe it to you in a letter but one of these days I'll tell you all about it."

This piece first appeared on Home of Heroes.

SAVING LIVES UNDER FIRE IN THE VIETNAM JUNGLE

Claude C. "Pete" Quick, Distinguished Service Cross

I waved goodbye to my friends in Bravo Company at 0820 hours. I was following Alpha Company into the jungle. Captain Howard, the company commander, was standing just to my left rear. He held up his right arm and everyone got down. I didn't know what was going on until four riflemen led four Vietnamese in black clothing into the command group's area. The Vietnamese were holding on to bicycles. They explained to the captain through our Vietnamese scout that they were woodcutters on their way to work on the other side of the jungle. The captain asked them if they had worked in the area yesterday and they replied that they had. The scout screamed at them, "VC" (Viet Cong) and pointed his finger into their face. The scout stepped back as a newsman stepped forward and took a photograph.

Captain Howard had the men blindfolded and the bikes checked to see if they were booby-trapped. Their hands and legs were shackled so that they could only take small steps, and they were led off to our battalion headquarters. A check of the area revealed six Chi Com grenades, three M1 carbines and a Chi Com sub-machine gun. A document bag was also located containing dispatches. One dispatch checked by the Vietnamese scout was an order for all Communist liberation forces to report to their headquarters. The dispatches were also forwarded up the chain. Everything calmed down. I followed Alpha Company into the jungle.

Joseph G. Forrester was our 1st platoon medic; Thomas Ingersoll, 2nd platoon; and a new kid, Charles Whitehead, was with 3rd platoon. William Klitchka was with weapons platoon, and he would remain behind in our firebase with the 81-mm mortar section. We moved through the woods down a trail Charlie Company had found the day before.

There are times in your life when you feel that everything in the world is about to go wrong. The hairs on the back of your stand up, and you get that itchy, crawly feeling all over your body. One soldier told his buddy, "I think that I'm going to die today." His buddy laughed and said, "Hey, we're just going to take a little tour in the jungle. Don't mean nothing." Yet everyone felt uncomfortable because we were using a trail that one of our units had used the prior day. This violated Rule 11 of Rogers' Rangers Standing Orders: "Don't ever march home the same way. Take a different route so you won't be ambushed."

We moved north through the woods till we came to a large L-shaped open area. It would be a perfect place for an ambush. We moved hastily through the open area and eased into the adjacent wood line. As we began to move deeper into the woods we found trip wires, but too late. The explosion brought horrendous screams. Two men had gone down from a booby trap. One was hit in the arm, which took it off just below the elbow. The other was hit right below the knee, and his right leg was gone. Hands were raised and the company came to a halt.

Whitehead, one of the platoon medics, moved forward to give aid. The next explosion saw him flying through the air. As company medic I moved toward the wounded with the captain. A lieutenant reported, "It's not safe to move anywhere in there." But he told me, "Doc, if you'll go with that sergeant, he'll get you to them." We found Private First Class Jesse Shull, who lost his leg. I applied a tourniquet. As I was pulling it tight and twisting it to tie it down, Whitehead was carried out. His right boot was missing. I completed tying off Shull while I was giving instructions for an infantryman to start a tourniquet on Whitehead. I took a dog tag from each man, gave them morphine and reached into Whitehead's pocket and removed five syrettes. I also took his .45-caliber pistol. I talked to both men, calmed them down, and gave them cigarettes. I did a quick stump dressing for Shull, using a cravat and safety pins that came with it. Then I gave them some water and carried them out to the edge of the clearing. I marked them and pinned the syrettes onto their shirts. Battalion had called for a Dustoff (medical evacuation) helicopter, and asked us to clear an area in the open for it.

Lieutenant Day was the leader of the reserve platoon that was securing the cleared area. The captain wanted the remainder of the company out of the open area. But everywhere we checked to make entry was a mess of trip wires, nearly impassable vines, Bouncing Betty explosive devices, large bomb and butterfly mines, all rigged to be command detonated. The enemy had secured this area about 30 yards deep. An ant couldn't walk through it without causing an explosion. It was impregnable.

The Dustoff came in. Time seemed to slow down. Everything seemed to be happening in milliseconds. Snipers opened up on the Dustoff. Antiaircraft guns fired from inside the jungle. The helicopter immediately swung around and headed back, the pilot telling us that the area was too hot for landing.

Soldiers moved to blow through the booby-trapped area by using hand grenades and claymores. We heard a loud explosion. It was a 1,500-pound command-detonated mine. "Let's go, Doc," the captain said. My walk turned into a run as I followed the platoon medic, Joseph Forrester. I slowed to a walk, since he was only about 30 yards in front of me, and I could see his back. I also saw the explosion that hit him. He walked into the minefield.

It was just continuous screaming. "Medic, Medic, oh, God help me. I'm dying. Oh, God, I'm dying, Medic. Doc, Doc over here. Help, help." It seemed to me that every tree was screaming, "Medic!" but I could only take one at a time. The closest was Forrester. If I could help him, maybe he could help me. I eased into the area where he was lying. I bent down to pick him up and my helmet fell off. It had rolled into a tangle of trip wires; I didn't have time to reach for it. He had some big wounds in his legs. They were not major, but they were bleeding a lot. I got dressings on them and told him he'd be all right, probably back to duty that day. I slung my aid bag and bent over slightly to lift him.

I didn't hear the shot. I just looked up, and my head hurt. I fell backward off my feet. I had no pain other than on my head. I thought something had flown through the air and hit me. Then I heard another shot, I looked up and again I went backward off my feet. To my amazement I had been shot twice in the head. Then I heard the rifle fire. One of our lieutenants had just shot a sniper out of a tree near me. Luckily I only had flesh wounds. I could see ok, and I had work to do. I drew my .45 and set it on the ground. I was going to be ready if I heard any more shots. I pulled the morphine out of Forrester's pocket and stuck it in my pocket. I told him he'd be ok. "Toughen up," I said, and lifted him because he didn't think he could stand. As I started to lift he grabbed my .45 off the ground and laid it on his chest.

As I stood—looking at the ground, not wanting to hit any trip wires—Forrester screamed in my ear, "Duck, Doc." I started to turn but didn't know what to do. He raised the .45. A VC was coming toward me with a Russian SKS rifle, its long cylindrical bayonet extended. It was over his head, coming in a downward motion toward me. Forrester stuck the .45 almost in my right ear and pulled the trigger. A squad leader was down and told me that all his people were down. He had wounds in both legs and his right hip but they were not bleeding heavily. My assessment was that he'd probably be ok. I dragged him to a bamboo outcropping near the lieutenant. The furthest man out had been blown off his feet and probably landed on the large magazine for his Browning Automatic Rifle (BAR). It had fractured his back. He was completely out of action and screaming in the middle of the trail. I didn't have much choice at this point to use the correct procedures for treating a spinal injury. I tried to keep him flat on the ground, but lifted his arms, and had him place them around my neck. I grabbed him by his shirt collar with his head cradled between my forearms and I pulled him back to the rear. I then ran out of the jungle, picked up Forrester's litter that was lying near the entry area and ran back in with it. Slowly, using the same drag method, I got him onto the litter and Then I took him on the litter out to where Forrester was.

I then went to the squad leader, who said, "Doc, we need that BAR." It was lying in the middle of a trail, near two VC bunkers. They were firing at our troops, and there were also snipers in the trees. The squad leader was shooting at them. The rest of this platoon was firing at the bunkers. I took a dive into the trail and crawled out to the weapon. My first thought was, "This damn thing ain't wounded." I picked it up but I could see machine-gun fire coming from the bunker on my right, and it was close. I pointed the weapon at it and pulled the trigger. Ten or twelve rounds went off. I turned to my left and fired at the other bunker. I grabbed a bandolier that was on the ground full of magazines and ran back to the squad leader. I then went back to another wounded soldier and, using a fireman's carry, got him out of the jungle.

Sometime you have to make a choice of when to do your job for the protection of your patient and yourself. If I died treating them then no one else would be there to help. A wounded soldier was yelling, "Medic!" when I lifted him and just ran. He felt like a feather in my arms. There were two more left. One of them was screaming and holding his abdomen. His intestines were spread out into the jungle in tree limbs and branches, but still connected to him. I gathered them up and slowly moved back to him putting them all in his shirt, and wrapped him with a stomach dressing and carried him out. As I put him down near a bamboo outcropping I could hear a Dustoff coming in. I had to get to the others and get them evacuated.

The chopper was fired on as I moved to and from each of the wounded. I told one of the lieutenants, "If we don't get these men out of here now, Sir, some of them will die." Back at battalion another captain was gathering a platoon to come to our aid. A lot of the litters that we captured the previous day were passed out to the platoon. One medic went with each litter group. They came into our area as soldiers were using chain saws to cut their way into the jungle. Snipers were close and something had to be done. A lieutenant gathered some soldiers and had them fire their weapons on full automatic into the treetops until the VC firing ceased. Rifle grenades sailed out of the jungle and in a moment four men were down. I dragged each man back. I was exhausted and collapsed from my own wound. I was placed on a litter.

There was another explosion. Someone had stepped on a mine. I could stay on this litter and go home, but I realized my duty was to stay there and help my wounded comrades. I got up and got to one of them. He was in kind of a pile, having been hit in the legs. I dragged him out of the area that was under fire. Two others were bleeding. I got it stopped, and put one of them on my back, a big Hawaiian. It was hard to carry him, but I got him out. I was now falling from exhaustion but went for two others.

I was running out of medical supplies.

A bullet had hit a friend in the chest but I told him he'd be ok. I took the morphine out of his left shirt pocket and ripped open his shirt. The bullet had entered his right chest and exited at his shoulder blade. I put Vaseline gauze on both wounds and then a piece of poncho to make sure it was sealed. I put dressings on both wounds. I took his dog tag, placed him on the litter on his injured side, and he was taken away.

I picked up one medic's aid bag and yelled to another, "Do you have any more morphine?" He threw me a pack of five syrettes and followed the company into the Boi Loi woods. They were invaluable as I continued to treat so many wounded. My pockets were filling up with dog tags. I picked up a piece of grenade wire and put the dog tags on it to make sure I wouldn't lose any of them.

We were told to keep bringing the wounded back to the same location. Every time I did so, we received sniper fire. It was 1000 hours. I had no medics left other than Forrester, who was treating the wounded as he hobbled around on his injured legs.

We continued to receive casualties. SP4 Manuel C. Flores, an M60 machine gunner, was hit by several bullets with such a degree of force that they knocked him several feet to the ground. A large-caliber weapon had played havoc with his stomach. I recovered his intestines and put them in his shirt, bandaged him and was assisted in carrying him to the rear. Luckily a litter team was waiting. Seeing his friend Flores go down, another soldier took the M60 and continued the attack but several more men in the platoon were hit by automatic weapons fire. He brought the injured men to the area where I had treated Flores, returning to get the others until all were out of danger. He then took up his weapon and charged a VC bunker, killing its occupants and several nearby snipers.

It was 1100 hours, and we had eighteen wounded. Three had refused evacuation and returned to duty. I had forgotten about my own injuries. As I brought men out our security force was involved in a firefight with snipers in the area. I desperately needed more medical supplies. Thankfully, two full aid bags eventually came down through the trees. As I went to get them I was pinned down by sniper fire. Grenades were flying out of the treetops. One of them got too close; a piece of shrapnel caught me in my right neck, under my cheek and jawbone. Other pieces hit me in both forearms. Then a mine exploded and a piece of that tore off my helmet.

At this point the VC 320th Local Force Battalion was joining forces with the VC 165 A Regiment and setting up in freshly dug and built positions inside the Boi Loi. They moved in with a large number of .51-caliber antiaircraft machine guns. Snipers were slowing us so fresh fire lanes for these machine guns could be cut into the jungle floor. They would not run. Instead they would employ overlapping fields of fire with deep kill zones in large areas of the jungle. They sent out scouts to watch our movements. They sent out fire teams to counter us as we maneuvered to destroy them. Their plan was to trap us with their machine-gun fire.

Each move now was like a game of chess.

Bravo Company and Alpha Company were getting sniper fire and we were moving to seek and destroy the enemy positions as they fired upon us from our front and flanks. Our two columns were just 150 to 175 meters apart. Both units were in close radio contact and the sniper fire became intense. It would require both companies to change their direction of travel. The commander felt that this was not acceptable and he ordered both units to halt and told them to call in artillery on the sniper positions and force them to withdraw.

I was with a company command group in the middle of all of this and the uncharacteristic quietness made me feel more secure. I pulled out a cigarette and all of a sudden there was a loud-pitched bird sound. Trees fell and people started screaming and rolling in the darkness. You could feel that final scream and gurgling sound that men make when they are critically wounded. Machine-gun bullets were literally cutting equipment and clothes off bodies. I was hit and knocked to the ground, as were others. I had been struck in the chest by a heart. It hit me so hard that I felt I'd been shot. An RTO (radio telephone operator) was hit in the right arm. The captain was hit in the left arm. The RTO on his right lost his arm at the shoulder. The first sergeant had been hit in the hip, smashing it at the joint. His leg was twisted backwards as he fell to the ground. Another soldier's left leg was gone. I had been hit in the right knee and left thigh.

I looked around. Forrester had returned to duty and was the only other medic I had in the company. He was rendering aid under intense

.51-caliber machine-gun fire. He moved from one man to another, treating them and pulling them to the rear until he came to the last. He knelt beside the wounded soldier and was struck in his right arm. There was nothing he could do now but try to cover.

I got to the captain, put a dressing on the arm and went on to other wounded men. One of them had been hit in the stomach. I fell into a triage mode. There were others I had to go to first. I felt that his wound was not survivable and that I might be able to save others who would live. I would come back to him later.

The first sergeant was not bleeding seriously but the soldier who lost his leg needed a tourniquet. There was no hope for it. Yet he was very calmly shooting into the VC positions. I did no further dressing on him except for the tourniquet. I helped him stand on his good leg, lifted him to my shoulder and carried him to the rear, putting him on the ground next to the captain. I turned my attention back to the first sergeant, finding his right leg turned completely around. I moved his other leg beside it, used my belt at his knee, a piece of my shirt at his ankle and I lifted him and dragged him to the rear despite his refusal, since he was tossing grenades and firing at the enemy. I told him that the captain had ordered him. He looked at me and said, "Well then, Doc, get me out of here." The .51-caliber bullet had entered his right hip and exited his right upper outer quadrant. I put dressings on both wounds and tied them and had him lie on his injured side. The captain gave him tasks to keep his mind off his injuries.

I got to a soldier who had moved behind a tree away from one of our downed lieutenants. He raised his right hand, and he was struck through it. I got a dressing on his right arm but we had close-in rifle fire that was pinning us down flat. He looked at me and said, "Doc, we've been captured." My attention was on dressing his hand and I told him, "No, we'll be ok." He said, "Doc, that VC has a rifle pointed at us." The VC's weapon was pointed directly at me. I was going to die. I laid my head over to the side, putting my helmet between the VC and me and told Boyd, "I'm going to die, jump over me and get back to our lines." The VC fired into my right shoulder and motioned with the bayonet for me to move toward the direction of fire. I lifted my left arm over to my shoulder and I screamed as loud as I could to the soldier, "Go now. Go!" In an instant he was gone. The VC tapped me on the helmet with his bayonet and motioned for me to move. I started to follow his instructions, but then a grenade exploded near him.

People were yelling for me to get out of there. I took a breath and moved out over the dead officer but saw the book, CEOI (Communications Electronics Operating Instructions) SECRET. I knew this couldn't be left here. They kept screaming at me to go. I picked up the CEOI; it was connected around his neck by a chain. I broke the chain and pushed the book into my shirt. I stood up and grabbed the lieutenant's arms and started to drag him in. But I was exhausted, in shock, scared and hardly able to stand myself. I had already been wounded seven times that day. I fell to the ground. Two lieutenants were yelling, "Leave him, Doc, we'll get him later." I looked at the lieutenant's face. He looked so young. I pulled a dog tag off his chest, stuck a dog tag in his mouth, pulled a safety pin from my pocket and pinned his lips closed. I put the other dog tag in my pocket, got up and ran to our lines.

As I came up to our men, an explosion knocked me to the ground. I had hit a trip wire. I tried to stand and I felt the Bouncing Betty go down and then rise and hit my hand. My hand knocked it away to the far side of the tree. It exploded. I looked around. One man's face was gone as was most of his head. The lieutenants were down. Another soldier's right arm was gone. He started to run toward the dead lieutenant and into VC fire. I screamed, "Knock him down and put a tourniquet on his arm." I tried to get up, but I had a large gash in my right leg and large laceration on my left knee. I dragged myself to the wounded man, who was being treated by the other soldier.

The VC .51-caliber gun suddenly fell silent and snipers started to fire intensely again. I was unaware that the VCs were charging and our combined units were knocking them down as they advanced. I was treating a soldier and asked another one to help me. He looked at me with glazed-over eyes and said quietly, "Help me, Doc." I opened his shirt and initiated treatment for a stomach wound. I screamed to the lieutenants that I needed a Dust Off now or I was going to lose this man. The captain said the Dustoff was on its way.

Artillery was firing and hitting the ground at all angles to keep the enemy at bay. The noise was chaotic and overwhelming. It was a beautiful sight, seeing the front of that helicopter with the words "Original Dust Off" inscribed around a Red Cross. I lifted the wounded man as the chopper settled to the ground and I carried a casualty into the door. The medic jumped out and helped me load him on the floor. I told him I had two more. He jumped out of the bird to help and another medic said, "You know, you really need to go out, too."

Then the chopper exploded. It had been hit by automatic weapons fire in the rotor blade. The crew chief was wounded, as was one officer. The blade had just cleared the other officer's heads and mine. We ran to the chopper and treated the wounded. We got the wounded soldier back on the ground. The medic pulled all his supplies from the ship. The other officer turned all the mechanical equipment off and sat there quietly. It would have to be lifted out by a flying crane. From this short battle we had thirteen wounded and two killed. It was 1420.

We got back to the aid station. The captain was evacuated on a Dustoff. As it flew out a flying crane took the downed helicopter. The battalion commander came over and asked if I was "Doc Quick." I said, "Yes, Sir." He saluted me, and said, "Thank you, Doc. Thank you."

NOTE: The 2nd Battalion 27th Infantry had inflicted heavy casualties on a regimental-sized VC force. The total number of enemy casualties would not be known until the war was over, when the area would be turned into a national graveyard like Arlington. We had suffered eighty-four wounded in action. It would later be corrected by Brigade and the Division public affairs office to read fifty-two for media purposes. We had one officer killed in action and all three company commanders wounded in action. All of our forward observers from 8th Artillery and their RTOs were wounded or killed. An attached Air Force forward air controller was wounded and would later die in the hospital.

From an account by Claude concerning his actions in May 1966 while serving as a medical aidman attached to a rifle company.

CONSCIENTIOUS OBJECTOR WHO SAVED LIVES ON OKINAWA

PFC DESMOND T. DOSS, MEDAL OF HONOR

Robert L. Ampula

When World War II began, Desmond T. Doss was working at a shipyard in Newport News, Virginia. His job afforded Desmond the opportunity to request a deferment from serving in the military service, but being in good health, he felt it was his duty as well as an honor to serve his country in the war. Desmond was also devoutly religious and his faith restricted him from taking a life under any circumstances, a fact he made known when he joined the Army.

Americans were appalled at the Japanese attack on Pearl Harbor and when the United States entered the war the majority of Americans rushed to support the war effort. Those who opposed the war were seen as unpatriotic. The term "Conscientious Objector" evoked many negative connotations during this period. There were primarily three categories of conscientious objectors. The first, like Doss, refused to take a life but were willing to join the military service in other than combat roles. The second were individuals that would perform alternative service in support of the war effort. Finally, there were those who were opposed to any support of the war. Some members of the latter group were imprisoned throughout the war.

As a result of the prejudices associated with the CO tag, Desmond endured much ridicule and harassment during his early time in the Army. Soldiers would throw shoes at him while he prayed and would make sarcastic remarks. Desmond preferred to be called a conscientious cooperator instead of objector because he believed in serving his country like everyone else. He just didn't want to take a life. He preferred to save lives, and while other soldiers were receiving combat training Desmond received medical training. The longer he was with his unit and the more the men got to know him, the better their relationship became.

Desmond's time in the military improved when he was assigned to the 77th Division, the Statue of Liberty Division. He felt it was an honor to serve with these men. They learned to trust each other and with the exception of a few individuals, he never again experienced difficulties as a conscientious objector.

Private First Class Desmond T. Doss is the only known conscientious objector to receive the Medal of Honor in World War II. Desmond passed away on March 23, 2006 in Piedmont, Alabama. On April 29, 1945, was serving as an aid man as the 1st Battalion assaulted a 400-foot-high Okinawan jagged escarpment. As the troops gained the summit, mortar and machine-gun fire inflicted over 75 casualties while driving the other soldiers back. He refused to seek cover and remained in the fire-swept area and carried the wounded, one by one, to the edge of the escarpment and lowering them on a rope litter down the face of the cliff. For the next twenty days, he braved enemy shelling and small-arms fire to save countless soldiers from death. Finally, on May 21, as he was being carried to cover, his group was caught in an enemy tank attack. Seeing a more critically wounded man, he crawled off the litter and directed the bearers to save the other man and leave him. Then, while awaiting their return, he was again hit and this time he suffered a compound fracture of one arm. He bound a rifle stock to his shattered arm and crawled 300 yards over rough terrain to safety.

Excerpted from the Army Medical Department (AMEDD) Historian by Robert L. Ampula and Legion of Valor General Orders. Based on his life, the film Hacksaw Ridge, directed by Mel Gibson appeared in U.S. theaters in November 2016 to excellent reviews. He was also the subject of a 2004 award-winning documentary The Conscientious Objector.

SAVING WOUNDED MARINES IN IRAQ

HOSPITALMAN LUIS E. FONSECA JR., NAVY CROSS

Raymond L. Applewhite

Secretary of the Navy Gordon R. England presented the Navy Cross to Hospitalman Luis E. Fonseca Jr. in a ceremony held at Naval Hospital Camp Lejeune, North Carolina, August 11.

Fonseca, a 23-year-old corpsman, was awarded the Navy Cross for his actions in support of Operation *Iraqi Freedom* on March 23, 2003, while serving with Amphibious Assault Vehicle Platoon, Company C, 1st Battalion, 2nd Marines, Task Force Tarawa, II Marine Expeditionary Force.

The Navy Cross, the U.S. Navy's second highest decoration, is awarded for extraordinary heroism while engaged in an action against an enemy of the United States. The act must be performed in the presence of great danger or at great personal risk.

During his company's assault and seizure of the Saddam Canal Bridge, five Marines were wounded when their amphibious assault vehicle was struck by a rocket-propelled grenade. Fonseca, in the face of small-arms, machine-gun and intense rocket-propelled grenade fire, evacuated the Marines from the burning vehicle and established a casualty collection unit inside his own medical evacuation vehicle. There, he stabilized two Marines with lower limb amputations and administered morphine. After his vehicle was rendered immobile by enemy fire and again, under intense gunfire, Fonseca organized litter teams and directed the movement of four of the Marines, while personally carrying one wounded Marine over open ground to another vehicle.

"I feel privileged to be here to recognize Hospitalman Fonseca for his extraordinary valor and courage," England said. "Corpsmen have a long tradition of service to the United States Marine Corps. You make all of us proud, and let me personally thank you for going above and beyond the call of duty. On behalf of the President of the United States and all of America, I thank you."

Fonseca's colleagues, who were also in attendance, expressed their pride in his actions.

"He is a very motivated corpsman and deserving of this award," said Hospital Corpsman 2nd Class (FMF) Erin Asidao. "I was overjoyed when I heard. I think many corpsmen go unrecognized. I think it's good for the Navy and good for the Hospital Corps."

"I was doing my job," said Fonseca. "I wish I could have done more."

This first appeared on the Navy News Service.

WHAT IS A NAVY CORPSMAN?

Robert Cowan

What is a Navy Corpsman, many people ask?
Well, I've decided to enlighten you; I've taken on the task
A Corpsman is a strange fellow; I'll tell you what I mean
He joined the U.S. Navy but he's more like a Marine

When Marines are asked to go to war to fight and maybe die
They have their "Doctor" with them; he's their "go to" guy
A special breed of sailors that Marines do call their own
His job is taking care of them so they can go back home

When the shooting starts and bullets fly and men all hit the dirt
The corpsman looks around to see if anyone's been hurt
He hears a feeble voice cry. "Doc, I'm over here".
The corpsman rushes forward, his mission crystal clear

He finds a wounded comrade, a Marine that has been shot
The corpsman working swiftly, giving all he's got
The young Marine whispers weakly, "Doc, will I die today?"
"Not a chance", the corpsman replies, "if I have my way".

The young Marine did survive to fight another day
On a miserable far off battlefield, a sailor saved his life
He'd soon be going home again to his children and his wife

So, if you ever meet a Corpsman say a silent prayer
For there are many Marines alive today who are glad that he was there
There's no way of telling just how much he's done and seen
As I said, he's in the Navy but he's more like a Marine.

This poem appeared on the Together We Served website and Facebook page.

NAVY CHAPLAIN ON THE FRONT LINES

Father Vincent Capodanno, Medal of Honor

Doyle D. Glass

Most of the grunts—even the salts—didn't know their commanding officer, Lieutenant Murray, very well. Now he was leading them into a precarious battle, and the urgency meant less planning and more danger. Walking among the men, Father Capodanno sensed tension and fear.

Father Vincent Capodanno was a Staten Island native who had been ordained in 1957, commissioned into the Navy Chaplain Corps in 1965, and sent to Vietnam with the 1st Marine Division in 1966. He was the former chaplain for the 1/5, so he knew the men who were battling for their lives; he had been with the 3/5 only a few weeks. He had completed a full tour with the 7th Marines south of Chu Lai before extending and arriving with the 1/5.

He could do little more than offer prayers for Bravo and Delta, but he knew he could do more for the men currently in his charge. He gave the Marines Communion and performed the rite of General Absolution, a form of absolution given when dire circumstances prevent a priest from hearing individual confessions.

At 38, Capodanno was older than the other Marines, including the commanding officers. Tall and good-looking, he had already served one tour in Vietnam and had requested an extension. In his short time with the 3/5, he had already made a strong impression. The other Marines knew by the look in his eyes, the way he carried himself, the way he radiated belief in his faith that he was a conduit for anyone who wanted to know Jesus Christ.

It wasn't just the words in his sermons. It was the way he lived his life, demonstrating his faith in his every act of concern for his fellow Marines. He spent more time with the troops than with the other officers and seemed to have unlimited energy.

The Marines were young and scared and never knew which bullet had their name on it. Father Capodanno was always available for casual conversation or spiritual guidance to ease their minds. He give the Marines cigarettes and tried to get extra rations to make them more comfortable.

But those were material items. Most importantly, the men felt Capodanno could guide them to find God's presence, and he frequently reassured them that God was with them. After providing comfort or guidance to the men, Capodanno would end the conversation by putting his hand on the Marine's head and saying a prayer for that Marine and Marines everywhere.

When he said Mass, he knew his audience was different from the followers who sat in formal pews back in the states. So his message was different. And simple—no long homilies or strict lectures.

"There's a lot going on here that you can't control," he would say, his voice tinged with a New York accent. "It's in God's hands, so the best you can do to prepare is to try to stay in the state of grace. You can't control what might happen once something starts. Do the right thing."

Father Capodanno caught up to Sully, who was overseeing 1st Platoon on its way to the LZ.

"Sergeant, I would like to say a prayer for your men, if it's all right," he said.

"Certainly." With a few quick orders, Sullivan gathered a group of men.

Capodanno bowed his head and said a prayer. Then he looked up at them. "The mission will be dangerous," he warned. "I just want to make sure you know the Lord is with you."

As Marines walked away, the father shook Sully's hand. "Just go out and do your job, and you'll be all right," he said.

Father Capodanno handed out St. Christopher medals to every man who wanted one. This was done mostly while they were in the LZ, waiting for choppers. Many Marines already carried medals of the protective saint, but others lined up to get one.

Soon choppers were setting down at the LZ, ready for action. At 11:10 a.m., less than two hours since the Regimental Fragmentation Order was issued, the Marines of Kilo Company lifted from the LZ on Hill 63 and disappeared across the countryside.

Not enough choppers were available for all the Marines. After Kilo left, it was "hurry up and wait" for the Marines of Mike Company. They sat on the grass in the hot, sunny LZ loaded with gear for another thirty minutes, nervously guessing about the upcoming mission.

"I hear they got it bad."

"Yeah, outnumbered."

"What do you think's gonna happen?"

"Maybe it'll be over by the time we get there."

"Yeah—we'll just set up a perimeter, help clean up."

Father Capodanno circled the LZ. He eyed one of the young Marines—something didn't seem right. He stopped. The young Marine started to rise in respect to his senior officer."

"No, son." Capodanno gestured for the Marine to stay seated. He sat down next to the young man. "Can I bum a cigarette?"

"Sure."

Capodanno lit the cigarette and took a long drag. "You don't look so good. What's wrong?"

"I've been in combat before, but today—I don't know. I just have this feeling, like something bad's going to happen to me today."

"Don't focus on your fears," the Father said. "Will you pray with me?"

"Sure."

The two men said a prayer, and Father Capodanno gave a blessing. Then he moved on to other Marines with the same worried look, offering prayers and counseling.

As the last group of 165 Marines of Mike Company boarded a chopper, Father Capodanno slipped in with them. He felt the men needed his support. He was also concerned for the 115 Marines he had served with under Colonel Hilgartner. He knew he could link up with the battalion command group when the units joined together at the LZ and could stay with the battalion command to keep abreast of the battle's developments. Mike's command group had already lifted out, so no one objected as he climbed in. But a few men exchanged looks that said, *He so not supposed to be here.*

By 11:50 a.m., the last Marines of Mike Company were lifted from Hill 63 and were officially under the operational control of Colonel Hilgartner and the 1/5 Alpha Command. Lieutenant Murray had a bad feeling about the rescue mission. *You just don't take units, split them up, give them to somebody else, and expect it to run fluidly,* he thought. But according to the plan, he and his men would be linking up with the 115 battalion commander shortly.

Little did he know that it would be twenty perilous hours before he would finally meet anyone from the 115 command group. And ten days before he would return to the safety of Hill 63.

In a fighting hole to the rear of 2nd Platoon's position, Lieutenant Blecksmith could see enemy soldiers sneaking out from the tree line and moving steadfastly up the knoll to take on his men. Suddenly a crouched runner came up to his position: Father Capodanno. Capodanno also surveyed the scene, already littered with wounded Marines. He started to crawl out of the hole.

Blecksmith grabbed his pack and pulled him back. "Stay here!"

Capodanno turned and said firmly, "I've got to go out there."

"Aye aye, Sir." Blecksmith released the priest, who scrambled onto the battlefield.

Blecksmith suddenly remembered a speech from USC head coach John McKay. It had been his senior year, and the war was heating up. "Boys, you've got to study," McKay had said. "You've got to get your grades up. If you don't, you'll get drafted in the Army and go to Vietnam. If you go to Vietnam, there's no halftime, there's no trainers, there's no orange wedges, there's no Cokes."

Blecksmith realized he was playing the ultimate game now, where the outcome was life or death.

Father Capodanno moved across the top of the knoll, kneeling next to wounded Marines, sometimes offering medical attention, other times administering Last Rites, making the sign of the cross and praying.

"Stay cool!" he shouted to some nervous Marines seeing combat for the first time. "Don't panic!"

The father moved away toward the front of the knoll.

Second Platoon radio operator Lovejoy was also still pinned down on the right side of the knoll, farther to the front of the fighting than the other men from 2nd Platoon on that side of the knoll. After his M16 had jammed, he and Santos had decided to wait for the enemy fire to subside, but it was only increasing.

His radio crackled. He could still receive messages but not transmit.

"Pull back and tighten the perimeter!" a voice commanded. Lovejoy decided to take action. The knoll dropped at a steep angle at his location. He struggled to crawl out of the crater with his radio gear. As soon as he started to climb the steep slope, a stream of automatic weapons fire sprayed around him. He hit the deck. He tried to crawl and still pull his heavy equipment up the hill. Bullets sprayed everywhere.

I'm going to die right here, he thought.

Suddenly, a pair of hands came out of nowhere, grabbed his radio pack, and pulled him up. Lovejoy and his rescuer scrambled up the knoll. Another burst of enemy fire, and the two men fell back to the ground. Lovejoy turned and saw his rescuer was Father Capodanno. Lovejoy was shocked—the priest wasn't supposed to be on the front lines. Even if he got trapped in battle, he was supposed to stay back with the command group. But here he was in the heat of battle with a look of complete determination. He was calm despite the chaos around him.

When the Marine and Navy Chaplain reached the top of the knoll, Lovejoy dropped into a bomb crater just over the crest. Lovejoy nodded his thanks. Father Capodanno nodded then moved to help another Marine on the battlefield. *He's a true Christian*, Lovejoy thought.

In his new crater near the top of the front right side of the knoll, Lovejoy saw some stray smoke drifting over his position. Father Capodanno climbed back into the crater after administering Last Rites to a fallen Marine. Lovejoy grabbed the gas mask from his pack and offered it to the chaplain.

"You'll need it more than I will." Capodanno waved away the offer and crawled out of the crater again to assist more Marines.

The small amount of smoke and gas dissipated before reaching the crater, and Lovejoy didn't need the mask, either.

Lovejoy watched the priest shout encouragement to fallen fighters while directing corpsmen to them. He realized that seeing Capodanno on the battlefield wasn't so surprising after all—back at the base, the priest always presented himself as one of the guys, striking up down-to-earth conversations. He would ask Lovejoy, "They feeding you right?" or "How about those football playoffs?" The chaplain was always quick with an offer to help, and apparently that offer didn't end when the company went into battle.

Ignoring the fierce gunfire, Father Capodanno scrambled out to Manfra. He was still wearing his white stole, but his helmet had been knocked off.

Lobur watched from the nearby crater and wondered if he should tackle the priest to keep him from getting shot. "Get down! Get down!" he shouted.

Rounseville also watched from the depression, amazed. It's like there's no war going on, no bullets are flying, he thought. The priest didn't give a second thought to the incoming fire as he began Last Rites, sprinkling holy water from a small silver cylinder in his hand over Manfra.

Rounseville tried to provide cover for the priest, but his M16 jammed.

"My rifle's jammed," he shouted.

Father Capodanno grabbed Manfra's rifle. Crouching, he ran back to the small depression.

"Here. Take the sergeant's rifle," Capodanno said, handing the weapon to Rounseville. He then scrambled back to Manfra's side. On the way, Capodanno was struck by an enemy round. He fell to the ground.

The men around him watched, stunned and worried. But the chaplain recovered and crawled the remaining distance to Manfra. The two men were head-to-head on their stomachs. The chaplain grabbed Manfra's hand. "Where are you hit?"

"In the foot, in the chest."

"Do you know the Lord's Prayer?"

"I—I don't know the whole thing." Manfra struggled to talk. His mouth welled up with blood.

"Well, I'll say it with you. Our Father, who art in heaven … "

While the two men recited the prayer, Doc Phelps arrived. As the priest continued his prayer, Phelps eased Manfra's torso up to keep him from drowning in his own blood. He did his best to stop the bleeding, then stuffed bandages on Manfra's chest as enemy rounds flew overhead.

"Corpsman up!"

At the sound of the cry, Phelps moved back toward the top of the knoll, where he saw Santos still alive after being shot in the head. Doc Phelps crawled to him, lying on his stomach across the slope. He reached out to Santos' wounded head, but a low-flying enemy round struck Phelps in the forehead, killing him instantly.

Farther down the knoll, Capodanno squeezed Manfra's hand. "Be strong, young man. We'll get through this."

Another voice screamed from the bottom part of the knoll. "I'm hit!"

"I have to move on," Capodanno said. "We'll get you out as soon as we can."

Capodanno scrambled away toward the foot of the knoll. In a nearby crater, Tancke was struck by the passion he saw in the priest's eyes as he moved from one wounded Marine to the next, never showing any regard for his own safety. The priest exchanged glances with Tancke as he passed then shifted direction when he saw Corpsman Leal on the ground at the foot of the knoll.

"Watch out for the gunner!" Tancke shouted. "Watch the gunner!"

The priest crouched as he ran to Leal.

The machine gun opened up. Father Capodanno fell to the ground, riddled with bullets.

Two Marines set a body covered with a poncho behind Field's position then left to retrieve another body. Curious to know who it was, he crawled over and pulled back the poncho. He couldn't see a face in the darkness, but a flare went off. The flare cast a golden glow on the scene. The dead Marine's head was tilted slightly to the right, and there was a calm look on his face. Fields didn't recognize the man, but he saw a gold glint on the collar. *This is an officer!* he thought. He scrutinized the emblem. It was a cross. *I didn't know we had a chaplain with us.*

He knew this news was important. He scrambled down the back side of the knoll to the edge of a crater. It was pitch black, so he wasn't sure where he was.

"Is somebody down there?"

"Yeah! This is the CP," someone said.

"We've got a chaplain up here who is dead."

"Damn! We didn't know he was with us!"

The news was relayed to Lieutenant Murray, who was shocked: in the chaos of the battle, he hadn't realized the chaplain had come along.

Father Capodanno was the first Navy chaplain killed in Vietnam.

NOTE: Private First Class Julio Rodriquez wrote a letter to the Capodanno family explaining that he was one of the men who recovered the father's body. "When we found him, he had his right hand over his left breast pocket. It seemed as if he was holding his Bible. He had a smile on his face, and his eyelids were closed as if asleep or in prayer," he wrote.

This piece is extracted from the book Swift Sword The Marines of Mike 3/5 *by Doyle D. Glass.*

NURSES ON THE WESTERN FRONT

Helen Grace McClelland, Distinguished Service Cross

The President of the United States of America, authorized by Act of Congress, July 9, 1918, takes pleasure in presenting the Distinguished Service Cross to Reserve Nurse Helen Grace McClelland, United States Army, for extraordinary heroism in action while serving with Nurse Corps, A.E.F. (Attached), while on duty with the surgical team at British Casualty Clearing Station No. 61, British area, France, August 17, 1917. Nurse McClelland occupied the same tent with Miss Beatrice MacDonald, another reserve nurse, cared for her when wounded, stopped the hemorrhage from her wounds under fire caused by bombs from German aeroplanes. *The History of American Red Cross Nursing*, published in 1922 by the American Red Cross, quotes her:

> When the first big drive came in, no one felt like going off duty while the men were still pouring in on us. One day we worked for 24 hours, stopping only for something to eat. After cleaning up our tables, we went to bed at 2 AM but were back on duty at 4 AM for another twelve-hour shift. During a drive there were always ambulance trains waiting to be loaded. Only the worst cases were brought into the clearing stations; the others were taken directly to the trains, which carried a certain number of cot cases and a certain number of "walkers." As soon as its quota was complete, the train was sent down to the base. I shall never forget those men; they never had a word of complaint. When you asked them if they were suffering much pain, they would answer: "It's drawing a bit, Sister." When

a lad would say to the doctor who was examining him, "Do you think it will be a Blighty, sir?" the hope in that boy's eyes made your heart ache, you knew how badly he wanted to get home, away from filth, agony and destruction for a little while at least.

This piece first appeared in the Legion of Valor General Orders.

Helen Grace McClelland died in December 1984.

Beatrice Mary MacDonald, Distinguished Service Cross

In August 17, 1917, while on duty with a surgical team at the British Casualty Clearing Station No. 61, during a German night air raid Nurse MacDonald continued at her post of duty, caring for the sick and wounded until seriously wounded by a fragment of a shell from German bomb, thereby losing one eye. She was the first woman to receive this award.

Adapted from Hall of Heroes information.

Beatrice Mary MacDonald died in September 1969.

Jane Jeffrey, Distinguished Service Cross

The President of the United States of America, authorized by Act of Congress, July 9, 1918, takes pleasure in presenting the Distinguished Service Cross to Nurse Jane Jeffrey, a United States Civilian for extraordinary heroism while she was on duty at American Red Cross Hospital No. 107, in France, July 15, 1918. She was severely wounded by an exploding bomb during an air raid. She showed utter disregard for her own safety by refusing to leave her post, though suffering great pain from her wounds. Her courageous attitude and devotion to the task of helping others was inspiring to all of her associates.

Jane Jeffrey was a British citizen working in the United States when she enlisted in the Red Cross as a nurse. She was one of the first recipients of the award. It was signed by another Legion of Valor member, General Pershing. It took her over a year to recover from the wounds she received on that tragic day.

Her medal and citation are in the care of the Maine Historical Society in Portland, Maine. She later married A. B. Ricker of the famous Poland Spring Hotels, so the Maine Historical Society lists her as Jane Jeffrey Ricker. Jane died in 1960 and her legacy was the money to build and furnish a library in Portland in memory of her husband.

This piece first appeared in the Legion of Valor General Orders.

THE COMBAT MEDIC PRAYER

Oh Lord, I ask for the divine strength
to meet the demands of my profession.
Help me to be the finest medic,
both technically and tactically.
If I am called to the battlefield,
give me the courage to conserve our
fighting forces by providing medical
care to all who are in need.
If I am called to a mission of peace,
give me the strength to lead by caring for
those who need my assistance.
Finally Lord, help me take care
of my own spiritual, physical
and emotional needs.
Teach me to trust in your
presence and never-failing love.

Amen

From the Army Medical Department Regiment site.

WOMAN AHEAD OF HER TIME

MARY EDWARDS WALKER, MEDAL OF HONOR

Rudi Williams

Whenever Ann Walker's brattish attitude emerged, her grandmother would often say, "You're just like your great-aunt Mary."

"When I was a teenager, I started to wonder, who is this great-aunt Mary?" said Walker, 74. "I sort of hungered for information about her, but I couldn't find much. Nobody, including my grandmother, seemed to care about her. She always said, 'Your aunt was always dressing like a man.'"

Her curiosity surged when one of her father's friends, a history professor, told her about her distant relative, actually her great-great-aunt, Dr. Mary Edwards Walker of the Civil War Union Army. He told her Mary Walker was the first American woman to be a military doctor, a prisoner of war and a Medal of Honor recipient. She was also a Union spy and a crusader against tobacco and alcohol.

"He told me she was always imitating men, and if she had dressed like a lady, she would have had a larger role in history," said Walker, a resident of Washington's Georgetown Aged Women's Home. A retired freelance journalist, Walker said she's working on a book, *Woman of Honor*, to tell the story of her aunt's Civil War exploits and her controversial life thereafter.

Through the family friend and research, Ann Walker learned her aunt was born on November 26, 1832, in Oswego County, N.Y., and graduated from Syracuse Medical College in 1855. She married fellow medical student Albert Miller, but declined to take his name. The couple set up a medical practice in Rome, N.Y., but the public wasn't ready to accept a woman physician. The practice and the marriage foundered.

When the Civil War started, the Union Army wouldn't hire women doctors, so Walker volunteered as a nurse in Washington's Patent Office Hospital and treated wounded soldiers at the Battle of Bull Run in Virginia. In 1862, she received an Army contract appointing her as an assistant surgeon with the 52nd Ohio Infantry.

The first woman doctor to serve with the Army Medical Corps, Walker cared for sick and wounded troops in Tennessee at Chickamauga and in Georgia during the Battle of Atlanta.

Confederate troops captured her on April 10, 1864, and held her until the sides exchanged prisoners of war on August 12, 1864. Walker worked the final months of the war at a women's prison in Louisville, Kentucky, and later at an orphans' asylum in Tennessee.

The Army nominated Walker for the Medal of Honor for her wartime service. President Andrew Johnson signed the citation on November 11, 1865, and she received the award on January 24, 1866. Her citation cites her wartime service, but not specifically valor in combat.

Walker's citation reads in part that she "devoted herself with much patriotic zeal to the sick and wounded soldiers, both in the field and hospitals, to the detriment of her own health. She has also endured hardships as a prisoner of war for four months in a Southern prison while acting as contract surgeon."

The War Department, starting in 1916, reviewed all previous Medal of Honor awards with the intent of undoing decades of abuse. At the time, for instance, the medal could be freely copied and sold and legally worn by anyone. Past awards would be rescinded and future ones would be rejected if supporting evidence didn't clearly, convincingly show combat valor above and beyond the call of duty.

Mary Walker and nearly 1,000 past recipients found their medals revoked in the reform. Wearing the medal if unearned became a crime. The Army demanded Walker and the others return their medals. She refused and wore hers until her death at age 87 in 1919.

In the late 1960s, Ann Walker launched an intensive lobbying campaign to restore her aunt's medal. A November 25, 1974, letter from the Senate Veterans Affairs Committee read, in part, "It's clear your great-grandaunt was not only courageous during the term she served as a contract doctor in the Union Army, but also as an outspoken proponent of feminine rights. Both as a doctor and feminist, she was much ahead of her time and, as is usual, she was not regarded kindly by many of her contemporaries. Today she appears prophetic."

President Jimmy Carter restored Mary Walker's Medal of Honor on June 11, 1977. Today, it's on display in the Pentagon's women's corridor.

Walker said her relative was controversial on the battlefield and in civilian life. During the war, she wore trousers under her skirt, a man's uniform jacket and two pistols. As an early women's rights advocate, particularly for dress reform, she was arrested many times after the war for wearing men's clothes, including wing collar, bow tie and top hat.

The Women in Military Service to America Memorial at Arlington (Va.) National Cemetery features the story of Dr. Mary E. Walker along with a photograph of her and her walking cane. Curator Judy Bellafaire called Walker "quite a character," and one whose ideas made her seem eccentric in her own day and age.

"But judging her from today's perspective, much of what she spoke and wrote about, that people made fun of at the time, is probably true today," Bellafaire said.

Excerpted from American Forces Press Service (April 30, 1999).

PARARESCUE IN AFGHANISTAN

Senior Airman Jason Dean Cunningham, Air Force Cross

On March 4, 2002 Airman Cunningham, a combat medic, was dispatched to help rescue a group of American soldiers who were pinned down by enemy fighters in the mountains near Marzak, Afghanistan. Cunningham, after surviving the helicopter crash, remained in the burning fuselage on the snowy mountain side to treat his wounded comrades. He put himself in the way of enemy fire more than a half dozen times to keep the wounded safe. Even after he was mortally wounded, Airman Cunningham continued to direct the movement of his patients.

The battle was the bloodiest operation of the war in Afghanistan. He was finally killed by enemy machine-gun fire as he darted out of the helicopter on one of his several efforts to remove the wounded to safety. His wife, Theresa Cunningham shared a letter Jason wrote to her just two weeks before his death. In it he said "if I die, I want you to know I died a happy man—happy because I met you, happy because I have two beautiful girls and happy because I got to do what I wanted to do." He was one of the Air Force's elite pararescuemen and a true American hero.

This piece first appeared in the Legion of Valor General Orders.

FATE, FORTUNE AND FUN

War is the province of chance
War is fought by human beings
                        Carl von Clausewitz

JAMES B. MOREHEAD SAVES A BOMBER BASE

James B. Morehead, a World War II fighter ace, earned the Distinguished Service Cross for extraordinary heroism in action near Darwin, Australia on April 25, 1942. While commanding a flight of four fighter planes, he sighted 28 enemy bombers protected by enemy fighters. He led his flight in an attack against the bombers and succeeded in shooting two down. He then engaged an enemy fighter and shot it down. In spite of the great Japanese superiority in numbers, he succeeded in returning home with all four planes. But there was another flight on February 23, 1942 which has, until recently, been a question mark in Jim's mind as to exactly what happened.

George Weller, a Pulitzer Prize war correspondent, wrote an article in the spring of 1942 stating that Morehead attacked and turned back an entire formation of Japanese bombers that were on their way to bomb the U.S. 19th Bomb Group field on Java, Dutch East Indies. Weller reported that, as three fellow P-40 pilots drew off the Zeros guarding 54 twin-engine bombers, Morehead charged and fired repeatedly on the lead and number two bombers. His daring action resulted in all the enemy bombers jettisoning their bombs and reversing course back to their home base. When Jim read this article back in 1942, he doubted Weller's account. "It was preposterous that a beat-up P-40 could have turned back an entire formation of Japanese bombers," he said.

But it appears Weller was correct. William H. Bartsch, a WWII historian and author of *Every Day a Nightmare: American Pursuit Pilots in the Defense of Java, 1941–1942*, pored over Japanese records and confirmed that the bomber, piloted by the leader of the second group of three G4M1s, took 80 hits and its left engine was knocked out. Concerned that the group leader had been badly wounded in the attack by Morehead, the attack commander gave the order to dump the formation's bombs and return to its field in Bali.

After becoming an ace in the Pacific theater, Jim went on to serve another tour of duty in Europe, flying the P-38 Lightning. On June 6, 1944, while leading a squadron of 16 fighters protecting the American bombers attacking the Ploesti oil fields in Romania, he was credited with downing a Messerschmitt for his eighth kill.

This piece first appeared in the Legion of Valor General Orders.

HOT SAUCE

Colonel Philip C. Conran, USAF, Ret., Air Force Cross

In 1969, an Army rifle company in Vietnam collected some military payment certificates and sent off for a case of Tabasco Sauce to enhance some of those horrible C-rations. The Tabasco Company not only sent a case, but also returned the MPCs.

The enclosed letter was signed by Walter S. McIlhenny, the company president. Needless to say, the sauce made their day and greatly improved unit morale.

Many years later, Rich Rinaldo—a member of that company, who went on to become a Distinguished Service Cross recipient—was doing a little public-relations work for Ralph Browner, who was organizing the 2008 Legion of Valor convention in Las Vegas. Rich sent letters to defense firms, movie studios, etc., seeking support. "The reunion was just around the corner and my efforts seemed to be in vain, after being wrung through various politically correct corporate philanthropy committees and the inevitable bureaucrats. At least all the companies replied except for the Disney Company, which made a fortune on war movies. They sent my letters back unopened. Then, right before the convention, a UPS truck showed up with a box containing 144 miniature Tabasco Sauce bottles and it made my day." Rich sent them to Ralph and they ended up in attendees' convention bags.

Jump to 2012, and Rich was reading a W. E. B. Griffin novel about the United States Marine Corps, *Close Combat*, which included information on a Walter S. McIlhenny who served with distinction at Guadalcanal, receiving the Navy Cross, Silver Star and the Purple Heart. Remembering the name from years past, Rich did some research and found out the McIlhenny family owned the Tabasco Company and Walter was President from 1959 until his death in 1985. He learned that Walter left most of his fortune to the Marine Military Academy.

McIlhenny was decorated for heroism and courage as Executive Officer of Company B, 1st Battalion, 5th Marines, 1st Marine Division, during a frontal assault upon a strongly fortified enemy Japanese position along the coast of Guadalcanal, Solomon Islands on August 27, 1942. After organizing a volunteer party to advance and evacuate the wounded from the hazardous position well forward of the company, First Lieutenant McIlhenny, armed only with a rifle and while under heavy enemy mortar and machine-gun fire, covered the advance and withdrawal of the rescue party, gallantly drawing enemy fire and silencing a Japanese machine-gun nest. Although ill at the time and suffering shock from concussion of an enemy mortar shell, he returned to a vantage point close to enemy lines. In the face of fierce sniper fire, he acted as an observer, relaying accurate information necessary for fire control until ordered by his superior officer to leave his post. His great personal valor, above and beyond the call of duty, not only made possible the rescue of nine wounded men but also contributed to the success of Marine mortar fire.

This piece first appeared in the Legion of Valor General Orders.

TENNESSEE TWO-STEP

A SMALL INCIDENT IN A LARGE WAR

Roger Norland

Warfare could be likened to a dance where each person's movement is followed closely by the movement of his partner, with one side taking the lead and the other following. Frequently, soldiers end up sitting out many of the "dances" and then suddenly find themselves in a swirl of combat when they least expect it.

During the Civil War it was common practice to recruit an entire company from one locale. In this case, Company H of the 2nd Minnesota Infantry was raised in Blue Earth County, Minnesota in the summer of '61. Most of the soldiers were young farm boys, with a sprinkling of merchants, printers, trappers and riverboat men. Among them was an orphaned farmhand from Garden City named Joseph Burger. Young Burger was only 13 years old but big for his age; when he lied and claimed to be 18, the recruiter must have winked when he let him sign the enlistment papers.

On a cold and grey Sunday morning in 1863, the 2nd Minnesota regiment was in Tennessee, encamped near the home of a rebel colonel named Battle along the Nolens Pike just outside Nolensville. Just a few days earlier snow and sleet had fallen, making this February 15th start out rather bleakly. The normal sounds of camp life brought the soldiers out of their frost-encrusted tents. Dying embers from last night's campfires were brought to life for hot coffee while crates of hardtack were pried open for a quick breakfast. The blanket-draped soldiers stood around the smoking fires and heard the duty assignments for the day. A squad of soldiers of Company H was detailed to guard some of the regiment's wagons, which were being sent out into the nearby countryside to gather forage for the regiment's mule teams. At the least, the expedition would give the guards an opportunity to get out of camp, with the distinct possibility of finding some eggs or a chicken or two for supper that night.

Accompanying four wagons, the squad from Company H encountered on the road a "contraband" soldier—slang for any black person—who told the Minnesotans they should be wary because five hundred Confederate cavalry were in the area.

The Company H foragers eventually came to their destination and turned into the entrance lane to a farm. At once the soldiers began emptying the corncrib and transferring its contents to the wagons.

Suddenly, the drumming of horse hooves and the belligerent rebel yell sounded from the road. Gray-clad troopers charged down the lane firing their carbines and yelling. "Surrender, you damned Yankees!"

First Sergeant Livilo Holmes hustled his squad into the corncrib. One soldier remembered him saying, "Stick to me and we will give them the best turn in the shop!" Confederate carbine fire peppered the corncrib, splintering wood and wounding three of the defenders. The Minnesota boys shouted insults at the now-dismounted rebels and fired their muskets as fast as they could load and shoot in the cramped confines of the crib. The Southerners replied in kind, their shouts and gunfire mixing with the groans of the wounded and the whinnying of riderless horses. Again they hailed the Yanks and demanded surrender. The boys in blue responded with more musketry. Inside the crib, the infantrymen were no longer cold but were choking from their own gun smoke, which barely allowed them to see their targets.

The Confederates comprised an oversized company of approximately 125 troopers armed with carbines, rifle, and pistols. Their gunfire equaled a veritable storm of lead bullets smashing into the small structure;

fortunately the logs of the crib were sturdy and offered much protection to the defenders.

The gunfire had not gone unheard in the camp of the 2nd Minnesota and soon the balance of the regiment came over a nearby hill deployed as skirmishers. Seeing them, the Rebs withdrew. As they did so, the squad in the corncrib emerged to round up seven horses, several weapons, and three wounded Confederates. One of Holmes' soldiers mounted a captured horse and rode across a field to warn the rest of the command. He was able to head off three Union officers on horseback whose route would have taken them directly into the path of the retreating Rebs. Among the officers was his brigade commander, Colonel F. Van Derveer.

Union casualties in the encounter were one dead mule and three minor wounds. When the Minnesotans counted their remaining ammunition, they found that they had averaged 32 shots per soldier, leaving a margin of only eight bullets each in their pouches.

Sergeant Holmes was promoted to second lieutenant and given an inscribed sword and officer's sash by the members of his company as a token of their regard and esteem for him. Colonel J. W. Bishop of the 2nd Minnesota said, "While as a battle it was a small affair, the prompt, plucky defense then made by our 2nd Minnesota squad was a stunning surprise to the enemy and an example for our foraging detachments that was greatly appreciated by our commanders." The brigade commander, Colonel Van Derveer, stated, "This little affair is one of the most creditable of the campaign and deserves to be remembered and cited as worthy the emulation of all." Finally, Brigadier General James B. Steedman made Lieutenant Holmes the personal gift of an ivory-handled revolver. Even President Lincoln was told of this spark of good news, which was reported widely in the eastern newspapers.

Other than recognition of Sergeant Holmes, the brief hot action at the corncrib brought the defenders no reward other than lively conversation around the campfires for many weeks after. In 1897 this oversight was corrected and the Medal of Honor was awarded to the eight living members of the squad who could be located. Livilo Holmes received this message, as did the other ex-soldiers:

WAR DEPARTMENT
Livilo N. Holmes Esq.,
Sir: You are hereby notified that by direction of the President and under the provisions of the Act of Congress approved March 3, 1863, providing for the presentation of Medals of Honor to such officers, non-commissioned officers and privates as have most distinguished themselves in action, a Congressional Medal of Honor has this day been presented to you for most distinguished gallantry in action.
Respectfully,
R. A. Alger, Secretary of War'

Livilo Holmes, William Clark, Milton Hanna, Samuel Wright, Joseph Burger, James Flannigan. John Vale, and Byron Pay all received the Medal of Honor. Not rewarded because of death or disappearance were Homer Barnard, Nelson Crandall, Charles Krause, Louis Loudrosh, and Samuel Loudon. The post-war whereabouts of Charles Liscom and Samuel Leslie were unknown.

Lieutenant Holmes was promoted to captain by the end of the war. He returned to Mankato and became a prominent contractor. Milton Hanna also stayed in Mankato and was a driving force in building the Mankato Fire Department into a professional organization. Corporal William Clark bought a farm just across the river in Nicollet County. Byron Pay moved to South Dakota and had a successful business and public service career.

Joseph Burger, wounded in the hand in the corncrib fight, became at age sixteen the youngest captain in the Union Army. After the war he served twice in the state legislature. Among his offspring was grandson Warren Burger, who became Chief Justice of the U.S. Supreme Court.

John Vale settled in Rochester, Minnesota after the conflict. Samuel Wright lived out his life in Indiana. And James Flannigan returned to his old home in New York.

This originally appeared in Military Images *(July–August 1999). The lead for its use came from Stephen Burger, the great-grandson of Joseph Burger, who was one of the wounded soldiers. "Captain Joe," as he was known in Minnesota, was an orphan who enlisted at the age of 13 while claiming to be eighteen. At 16, he became the youngest captain in Army history. He lost his arm in combat, but continued in Hancock's Invalid Corps and marched with Sherman to the sea. His grandson, Warren E. Burger, the 15th Chief Justice of the United States, learned law from Joe's law books.*

GEORGE H. W. BUSH THE "ACE," THE NIGHT THE LIGHTS WENT OUT AT VLADIVOSTOK, AND THE LOBSTER RUN

William C. Raposa, USN, Ret., Navy Cross with Gold Star

George H. W. Bush

I attended the charter meeting of the Association of Naval Aviation at NAS Oceania about 25 years ago and a relatively unknown former congressman by the name of Bush was the principal speaker. George told that he was an Avenger TBF/TBM driver in WWII, like me, and that he had been credited with four planes. I knew this was not true since the Avenger was not a fighter and would have had a problem getting out of its own way. Then he explained. He had been shot down twice, spun in one time trying to land aboard and racked up another one totaling it on a carrier landing. He finished by saying he would have been made an ace by the Japanese if he had one more to his credit. I have heard it said that George Bush was the youngest Naval aviator to fly from carriers during the big war in the Pacific. I was six months younger than George but I understand there is a retired Navy captain in the Michigan area that was really the youngest in combat who claimed to be 18 when he was sworn in. I just could not tell a lie.

The Night the Lights Went Out at Vladivostok

Toward the end of our Korean combat tour in the summer of 1951 we had established a routine for the night heckler and intruder flights in flying off the USS *Boxer*, CV-21. The usual ordnance load was one 500-pound GP and eight 260- or 220-pound VT fragmentation bombs plus flares and a full load of 20mm ammo. Earlier on we had used napalm, a few Tiny Tim 1,200-pound rockets and assorted loads of butterfly bombs and tetrahedrons to drop on main traffic points. I had liked the napalm and had spotted a humongous pile of coal at a major power plant just south of Hamhung. It must have been a supply for a year or two about 100 feet high and 1,000 feet long. Since our targets at night were largely left up to us, I had intended to start a world-class conflagration at the appropriate opportunity but the powers to be decided it was too dangerous to let us make napalm runs at night.

Our AD4N aircraft on the *Boxer* CV- 21 were old and tired when we inherited them and no replacement was available in the Pacific for one of our machines when the wing spar was shot out and we needed a third bird. They assigned us an AD4Q with only one rear seat and old gyros that sometimes tumbled on a night cat shot. The new AD4NL aircraft with beefed-up armor plate under the engine and cockpit were being sent from the factory to the Sixth Fleet in the Med to be available if the Russians hiccupped. Our original team leader, Dave Arrivee, was shot down and lost at night flying a straight AD2 with no aircrew capability.

We were usually assigned a route to run at night and go after targets of opportunity especially trucks or trains. I would try to find something worthwhile such as a large warehouse or rail terminal early in the flight to get rid of the 500-pounder. We could run the assigned route in an hour or less and then be free to move around looking for more lucrative targets.

The AD4Q replacement arrived August 30, 1951 and it had a limited Radar Countermeasure (RCM) capability and only one seat in the belly. I launched about 9 p.m. in the middle of September on a very clear moonless night with my air crewman, Joe Neithercut. Joe finished with 41 combat missions and was selected as the enlisted representative for the Navy on a 60-city War Bond tour that almost killed him with "fried chicken" banquets in the states. For this he was flown back a week early from the combat tour.

Our assigned route this night was much further north than usual because the intelligence folks wanted traffic information and a try at some RCM work with the 4Q. We came in feet dry just south of Chongjin, close to 200 miles north of Hamhung. We were totally blacked out as we ran north and did our usual heckling dropping a bomb here and there. My regular wingman, Jammie Morris with his air crewman, Lee Sausser, had a mechanical abort so we were alone on this flight. Visibility was excellent and I was to have turned around before reaching a place called Najin, which was about 50 miles from the borders of China and Russia. Since we had plenty of time before recovery, I told Joe I would head a bit further north to see what kind of road traffic was coming south. As I climbed through 10,000 feet the city lights of a rather large place began to come into view so I started a turn since I was afraid I might have gone a few clicks too far. Then the entire city disappeared. It happened as if one switch had turned off every light in the area. Joe and I surmised that the air defense folks had a master control of all electricity in the entire region.

I was now southbound at a good clip descending and agreeing with Joe that we should not debrief this incident because of the possible politics. Just then a flaming cannon ball passed under the right wing, followed by some tracers. I jerked hard left and went down as a few more heavy cannon balls went by but further to the right. I told Joe that we had just had a MIG 15 firing at us. He replied that the shells were a lot closer to him although he was only ten feet in back of me. The MIG must have been under complete ground control including when to fire since they had no radar capability. I had a lot of respect for that airplane and pilot as well as their ground controllers to be able to tail me and get that close in the black of a black night. I was doing about 230 knots going downhill so he must have had to throttle back to 60/70 percent with some flaps and speed brake control to even get close. They were formidable foes for the under-gunned F86s since they had 37mm cannon and 20mm guns versus the Saber jet's 50 caliber machine guns.

The trip home to Boxer was uneventful from this point and we did debrief the MIG attack. We agreed not to say anything about putting out the lights at Vlad because the politicians would get excited.

The Russians evidently never said anything to the State Department and we heard nothing more on this, which could have caused an international incident.

The Lobster Run

Back in 1958–1959, I enjoyed running the new instrument flight program for the Replacement Air Group (RAG) at Navy Jacksonville. We had 16 F9F8T Cougars, six T-28s and about a dozen TV-2 types to process all incoming fleet pilots for all weather jet and prop carrier work. The other half of our squadron consisted of A4 Skyhawk and AD Skyraider aircraft for tactical training. Part of my job was flying all five types and keeping up with the world of attack as well as instrument work. As a collateral duty, I had total squadron responsibility for the occasional lobster runs to NAS Brunswick, Maine. About once a quarter we would collect a few bucks a head and schedule a Friday instrument check flight to Brunswick and return in the TV-2s. We accommodated about 20 to 30 fresh live lobster in each of the ammo cans in the nose of the Lockheed so usually we had a two-plane flight and a Friday night lobster bake at NAS Jax. On one run we were oversubscribed with orders for about a hundred lobsters but as fate had it, one aircraft had no back seat occupant so we figured on about 40 lobsters to be strapped into the rear ejection seat. All went well until we reached the takeoff end of the runway and my wingman, Frank Mudgett, could not get his canopy locked with all the lobster boxes in his back seat. He returned to the line and they squashed the boxes down and made sure the canopy was relocked.

Climbing out past 10,000 feet, I heard, "I have lobsters loose in the rear." There was a bit of panic for a few moments but as we climbed Frank said the lobsters were getting less aggressive. So I said let's go to 40,000 and see if we can put them to sleep. By turning up the cockpit temperature we found that they became dormant. The delivery was made on time and on schedule. The beach party that night was one of the better ones but we all agreed the TV-2 should be retired from future lobster runs.

As pressure grew for another squadron Friday night lobster ball, I worried how to get to Brunswick and back to Jax. Orders were taken and were double our last run. Now it was 200 live lobster and Hutch Cooper, the RAG CO had invited some of the station wheels to the party so it was up to me to produce. The Cougars could not handle that many and the run was a tad long for the T-28s and they were too slow. The A4s were just not the plane for this flight. Behold, here was an A4D to be transferred to NAS Quonset Point and they had an AD for me to take back to Jax. I flew up on the A4 on Thursday and picked up the AD, going to Brunswick early Friday morning for loading up the 200 lobsters. No problem in the AD ammo cans and in the belly of the plane so off I headed for NAS Oceania. Without drops I planned a real quick gas and go at Oceania where my old VC-35 Korean War wingman, Jamie Morris, was OPS officer. Passing Pax River, I called on the operations frequency and asked Jamie to work up my onward flight plan to Jacksonville and have a refueling truck ready for me since I had a delicate load aboard. As I pulled up, Jamie got on the wing for me to sign the flight plan and I was airborne in less than 15 minutes with clear sailing on time and on schedule for the beach party. Then the engine stopped.

Those of you who have flown the Able Dog know it does not glide well with a 14-plus foot prop not turning. We, the 200 lobsters, and me were 60 miles south of Norfolk and 60 miles north of the Marine Corps Air Station at Cherry Point, N.C. and we had 8,000 feet to play with. The mayday alerted the Coast Guard at Elizabeth City who launched an Albatross and the Marines who put up a rescue chopper heading out to me over Pamlico Sound. The lobsters remained mute. Working the primer, I was able to get a few turns every 500 feet or so and at 30 miles to go I still had 4,000 feet so it looked as if we just might make land if I could keep the engine partially running on the primer.

The last gasp brought me over the end of the runway for a straight in and a tow to the flight line. Now I wondered if my friend from Oceania had given me a generous portion of water with the gas or if the O&R at Quonset had done me in with the engine. The major consideration was 200 live lobsters. My call to Jax alerted them to cancel the Friday bash, and the generous Marines at the O'Club "volunteered" to take care of the lobsters and get them cooked for me while the maintenance folks worked over the plane that night. Incidentally, it was the O&R and not the gas so by 10AM Saturday I was ready to roll again. A call to the O'Club failed to alert anyone, but with a little persistence a resident O'Club manager determined that, yes, they had my lobsters and that they would be delivered shortly to flight operations. Presently, an O'Club pickup truck arrived at operations manned by two six-foot six-inch Marines without guns but with exactly 200 lobsters, cooked as promised.

The Saturday night lobster beach bash at NAS Jax was not quite as great as before and I received orders to a desk job shortly thereafter. It took two years to get another cockpit assignment but there were no more lobster runs in my future.

Excerpted from An Aviator's Journey *by William C. Raposa, USN, Ret., Navy Cross with Gold Star. William Clayton Raposa was a survivor of World War II, Korea and Vietnam. He was highly decorated for extraordinary heroism earning a Navy Cross with Gold Star (second award) and a Distinguished Flying Cross.*

"THE WHOLE DAMN BATTLEFIELD IS MY MONUMENT"

MAJOR GENERAL DANIEL E. SICKLES, MEDAL OF HONOR

It could never be said Daniel Sickles did not lead a full life. He was a Congressman, tried for murder, a Union general, diplomat, recipient of a Medal of Honor, "King of Spain," and instrumental in founding the Gettysburg Military Park. In all his busy days, controversy followed him and he *reveled in it.*

Born October 20, 1819 in New York City, Sickles studied law as a youth and quickly became embroiled in the graft-ridden world of Tammany politics. He met his future wife, Teresa Bagnoli, when he was a student and she an infant. They were married September 27, 1852. Sickles was already a man of many tastes and nearly 33 years old. Teresa was 16, and considered quite beautiful.

Between 1857 and 1861 Sickles was a Democrat Congressman from New York. He and his attractive young wife joined the Washington social whirl until Teresa met handsome Philip Barton Key (playboy son of Francis Scott Key) who rented a rundown house for his various activities, including meetings with Teresa. Sickles eventually found out and, being a "man of honor," shot Philip to death in Lafayette Park within view of the White House.

Authorities had no choice but to arrest Congressman Sickles. When offered bail, he refused it and awaited trial. His defense attorney was Edwin Stanton, later secretary of war under President Lincoln. Prosecuting was

Robert Ould, later the Confederate agent of prisoner exchange. Sickles was found not guilty owing to the "unwritten law" that a man had a right to defend the honor of his wife and home. It was a landmark case, setting the "temporary insanity" precedent. Sickles promptly locked Teresa away for good, after forcing her to sign a confession and publicly forgiving her.

When the Civil War began, Sickles raised a brigade in New York and was rewarded by President Lincoln with an appointment as brigadier general, September 3, 1861. On November 29, 1862 Sickles was promoted to major general. He fought and led men during the Peninsula Campaign, at Antietam under Hooker, and commanded a division at Fredericksburg. At Chancellorsville, Sickles was in command of the Third Corps.

Astride his horse, Sickles watched the Gettysburg battle from the Trostle Farm on July 2, 1863. An errant cannonball shattered his right leg at about 6:30 p.m., and he was carried from the field, jauntily smoking a cigar as he lay on the stretcher. Arms and legs were piled all around the hospital at Daniel Shaffer's farmhouse on Taneytown Road but Sickles' amputated leg was not thrown on the heap but saved and donated to a museum where Sickles could visit the shattered bones from time to time.

As he recovered, Sickles went on a fact-finding mission for President Lincoln in Union-held areas of the South. He also became a diplomat to Columbia in South America. Postwar he was appointed military governor of South Carolina and served as minister to Spain from 1869–1875. In Spain he caused some embarrassment by requesting the United States annex Cuba, a Spanish possession. Meanwhile, Teresa had died (1869) and Sickles became enamored with Isabella II, the former Spanish queen in exile. He even married her lady-in-waiting when rumors of his affair with the queen were published.

Finally returning to the United States, Sickles continued his assertions that he alone was responsible for the victory at Gettysburg. He returned to Congress in 1893 for one term and was awarded the Medal of Honor (1897), a form of vindication. During this period he was also instrumental in having the Federal government acquire Gettysburg acreage for a national military park. He was also chairman of the New York

Monuments commission, until removed in 1912, and attended the 50th anniversary celebration at Gettysburg in 1913. When someone asked why he had no monument at Gettysburg if he had indeed won the battle, Sickles supposedly said, "The whole damn battlefield is my monument."

Sickles died on May 3, 1914. His funeral was held at St Patrick's Cathedral on Fifth Avenue in New York City, and he was buried at Arlington National Cemetery.

This piece first appeared in the Legion of Valor General Orders.

CHIVALRY OR CERTAIN DOOM ABOVE GERMANY

CHARLES L. BROWN, AIR FORCE CROSS

Charles L. Brown was awarded the Air Force Cross for extraordinary heroism in military operations as a B-17 pilot of the 527th Bombardment Squadron, 379th Bombardment Group (Heavy), in action over Germany, December 20, 1943. While attacking a heavily defended target over occupied Germany, Lieutenant Brown's aircraft sustained severe flak damage, including destruction of the Plexiglas nose, wing damage, and major damage to the number two and four engines. Lieutenant Brown provided invaluable instructions to the copilot and crew requiring the number two engine to be shut down. He then expertly managed to keep the number four engine producing partial power. That enabled his crew to complete the improbable bombing run and bomb delivery on this important strategic target. Immediately upon leaving the target, severe multiple engine damage prevented maintaining their position in formation.

His violent, evasive tactics to counter the multiple enemy efforts to destroy their airplane directly contributed to his crew and his aircraft's survival. Alone and outnumbered, the aircraft was mercilessly attacked by the enemy. The crew's difficulties were compounded when they discovered that only three defensive guns were operational, the others frozen in the -75 degree Fahrenheit temperatures. The result of this brief but devastating aerial battle was one crew member dead, another with critical injuries that would require amputation of his leg, serious damage of the third engine, the complete destruction of the aircraft's left elevator and stabilizer, the inoperability of the bomber's oxygen and communications systems, and the complete shredding of the rudder by enemy fire that produced a death roll of the plane as it spiraled helplessly out of control causing the entire crew to temporarily lose consciousness.

Miraculously, prior to ground impact, Lieutenant Brown and the copilot regained consciousness and managed to regain full flight control by pulling the heavily damaged aircraft out of its nose-dive. Although managing to recover this aircraft from certain doom, the crew's plight was further complicated when a lone German fighter witnessed the maneuver, now attempted to force the crippled aircraft to land. Displaying coolness, courage and airmanship of more senior pilots, he boldly rejected the enemy fighter's attempts at a forced landing and directed the struggling aircraft to the North Sea. While attempting this improbable, treacherous return to home station, Lieutenant Brown's command and control was instrumental to the remaining crew's survival. While in the cockpit, he provided the essential engine control, fuel management, and piloting skills necessary to the cockpit team during their hazardous, yet miraculous return of the aircraft's perilous crossing of the North Sea back to home station in England.

Brown might not have survived this action but for the chivalrous actions of an ace German fighter pilot, according to his obituary in the *Miami Herald* on December 7, 2008: "Upon limping back to England they were intercepted by yet another enemy fighter over Germany. Recognizing their helpless state, the German pilot did not shoot them down.... The chivalrous German pilot ... escorted the crippled bomber to the coast ... and saluted his adversary. Forty-five years later the two pilots were re-united and became as close as brothers. Their story continues to receive international acclaim. The chivalrous German pilot, Luftwaffe ace Franz Stigler passed away on March 22, 2008."

This amazing story is further described in an article by John J. Frisbee in *Air Force Magazine*, published by the Air Force Association, in January 1997: "[T]here had been two persuasive reasons why Stigler should have shot down the B-17. First... [He] needed only one more that day to earn a Knight's Cross. Second, his decision ... was a court-martial offense in Nazi Germany and if revealed could have led to his execution. He considered these alternatives.... He could see the wounded aboard and thought; 'I cannot kill these half-dead people. It would be like shooting at a parachute.'"

Upon retirement from the Air Force, Brown enjoyed a distinguished career as a Foreign Service Officer with the U.S. Department of State and as an inventor in the environmental area, receiving numerous national and international awards in that endeavor.

From the Air Force Cross citation and stated materials.

FINAL THINGS

Remember, you may in God's mercy have had your day.... You may live until over it all comes the glamour of the years, and you may tell the tale so often that you'll hardly be able to distinguish the fabric from the embroidery.... On the other hand, your challenge may lie ahead....

Douglas Southall Freeman

MEMORIAL

Brigadier General William J. Mullen III, USA Ret., Distinguished Service Cross

Every year we look forward to this opportunity to refresh friendships of many years and to begin new ones. We relish the company of comrades whom we trust to understand us today as we once trusted each other in combat. Conversations in hallways and command posts turn quickly to memories of soldiers with whom we served. We talk about happy times and we talk about terrible moments. We celebrate life while we grieve death.

General "Vinegar Joe" Stillwell once said, "No matter how a war starts, it ends in mud. It has to be slugged out—there are no trick solutions or cheap shortcuts."[1]

Today we honor the memories of 1st Infantry Division soldiers who slugged it out in the mud. We mourn those no longer alive. Some were our friends. Most, we never met.

Some were killed in battle while others survived combat, returned to what we in Vietnam called "the world," and have now passed from this life. Whether or not we knew our dead personally, we honor their lives, their service, and their sacrifice.

Linda Ellis' poem *The Dash* takes its title from the mark on a gravestone that separates the dates of birth and death. She identifies the significance of the dash as the time the deceased lived; she tells us that the worth of that time is not the value of worldly goods gathered in life but how that person lived. She wrote in part:

> I read of a man who stood to speak at the funeral of a friend.
> He referred to the dates on her tombstone from the beginning to the end.
> He noted that first came the date of her birth and spoke of the following date with tears,
> But he said what mattered most of all was the dash between those years.
> For that dash represents all the time she spent alive on earth …
> And now only those who loved her know what that little line is worth.[2]

We honor our deceased veterans and the value of their dashes. To paraphrase President Lincoln at Gettysburg—we honor them because each of them gave, or offered to give, his or her last full measure so that the nation might live.

Since 1917 our patch has been seen on a hundred battlefields. Today, it is still being worn by soldiers who have gone into harm's way to defend the nation. Many of the thousands and thousands who have worn the Big Red One are no longer with us. They are the men, the women—the flesh and blood behind the grim numbers of the Division's dead in battle since 1917 and the thousands of veterans whose obituaries appear in hometown newspapers across our country.

Dick Cavazos, 18th Infantry, once told me, "You can tell a lot about a man when there is steel flying around his head." Dogface Six was right about that.

I began learning about our veterans when I began attending Division reunions in the late 60s. Because I had been where steel flew I could relate to stories from men who had slogged it out in the mud of France during WWI and those of soldiers who fought across Europe in WWII. Because I am a veteran I can appreciate the significance of General Eisenhower's statement when he described heroism as "the uncomplaining acceptance of unendurable conditions."[3] I listened to, related to, and identified with the experiences of my generation who had tramped through jungle, rice paddy, and rubber, or ridden on Thunder Road because Vietnam was my war, too. Because I am a veteran I can begin to understand what it took to break through the berm and lead the VII Corps into Kuwait and, what it now takes to patrol the countryside and towns of Iraq and

Afghanistan. Because I am a veteran I admire and respect the lives of all Big Red One soldiers who accepted the unendurable conditions of which Ike spoke. (Because I was a soldier, however, I question Ike's characterization that the acceptance was without complaint.)

Most soldiers in combat try to do what's right. In so doing they live up to our Division's motto. Doing what's right is seen in small things like sharing water, comforting a buddy who has reached his breaking point, taking the point when it's your turn, and easing tension with a joke when the world is exploding all around. Doing what's right is seen in big things like standing up and moving forward under fire, or charging into the beaten zone to pull a buddy to safety, or crawling into a cramped tunnel when it's certain that VC lurk in the darkness. Sometimes, living up to our motto is manifested in extraordinary actions such as those of Private First Class Bechtel whom I did not know and Private First Class Freese, whom I did know. Permit me to tell you about those two soldiers and what they did between their dashes.

On August 25, 1966, Charlie Company, 1–2 Infantry, and a platoon from Charlie Troop, 1–4 Cav started a fight in the base camp of what turned out to be the Phu Loi Battalion reinforced by a regional company. We had been trying to reach an ambush patrol which was surrounded when we made contact ourselves. We took heavy casualties in the first minutes of an intense, close-quarters fight. We were in some of the VC positions. We intended to stay; the Bad Chaps wanted their holes back.

B Company, 1–2 Infantry was one of the first two companies to fight its way into our location. Dracula Bravo quickly became heavily engaged. Private First Class Herbert Bechtel was a Bravo Company machine gunner. His platoon took heavy casualties and could not stay where it was. Recognizing that his comrades could not withdraw unless the enemy's fire was countered, Private Bechtel established a firing position with his team between the platoon and the entrenched VC. His accurate fire suppressed the VC, enabled wounded to be retrieved, and the platoon to pull back a little way. As this was going on, Private Bechtel was severely wounded by a VC rifle grenade. Nonetheless, he got back behind his machine gun and kept up his fire. He refused to seek treatment for his wounds. Instead he crawled 30 meters under fire to retrieve three cans of ammunition from a machine gun that had been destroyed. When he got back, his assistant machine gunner was dead. The ammo bearer was manning the weapon. When the ammunition supply again began to run low Private Bechtel once more braved furious fire to obtain more ammunition. The ammunition bearer was then seriously wounded. Private First Class Bechtel told him to crawl back to where the rest of the platoon was. Private First Class Bechtel took the weapon and continued to fire in short, well-aimed bursts. He was wounded again by a second grenade. His platoon sergeant shouted to him to pull back but he stayed at his post to cover the continuing evacuation of the wounded. Finally, the machine gun fell silent. Later, Dracula Bravo regained his position; Private First Class Bechtel was dead behind his gun. His finger was still on the trigger. His ammunition had been expended. No Mission Too Difficult! No Sacrifice Too Great![4]

Shortly before Private Bechtel's last stand, while Dracula Charlie and Dragoon Charlie were still alone in the base camp, I was working the radio trying to cut through all the traffic on the battalion net. We were pretty beat up. A lot of men were down. The Fourth Platoon, the mortar platoon, had 100 per cent casualties—or so I thought until I was interrupted by a voice calling, "Charlie Six, Charlie Six." I looked up. There was Private First Class Tom Freese, a mortarman. He stood there on that fireswept patch of open ground with a 60 mm mortar on one shoulder and a sack of ammunition hanging from the other. When he had my attention, he said, "Sir, the Fourth Platoon is ready for action. Where do you want me to shoot?" I gave him an azimuth. Private First Class Freese, now Dracula Charlie's Fourth Platoon, went to work. Duty First!

After I left Charlie Company I never saw Private First Class Freese again, although I thought of him often. A few years ago I learned that he had passed away at home.

Private First Class Bechtel and Private First Class Freese exemplify the sorts of lives we honor today. One soldier died in battle beneath a soldier's blow. One died in peaceful surroundings.

Linda Ellis ended her poem with the lines,

> So, when your eulogy's being read with your life's actions to rehash ...
> Would you be proud of the things they say about how you spent your dash?

We Big Red One veterans understand the worth of the dashes between dates on the headstones of fellow veterans. We are proud of how they soldiered; we honor and salute their service to our nation. How could we do anything else?

When my course on earth is run, I would be proud if the eulogist includes that I was once a soldier in the Big Red One and that I once was a mud soldier in a beautiful place at an ugly time with soldiers like Private First Class Herbert Bechtel, Private First Class Tommy Freese, and the comrades of my youth.

God bless our honored dead and their families. God bless you. May God protect the Big Red One soldiers who now defend the United States of America.

These remarks were made at the memorial service conducted during the Society of 1st Infantry Division 2009 reunion, Dearborn, Michigan.

William J. Mullen III, National Commander of the Legion of Valor in 2015–2016, graduated from the United States Military Academy, West Point, NY, in 1959. Commissioned in the infantry, he retired from the Army in 1992 in the grade of brigadier general. His awards and decorations include the Combat Infantryman Badge, the Distinguished Service Cross, the Distinguished Service Medal (OLC), Soldier's Medal (OLC), and the Ranger Tab. He lives in California.

Notes

1 Cited in Max Hastings, *Retribution, The Battle for Japan 1944–45*, Alfred A. Knopf, New York, 2007.
2 Linda Ellis. © 1998 by permission.
3 Cited in Gerald E. Linderman, *Embattled Courage*, The Free Press, New York, 2007.
4 Motto of the 1st Infantry Division (The Big Red One): No Mission Too Difficult! No Sacrifice Too Great! Duty First!

SOME SUFFER IN SURVIVAL

Colonel Bruce W. Reagan, Distinguished Service Cross

The trauma of warfare lies on the survivors as well as on the loved ones of those who do not survive. Who can cherish the thought of having ordered anyone, however inadvertently, to his death?

The overriding mission in the World War II mobilization period was training troops—imparting the basic skills and, by a form of regimentation, discipline to promote cohesiveness such that each man or unit could rely on those working alongside in working toward a common goal.

As an adjunct there was physical fitness to prepare for extended periods of exertion, but most important was instilling mental attitude for instinctive reaction to stressful situations—one that tolerated no intruding concern for consequences. True, it was Pavlovian in part but along with imparting a feeling of working for a just cause, there had to be an inner adjustment to the imminence of hazard to death. The emotion of fear, and to a lesser extent, of compassion had to be suppressed.

A most vivid example of such lack of inner adjustment came while fronting the well-protected fortifications of the Siegfried Line on the German border.

It was January 1945, and the initial thrust to the Ardennes Forest attack, leading to the Battle of the Bulge, had been blunted. They had retreated, however, into the forts of the Siegfried Line for a last *Gotterdammerung*—and a determined one it was.

Only a small measure of protection was afforded by the banks of the ravines leading to the swollen, ice-laden river fronting the concrete emplacements. Intense mortar and artillery at every well-zeroed-in approach route portended more hazard at the stream banks.

The stygian darkness, the drizzle of icy rain, and the treacherous footing of the stream beds, amidst the constant din of opposing weaponry was enough to test the valor of the most hardened of men.

Ours was a bunch of newly arrived recruits with scarcely 90 days in the service. The unexpected infantry losses characterized by the loss of almost a full division at the initiation of the Bulge Battle had forced drastic manpower measure—and we were at the cutting edge.

The planned sequence of events for the night was to be as follows: First, at dusk, the clearing of minefields and their impeding barbed wire from avenues of approach. Since under such conditions troops cannot be led over cliffs or open fields, such approaches were down the water courses. Second, to lead the assault troops burdened by 10- to 12-man capacity assault boats through the minefields and down the ravines to the water's edge. Third, to put the carriers into the boats for rowing across to gain access to the far side gun emplacements. All was to be done with stealth and on a relatively broad front. It didn't quite work out that way.

The sudden thrust into strange surroundings, a lack of mental adjustment, the fear and sense of greater danger with each forward step took their toll. They knew that the boats being carried could only lead to worse to come.

After slipping and scratching a hand or an elbow on the jagged rocks of the stream bed, the immature troops, hardly more than boys, hugged Mother Earth's surface with mournful cries of "Mother, Mother." Most were put back on their feet and told to keep contributing to the load and to keep going. It was an ordeal keeping with groups, with some members inclined to wander and their loads with them.

The scene at the water's edge was on of chaos amidst stealth. Muffled roll calls and orders were the only sounds as paddles were put into the hands of the men to row across. Some boats were overturned in the loading process, others disappeared down the swirling stream and few got across.

All efforts to get a guide rope across the 300 feet of raging water were thwarted by its inability to withstand the force of the current.

The river bottom was being paved with discarded equipment and the bank with straggling men who were quickly rounded up, handed another rifle, and reloaded into boats for a duplicated effort.

Such actions occurred at several sites with effort intensified as dawn approached and the knowledge they would be exposed to even more deadly fire from the far side concrete bunkers.

This was the pattern for three nights. On the fourth, a wire cable finally held and enough, although thoroughly drenched, troops were put across to reduce the nearby forts with their interlocking fires.

This was a traumatic baptism of fire for a number of recruits and we who stayed on the banks suffered mental as well as physical wounds.

There were times when one felt a more personal responsibility for death's song.

In the early days of training for action there was a dearth of visual aides to impress the required lessons for survival. The need for drafted blow-ups so that 20 rather than two or three could observe the processes of safety in clearing a minefield or first aid was apparent. Somehow there came to the attention of the responsible training officer the name and skills of a young draftee who could produce the sequential pictures of the limited texts available.

He was with some hesitancy removed from the training ranks and his talents applied to a broader purpose—preparing charts to teach others the necessary skills. As changes would have it, the training officer went on to a differing position. The young artist continued as an assistant to his replacement who soon became the operation officer in combat.

A few weeks after the Bulge started, and with heavy infantry losses, there was a five percent levy on all non-infantry units to fill the riflemen's ranks.

Shortly after there was an inquiry: "Where is young F? I haven't seen him for several days."

"Oh we had to send him out on the levy for riflemen."

Two weeks later, word was received that he had been killed in action.

Needless to say, guilt lay on the one who had pulled him out of his basic training for what was thought to be a more essential purpose. Was it? But who would ever know what insights to survival were implanted into others by his visual education supplements?

Yet another guilt trip involved a newly arrived lieutenant.

Well into the war, with losses of platoon leaders running very high—a complete turnover in the preceding half year with few replacements—we welcomed a new member.

He was a recent graduate forester from one of our western universities. It was sensed that the potential for danger was too high for one of his spirit so he was directed to stay close to the headquarters for a few weeks to only observe and get acclimated.

The pressures for his services as a platoon leader built up quickly.

"Boss, sir, I have only two of my authorized four second lieutenants. I am hurting. Why don't you let me have that one who is hanging around?" So he was assigned out. A week later, in part because of the lack of orientation and taking unnecessary risks, he was killed in action.

At least, he was known and could be accounted for.

Others were not. On one river crossing, a fellow battalion commander, although of infantry, informed that a few nights before two lieutenants unexpectedly showed up, just assigned, as replacements. With only an hour to go before the assault and all planning having been made, there was a quick greeting and handshake with "You go to Company C and you go to A. We have a river crossing tonight. Good Luck." They had no files, no paper, nothing and were known only as Tom and Joe.

Neither were found after the assault, so were presumed killed, and so noted when their files caught up with the unit.

Just before gasoline became available to Patton's forces in November 1944, two new but more experienced lieutenants arrived. Both had been withdrawn from instruction duties in the U.S. and were delighted at the opportunity to be able to say to their grandchildren, "Oh, I did more than teach explosives at Fort Belvoir. I was with the Third Army in Europe."

One, physically very impressive, was indeed a leader in spirit as well as in body. While it was often difficult to motivate men to depart the security of a cellar to go to work on a contested bridge or mine field, Lieutenant B had only to stand up and all his cohorts were alert and ready to go. On the site, they hovered around him, when otherwise not employed, like a bunch of bees protecting a queen. His presence and direction and their knowledge of what needed to be done was enough to get done.

It was an amazing lesson in the esoterica of leadership.

There was times when he felt he had to set the example. Thus at a minefield fronting the Siegfried, he ventured too far into a new type of booby-trapped mine field and lost a foot. To our regret, he was never seen again.

Still another unpleasant memory involves the battalion commander's Jeep driver. New and more advanced radios had been issued with the first two connecting his vehicle with the communications truck.

A brief lull in the action prompted the signal officer to request a check of the system—he was to make a recon in the commander's jeep.

He returned without the driver. His story—while scouting a possibly needed bridging site, he had dismounted and walked down a rock trail to the river. On return he found his driver on the road with his upper body shattered. There had been a *fougasse* (a head-high hole filled with stones and explosives) which he had somehow missed but the driver had tripped as he surreptitiously followed the captain.

The element of personal guilt was not lacking on another stream crossing into the same Siegfried Line. A long winter night was to provide concealment for two efforts. I hoped that at least one would succeed.

The first was bridging at a destroyed site and the other a heavy-duty ferry a mile downstream on the same river. An assistant was charged with the latter.

Every attempt to work on the two sites was met unsparingly by fire from pill boxes and supporting tanks on the far bank.

After that first friendly tank rolled across just before the morning fog lifted, the battalion commander settled down for some rest in a welcome straw pile of a nearby barn.

Soon came a medic with "Major K got hit a few minutes ago on the ferry site and is outside in the ambulance. Do you want to see him:"

"How bad and is he conscious?"

"Bad, a big chunk of his side is gone."

I thought of one of General Patton's admonitions—when you are out there in that foxhole and reach over to touch what was once the face of your best buddy, don't get morbid, get mad and get with it.

With regret, the response was "Evacuate him."

The sight of a dying personal friend, I feared, would evoke emotions, to include compassion, that were not conducive to carrying on our part of the war.

This piece first appeared on http://www.150th.com.

Colonel Reagan commanded the 150th Engineer Combat Battalion in World War II. The full citation for his award of the Distinguished Service Cross along with a description of the action in which it was earned may be found at http://legionofvalor.org/lov_citation/bruce-w-reagan/

Recent awards of the Medal of Honor show the burden of survivorship and guilt about combat, sometimes leading to post-traumatic stress.

For example, Army specialist Ty Carter tells us in a Stars and Stripes *article by Chris Carroll, "'I believed everything I did, all the good and bad choices in my life, all the training, would prepare me to save a life in combat....' But after evacuating a wounded friend and learning that he died anyway, Carter said, 'I believed I was a failure. Not just for the military, but in life in general.'"*

Similarly, Marine corporal Dakota Meyer reveals in his book Into the Fire *with Bing West, about the action that earned him his Medal of Honor, "But when it counted the most, I wasn't with them.... My country was recognizing me for being a failure...."*

A LIFE'S PASSION

LIEUTENANT COLONEL THOMAS A. RICHARDS, USMC, RET., NAVY CROSS

Tom was raised on the west side of Madison, Wisconsin and attended Randall Elementary School and West Middle and High School. As a high school sophomore, he discovered his aptitude for long-distance running and became a star runner on both the cross-country and track teams. His love of running continued throughout his life, including competing in several marathons. Following his graduation from high school, he worked as a machinist.

In 1967, Tom joined the Marine Corps and found his life's passion. After completing recruit training he was selected to attend scout sniper school and Vietnamese Language School at the Defense Language Institute in Monterey. He was then assigned to Company H, 2nd Battalion, 9th Marines in the Republic of Vietnam where he earned a meritorious combat promotion to the rank of sergeant, the Navy Cross Medal for valor in combat, and the Purple Heart Medal for his wounds. According to a story about him in the *Washington Post* by Dan Lamothe: "His award citation credits him with leading his small group of Marines against a much larger enemy force, braving gunfire-swept fields multiple times to help others to safety and manning a machine gun while under assault to prevent them from being overrun." Lamothe also talked about Tom's own struggle with post-traumatic stress, and how he shared his wartime experiences with young Marines like then "Marine Staff Sergeant Cliff Wooldridge, who was awarded the Navy Cross in May 2012 for valor on

June 18, 2010, a day in which he beat an enemy fighter to death with his own machine gun." Wooldridge said, according to Lamothe, "He made sure he set me up for success and sent me in the right direction, consistently checking up on me, asking for [situation reports] and meeting up whenever we could. I owe a lot to Tom. He was a role model for me."

Upon completing his assignment with the 9th Marines, Tom served as a drill instructor at Marine Corps Recruit Depot San Diego. While serving as a drill instructor he was selected for the Marine Associate Degree Completion Program, received his associate's degree, and was selected to attend Officer Candidate School through the Marine Corps' Enlisted Commissioning Program. He was commissioned as a second lieutenant.

Tom served four tours in infantry units and in various staff positions from battalion to division level.

He served twice on recruiting duty, in Pittsburgh, Pennsylvania and Lansing, Missouri; was an instructor at Marine Corps Command and Staff College; and as the Head, Historical Branch, Marine Corps History and Museums division of Headquarters, U.S. Marine Corps.

In addition to the Navy Cross and Purple Heart, Tom was awarded numerous other personal decorations and service medals, including the Meritorious Service Medal, Navy Commendation Medal (two awards), the Army Achievement Medal, the Combat Action Ribbon and the Marine Corps Good Conduct Medal, of which he was most proud. He retired in 1995 as a lieutenant colonel.

Both during and after the Corps, Tom's civic service and pursuit of academic excellence was legendary. He actively participated in the Legion of Valor and served as its National Commander, 2008. He was widely known for his nine years serving with Spirit of the Fourth, Inc. in the Rancho Bernardo community of San Diego, California. He was active in the Rotary Club and established the Miramar Semper Fidelis Rotary Club on the Marine Corps Air Station, Miramar; only the second service club on an active military base anywhere in the world. He was an active member of the San Diego County United Veterans Council (UVC) and served as the UVC chairmanship for 2010. He co-founded the Soldiers of the Sea, Band of Brothers Inc., an organization dedicated to bridging the gap between the Marine Corps and business communities. Tom served as a mentor to the San Diego State University Student Veterans Organization (SVO) and was presented with its "Mentor for Life" Award, its highest honor. He was appointed by Governor Arnold Schwarzenegger to the California Veterans Board.

He spearheaded nationwide efforts to discover incidents of Stolen Valor and prepared a "Friend of the Court" brief for submission to the Supreme Court in support of a finding that the Stolen Valor Act of 2005 was constitutional. In recognition of his community service, Tom was selected in 2005 for membership in the Rancho Bernardo Hall of Fame, one of only ninety selectees since 1974. In June 2009, he was named the California 75th State Assembly District Veteran of the Year. He also received the "Lifetime Support of Veterans Award" from the San Diego Veteran of the Year committee in 2009. He relocated from Southern California to Virginia Beach in 2012 and was appointed by Governor McDonnell in 2013 to the Virginia Joint Leadership Council of Veterans. He was also commandant of the Bulldog Detachment 835, Marine Corps League. An avid student, Tom earned both his baccalaureate and master's degrees in history, and his masters of business administration, all from San Diego State University. While in Virginia Beach, Tom followed his passion for teaching history as an adjunct professor at Tidewater Community College.

Tom maintained a rigorous physical fitness regimen throughout his life, permitting him to engage in numerous outdoor activities including diving, kayaking, camping, and hiking. During the past eleven years he climbed California's 14,497-foot Mt. Whitney ten times.

Tom never quit anything that he set his mind on. He was a consummate advocate for veterans' issues, was a devoted and dedicated husband, and was the best and sincerest friend a man could have. He was the epitome of a renaissance man who loved opera, fine art, classical and Celtic music, and world travel.

Material compiled from various sources.

Thomas Richards died in 2014.

ODE TO JOE

Joseph Bruni

Seventy plus years given me
Beyond your twenty
That precious gift
Denied you that hellish day
On the bloody sulfuric sands
Your right to survive
As great as mine
Was denied by torn, jagged shell
That claimed you and others
And spared me to retell
Your smile as friendly as mine
Your girl as warm as mine
Your future as promising as mine
Yet, I returned And you were left behind
How do I respond To those soulful questions From your Mom?
"Did my Son suffer Before he died?"
I said No but I know I lied
A youthful prayer comes to mind
Lord make me worthy
Now cries out A Universal prayer
"Lord make US worthy

Of his death, his suffering
And those of others"
Although I presently live
Part of my future death
Already remains with him

At a Legion of Valor Mid-Atlantic Chapter meeting, guest Joe Bruni concluded the meeting by reading this poem in memory of his buddy who was killed on February 19, 1945, on Iwo Jima. His poem is dedicated to all fallen service personnel.

Joseph Bruni proudly served with the 4th Marine Division and participated in the invasions of the Marshall Islands, Saipan, Tinian, and Iwo Jima. Joe's division was awarded two Presidential Unit Citations for Saipan and Iwo Jima.

DEAD SOLDIERS' BREATH

Ron Tranmer

The flag of our country waves proudly
for all of the world to see.
But it's not the wind, that makes it wave
as an emblem of the free.

It waves by the breath of our soldiers
who died for freedom's right.
Take off your hat and think of that
when one comes into sight.

HONORING RABBI ROLAND B. GITTELSOHN AND HIS STIRRING EULOGY ON IWO JIMA

Bruce Braley

This address was made Bruce Braley of Iowa in Congress on May 23, 2007.

Mr. Speaker, I rise today during Jewish American Heritage Month to honor the life and memory of Rabbi Roland B. Gittelsohn, who was the first Jewish chaplain ever appointed by the Marine Corps. Most Americans don't recognize the name of Rabbi Gittelsohn, but they should. Rabbi Gittelsohn delivered a stirring eulogy to the war dead on Iwo Jima that is second only to the Gettysburg Address of President Lincoln as a stirring ode to the principles of democracy that are the bedrock of this country and the young men and women who paid the ultimate price for our freedom.

During World War II, Rabbi Gittelsohn was assigned as a Jewish divisional chaplain of the 5th Marine Division. During the battle of Iwo Jima, Rabbi Gittelsohn was right in the heart in the action, ministering to the needs of Marines of all faith, with the knowledge that his life was in grave danger.

After the fighting was over, Rabbi Gittelsohn was asked to give a sermon at an ecumenical memorial service dedicating the 5th Marine Division cemetery on Iwo Jima, but due to prejudice he only gave remarks at a small Jewish service. My father served in the 5th Marine Division on Iwo Jima, and it is to his memory and the memory of Rabbi Gittelsohn that I offer these poignant words:

Here before us lie the bodies of comrades and friends, men who until yesterday or last week laughed with us, joked with us, trained with us, men who fought with us and feared with us. Somewhere in this plot of ground there may lie the man who could have discovered the cure for cancer. Under one of these Christian crosses or beneath a Jewish Star of David, there may now rest a man who was destined to be a great prophet, to find the way perhaps for all to live in plenty, with poverty and hardship for none. Now they lie here silently in this sacred soil, and we gather to consecrate the earth in their memory.

It is not easy to do so. Some of us have buried our closest friends here. To speak in memory of such men as these is not easy. No, our poor power of speech can add nothing to what these men have already done. All that we can even hope to do is to follow their example, to show the same selfless courage in peace that they did in war; to swear that by the grace of God and the stubborn strength and power of the human will, their sons and ours will never suffer these pains again. These men have done their job well. They have paid the ghastly price of freedom.

We dedicate ourselves, first, to live together in peace the way they fought and are buried in this war. Here lie officers and men, Negroes and whites, rich men and poor, together. Here, no man prefers another because of his faith or despises him because of his color. Here, there are no quotas of how many from each group are admitted or allowed. Among these men there is no discrimination, no prejudices, no hatred. Theirs is the highest and purest democracy.

Any man among the living who fails to understand that will thereby betray those who lie here dead. Whoever of us lifts up his hand in hate against a brother or thinks himself superior to those who happen to be in the minority makes of this ceremony and the bloody sacrifice it commemorates an empty, hollow mockery. To this, then, as our solemn, sacred duty, do we the living now dedicate ourselves to the rights of Protestants, Catholics, and Jews, of white men and Negroes alike, to enjoy the democracy for which all of them have paid the price.

When the last shot has been fired, there will be those whose eyes are turned backward, not forward, who will be satisfied with wide extremes of poverty and wealth in which the seeds of another war can breed. We promise you, our departed comrades, this too we will not permit. This war has been fought by the common man. Its fruits of peace must be enjoyed by the common man. We promise, by all that is sacred and holy, your sons, the sons of miners and millers, the sons of farmers and workers, the right to a living that is decent and secure.

When the final cross has been placed in the last cemetery, once again there will be those to whom profit will be more important than peace. To those who sleep here silent, we give our promise: We will not listen. We will not forget that some of you paid the ultimate price for men who profit at your expense. We will remember you as you looked when we placed you reverently, lovingly, in the ground.

Thus do we memorialize those who, having ceased living with us, now live within us again. Thus do we consecrate ourselves to the living to carry on the struggle they began. Too much blood has gone into this soil for us to let it lie barren. Too much pain and heartache have fertilized the earth on which we stand. We here solemnly swear, this shall not be in vain. Out of this, and from the suffering and sorrow of those who mourn this, will come, we promise, the birth of a new freedom for the sons of men everywhere.

From Congressional Record Volume 153, Number 85 (Wednesday, May 23, 2007) [House][Page H5688].

LAST RETREATS

A small sampling of the all too numerous truly permanent changes of station from our ranks over the years that are listed in our Legion of Valor General Orders.

Richard "Dick" Durkee, Distinguished Service Cross (DSC) died on September 14, 2004 in Berwyn Heights, Maryland. He is remembered as a hero of the "Lost Battalion" in the Battle of the Bulge. On January 4, 1945, he led 30 soldiers in a bayonet charge and, in less than 30 minutes of hand-to-hand fighting, 60 German soldiers lay dead. Six years later, on March 23, 1951, he led his soldiers in an attack near Uijongbu, Korea. When his ammunition was gone, he single-handedly assaulted an enemy position and killed the soldier with his bayonet. Unable to remove the bayonet, he went unarmed to another enemy position and seized an enemy soldier's rifle by the bayonet, wresting it from his hands and clubbed him to death. Although Dick's hand was seriously lacerated, he continued to lead the assault until the objective was secured.

David H. Hackworth, DSC with Oak Leaf Cluster (OLC) for a second award, died on May 5, 2005. Dave received his first DSC for action on February 7, 1966. He successfully organized and led his unit in saving a rifle company which had been pinned down for four hours. After personally conducting a reconnaissance of the battle area while under intense hostile machine-gun fire he then calmly maneuvered his unit to cut down the entrenched and determined Viet Cong. On March 23–25, 1969, while serving as battalion commander, Dave earned his second DSC. After one of his companies came under attack, he landed his helicopter to provide ammunition and to evacuate casualties. Remaining on the ground, he led a patrol in pursuit of the enemy and continued in this mode until the enemy was soundly defeated and their weapons and supplies confiscated.

This reflection about the controversial Colonel Hackworth is not from our Last Retreats. It is from retired Army Lieutenant Colonel Steven M. Yedinak, who served with him in Vietnam. Colonel Yedinak authored *Hard to Forget: An American with the Mobile Guerrilla Force in Vietnam* (1998).

> David Haskell Hackworth … *Hack* … *led from the front.* His entire career in the United States Army was devoted to proving that America was the best.
>
> He was an *unbridled warrior* who knew no bounds. A *renegade*, if you will, who would have been better placed during the Revolutionary War instead of among those he often called *Perfumed Princes. Hack's* ideas about war began with a concrete understanding that, among we humans called to service, *all soldiers were equal.* Rank, thought *Hack*, was a confusing portrayal of a soldier's worth. In *Hack's* Army, there would have been *no insignia* to signal the enemy when captured. His simple model reflected a *knowing and caring leader* who knew his men well enough to fight and die among them if necessary. His eight *Purple Hearts* for wounds suffered in battle were both a testament to his bravery and his leadership style. He routinely placed himself with the front elements of an engaged struggle. And, *he took the fight to the enemy.*
>
> *Hack* was also an unusual human being who took the time … *and the chance …* to self-identify and better know his position among his troops. Pentagon rules to the contrary, *Hack* knew no distinction either between or among those he was assigned to lead. He often divulged that the Army's rules *against fraternization* were a bunch of crap. Three clubs … one for lower-ranking enlisted men, one for seasoned non-commissioned officers and, of course, one for officers were all *on-limit for all soldiers. Hack* knew instinctively that there was gold to be mined among even the less experienced soldier and that, eventually, *it would pay off in spades in the field of lost shoes.* And how best to cultivate the mining process than to intermingle on a regular basis … *yes, in the club when drinking …* with his men.
>
> *Hack* always did his homework. I first met *Hack* in 1971 Cao Lanh, South Vietnam in the water-based *Delta* region. On arrival in Saigon and sitting with 200 other soldiers for an in-country briefing, I was approached by a Sergeant Major who said, Captain Yedinak, you won't have to sit through the briefing…. Colonel David Hackworth has personally asked for you, sir. His chopper is waiting on the pad for a quick ride to *Team-50*. On arrival, there was a jeep waiting for a short trip to the front gate of the compound. *Hack* in person at the

front gate said, Captain Yedinak, *welcome to Team-50 … I'm Dave Hackworth*. At that very moment, a Specialist Four took a polaroid picture which immediately printed out. *Hack* handed me the photo and said, *Yed*, mail this to Donna this afternoon and let her know you have safely arrived. That was *Hack*.

Hack's Discipline Model was both compassionate and balanced. Understanding the repercussions of combat stress on the human psychic, it was *Three Strikes and You're out!* Except for more egregious offenses, the first two transgressions were on *Hack* himself … the third was squarely on the perpetrator.

Any comparison of combat records … enlisted to officer in Korea and five years in Vietnam … would place *Hack* near the top. He was put in for the *Medal of Honor … our Nation's highest award for bravery three times, according to an article on his website and received* two *Distinguished Service Crosses* (second highest award), ten *Silver Stars* (third highest award) and eight Bronze Stars (fourth highest). *Hack* sits among our country's most highly decorated combat veterans. Yet, he would forfeit all by *taking a chance* … and *taking a stance* … openly speaking out in public about what he viewed as our *misguided effort in Vietnam* … using tanks in the jungle, bombing halts, large centralized operations versus clandestine guerrilla tactics and, of course, trying to win the hearts and minds of the people whose cultural instincts suggested otherwise. In *Hack's* mind … *no war-to-win if we just continued to kick the can down the road!*

Bottom line: You either *loved Hack* for who he was and that for which he firmly stood … or you *hated Hack* for finding fault with and openly disclosing his opinions regarding the system. Of course, I was among the thousands who loved *Hack* and was privileged to have served as his G-3 (Operations) and among his family's Honor Detail in Arlington 2005. *Thanks, Hack!*

James F. Hollingsworth, DSC (2 OLC) died in San Antonio, Texas on March 3, 2010. His first valorous action took place on April 11, 1945 when he led a task force for fourteen hours in a dash of 71 miles from Douren to the Elbe River at Schopebeck. On three occasions he went into towns and effected a complete German surrender. At the Elbe he was twice wounded and barely able to walk but continued to fight until the Germans blew the bridge. The second action was on November 5 and 8, 1966 when his masterful and unerring battle strategy accounted for one of the most significant victories in the Vietnam conflict. The third action took place on March 20, 1967 when Bau Bang, Vietnam came under intense attack a few hours after bUMmidnight. He immediately flew to the besieged unit and continued to expose himself while he located the Viet Cong and guided the support aircraft and adjusted artillery fire into the charging enemy forces which resulted in victory.

Harry W. O. Kinnard, DSC, died on January 5, 2009 in Arlington, Virginia. He parachuted into Normandy in the first hours on D-Day and received the DSC for heroism during Operation *Market-Garden*, the airborne attack in the German-occupied Netherlands. He was best remembered for his action on December 22, 1944 at Bastogne when the 101st Division was outnumbered and surrounded by German troops. Two German officers approached the American lines and demanded the American commander surrender within two hours or face annihilation. The message was received by Brig. General McAuliffe, acting division commander, who said: "Us surrender? Aw, nuts." According to official Army sources, General McAuliffe then asked for input from his staff about what to say and Kinnard spoke up saying the general's first remark would be hard to beat. When asked to clarify Kinnard stated: "Sir, you said Nuts" and that answer was sent back to the Germans. The German officers, not understanding the phrase, were told that it meant "go to hell."

Robert "Bob" C. Knight, DSC died on August 28, 2013 while living in West Melbourne, Florida. On January 31, 1968, during the Lunar New Year enemy surprise night assault on the airfield and city of Soc Trang, he dashed through a hail of impacting rounds to reach his helicopter as others were taking cover. He then risked his life and braved withering enemy fire over the next 28 hours to knock out hostile weapons positions while inflicting heavy casualties on the Viet Cong guerrillas. His fearless efforts were critical in repelling the massive enemy offensive.

Victor H. Krulak, Navy Cross, died on December 29, 2008 in La Jolla, California. On October 28, 1943 he landed his Marine battalion on Choiseul Island in the Solomon chain to divert hostile attention from the main attack force en route to Bougainville. Although wounded on October 30, he refused to relinquish command and succeeded in the objective to destroy hundreds of tons of Japanese supplies and burning camps and landing barges. The operation was completed on November 3. The Navy sent patrol boats to evacuate wounded Marines.

Krulak befriended one of the young commanders, John F. Kennedy. Decades later the two shared a drink of whiskey in the Oval Office after Kennedy was elected president.

Jose M. Lopez, Medal of Honor (MOH), died on May 16, 2005 in San Antonio, Texas at the age of 94. He received his award for his heroic action while manning a machine gun on December 17, 1944 near Krinkelt, Belgium. Jose's gallantry and intrepidity, on four seemingly suicidal missions, earned him the Medal of Honor. He was credited with killing over 100 German soldiers, was almost solely responsible for allowing his company to avoid being enveloped, to withdraw successfully and to give other forces coming up in support, time to build a line which repelled the enemy drive.

John S. McKim, DSC died on July 16, 2004 in Sunland, California. On February 14, 1951, John's platoon was attacked by over 75 enemy soldiers in the vicinity of Kyongan-ni, Korea. When the 57mm recoilless rifle section was overrun, John rushed forward under intense enemy automatic-weapons and mortar fire and set up a 60mm mortar in an exposed V position directly on the skyline and fired at the enemy. When his ammunition was exhausted, he stood completely exposed to the enemy and began hurling grenades. Through his efforts, the enemy force was repelled with heavy casualties and the vital positions were held. He worked directly for Walt Disney and was responsible for much of the original artwork seen at Disneyland in California.

Everett P. Pope, MOH, died on July 16, 2009. During combat on September 19–20, 1944 on Peleliu Island, he, after being subjected to point-blank cannon fire which caused heavy casualties, rallied his men and gallantly led them to the summit in the face of enemy machine-gun, mortar and sniper fire. Then, with only 12 men and insufficient water and ammunition, he held the summit through the night while fiercely beating back the enemy with hand-to-hand combat as the supply of ammunition dwindled.

Edwin Price Ramsey, DSC, after joining the Army in 1941, volunteered to serve with the 26th Cavalry of the Philippine Scouts. After Japan invaded the Philippines in January 1942, he led the last mounted Army Horse Cavalry charge on Bataan which earned him a Silver Star. After the charge he escaped to mobilize and later lead as many as 40,000 guerilla fighters in central Luzon. In June 1945 General Douglas MacArthur awarded him the Distinguished Service Cross. In 1991 Ramsey co-authored *Lieutenant Ramsey's War*. He died on March 7, 2013 and is buried at Arlington National Cemetery. His wife, Dr. Raquel Ramsey, joined the Legion of Valor as an Associate Life Member.

During Veterans Day weekend, 2016, *Never Surrender: The Ed Ramsey Story*, a documentary produced by Vanilla Fire Productions, with Dr. Ramsey as co-executive producer, had its World Premiere screening at the Simon Wiesenthal Center. Los Angeles, CA. and will be shown in other locations. It's about patriotism and the two countries he loved–the U.S. and the Philippines. It shows that he was more than just a war hero and guerilla leader. Ramsey distinguished himself as a polo player, business executive, author, friend and family man.

EPILOGUE

Lieutenant Colonel Richard D. Wandke, US Army

Several years have passed since the Vietnam War has ended, but the scars for many will always remain. There is one thing in war that is certain. It doesn't make a difference whether an individual is the bravest or the meekest on the battlefield. When the shells start exploding and the bullets start flying, the soldier will turn to God for assistance in the conflict. Perhaps General George Patton said it best in this prayer:

> God of our Father, who by land and sea has ever led us to victory, please continue your inspiring guidance in this, the greatest of our conflicts. Strengthen my soul so that the weakening instincts of self-preservation, which beset all in battle, shall not blind me in my duty to my own manhood, to the glory of my calling, and to my responsibilities to my fellow soldiers. Grant to our armed forces that disciplined valor and mutual confidence that mean success in war.
>
> Let me not mourn for the men who have died fighting, but rather let me be glad that such heroes have lived. If it be my lot to die, let me do so with courage and honor and in a manner that will bring the greatest harm to the enemy, and please, oh, Lord, protect and guard those I shall leave behind. Grant us the victory, Lord.

And then one day we are retired. Our friends are retired and getting grey ... we move slower and we see the young folks behind us and wonder if they notice that we have aged.... Some of our friends are in better shape and some not so good ... and we see the great change. Not like the ones that we remember when we were young and vibrant.

But, at least we know, that though the winter has come, and we are not sure how long it will last … this we know, that when it's over on this earth…. God has a place reserved for us and a new adventure will begin! Yes, we have regrets. There are things we wish we had done. Perhaps some things we had not done or done better. Yet, as we reflect on the good things and the friends and family that are special, we know we have had a good life.

Excerpted from the novel, Vietnam Remembered *by Lieutenant Colonel Richard D. Wandke, US Army.*

APPENDICES

APPENDIX 1

A Brief History of the Legion Of Valor

"For conspicuous gallantry and intrepidity at risk of life, above and beyond the call of duty...." With words similar to these and a bit of ribbon and metal, the nation honors those in its armed forces who, engaged with the enemy, forgot personal danger and accomplished their mission.

The awarding of medals to our national heroes dates back to the Revolutionary War when George Washington recommended decorations be given to John Paulding, David Williams and Jacob Van Wert, captors of the British spy Major Andre. In 1782 in Newburg, N.Y., George Washington had created the Purple Heart as a decoration for "singular meritorious action." Three men received the award in 1783. Congress authorized the first Medal of Honor in 1861.

In World War I, the President was authorized to present the Distinguished Service Cross to any person "who distinguished himself by extraordinary heroism in connection with military operations against an armed enemy." In 1919, a similar decoration was conceived for the Navy, known as the Navy Cross. The Air Force Cross was authorized by Congress in 1960.

The wearing of one of the above medals has grown in prestige since many of the recipients are awarded the medal posthumously. As the time of writing, only around 412 members of the Legion of Valor of the United States of America, Inc. are still alive.

The Legion of Valor was organized on April 23, 1890, in Washington D.C. by a group of Civil War and Indian Campaign veterans who had been awarded the Congressional Medal of Honor. In 1918, recipients of the Distinguished Service Cross were declared eligible for membership. In 1933, Navy Cross recipients were admitted to the organization, and Air Force Cross recipients in 1962.

The Legion has met in an annual convention ever since 1890, moving between venues each year. We include in the program at all reunions the hushed moment when the members stand uncovered in respectful silence to commemorate the deeds of those members who passed away during the preceding year.

The Legion of Valor is perhaps the most unique organization in the United States of America. Membership is not achieved by birth, social position, wealth, or academic achievement. Eligibility is confined to recipients of our nation's two highest decorations for valor. The official presentation of these medals to individuals of the United States Armed Forces determines who its members shall be.

Additional information may be obtained by visiting legionofvalor. com. or by contacting the National Adjutant: Donald L. Marx, Air Force Cross, 3927 Rust Place, Fairfax, VA 22030.

APPENDIX 2

BOOKS AND SITES BY OR ABOUT MEMBERS AND FRIENDS OF THE LEGION OF VALOR

John C. "Doc" Bahnsen, DSC with Wess Roberts, *American Warrior: A Combat Memoir of Vietnam* (Citadel, 2007)

Abe Baum, Richard Baron and Richard Goldhurst, *Raid!: The Untold Story of Patton's Secret Mission* (G. P. Putnam's, 1981)

Frederick C. Blesse, DSC, *"Check Six": A Fighter Pilot Looks Back* (Champlin Fighter Museum Press, 1988)

Frederic L. Borch, *Judge Advocates in Combat: Army Lawyers in Military Operations from Vietnam to Haiti* (Office of the Judge Advocate General and Center of Military History, U.S. Army, 2001)

Frederic L. Borch, *The Silver Star: A History of America's Third Highest Award for Valor* (Borch and Westlake Pub., 2001)

Frederic L. Borch, *Judge Advocates in Vietnam, a History of Army Lawyers in Southeast Asia from 1959 to 1975* (University Press of the Pacific, 2004)

Frederic L. Borch and Daniel Martinez, *Kimmel, Short and Pearl Harbor: The Final Report Revealed* (Naval and Institute Press, 2005)

Frederic L. Borch, *For Military Merit: Recipients of the Purple Heart* (Naval Institute Press, 2010)

Frederic L. Borch, Medals for Soldiers and Airmen: Awards and Decorations of the United States Army and Air Force (McFarland and Company, 2013)

Frederic L. Borch, *Targeting After Operation Allied Force: Has the Law Changed for CINCs and Their Planners?* (Naval War College, 2001)

Frederic L. Borch, *The Bronze Star Medal* (Orders and Medals Society of America Monograph) (OMSA Book Service, 1994)

Patrick Henry Brady, MOH, with Meghan Brady Smith, *Dead Men Flying: Victory in Viet Nam: The Legend of Dust Off: America's Battlefield Angels* (WND Books, 2012)

Jack Broughton, AFC, *Thud Ridge* (J. B. Lippincott Co., 1969)

Jack Broughton, AFC, *Going Downtown: The War Against Hanoi and Washington* (Pacifica Military History, 1988)

Jack Broughton, AFC, *Rupert Red Two: A Fighter Pilot's Life from Thunderbolts to Thunderchiefs* (Zenith Press, 2007)

David Christian, DSC and William Hoffer, *Victor Six: The Saga of America's Youngest, Most Decorated Officer in Vietnam* (McGraw-Hill, 1990)

George E. Day. MOH, AFC, *Return With Honor* (Champlin Museum Press, 1989)

William E. Davis, NC, *Sinking the Rising Sun: Dog Fighting & Dive Bombing in World War II* (Zenith Press, 2007)

Dieter Dengler, NC, *Escape From Laos* (Presidio Press, 1996)

Gil Dorland, DSC, *Legacy of Discord: Voices of the Vietnam War Era* (Potomac Books, 2002)

John J. Duffy, DSC, http://epoetryworld.com/

John J. Duffy, DSC, *The Battle for Charlie* (CreateSpace IPP, 2014)

John J. Duffy, DSC, *Bush Chronicles* (BookSurge, 2005)

John J. Duffy, DSC, *Chromosome 23* (CreateSpace IPP, 2013)

John J. Duffy, DSC, *Peaceman* (1976)

John J. Duffy, DSC, *Sageman* (BookSurge, 2005)

John J. Duffy, DSC, *Warman* (1975)

Joe Foss, MOH, with Donna Wild Foss, *A Proud American—The Autobiography of Joe Foss* (Pocket Books, 1992)

Joseph L. Galloway and Lt. Gen. Harold G. Moore, *We Were Soldiers Once...And Young: Ia Drang—The Battle That Changed the War in Vietnam* (Random House, 1992)

Joseph L. Galloway and Lt. Gen. Harold G. Moore, *We Are Soldiers Still: A Journey Back to the Battlefields of Vietnam* (Harper Collins, 2008)

Joseph L. Galloway as part of U.S. News and World Report, *Triumph Without Victory: A History of the Persian Gulf War* (Times Books, 1992)

John E. Gray, DSC, *Called To Honor: Memoirs of a Three-War Veteran—World War II, Korea, Vietnam* (R. Brent & Co, 2006)

John Grider Miller, *The Bridge at Dong Ha* (Naval Institute Press, 1996)

David H. Hackworth, DSC w OLC and Julie Sherman, *About Face: The Odyssey of an American Warrior* (Simon & Schuster, 1989)

David H. Hackworth, DSC w OLC and Eillhys England, *Steel My Soldiers' Hearts: The In-Country Transformation of U.S. Army, 4th Battalion, 39th Infantry, Vietnam* (Rugged Land, 2002)

David H. Hackworth, DSC w OLC with Tom Mathews, *Hazardous Duty: America's Most Decorated Living Soldier Reports from the Front and Tells it the Way it is* (William Morrow, 1996)

David H. Hackworth, DSC w OLC, *Price of Honor* (Berkley, 2001)

David H. Hackworth, DSC w OLC and Julie Sherman, *Brave Men: The Blood and Guts Combat Chronicle of One of America's Most Decorated Soldiers* (Simon & Schuster, 1993)

David H. Hackworth, DSC w OLC, and General S. L. A. "Slam" Marshall, *The Vietnam Primer* (U.S. Government Printing Office, 1967)

Albin F. Irzyk, DSC, *A Warrior's Quilt of Personal Military History* (Pentland Press, 2011)

Karl Marlantes, NC, *Matterhorn: A Novel of the Vietnam War* (Atlantic, 2010)

Karl Marlantes, NC, *What It Is Like To Go To War* (Atlantic, 2011)

Mike McDermott, DSC, *True Faith and Allegiance: An American Paratrooper and the 1972 Battle for An Loc* (University Alabama Press, 2012)

James Megellas, DSC, *All The Way To Berlin: A Paratrooper at War in Europe* (Presidio Press, 2003)

Jim Morehead, DSC, In My Sights: The Memoir of a P-40 Ace (Presidio Press, 1997)

William J. Mullen, III, DSC Romie L. Brownlee, *Changing an Army, An Oral History of General William E. DePuy, USA Retired* (Center of Military History, 1988)

Edwin Ramsey, DSC, *Lieutenant Ramsey's War: From Horse Soldier to Guerrilla Commander* (Potomac Books, 1996)

Willaim C. Raposa, NC w Gold Star, *An Aviator's Journey* (privately published)

Robert Tonsetic, DSC, *Warriors: An Infantryman's Memoir of Vietnam* (Presidio, 2004)

Robert L. Tonsetic, DSC, *Forsaken Warriors: The Story of an American Advisor who Fought with the South Vietnamese Rangers and Airborne* (Casemate, 2009)

Robert L. Tonsetic, DSC, *Days of Valor: An Inside Account of the Bloodiest Six Months of the Vietnam War* (Casemate, 2007)

Robert L. Tonsetic, DSC, *1781: The Decisive Year of the Revolutionary War* (Casemate, 2011)

Robert L. Tonsetic, DSC, *Special Operations in the American Revolution* (Casemate, 2013)

Jeremiah Workman, NC, *Shadow of the Sword: A Marine's Journey of War, Heroism, and Redemption* (Ballantine Books, 2009)

James Webb, NC, *Fields of Fire* (Prentice Hall, 1978)

James Webb, NC, *A Sense of Honor* (Harper Collins, 1983)

James Webb, NC, *A Country Such as This* (Doubleday, 1983)

James Webb, NC, *Something to Die For* (William Morrow & Co, 1991)

James Webb, NC, *The Emperor's General* (Broadway Books, 1998)

James Webb, NC, *Lost Soldiers* (Bantam, 2001)

James Webb, NC, *I Heard My Country Calling: A Memoir* (Simon & Schuster, 2014)

C. Douglas Sterner, Honorary, http://www.homeofheroes.com/

C. Douglas Sterner with Pamela Sterner, *Restoring Valor—One Couple's Mission to Expose Fraudulent War Heroes and Protect America's Military Award System* (Skyhorse, 2014)

C. Douglas Sterner, *Go For Broke: The Nisei Warriors of World War II Who Conquered Germany, Japan, and American Bigotry* (American Legacy Press, 2007)

C. Douglas Sterner with Pamela Sterner, *The Defining Generation: Stories of a generation that challenged the traditions of the past and in its search for meaning and purpose, redefined the world we live in today* (Home of Heroes Publishing, 2016)

C. Douglas Sterner, *Shinmiyangyo: The OTHER Korean War* (Amazon, 2015)

C. Douglas Sterner, *God is Good—Jaime's Story: A True Story of Friendship and Faith* (CreateSpace, 2015)

C. Douglas Sterner, *Wings of Valor Volume I—Army Air Medals of Honor WWI* (CreateSpace, 2015)

C. Douglas Sterner, *Wings of Valor Volume II—Army Air Medals of Honor WWII Pacific* (CreateSpace, 2015)

C. Douglas Sterner, *Wings of Valor Volume III—Army Air Medals of Honor WWII Europe* (CreateSpace, 2015)

C. Douglas Sterner, *United States Air Force Heroes in the War on Terrorism* (CreateSpace, 2015)

C. Douglas Sterner, *United States Marine Corps Heroes in the War on Terrorism & Attached Navy Corpsmen* (CreateSpace, 2015)

C. Douglas Sterner, *United States Army Heroes in the War on Terrorism— Operation Iraqi Freedom* (CreateSpace, 2016)

C. Douglas Sterner, *United States Army Heroes in the War on Terrorism— Operation Enduring Freedom* (CreateSpace, 2015)

C. Douglas Sterner, *United States Army Heroes Volume I—Medal of Honor* (CreateSpace, 2015)

C. Douglas Sterner, *United States Army Heroes Volume II—DSC 1862– WWI (A–G)* (CreateSpace, 2015)

C. Douglas Sterner, *United States Army Heroes Volume III—DSC WWI (H–R)* (CreateSpace, 2015)

C. Douglas Sterner, *United States Army Heroes Volume IV—DSC WWI (S–Z)* (CreateSpace, 2015)

C. Douglas Sterner, *United States Army Heroes Volume IX—DSC Korea* (CreateSpace, 2015)

C. Douglas Sterner, *United States Army Heroes Volume X—DSC Vietnam War to Present* (CreateSpace, 2015)

C. Douglas Sterner, *United States Army Heroes Volume XI—DSM (1918– 1941)* (CreateSpace, 2015)

C. Douglas Sterner, *United States Army Heroes Volume XII—DSM WWII* (CreateSpace, 2015)

C. Douglas Sterner, *United States Army Heroes Volume XIII—DSM (1946–Present)* (CreateSpace, 2015)

C. Douglas Sterner, *United States Navy Heroes Volume I—Medal of Honor and DSMs* (CreateSpace, 2015)

C. Douglas Sterner, *United States Navy Heroes Volume II—Navy Cross (1915–WWII)* (CreateSpace, 2015)

C. Douglas Sterner, *United States Navy Heroes Volume III—Navy Cross WWII (A–L)* (CreateSpace, 2015)

C. Douglas Sterner, *United States Navy Heroes Volume IV—Navy Cross WWII (M–Z)* (CreateSpace, 2015)

C. Douglas Sterner, *United States Navy Heroes Volume V—Navy Cross (Korea–Present)* (CreateSpace, 2015)

C. Douglas Sterner, *United States Marine Corps Heroes Volume I—Medal of Honor, Brevet Medals and DSMs* (CreateSpace, 2015)

C. Douglas Sterner, *United States Marine Corps Heroes Volume II—Navy Cross (1915–WWII)* (CreateSpace, 2015)

C. Douglas Sterner, *United States Marine Corps Heroes Volume III—Navy Cross (WWII–Present)* (CreateSpace, 2015)

C. Douglas Sterner, *United States Marine Corps Heroes Volume IV—Silver Star (WWI)* (CreateSpace, 2015)

C. Douglas Sterner, *United States Marine Corps Heroes Volume V—Silver Star WWII (A–K)* (CreateSpace, 2015)

C. Douglas Sterner, *United States Marine Corps Heroes Volume VI—Silver Star WWII (L–Z)* (CreateSpace, 2015)

C. Douglas Sterner, *United States Marine Corps Heroes Volume VII—Silver Star (Korea)* (CreateSpace, 2015)

C. Douglas Sterner, *United States Marine Corps Heroes Volume VIII—Silver Star Vietnam (A–L)* (CreateSpace, 2015)

C. Douglas Sterner, *United States Marine Corps Heroes Volume IX—Silver Star Vietnam (M–Z) to Present* (CreateSpace, 2015)

C. Douglas Sterner, *United States Air Force Heroes—Medal of Honor, DSC, Air Force Cross & DSMs* (CreateSpace, 2015)

C. Douglas Sterner, *United States Coast Guard Heroes—Awards above the Bronze Star* (CreateSpace, 2015)

APPENDIX 3

Members Past and Present and Volunteers[1]

Key:

MOH	Medal of Honor
DSC	Distinguished Service Cross
NC	Navy Cross
AFC	Air Force Cross
A	Army
N	Navy
M	Marines
AF	Air Force
CG	Coast Guard
RV	Republic of Vietnam
RA	Royal Australian
N/A	Not Available

Civil War 1861–1865

Custer, Thomas Ward	MOH - A	Union A
Dickey, William	MOH - A	A
Howard, Oliver O.	MOH - A	Union A
Karpeles, Leopald	MOH - A	Union A
Miles, Nelson A.	MOH - A	Union A
O'Beirne, James R.	MOH - A	Union A
Peck, Theodore S.	MOH - A	Union A
Platt, George C.	MOH - A	Union A
Porter, Horace	MOH - A	A
Reddick, William H. H.	MOH - A	A
Sickles, Daniel E.	MOH - A	Union A
Thorne, Walter	MOH - A	Union A
Urell, M Emmet	MOH - A	Union A

Veale, Moses	MOH - A	Union A
Whitman, Frank M.	MOH - A	Union A

Interim 1866–1870

Rarreick, John	MOH - A	A

Interim 1871–1898

Godfrey, Edward S.	MOH - A	A
Knight, Joseph F.	MOH - A	A
Taylor, Richard H.	MOH - N	N

Indian War Campaign 1872

Cody, William Frederick	MOH - A	A

Spanish–American War 1898

Davis, John	MOH - N	N
Roosevelt, Theodore T.	MOH - A	A
Russell, Henry P.	MOH - N	N

China Relief Expedition (Boxer Rebellion) 1898–1901

Dahlgren, John Olof	MOH - N	M
Horton, William Charlie	MOH - N	M
McCloy, John	MOH - N	N
Titus, Calvin Pearl	MOH - A	A

Note

1 Multiple awards are listed separately.

Philippine Insurrection 1899–1902

Anders, Frank L.	MOH - A	A
Bassett, Daniel S	DSC	A
Coston, Tony	DSC	A
High, Frank C.	MOH - A	A
Kilbourne, Charles E.	MOH - A	A

Interim 1901–1911

Corahorgi, Demetri	MOH - N	N
Kahn, Joseph F.	DSC	A
Schroeder, Henry F.	MOH - A	A
Staples, Frank	DSC	A

Mexican Campaign (Vera Cruz) 1914

Bradley, George	MOH - N	N	N
Fryer, Eli Thompson	MOH - N	M	M
McCloy, John	MOH - N	N	N
McNair, Frederick Vallette Jr.	NC	N	N
McNair, Frederick Vallette Jr.	MOH - N	N	N
Nickerson, Henry Nehemiah	MOH - N	N	N
Zuiderveld, William	MOH - N	N	N

World War I 1914–1918

Abbott, Robert L.	DSC	A
Abbott, William Y. Sr	DSC	A
Abernathy, Charles V.	DSC	A
Adams, Ashley D.	NC	N
Aghababian, Y. A.	DSC	A
Aldridge, Joseph S.	DSC	A
Allen, Fred	DSC	A
Allen, Joseph E.	DSC	A
Alt, Walter F.	DSC	A
Ambercrombie, Hugh	DSC	A
Ambrunn, William C.	DSC	A
Anderson, Charles R.	DSC	A
Andrews, M Morris	DSC	A
Ascher, Oscar	DSC	A
Ash, Harold J.	DSC	A
Ashburn, Ike	DSC	A
Atkinson, Joseph T.	DSC	A
Ayotte, Edward	DSC	A
Bailey, George W	DSC	A
Bain, Edgar H.	DSC	A
Bainbridge, R. J.	DSC	A
Bald, Edward N.	NC	A
Bald, Edward N.	DSC	M
Baldridge, Troy J.	DSC	A
Ball, Ernest B.	DSC	A
Banks, Harley E.	DSC	A
Bann, Edward J.	DSC	A
Barkley, John L.	MOH - A	A
Barnes, Lester J.	DSC	A

Barrett, Herbert W.	DSC	A
Bartels, Herman	DSC	A
Barton, Harry D.	DSC	A
Bates, Charles Edward H.	DSC	A
Benjamin, Henry R.	NC	N
Bergasse, H. J.	DSC	A
Bernstein, Dudley	NC	N
Bevan, Stanley	DSC	A
Bice, Fred G.	DSC	A
Bicknell, Leroy E.	DSC	A
Binkley, David V.	DSC	A
Bird, Felix	DSC	A
Blood, Robert O.	DSC	A
Boas, Ross H.	DSC	A
Bolen, Jacob	DSC	A
Bonney, T. D.	DSC	A
Boone, Joel Thompson	MOH - N	N
Boone, Joel Thompson	DSC	N
Booth, James O.	DSC	A
Bordwick, M. A.	DSC	A
Bos, Lambert B.	NC	M
Bos, Lambert B.	DSC	M
Boughen, Joseph E.	DSC	A
Bougie, James E.	DSC	A
Bradley, Willis Winter	MOH - N	N
Breen, Vincent C.	DSC	A
Brennan, Matthew J. Sr	DSC	A
Brewer, Louis Morton	DSC	A
Brickley, David J.	DSC	A
Bridgers, Alvin O.	DSC	A
Brigham, George	DSC	A
Bright, Horace O.	DSC	A
Britt, Charles	DSC	A
Brittain, William S.	DSC	A
Brocopp, Herman A.	DSC	A
Bronson, Deming	MOH - A	A
Brown, Fletcher W.	NC	CG
Brown, Samuel A. Jr.	DSC	A
Bunge, Robert C.	DSC	A
Bunkley, Joel W.	NC	N
Burdick, Howard	DSC	A
Burns, Edward N.	DSC	A
Bush, Herman L.	DSC	A
Butler, Smedley D.	MOH - N	M
Cain, Robert S.	DSC	A
Campanaro, Fred F.	NC	N
Campbell, Alexander	DSC	A
Campbell, Willis Moser Sr	DSC	A
Capen, Ralph A.	DSC	A
Cappadocio, Louis	DSC	A
Carlson, Charles G.	DSC	A
Carlson, Emil A.	DSC	A
Carter, Franklin	DSC	A
Carter, Paul D.	DSC	A
Carver, Paul Munroe	DSC	A

Casaga, Samuel E.	DSC	A		Dunn, Don	DSC	A
Cassidy, Henry K.	DSC	A		Dunnington, Walter G.	DSC	A
Cattus, John C.	DSC	A		Durham, James E.	DSC	A
Cavanaugh, Thomas J.	DSC	A		During, Fred	DSC	A
Cayer, A. J.	DSC	A		Earle, George H.	NC	N
Cheney, Henry A.	DSC	A		Eastman, Ray	NC	N
Child, Howard J.	NC	M		Eberlin, Ralph	DSC	A
Child, Howard J.	DSC	M		Edell, Chris L.	DSC	A
Chiles, Walter K.	DSC	A		Edgar, Fred W.	DSC	A
Christiansen, Henry E.	DSC	A		Edwards, Hugh F.	DSC	A
Clauson, Oscar	DSC	A		Eichelsdoerfer, R. M.	DSC	A
Cleverly, Irving N.	DSC	A		Eichorn, Victor L.	DSC	A
Clinton, Walter E.	DSC	A		Eisenhart, E. S.	NC	N
Coakley, John L.	DSC	A		Ellison, Walter	NC	N
Cogswell, Theodore	DSC	A		Ervin, Sam J. Jr.	DSC	A
Cohee, Ora J.	DSC	A		Ethier, Ralph	DSC	A
Cole, Charles E.	DSC	A		Evans, Harry C.	DSC	A
Colley, Dwight T.	DSC	A		Evans, John E.	DSC	A
Collins, Walter T.	DSC	M		Evans, William C.	DSC	A
Colton, James S.	DSC	A		Evens, Cornelius	NC	N
Cooper, Edwin H.	DSC	A		Eversole, Henry Clay	DSC	A
Cornell, Thomas L.	DSC	A		Faison, James K.	DSC	A
Cox, Aulbert D.	DSC	A		Fanning, Harry I.	DSC	A
Crandall, Dewitt H.	DSC	A		Farris, Oscar L.	DSC	A
Crane, John	DSC	A		Fenwick, Edward G.	DSC	A
Crawford, H. E.	DSC	A		Ferentchak, Martin	DSC	A
Cronkhite, Leroy G.	DSC	A		Ferguson, John E.	DSC	A
Cullen, William J.	DSC	A		Ferrell, William M.	DSC	A
Curtin, David F.	DSC	A		Figgins, Charles R.	DSC	A
Cushing, Frederick R.	DSC	A		Finn, John J.	DSC	A
D'Olive, Charles R.	DSC	A		Finucane, Peter	DSC	A
Darling, Homer C.	DSC	A		Fisher, Russell S.	DSC	A
Davidson, L. Clifford	DSC	A		Fitzgerald, R. J.	DSC	A
Dawson, Leo H.	DSC	A		Fleet, George T.	DSC	A
Day, Louis T.	DSC	A		Fleitz, Morris F.	DSC	A
De Rogatis, Albert	DSC	A		Fleming, Thomas W.	DSC	A
De Rosselli, Peter	DSC	A		Flint, John H.	DSC	A
DeLoiselle, H. C.	DSC	A		Floyd, William M.	DSC	A
DeWalt, Clyde H.	DSC	A		Fogg, Preston D.	DSC	A
Deckert, Robert	DSC	A		Fogo, E. T.	DSC	A
Dettre, Rex H.	DSC	A		Foley, Thomas F.	DSC	A
Dilliard, John A.	DSC	A		Fore, James E.	DSC	A
Dillon, John T.	DSC	A		Fore, Witt S.	DSC	A
Dion, Arthur J.	DSC	A		Formica, Pietro E.	DSC	A
Dolce, Louis	DSC	A		Forrest, Arthur J.	MOH - A	A
Dombrowski, Leon A.	DSC	A		Fossett, Edward Joseph	DSC	A
Donley, Charles Frederick	NC	N		Fox, Harry Victor	NC	N
Donovan, William J.	MOH - A	A		Frary, Frank M.	DSC	A
Donovan, William J.	DSC	A		Freehoff, William F.	DSC	A
Douglass, Joseph U.	DSC	A		Friel, J. Whiting	DSC	A
Downer, J. W.	DSC	A		Fritz, Albert	DSC	A
Doyle, John J.	DSC	A		Frundt, Oscar C.	DSC	A
DuBoise, Victor A.	DSC	A		Furlong, Harold A.	MOH - A	A
Duffy, Francis A.	DSC	A		Gahring, William R.	DSC	A
Duly, J.	DSC	A		Gannon, Joseph	DSC	A

Gariepy, Ted	DSC	A	Jackson, Horatio Nelson	DSC	A
Gee, Othel J. MD	DSC	A	Jager, H. Neil	DSC	A
Gehris, Jack D.	DSC	A	Janssen, Martin J.	DSC	A
Gibney, John J.	DSC	A	Jerabek, Jerry J.	DSC	A
Gilchrist, Edward	DSC	A	Jervey, Thomas M.	DSC	A
Goldberg, Sam	DSC	A	Johnson, A. Allen	DSC	A
Goodall, Robert M.	DSC	A	Johnson, Henry	MOH - A	A
Goodman, Lionel F.	DSC	A	Jolley, Thomas	DSC	A
Grahek, Matthew G.	DSC	A	Jones, Arthur Carroll	DSC	A
Granger, Warren L.	NC	N	Jones, T. E.	DSC	A
Greene, Edward B.	DSC	A	Jones, Walter B.	DSC	A
Greer, George B.	DSC	A	Kaper, Joseph	DSC	A
Grimes, Eustis B.	DSC	A	Katz, Phillip Carl	MOH - A	A
Grow, Robert W.	DSC	A	Kee, Sing	DSC	A
Grumley, Fred R.	DSC	A	Kemmerer, Bertrus	DSC	A
Gullickson, Olaf J.	NC	N	Kenaston, Hal	DSC	A
Gustafson, Charles	DSC	A	Kendall, Paul W.	DSC	A
Habecker, Guy M.	DSC	A	Kepner, William E.	DSC	AF
Hagan, J. Addison	DSC	A	Kerrigan, Patrick J.	NC	N
Hagan, Luther J.	DSC	A	Kielpinski, Vincent P.	DSC	A
Hakala, Edwin U.	NC	M	Kilbourne, Charles E.	DSC	A
Hale, David C.	NC	AF	Kimball, Roy E.	DSC	A
Hall, Walter H. Jr.	NC	N	Klein, Irving	DSC	A
Hamilton, Reuben G.	DSC	A	Klier, George J.	DSC	A
Handy, Thomas	DSC	A	Kmiotek, Aloysius	DSC	A
Hanna, Leon M.	DSC	A	Knight, John (Jack) T.	DSC	A
Hanson, Laman W.	NC	M	Kochli, Fred	DSC	A
Hanson, Raymond W.	NC	N	Kohn, Marion	NC	A
Hardie, William C.	DSC	A	Koleman, Norman D.	DSC	A
Hardy, Leslie T.	DSC	A	Korman, Frank A.	DSC	A
Harrell, Benjamin H.	DSC	A	Kostak, Frank J.	DSC	A
Hartman, William A.	DSC	A	Krigbaum, William L.	DSC	A
Harwood, Ralph W.	DSC	A	LaCroix, Orie H.	DSC	A
Hassig, Albert U.	DSC	A	LaDue, R. E.	DSC	A
Hayes, Edward S.	DSC	A	Lake, Horace A.	DSC	A
Healy, James A.	DSC	A	Lanergan, John F.	DSC	A
Hedlund, Fritz E.	DSC	A	Langdon, Russell C.	DSC	A
Heintz, Victor	DSC	A	Lawless, Howard R.	DSC	A
Hempe, Joseph C.	DSC	A	Lawton, Sanford	NC	N
Hendricks, Patrick	NC	A	Lee, James E.	DSC	A
Hermle, Leo D.	DSC	M	Lee., James E.	DSC	A
Herter, Edward	DSC	A	Lemon, Dwight E.	DSC	A
Hines, Paul H.	DSC	A	Lennox, Herbert K.	DSC	A
Hirschfelder, Chester J.	DSC	A	Leroy, George J.	NC	N
Hobscheid, Paul	DSC	A	Levine, Abel J.	DSC	A
Holland, Spessard Lindsey	DSC	A	Levy, Joseph	DSC	A
Holt, Frank M.	DSC	A	Lewis, Madison H.	DSC	A
Howard, James L.	DSC	A	Licklider, John D.	DSC	A
Howe, Arthur W.	NC	N	Liebeskind, H.	DSC	A
Hubbard, Harold G.	DSC	A	Lindberg, A. W.	DSC	A
Huelser, Charles A.	DSC	A	Lindsay, Grant S.	DSC	A
Hunt, David B.	DSC	A	Linton, Charles W	DSC	A
Hurley, Philip Sr	DSC	A	Lohmann, Lewis E.	DSC	A
Ingalls, Ray L. H.	DSC	A	Longfield, Simon A.	DSC	A
Inks, Charles L.	DSC	A	Lott, John H.	DSC	A

Love, Charles J.	DSC	A	Merriman, Clifton	DSC	A
Lyerly, William B.	DSC	A	Merritt, Charles B.	DSC	A
Lyons, Charles J.	NC	N	Merritt, Henry C.	DSC	A
Lyons, Walter F.	DSC	A	Messina, John	DSC	A
MacArthur, Douglas	DSC	A	Mezoff, John J.	DSC	A
MacBrayne, W. C.	DSC	A	Miller, Charles	DSC	A
MacDonnell, John	DSC	A	Miller, Harry W.	DSC	A
Macauley, Malcolm A.	DSC	A	Miller, Herbert H.	DSC	A
Mader, Tom O.	DSC	A	Miller, Lawrence G.	DSC	A
Mahar, Daniel J.	DSC	A	Mills, Bruce H.	DSC	M
Malcomson, Bruce K.	DSC	A	Mills, Bruce H.	NC	M
Manco, Artie G.	DSC	A	Moan, Ralph T.	DSC	A
Mannion, Joseph F.	DSC	A	Morelock, Sterling L.	MOH – A	A
Mansfield, James R.	DSC	A	Moro, Charles L.	NC	N
Manton, Walter Williamson	DSC	A	Morrison, William L.	DSC	A
Marks, Erwin J.	DSC	A	Morse, Daniel A.	DSC	A
Markus, Norbert W.	DSC	A	Moskowitz, Herman	DSC	A
Marshall, Willard H.	DSC	A	Murphy, Frank P.	DSC	A
Martin, Edward	DSC	A	Murphy, James V.	NC	N
Martin, Henry F.	DSC	A	Nagowski, A. J.	DSC	A
Martin, Oscar E.	DSC	A	Neelon, Raymond V.	DSC	A
Martz, Forrest L.	DSC	A	Nelson, Herbert W.	DSC	A
Marx, R. S.	DSC	A	Nichol, William O.	DSC	A
Mason, Francis W.	DSC	A	Nichols, Claude Morrison	DSC	A
Mathey, Maurice L.	DSC	A	Nicol, William O.	DSC	A
Matter, Peter	DSC	A	Nixon, William J.	DSC	A
Maurer, Phillip E.	DSC	A	Norris, Ravee	DSC	A
May, George J.	DSC	A	Norton, Earle D.	DSC	A
Mays, Dooley	DSC	A	Norton, Frank B.	DSC	A
McCandless, Byron	NC	N	Norton, Robert W.	DSC	A
McCarthy, Michael J.	DSC	A	Nourse, William H.	DSC	A
McCauley, Philip J.	DSC	A	Nuzzolo, Ficorentino	DSC	A
McClelland, Helen Grace	DSC	A	O'Connor, Harry G.	DSC	A
McCloy, John	NC	N	O'Dell, J. D.	DSC	A
McCracken, Lynn	DSC	A	O'Brien, Joseph P.	DSC	A
McCulloch, Robert	NC	N	Oliphant, David Arthur	DSC	A
McCullough, C. A.	DSC	A	Olsen, S. R.	DSC	A
McCullough, Clare A.	DSC	A	Olson, Stanley R.	DSC	A
McDevitt, James A.	DSC	A	Ord, Ralph E.	DSC	A
McDowell, Elliott E.	DSC	A	Osborn, James C.	NC	N
McEwen, Glenn O.	DSC	A	Osmond, Frank W.	DSC	A
McGarty, Michael J.	DSC	A	Owens, John J.	DSC	A
McGee, Lawrence T.	DSC	A	Page, Kenneth B.	DSC	A
McGinnis, George E.	DSC	A	Parissi, Joseph	DSC	A
McGuire, Earl R.	DSC	A	Parker, George E. Jr.	DSC	A
McGuire, Leo F.	DSC	A	Parker, Samuel I.	MOH – A	A
McIntyre, James B.	DSC	A	Parker, Samuel I.	DSC	A
McLaughlin, Edwin W.	DSC	A	Passafiume, Joseph	DSC	A
McMurray, Ora R.	DSC	A	Paton, Noel	DSC	A
McNicholas, Thomas G.	DSC	A	Patrick, William E.	DSC	A
McNulty, H. L.	DSC	A	Peardon, Roswell C.	NC	N
McSweeney, Dan S.	DSC	A	Pendell, Elmer	DSC	A
Melfi, Jerry	DSC	A	Perkins, Earl H.	DSC	A
Mellen, Clifford D.	DSC	A	Peronace, Anthony	DSC	A
Merrick, Robert G.	DSC	A	Pershing, John J.	DSC	A

Personett, John F.	DSC	A	Schiana, Alfred	NC	M
Peterman, Walter G.	NC	N	Schiana, Alfred	DSC	M
Petrovic, Joseph F.	DSC	A	Schiani, Alfred	NC	M
Petty, Orlando Henderson	MOH - N	N	Schiani, Alfred	DSC	M
Pope, Thomas A.	MOH - A	A	Schick, Frederick	DSC	A
Porter, Earl W.	DSC	A	Schmidt, Oscar Jr.	MOH - N	N
Posser, Frederick Jr.	DSC	A	Schreech, George W.	DSC	A
Powell, George W.	DSC	A	Schwartzwaelder, C. A.	DSC	A
Powell, James Thomas	DSC	A	Scialabba, Ignazio	DSC	A
Prager, Ben	DSC	A	Scionti, Louis	DSC	A
Purrington, Alden C.	DSC	A	Scott, David S.	DSC	A
Rafferty, R. W.	NC	N	Scott, John E.	DSC	A
Rafter, Edwin J.	DSC	A	Seeler, Wilfred J.	DSC	A
Randles, Harold J.	DSC	M	Seibert, Lloyd M.	MOH - A	A
Ransom, Warren A.	DSC	A	Seligman, M. T.	NC	N
Rapport, George D.	DSC	A	Semmes, Harry H.	DSC	A
Rath, Howard G.	DSC	A	Semple, Frank J.	DSC	A
Reece, B. Carroll	DSC	A	Senay, Charles T.	DSC	A
Reed, Raymond E.	DSC	A	Setliff, Guy M.	NC	N
Reid, G. B.	DSC	A	Shaskan, David M.	DSC	A
Reilley Charles R.	DSC	A	Shedlock, Anthony F.	DSC	A
Reilley, Charles R.	DSC	A	Shemin William	MOH - A	A
Reinburg, Leroy	NC	CG	Shemin, William	DSC	A
Reugg, Robert	DSC	A	Shenkel, John H.	DSC	A
Reynolds, Eugene C.	DSC	A	Shepherd Lemuel	DSC	M
Richards, Calvin D.	DSC	A	Shepherd, Royal H. C.	DSC	A
Richards, Walter R.	DSC	A	Shipman, Harold L.	DSC	A
Rickenbacker, Edward V.	DSC	A	Shuey, Perry R.	DSC	A
Rickenbacker, Edward V.	MOH - A	A	Signor, Henry Leslie	DSC	A
Riley, Raymond W.	DSC	A	Sill, Fred D.	DSC	A
Ringelman, G. A.	NC	N	Simpson, C. Isaac	NC	N
Robart, Ralph W.	DSC	A	Sinatra, Marion	DSC	A
Robbins, Burton Aldrich Jr.	NC	N	Skrypeck, Andy	DSC	A
Robbins, Walter	NC	N	Slate, Ralph	DSC	A
Roberson, J. N.	DSC	A	Smallyon, Edward H.	DSC	A
Robinson, John J.	DSC	A	Smith, Ford D.	DSC	A
Robison, Edward M.	DSC	A	Smith, Harry L.	DSC	A
Rodemich, L. F.	NC	N	Smith, Harry S.	DSC	A
Rohan, Edgar A.	DSC	A	Smith, Ivan H.	DSC	A
Ross, Earl A.	DSC	A	Smith, John W.	DSC	A
Ross, H. E.	DSC	A	Smith, Nat R.	DSC	A
Rover, Harry J.	DSC	A	Snyder, M. Allan	DSC	A
Rowbottom, R. S.	DSC	A	Sonastelie, Carl J.	DSC	A
Rubel, Albert C.	DSC	A	Spaatz, Carl	DSC	A
Ruge, Edwin G. W.	DSC	A	Spencer, Edward L.	DSC	A
Ruland, Henry F.	DSC	A	Spencer, William M.	DSC	A
Rumbaugh, E. R.	DSC	A	Stackpole, E. J. Jr.	DSC	A
Russell, N. Jr.	NC	N	Stair, Willett A.	DSC	A
Russell, T. N.	NC	N	Stawitzke, John F.	NC	N
Russell, T. N.	DSC	N	Steele, Frank S.	DSC	A
Ryan, Oscar H.	DSC	A	Steinkraus, Herman W.	DSC	A
Ryan, Patrick T.	NC	N	Stenseth, Martinus	DSC	A
Sakrison, Roy H.	DSC	A	Sterling, Thomas	DSC	A
Sartain, George	DSC	A	Stewart, David B.	DSC	A
Schaperow, James H.	NC	N	Stiff, William	DSC	A

Stika, Joseph E.	NC	CG
Stinson, James K	DSC	A
Stirling, Thomas	DSC	A
Stone, Otis L.	DSC	A
Stowers, Freddie	MOH - A	A
Stubbs, Edwin J.	DSC	A
Sutherland, Frank S.	DSC	A
Swain, Jack R.	DSC	A
Thayer, Sidney Jr.	DSC	A
Thiede, Michael	DSC	A
Thomas, Fred J.	DSC	A
Thompson, John W.	DSC	A
Thompson, William D.	DSC	A
Thorngate, George	DSC	A
Thornhill, W. P.	DSC	A
Thurston, Clair H.	DSC	A
Todd, Walter H.	NC	N
Tousic, Frank	DSC	A
Townsend, George L.	NC	A
Troska, Charles P.	DSC	A
Troup, Clarence D.	DSC	A
Trovel, Emil W.	NC	N
Trovell, E.	NC	N
Turner, Dennis C.	DSC	A
Tuttle, Mellen F.	DSC	A
Tveten, Hans L.	DSC	A
Tydings, Millard	DSC	A
Vail, William H.	DSC	A
Van Horn, C. W.	DSC	A
Van Iersel, Louis	MOH - A	A
Vaughn, George A.	DSC	A
Vaught, Glen	DSC	A
Vollmer, Frank D.	DSC	A
Vonland, George O.	DSC	A
Vosburgh, Fred	DSC	A
Waldron, Joseph F.	DSC	A
Wallace, Anthony M.	DSC	A
Waller, Luther H.	DSC	A
Walsh, James G.	DSC	A
Walsh, John R.	DSC	A
Walton, Robert	DSC	A
Ward, M. C.	DSC	A
Ware, James V.	DSC	A
Watkins, F. C.	DSC	A
Weaver, Charles H.	DSC	A
Weaver, Ross E.	DSC	A
Weaver, William G.	DSC	A
Weeks, Mody A.	DSC	A
Wesselhoeft, Conrad	DSC	A
Whipple, Columbus	DSC	A
White, Richard J.	NC	A
Whitney, Leroy F.	DSC	A
Wilbor, Thomas W.	DSC	A
Wild, Edward W.	DSC	A
Williams, Frank J.	DSC	A

Williams, Henry J.	NC	N
Williams, John F.	DSC	A
Winchenbaugh, Wolcott	DSC	A
Winchenbaugh, Wolcott	NC	M
Winship, Blanton	DSC	A
Wise, Charles E. Jr.	DSC	A
Withers, Loris A.	DSC	A
Wolffe, Murry	NC	N
Woodside, Robert G.	DSC	A
Woolshagler, J. F.	DSC	A
Worthy, Elmer T.	DSC	A
Wyatt, Edward H.	DSC	A
Yeager, Louis	DSC	A
Yeager, Roy	DSC	A
Young, Charles I.	DSC	A
Youngbar, Andy F.	DSC	A
Zimmerman, Arthur P.	DSC	A

Haiti 1915

Butler, Smedley D.	MOH - N	M

Interim 1915–1916

Bratton, M. Gans	NC	N

Haiti Campaign 1919–1920

Paul, William	NC	M

Interim 1920–1940

Ackers, Charles	NC	N
Anders, Arthur F.	NC	N
Badders, William	MOH - N	N
Badders, William	NC	N
Ballinger, Ernest F.	NC	M
Carbone, Alphonse	NC	M
Eadie, Thomas	N	
Eadie, Thomas	MOH - N	N
Eadie, Thomas	NC	N
Fickes, Ted D.	NC	N
Gilbert, John	NC	N
Hebard, Robert R.	NC	N
Hennessy, John N.	NC	N
Huber, William R.	MOH - N	M
Kensick, Casmer	NC	N
Lang, John H.	NC	N
Michels, Fred G.	NC	N
Murphy, James T.	NC	N
Peterson, Reginald	NC	N
Sibitzky, M. C.	NC	N
Wilson, John Dahlgren	NC	N
Winslow, Cameran McRae Jr.	NC	N

Nicaraguan Campaign 1930–32

Puller, Lewis B.	2NC	N

World War II 1941–1945

Abbott, Gordon	NC	N
Abele, Mannert Lincoln	NC	N
Abercrombie, Hugh	DSC	A
Abernethy, E. P.	NC	N
Abrams, Creighton	DSC	A
Adams, Lucian	MOH - A	A
Ahrens, Walter E.	DSC	A
Akin, Spencer B.	DSC	A
Alden, Carlos C.	DSC	A
Aldrich, Charles W.	NC	N
Alexander, John A.	DSC	A
Alexander, Paul E.	DSC	A
Anderson, Beauford T.	MOH - A	A
Anderson, Bernard E.	DSC	A
Anderson, Eric C.	DSC	A
Anderson, Paul W.	DSC	A
Anderson, Wilford C.	DSC	A
Archer, Robert John	NC	N
Arison, Rae	NC	N
Armstrong, Gene L.	DSC	A
Armstrong, Robert G.	NC	N
Arnold, Edgar L.	DSC	A
Arnold, Jackson D.	NC	N
Arooth, Michael L.	DSC	AF
Arsenault, Frederick L.	NC	N
Ashley, Earl D.	DSC	A
Atkinson, Gwen G.	DSC	A
Atkinson, Paul G.	DSC	AF
Aurand, Evan P.	NC	N
Awakuni, Masao	DSC	A
Babson, Robert F.	DSC	A
Bach, Frederick L.	DSC	A
Bail, Bernard W.	DSC	A
Bailey, Kenneth D.	MOH - N	M
Baker, Earl P. Jr.	NC	N
Baker, Earl Philip Jr.	NC	N
Baker, Frederick K.	DSC	A
Ball, Charles	DSC	A
Balza, William J.	DSC	A
Bangs, Louis Lee	NC	N
Barber, Alex W.	DSC	A
Barber, Rex T.	NC	A
Barbiero, Samuel S.	DSC	A
Barcellona, Gaetano R.	DSC	A
Barfoot, Van T.	MOH - A	A
Barker, William R.	DSC	A
Barnes, Robert M.	NC	N
Bartlett, John W.	NC	M
Basilone, John	NC	M

Basilone, John	MOH - N	M
Basore, Harry H. Jr.	NC	N
Batchelder, Merten J.	NC	M
Bates, Richard S.	NC	N
Battalio, Samuel T.	DSC	A
Baum, Abraham J.	DSC	A
Baxter, James Landron	NC	N
Beach, Edward L.	NC	N
Beamish, Warren W.	DSC	A
Beck, James R.	NC	M
Becton, F. Julian	NC	N
Beightler, Robert S.	DSC	A
Beitler, Kenneth E.	DSC	A
Belfor, Max	DSC	A
Bell, John J.	NC	N
Belmont, Gail H.	DSC	A
Benner, Charlie R.	NC	M
Bennett, John E.	NC	N
Berkowitz, Henry	DSC	A
Berlin, Walter I.	DSC	A
Bertoldo, Vito R.	MOH - A	A
Biddle, Melvin E.	MOH - A	A
Bischoff, Lawrence P.	DSC	A
Bishop, Claude U. Jr.	NC	N
Bitchell, Stanley L.	NC	M
Bjarnason, Paul H.	NC	N
Blair, Melvin Russell	DSC	A
Blais, Francis James	DSC	A
Blaisdell, Donald B.	DSC	A
Blakely, Jay C.	NC	M
Bluemel, Clifford	DSC	A
Blumhagen, Robert F.	DSC	A
Boggs, Kenneth L.	DSC	A
Bolton, Cecil H.	MOH - A	A
Bonnyman Alexander	MOH - N	M
Booth, Charles H. Jr.	DSC	A
Borgia, Anthony E.	NC	M
Bottomley, Harold S. Jr.	NC	N
Botts, Douglas Arthur	NC	N
Bouchardon, Andre J.	DSC	A
Bouck, Lyle J. Jr.	DSC	A
Boulware, J. W.	NC	N
Bowen, Frank S. Jr.	DSC	A
Boyer, Randolph B.	NC	N
Boyington, Gregory	MOH - N	M
Boyle, William J.	DSC	A
Bradberry, Clarence F.	DSC	A
Bradley, Jack T.	DSC	A
Brady, Hugh	DSC	A
Brady, Wallace Anthony	NC	N
Braga, George F.	DSC	A
Brandt, Charles A.	DSC	A
Brehm, Harold Paul	NC	N
Brennan, John J.	DSC	A
Brenner, William E.	DSC	A

Bretton (Beugnon), Raphael G.	DSC	A		Cestoni, Angelo Jr.	DSC	A
Brice, Arthur T.	DSC	A		Chaffin, Bradford W. Jr.	NC	M
Bridges, Robert A.	NC	N		Chaisson, James J.	NC	M
Bringle, William F.	NC	N		Chamberlain, George D.	DSC	A
Brookes, Charles S.	NC	N		Chamblee, Graham V.	DSC	A
Brooks, William C. Jr.	NC	N		Champagne, Joseph D.	NC	M
Brosokas, Victor P.	DSC	A		Champlin, Malcolm M.	NC	N
Brown, Bobbie E.	MOH - A	A		Chapin, Neil M.	DSC	A
Brown, Carl Allen Jr.	NC	N		Cheston, Elliot B.	DSC	A
Brown, Charles L.	AFC	A		Childers, Ernest	MOH - A	A
Brown, Ernest L.	DSC	A		Chilson, Llewellyn M.	DSC	A
Brown, Frank Melville Jr.	DSC	A		Chudej, Robert L.	DSC	A
Brown, James Harvey	NC	N		Claggett, B. Dulany	NC	N
Brown, William Perry Jr.	NC	M		Clancy, Robert Lawrence	NC	N
Browner, Ralph L.	NC	M		Clapp, Edward S.	NC	N
Brunelle, Albert W.	NC	N		Clarey, Bernard A.	NC	N
Bruton, Henry C.	NC	N		Clark, Douglas Alan	NC	N
Bryan, Charles B.	DSC	A		Clark, Mark W.	DSC	A
Buell, Harold L.	NC	N		Clark, Paul L.	NC	CG
Bulkeley, John Duncan	MOH - N	N		Clarke, John F.	DSC	A
Bulkeley, John Duncan	NC	N		Classen, Thomas J.	DSC	AF
Bullock, Jesse H.	DSC	A		Clement, Wallace L.	DSC	A
Burdue, Clayton C.	DSC	AF		Clinton, Robert J.	NC	N
Burke, Arleigh A.	NC	N		Cobb, Henry H. Jr.	DSC	A
Burke, Francis T.	NC	M		Cobb, Robert B.	DSC	A
Burke, Lloyd L. (Scooter)	DSC	A		Cobbett, Warren E.	DSC	A
Burke, Louis Edward.	NC	N		Cochran, Jack C.	NC	N
Burke, Phillip R.	NC	M		Cohen, Harold	DSC	A
Burke, Robert C.	DSC	A		Colalillo, Mike	MOH - A	A
Burkhart, Calvin	NC	N		Cole, William M.	NC	N
Burns, Walter J.	DSC	A		Collins, James F.	DSC	A
Burnshaw, Edward C.	DSC	A		Collinson, Joseph F.	DSC	A
Burt, James M.	MOH - A	A		Compton, Keith K.	DSC	A
Bush, Robert E.	MOH - N	N		Conkey, George L.	NC	N
Butler, Benjamin J.	DSC	A		Connors, Gerald Martin	NC	N
Butt, Noah B. Jr.	NC	N		Cook, Lawrence Blanchard	NC	N
Cady, Joseph	NC	N		Coolidge, Charles H.	MOH - A	A
Cagwin, Leland G.	DSC	A		Cordiner, Douglas	NC	N
Caldwell, Frank C.	NC	M		Cota, Norman D.	DSC	A
Caldwell, R. H.	NC	N		Cox, John A.	DSC	A
Callaghan, Daniel Judson	MOH - N	N		Craft, George H.	DSC	A
Callahan, Joseph W.	NC	N		Cragg, Edward	DSC	A
Camp, Lloyd Vernon	DSC	A		Craig, James A. Jr.	DSC	A
Canham, Charles D. W.	DSC	A		Craven, Howard R.	NC	M
Cannon, George Ham	MOH - N	M		Crawley, Lawrence N.	NC	M
Cano, Pedro	MOH - A	A		Crews, John R.	MOH - A	A
Capri, Samuel J.	DSC	A		Crosbie, Maurice G.	DSC	AF
Carew, John J.	DSC	A		Crosby, John Theodore	NC	N
Carmichael, Richard H.	DSC	AF		Crow, Roger C.	NC	N
Carroll, J.	DSC	A		Cruikshank, Chester G.	DSC	A
Carroll, Phillip H.	DSC	A		Cruze, Jack D.	NC	N
Carson, D. A.	NC	M		Cunningham, Charles D.	DSC	A
Carter, Edward A.	MOH - A	A		Cupp, James N.	NC	M
Carter, Melvin R.	NC	N		Curran, John L.	DSC	A
Caton, Edward H.	DSC	A		Cushman, Kent M.	NC	N

Cushman, Robert E. Jr.	NC	M	Durand, Robert Frank	NC	N
Cyr, Paul	DSC	A	Dye, Billy H.	NC	N
Dahlberg, Kenneth H.	DSC	A	Eareckson, William O.	DSC	A
Daly, Michael J.	MOH – A	A	Eareckson, William O.	NC	A
Danis, Anthony L.	NC	N	Eastland, William H.	DSC	A
Darago, Albert A. Jr.	DSC	A	Eckenrod, Gervase A. (Gerry)	DSC	A
Darby, William Orlando	DSC	A	Edmunds, Edward	DSC	A
Daskevich, Anthony F.	DSC	A	Edwards, Dan	MOH – A	A
Davidowicz, C. J.	DSC	A	Edwards, Dan	DSC	A
Davies, Donald	DSC	A	Eggleston, Leonard L.	DSC	A
Davila, Rudolph B.	MOH – A	A	Ehlers, Walter D.	MOH – A	A
Davis, Arthur V.	NC	M	Eisele, George R.	NC	N
Davis, Charles L.	DSC	A	Eisenhart, Frank J.	NC	N
Davis, Charles W.	MOH – A	A	Elder, Arthur G.	NC	N
Davis, Clayton E.	DSC	A	Eller, Donald T.	NC	N
Davis, Raymond G.	NC	M	Elling, James C.	DSC	A
Davis, Samuel Adams	NC	N	Ellis, Charles A.	DSC	A
Davis, William Edgar III	NC	N	Ellis, Richard A.	DSC	AF
Day, James L.	MOH – N	M	Ellsworth, Theodore R.	DSC	A
DeGraaf, George	DSC	A	Emerson, William S.	NC	N
DeMoss, Charles William	NC	N	Enright, Joseph Francis	NC	N
Dearolf, Thomas W.	DSC	A	Erdman, Herman	DSC	A
Dempsey, James Charles	NC	N	Erwin, Henry E.	MOH – A	A
Deshayes, Albert P.	DSC	A	Esders, Wilhelm G.	NC	N
Devereux, James P. S.	NC	M	Ettinger, Ralph D.	NC	N
Dexter, Robert F.	DSC	A	Evans, John S.	NC	N
DiSalvo, Santo J.	DSC	A	Evans, Raymond J.	NC	CG
Dillon, William T.	DSC	A	Evans, Thomas J.	DSC	A
Dixon, Harold F.	NC	N	Faltyn, Hubert J.	NC	M
Dixon, Harold M.	DSC	A	Farmer, James Willie	DSC	A
Dodson, Charles O.	NC	N	Farrar, Archibald Alexander	DSC	A
Doherty, Timothy C.	DSC	A	Farrar, Joseph B.	DSC	A
Doman, Glenn J.	DSC	A	Feeney, Joseph	NC	N
Doolittle, James H. "Jimmy"	MOH – A	A	Fenno, Frank W. Jr.	NC	N
Doss, Desmond T. Sr	MOH – A	A	Fieguth, Walter	NC	M
Doughtie, James D.	DSC	A	Finke, John G.	DSC	A
Doughty, Edward D.	DSC	A	Finn, John William	MOH – N	N
Douglas, Paul P. Jr.	DSC	AF	Fisher, Almond E.	MOH – A	A
Dove, Vinton Walsh	DSC	A	Fisher, Ellis J.	NC	N
Downey, Ernest W.	NC	N	Fisher, Lewis B.	DSC	A
Downing, Arthur L.	NC	N	Fitch, Alva R.	DSC	A
Dowthitt, John A.	DSC	A	Fletcher, Charles B.	NC	N
Drago, Thomas R.	NC	N	Floege, Ernest F.	DSC	A
Drew, Urban L.	AFC	AF	Fluckey, Eugene B.	MOH – N	N
Drowley, Jesse R.	MOH – A	A	Fluckey, Eugene B.	NC	N
DuBose, Edwin A.	NC	N	Foley, John P.	DSC	A
Duffee, Raymond D.	NC	N	Forbuss, Elmer L.	DSC	A
Dugas, Albert J.	DSC	A	Fordyce, Ralph W.	NC	M
Duncan, Robert W.	NC	N	Forsythe, Abe Jr.	NC	M
Dungan, Fred Leroy	NC	N	Foss, Joseph Jacob	MOH – N	M
Dunham, Russell E.	MOH – A	A	Frederick, Eugene J. Jr.	NC	M
Dunham, William D.	DSC	AF	Frederick, Paul H.	DSC	A
Dunn, Jack DeVore	DSC	A	Freeman, J. S.	NC	N
Dunn, James Jr.	NC	M	Fridge, Benjamin W.	DSC	A

Fries, Robert A.	DSC	A		Gowdy, George H.	DSC	A
Fry, James C.	DSC	A		Greely, Joseph	NC	N
Fuller, Arthur M.	DSC	A		Green, Charles Edward	NC	M
Fuller, Robert G.	NC	M		Green, Jack E.	DSC	A
Funk, Edward	DSC	A		Greer, Howard W.	DSC	A
Funk, Harold Nathan	NC	N		Gregg, Max Eugene	NC	N
Funk, Leonard A. Jr.	MOH - A	A		Gregg, Stephen R.	MOH - A	A
Funk, Leonard A. Jr.	DSC	A		Gregor, Orville F.	NC	N
Furney, Maynard M.	NC	N		Grenfell, Elton Watters	NC	N
Gabbamonte, John H.	DSC	A		Griffin, William Andrew	NC	M
Gabreski, Francis S.	DSC	A		Griffith, Welborn B.	DSC	A
Gaines, Kenneth Lamar	DSC	A		Grimes, William W. Jr.	DSC	A
Galer, Robert E.	NC	M		Gruver, Harry L.	NC	N
Galer, Robert E.	MOH - N	M		Guest, William M.	DSC	A
Gallant, Wallace M.	DSC	A		Gustafson, Luther Sidney	DSC	A
Gambonini, Paul B.	DSC	A		Habal, Dulcesimo	DSC	A
Gano, Roy A.	NC	N		Hackett, Thomas A.	DSC	A
Garafano, Frank P.	DSC	A		Hagney, Frank J.	DSC	A
Garberg, James S.	DSC	A		Hall, Robert Kerr	NC	A
Garcia, Marcario	MOH - A	A		Hall, Virginia	DSC	A
Gardler, Harrison M.	DSC	A		Hamilton, Edward S.	DSC	A
Garofano, Frank P.	DSC	A		Hamilton, Pierpont M.	MOH - A	A
Garretson, Frank E.	NC	M		Hanks, Euguene Ralph	NC	N
Gary, Donald A.	MOH - N	N		Hanna, Robert M.	NC	M
Gary, Donald A.	NC	N		Hansen, Harry F.	DSC	A
Gavin, Thomas P.	NC	N		Hansen, Robert Jr.	DSC	A
Gay, William M.	DSC	AF		Hanson, Eugene R.	NC	N
Gaynor, Paul F.	DSC	A		Hantman, Sidney	DSC	AF
Gaynor, Robert M.	DSC	A		Harbert, John E.	DSC	A
Gehres, Leslie F.	NC	N		Hardee, David L.	DSC	A
Gehrke, Wilbur J.	NC	M		Hardison, Felix M.	DSC	AF
Gehrman, Frank R.	DSC	A		Hardy, Willis E. (Bill)	NC	N
Gellman, Albert E.	DSC	A		Hargrove, Robert C.	DSC	A
Gentile, Ernest J.	NC	N		Harmon, Walter E.	NC	N
Gentry, Harry L.	DSC	A		Harral, Brooks J.	NC	N
Geran, Raymond Z.	DSC	A		Harrer, Keith J.	NC	M
Germershausen, William J.	NC	N		Harris, Fred R.	NC	N
Gibbs, David Raymond	DSC	A		Hartvig, Donald H.	NC	N
Gibson, Robert D.	NC	N		Hatler, Elton L.	NC	N
Gilbert, Clifford R.	NC	M		Hawk, John D.	MOH - A	A
Gilbert, Laurence Edwin	NC	N		Hayashi, Shizuya	MOH - A	A
Gilchrest, Dexter S.	NC	N		Heck, Edward Jr.	NC	N
Gilreath, J. Frank Jr.	NC	N		Hedlund, Oswald J.	NC	M
Ginish, Stanley L.	DSC	A		Heindl, Elmer W.	DSC	A
Glober, George E.	DSC	A		Heller, Edwin L.	DSC	AF
Glynn, William J.	DSC	A		Henderson, Torsten E.	DSC	A
Goldberg, Hyman M.	DSC	A		Hendrix, James R.	MOH - A	A
Goldstein, Sidney	DSC	A		Hermle, Leo D.	NC	M
Good, William T.	NC	N		Herrera, Silvestre S.	MOH - A	A
Goode, Lemuel	DSC	A		Herring, Rufus G.	MOH - N	N
Goodsell, Vincent F.	DSC	A		Herriott, Harold T.	DSC	A
Goranson, Ralph E.	DSC	A		Hewitt, H. Kent	NC	N
Gorder, Merle H.	NC	N		Higgins, William J.	DSC	A
Gordon, Nathan	MOH - N	N		Hightower, Louis V.	DSC	A

Hill, Andrew J.	NC	N	Johnson, Dale L.	NC	N
Hill, David L.	DSC	A	Johnson, Dwight L.	NC	N
Hill, Edwin Joseph	MOH - N	N	Johnson, Leon W.	MOH - A	A
Hilsky, Robert J.	NC	M	Johnson, Maro P.	DSC	A
Hirschfelder, Chester J.	A		Johnson, Oscar G.	MOH - A	A
Hodgon, Fred	DSC	A	Johnson, Wayne L.	DSC	A
Hoffman, Charles K.	NC	N	Johnston, Ruby E.	DSC	A
Hofmann, Fred Jr.	NC	M	Jolly, John C.	NC	N
Hogden, Raymond L.	NC	N	Jones, George M.	DSC	A
Hohnson, Dale	NC	N	Jones, Robert E.	NC	M
Holladay, Sam M. Jr.	NC	N	Jordan, Henry S.	DSC	A
Holland, Robert H.	DSC	A	Jordan, Vernon C.	DSC	A
Holliday, Robert L.	DSC	A	Jorgenson, John H.	NC	N
Hollingsworth, James F.	DSC	A	Joyce, John D.	DSC	A
Holmes, Kenneth A.	NC	N	Kaelin, Joseph	NC	N
Holsberg, Wilford G.	DSC	A	Kahn, Lauren Herman	NC	M
Holt, Phillip C.	NC	N	Kasper, Carl J.	DSC	A
Hoover, G. C.	NC	N	Katalinas, Joseph Anton	DSC	A
Hoover, John R.	DSC	A	Kauffman, A. Henry	DSC	A
Hopkins, Lewis A.	NC	N	Kauffman, Eldeen H.	DSC	A
Horenburger, Carl H.	NC	N	Kay, Francis	NC	N
Horner, Freeman V.	MOH - A	A	Keeler, Robert C.	DSC	A
Hornsby, Jack	DSC	A	Keith, L. W. Jr.	NC	N
Hornsby, Jasper T.	DSC	A	Kellogg, Frederick A.	NC	M
Howell, John D.	NC	N	Kelly, Colin P. Jr.	DSC	A
Hubbard, Ronald D.	DSC	A	Kelly, Fonville	NC	N
Hudson, Charles S.	DSC	A	Kemper, George Emil	NC	N
Huff, Paul B.	MOH - A	A	Kenney, Edward C.	NC	N
Huffman, Gerald M.	NC	N	Kenton, Roland H	NC	N
Huggins, Gordon E.	DSC	A	Keszthelyi, Tibor K.	DSC	A
Huggins, Jesse C. Jr.	NC	N	Kidd, Isaac C.	MOH - N	N
Hughes, Lloyd "Pete" Herbert	MOH - A	A	Kiernan, James A.	DSC	A
Hunt, James I.	DSC	A	Kimberlin, Vincent A.	DSC	A
Hunt, Raymond C.	DSC	A	Kincaid, J. Leslie	DSC	A
Hurd, Kenneth C.	NC	N	King, John J.	DSC	A
Hurst, Edward Hunter	NC	M	Kinney, Sheldon Hoard	NC	N
Huttenberg, Allen J.	NC	N	Kinsey, Paul S.	DSC	A
Huttenburg, Allen John	NC	N	Kirkland, Raymond M.	DSC	A
Hyde, Louis G. V.	DSC	A	Kisters, Gerry H.	MOH - A	A
Ingle, Donald F.	DSC	A	Kisters, Gerry H.	DSC	A
Inouye, Daniel K.	MOH - A	A	Kizirian, Harry	NC	M
Irwin, Henry J.	NC	N	Kleiss, Norman J. Sr	NC	N
Irzyk, Albin F.	DSC	A	Knight, Everett C.	DSC	A
Ivary, Toivo Henry	NC	M	Knowlton, Donald E.	DSC	A
Iversen, Ivan B.	NC	M	Kosmyna, Steven	DSC	A
Jackson, James Douglas	DSC	A	Kossler, Herman J.	NC	N
Jacobucci, John R.	DSC	A	Kouma, Anthony B.	NC	M
Jamail, Abe	DSC	A	Krasman, Albert J.	DSC	A
Jamison, Lee R	DSC	A	Kravontka, M. V.	DSC	A
Jarrell, A. E.	NC	N	Krepski, Theodore E.	NC	N
Jester, Maurice D.	NC	CG	Krouse, Michael H.	NC	N
Johns, Samuel N.	DSC	A	Kruck, Warren J.	NC	N
Johnsmiller, Robert W.	NC	M	Kunkle, James K.	DSC	A
Johnson, Clark E.	DSC	A	Kunkle, Robert D.	NC	N

Lackness, Berdines	DSC	A		Marion, Lawrence B.	DSC	A
Lahodney, William J.	NC	N		Marquez, Eleuterio Joe	NC	N
Lally, John G.	DSC	A		Marsh, Wilbur L.	NC	N
Lance, Alden S.	DSC	A		Marshall, William J.	DSC	A
Landry, Milton J.	DSC	A		Martin, Kenneth R.	DSC	AF
Lang, Lawrence	NC	M		Martinek, Peter Paul	NC	N
Langrall, James H.	NC	N		Martinez, Joe P.	MOH - A	A
Lapham, Robert B.	DSC	A		Masny, Otto	DSC	A
Laven, George Jr.	DSC	A		Massello, William Jr.	DSC	A
Lawrence, Henry G. Jr.	NC	M		Maxwell, Robert D.	MOH - A	A
Lawrence, John C.	NC	N		Mayberry, Clarence L.	DSC	A
Lazarski, Joseph J.	DSC	A		McCampbell, David	NC	N
LeMay, Curtis E.	DSC	AF		McCampbell, David	MOH - N	N
Leach, James H.	DSC	A		McFarland, Alan Roberts	NC	N
Lee, Daniel W.	MOH - A	A		McGann, Patrick H.	NC	N
Leeper, Charles David	NC	N		McGarity, Vernon	MOH - A	A
Lemke, Edwin J.	DSC	A		McIlhenny, Walter S.	NC	M
Leonard, William R.	NC	N		McInerney, William E.	DSC	A
Leverette, William L.	DSC	A		McKelvey, Russell	DSC	A
Lewis, Donald	NC	N		McLean, E. R. Jr.	NC	N
Lieberman, Nate	DSC	A		McLellan, Paul F.	NC	M
Lightner, Earl Fred	NC	N		McMahon, Robert F.	DSC	A
Lindsay, Elvin L.	NC	N		McNeese, Harold G.	DSC	AF
Lindsey, Eugene Elbert	NC	N		McPhee, Albert E.	DSC	A
Lindsey, Jake W.	MOH - A	A		McRoberts, John H.	DSC	A
Lindstrom, Ross A.	NC	N		Mcdaniel, Hector Singleton	NC	N
Line, John H.	NC	N		Mead, Harry R.	NC	N
Linn, Richard F.	DSC	A		Medina, Rumaldo B.	DSC	A
Linso, John	NC	N		Megellas, James	DSC	A
Little, Clayton N.	DSC	A		Melnitsky, Edward P.	NC	M
Little, Edwin Charles	NC	N		Merli, Gino J.	MOH - A	A
Livesey, Benjamin R.	NC	M		Merrill, Bobbie L.	DSC	A
Llewellyn, Stanley D.	DSC	A		Michael, Edward S.	MOH - A	A
Locke, Chester M.	NC	N		Mihalowski, John "Mike"	MOH - N	N
Lomell, Leonard G.	DSC	A		Milesnick, John S.	DSC	A
Lopez, Jose M.	MOH - A	A		Miller, Doris	NC	N
Losten, Steven W.	DSC	A		Miller, Edwin S.	NC	N
Lovett, Claude E. Jr.	DSC	A		Miller, George H.	NC	N
Lowden, James J.	DSC	A		Miller, Victor LaVerne	NC	N
Lowe, Walter	DSC	A		Mills, Richard D.	DSC	A
Lundquist, Carl E.	DSC	A		Misner, Charles C.	DSC	A
Lytle, Cleveland	DSC	A		Mitchell, James T.	NC	M
MacArthur, Douglas	MOH - A	A		Mitchell, John	DSC	A
MacGillivary, Charles A.	MOH - A	A		Mitchell, Willard M.	DSC	A
Mack, David	DSC	A		Mitchell, William F.	NC	N
Maghakian, Victor	NC	M		Moats, Sanford K.	DSC	A
Magoffin, M. D.	DSC	A		Momsen, Charles B.	NC	N
Mahlmann, Ernest R.	NC	N		Monaghan, James Francis	NC	N
Mahoney, Grant S.	DSC	A		Monges, Charles J.	NC	M
Mahony, Grant	DSC	A		Montgomery, Jack C.	MOH - A	A
Makstutis, John B.	NC	M		Moore, Edward Charles	NC	N
Maloney, John S.	DSC	A		Moore, Pren L.	DSC	A
Maltby, Arthur L. Jr.	NC	N		Moore, William L.	NC	N
Mand, Alois J.	DSC	A		Moore, William W.	DSC	AF

Morehead, J. B.	DSC	A	Ough, Webster J.	DSC	A
Morgan, Corwin F.	NC	N	Owens, Marion Pope (Dutch)	DSC	A
Morgan, Samuel A.	DSC	A	Owens, Seymour D.	NC	N
Morrill, John H.	NC	N	Pagel, Joseph Lloyd	NC	N
Morris, Donald W.	NC	N	Paige, Mitchell	MOH – N	M
Morris, Victor M.	DSC	A	Palm, Carl C.	DSC	A
Morton, Gilbert L.	NC	M	Parish, Herman O.	NC	N
Moto Kaoru	MOH – A	A	Parks, Lewis S.	NC	N
Mott, Hugh B.	DSC	A	Parris, Harold L.	DSC	A
Munro, Douglas Albert	MOH – N	CG	Partridge, Donald D.	DSC	A
Muri, James Perry	DSC	A	Patch, Lloyd E.	DSC	A
Murphy, Audie Leon	DSC	A	Patterson, William W.	NC	N
Murphy, Audie Leon	MOH – A	A	Pauk, John Frederick	NC	N
Murphy, Philip J.	DSC	A	Paxton, Floyd M.	DSC	A
Murray, Samuel J.	DSC	A	Payne Frederick R.	NC	M
Murray, Thomas O.	NC	N	Peabody, Herbert Gale	DSC	A
Mushik, Donald	DSC	A	Pearson, John M.	DSC	A
Muth, James C.	DSC	A	Pecquet, Andre E.	DSC	A
Natoli, Constantino V.	DSC	A	Pence, Donald C.	DSC	A
Nau, Charles E.	DSC	A	Perkins, Norris H.	DSC	A
Naul, Jesse W. Jr.	NC	N	Perrin, Herbèrt T.	DSC	A
Nendza, Albert I.	DSC	A	Petersen, Wallis F.	NC	N
Neppel, Ralph G.	MOH – A	A	Peterson, Herbert A.	NC	N
Newman, Aubrey S.	DSC	A	Pfleger, James Richard	DSC	A
Newman, Beryl R.	MOH – A	A	Pharris, Jackson Charles	MOH – N	N
Newton, Roy A.	NC	N	Phillips, Charles Emery	NC	N
Niemic, Walter J.	NC	N	Phillips, Claude B.	DSC	A
Niemiec, Walter J.	NC	N	Phillips, Hubert Edward	DSC	A
Nisewaner, T. A.	NC	N	Phillips, James Holden	DSC	A
Nishimoto, Joe M.	MOH – A	A	Phillips, Richard H.	NC	N
Noon, Theodore W. Jr.	DSC	A	Pickette, William Lee	DSC	A
Norgaard, Rollo Niel	NC	N	Pierce, George E.	NC	N
Nowak, Stephen	NC	M	Pierce, Sammy A.	DSC	A
Nowak, Walter J.	DSC	A	Pittman, William R.	NC	N
O'Dea, Padraig M.	DSC	A	Pleam, Daniel W.	DSC	A
O'Dowd, Jerome J.	NC	N	Podsiadly Joseph J.	DSC	A
O'Keefe, A. J.	DSC	A	Pohtilla, William C.	NC	N
O'Leary, Eugene Bernard	DSC	A	Poitras, Edwin W.	NC	N
O'Neill, John T.	DSC	A	Polk, Jack O.	NC	N
Obermeyer, Charles R.	DSC	A	Pollard, Samuel W. Sr	DSC	A
Oden, Delk M.	DSC	A	Pollard, Thomas D.	DSC	M
Odenbrett, Harvey George	NC	N	Pollard, Thomas D.	NC	M
Odom, Hubert	DSC	A	Pollock, Daniel C.	NC	M
Ogden, Carlos C. Sr	MOH – A	A	Pope, Everett P.	MOH – N	M
Okutsu, Yukio	MOH – A	A	Poschner, George W.	DSC	A
Oleson, Lloyd F.	DSC	A	Possinger, Harvey M.	DSC	A
Oller, Gerald W.	DSC	A	Powell, Nolan L.	DSC	A
Olson, Eugene Robert	NC	N	Pratt, Richard Rockwell	NC	N
Ono, Frank H.	MOH – A	A	Prendergast, George Jr.	NC	N
Ono, Thomas	DSC	A	Presley, William M.	DSC	A
Ononorato, J. P.	NC	N	Preston, Benjamin G.	NC	N
Oresko, Nicholas	MOH – A	A	Price, Donald R.	DSC	A
Orr, William D.	DSC	AF	Priest, Royce W.	DSC	A
Ortiz, Pierre (Peter)	NC	M	Pryor, William L.	DSC	A

Puller, Lewis B.	2NC	M	Savino, Frank A	DSC	A
Pulver, Murray S.	DSC	A	Sayre, Edwin B.	DSC	A
Quirk, Brian J.	NC	M	Scanland, Worth M.	NC	N
Radzwich, Edward R.	DSC	A	Schaefer, Harold F.	DSC	A
Ralston, Emerald M. MD	DSC	A	Schaefer, Joseph E.	MOH - A	A
Ramage, James D.	NC	N	Schallmoser, Joseph M.	DSC	A
Ramage, Lawson Paterson	MOH - N	N	Scheidleman, Cedric J.	NC	M
Ramage, Lawson Paterson	NC	N	Scherrer, E. C. D.	DSC	A
Ramsey, Edwin Price	DSC	A	Schlesinger, A. L.	DSC	A
Randle, Edwin H.	DSC	A	Schonland, Herbert Emery	MOH - N	N
Raposa, William C.	NC	N	Schultz, Arthur J. Jr.	NC	N
Rauschkolb, Frank	DSC	A	Schultz, George W. Jr.	DSC	A
Ray, Dewey Franklin	NC	N	Scott, Leonard E.	DSC	A
Reagan, Bruce W.	DSC	A	Seaward, Eugene Trefethen	NC	N
Reed, Edward B.	DSC	A	Seligman, M. T.	N	
Reed, Robert S.	NC	M	Shaheen, Albert J.	NC	M
Reich, Eugene B.	DSC	A	Shameklis, Algy C.	DSC	A
Reiser, Frank J.	NC	N	Shannon, William L.	NC	M
Rennebaum, Leon August	DSC	A	Shattuck, Charles W.	NC	N
Retzlaff, George T.	DSC	A	Shearon, Bruce C.	NC	N
Reusser, Kenneth L.	NC	M	Sheedy, Daniel C.	NC	N
Reynolds, George W.	DSC	A	Sheehan, Thomas P.	DSC	A
Ridlon, Walter J.	NC	M	Shoup, David Monroe	MOH - N	M
Riera, Robert Emmett	NC	N	Sigler, Franklin Earl	MOH - N	M
Rinen, Apolonio R.	DSC	A	Silva, Augustine S.	DSC	A
Ritchey, Andrew Jackson	DSC	A	Silva, John B.	DSC	A
Roberts, Eskell F.	DSC	A	Simeral, George A.	DSC	A
Roberts, Wilbur E.	NC	N	Singlestad, S. Donald	DSC	A
Rodenburg, Eugene E.	NC	N	Singletary, George F.	DSC	A
Rodwell, James S.	DSC	A	Sjogren, John C.	MOH - A	A
Rogers, Arthur H.	DSC	A	Skerry, Harry J.	DSC	A
Roosevelt, Theodore Jr.	MOH - A	A	Slagle, John W.	NC	M
Rosborough, James C.	DSC	A	Slicken, Marvin	DSC	A
Rosenthal, Robert	DSC	A	Slusser, John H.	NC	M
Ross, Donald K.	MOH - N	N	Smith, E. Lee Jr.	DSC	A
Ross, Wesley R.	DSC	A	Smith, Edward L.	DSC	A
Rosskamm, Leo	DSC	A	Smith, Robert J.	DSC	A
Rouse, Henry F.	DSC	A	Smith, Robert W.	DSC	A
Roy, Raymond G.	DSC	A	Smith, Stephen B.	NC	N
Rubel, David M.	NC	N	Smith, William Oliver	DSC	A
Ruby, Gottlieb	DSC	A	Snedeker, Edward W.	NC	M
Rudder, J. Earl	DSC	A	Snell, Clifford E.	NC	N
Rudolph, Donald E.	MOH - A	A	Soderman, William A.	MOH - A	A
Ruegg, Robert G.	DSC	A	Solley, Charles M.	DSC	A
Ruggiero, Matthew F.	DSC	A	Sorenson, Richard Keith	MOH - N	M
Ruiz, Alejandro R. Renteria	MOH - A	A	Soumas, George P.	DSC	A
Rush, Charles W.	DSC	A	Specht, Harry J.	DSC	A
Ryan, Francis X.	NC	N	Sperry, Edwin	NC	N
Sakato, George T.	MOH - A	A	Sprecher, Kenneth Ned	DSC	A
Salomon, Ben L.	MOH - A	A	Staff, Louis A.	DSC	A
Sampson, Francis L.	DSC	A	Stanford, Norman R.	NC	M
Sanford, William L.	DSC	A	Stegemeyer, Gerald B.	DSC	A
Sargent, Frank H.	DSC	A	Stephan, Charles R.	NC	N
Savage, Merritt M.	NC	M	Stephan, Edward C.	NC	N

Stevens, Clyde B.	NC	N	Vlung, Dirk J.	MOH – N	M
Stevens, Paul F.	NC	N	Voss, Clair H.	NC	M
Stone, Harry J.	DSC	A	Voss, Evan C.	DSC	A
Stout, Earl L.	NC	N	Vraciu, Alexander	NC	N
Stout, Herald Franklin	NC	N	Wagner, Arthur	NC	N
Stover, Wilmer Wallace	DSC	A	Wagner, Boyd	DSC	AF
Strean, Bernard M.	NC	N	Wagner, Ernest G.	DSC	A
Street, George Levick III	MOH – N	N	Wagoner, George E.	DSC	A
Street, George Levick III	NC	N	Wahlen, George E.	MOH – N	N
Strojny, Raymond F.	DSC	A	Waldrop, Leonard Ernest	NC	N
Sullivan, D. J.	NC	N	Walker, Beasor B.	DSC	A
Swann, Alonzo A.	NC	N	Walker, John Denley	NC	N
Sweeney, Walter Campbell Jr.	DSC	AF	Wallace, John G.	NC	N
Swenson, Jay L.	DSC	A	Wallace, Robert D.	DSC	A
Swett, James Elms	MOH – N	M	Wallis, Lynn T.	DSC	A
Switzer, George	NC	N	Walraven, Albert T. Jr.	NC	N
Talbott, C. M.	DSC	A	Walsh, Quentin R.	NC	CG
Tanner, John L.	DSC	A	Walsh, Thomas J.	DSC	A
Tapp, James B.	DSC	A	Walters, Richard B.	NC	N
Tatko, Walter A.	DSC	A	Ward, Henry P.	DSC	A
Taylor, Emmett M.	DSC	A	Warren, Sammie L.	DSC	A
Terry, Joseph	DSC	A	Wasneski, Joseph	NC	N
Terzi, Joseph A.	NC	M	Waters, John K.	DSC	A
Thayer, Kenneth C.	DSC	A	Watland, Lloyd A.	DSC	A
Theisen, George M.	DSC	A	Watts, Charles E.	NC	N
Thomas, Robert E. Jr.	NC	N	Waugh, Robert T.	MOH – A	A
Thomason, J .W.	NC	N	Weaver, Howard E.	DSC	A
Thompson, Francis H.	DSC	A	Weaver, William G.	2DSC	A
Thompson, Paul W.	DSC	A	Weems, Thomas N. DDS	DSC	A
Thornell, John Francis Jr.	DSC	AF	Weiss, Donald F.	NC	N
Thurston, Earl F.	DSC	A	Welch, Gordon A.	NC	N
Tice, John P.	DSC	A	Wellen, William Henry Jr.	NC	N
Tilson, Lemuel G.	DSC	A	Wellwood, Robert E.	NC	M
Timmes, Charles J.	DSC	A	Westin, Howard J.	NC	N
Todd, H. Allan	DSC	A	Westin, Howard S.	NC	N
Tofuri, Charles A. Sr	DSC	A	Wetmore, Ray S.	DSC	A
Tolley, Cecil Ray	NC	M	Whitcomb, Cecil B.	DSC	A
Torian, Paul T.	NC	M	White, Arthur	DSC	A
Townsend, Dured E.	DSC	A	White, George Oliver	NC	M
True, Clinton U.	DSC	A	White, Lawrence K. (Red)	DSC	A
Tucker, R. H.	DSC	A	Whitehill, John A. Jr.	DSC	A
Tucker, Robert E.	DSC	A	Whitlow, Walter	DSC	A
Turner, George B.	MOH – A	A	Wicklander, Edgar B.	NC	N
Tyler, Warner W.	NC	N	Wiedorfer, Paul J.	MOH – A	A
Urban, Matt L.	MOH – A	A	Wilhoit, William L.	NC	N
Vahle, Ralph W.	NC	M	Willaimson, Leon M.	NC	M
Van Brunt, Thomas Byrd	NC	N	Williams, Hershel Woodrow	MOH – N	M
Van Fleet, James A.	DSC	A	Willoughby, C. A.	DSC	A
Van Nice, Daniel B.	DSC	A	Wilson, Louis Hugh Jr.	MOH – N	M
Van Orden, George O.	NC	M	Wilson, Ray E. Jr.	NC	M
Van Stone, Clifford G.	NC	N	Wilson, S. J.	DSC	A
Vandervoort, Benjamin H.	DSC	A	Winchell, Albert W. (Walt)	NC	N
Veuve (Joyeuse), Rene	DSC	A	Winston, Sanford H.	DSC	A
Viale, Angelo S.	DSC	A	Winters, Elmer R.	DSC	A

Wise, Homer L.	MOH - A	A
Wisniewski, Edward L.	NC	N
Wohner, John H.	DSC	A
Wood, Hunter Jr.	NC	N
Wood, Leon	DSC	A
Wood, Ralph K.	NC	M
Wood, Thomas D.	DSC	A
Worthing, Wilbur F.	DSC	A
Worthington, Robert K. R.	NC	N
Wright, Allen L.	DSC	A
Wright, Elam W. Jr.	DSC	A
Wright, Wendell P.	NC	N
Young, Robert	DSC	A
Young, Walter A.	DSC	A
Zacek, Edward C.	NC	N
Zalewski, Frank C.	DSC	A
Ziegele, Paul	DSC	A
Zielenske, Walter J.	NC	N
Zinser, Roy F.	DSC	A
Zymros, Chester	NC	N
Benson, John O.	N	
Darby, William Orlando	N	
Wright Raymond R.	MOH - A	

Korean War 1950–1954

Abell, Welton Ralph	NC	M
Agnew, Richard S.	DSC	A
Alexander, George W. Jr.	NC	M
Alley, David W.	NC	M
Arthur, Donald J.	DSC	A
Bailey, Don V.	DSC	A
Barber, William E.	MOH - N	M
Barbosa, Arthur G.	NC	M
Beahler, Lee E.	DSC	A
Beall, Olin L.	DSC	A
Beatty, Robert E.	NC	M
Bell, Weldon Ralph	NC	M
Benavides, Adolfo	NC	M
Bernard, Carl R.	DSC	A
Blair, Melvin Russell	A	A
Blasongame, Richard N.	NC	M
Bleak, David B.	MOH - A	A
Blesse, Frederick C.	DSC	AF
Blick, Joseph A.	NC	M
Bolt, John F.	NC	M
Brannon, Charles E.	DSC	A
Brown, William Perry Jr.	M	M
Burke, Lloyd L. (Scooter)	MOH - A	A
Burr, Philip J.	NC	M
Cathcart, William D.	DSC	A
Chamberlain, George D.	2DSC	A
Chamberlain, Smith B.	DSC	A
Charette, William R.	MOH - N	N

Chenoweth, Theodore H.	NC	M
Clapp, Edward A.	DSC	M
Clark, William D.	DSC	A
Clawson, Paul E.	DSC	A
Clemons, Joseph G. Jr.	DSC	A
Conaway, Lyle F.	NC	M
Corcoran, Laurence M.	DSC	A
Counselman, John D.	NC	A
Craig, Thomas Kervin	DSC	A
Crispino, Ted	DSC	A
Daigneault, Donald A.	NC	M
Daly, John H.	DSC	A
Davis, Raymond G.	MOH - N	M
Desiderio, Reginald B.	MOH - A	A
Dewey, Duane E.	MOH - N	M
Dick, Joseph D.	DSC	A
Dixon, Kenneth B.	DSC	A
Doezema, Richard M.	NC	A
Donahue, Daniel J.	DSC	A
Dukes, Matthew D.	NC	M
Dunay, Andrew F.	NC	M
Dunwoody, Harold H.	DSC	A
Durkee, Richard W.	DSC	A
Eanes, Moir Earl	DSC	A
Elthon, Eldon J.	DSC	A
Faith, Don C.	MOH - A	A
Fenwick, John L.	NC	M
Fielding, Teddy Roosevelt	NC	N
Fischer, Harold E.	DSC	A
Flerchinger, Hubert P.	DSC	A
Flowers, Donald Victor	DSC	A
Foster, Fred Townsend	NC	N
Franklin, Joseph R.	DSC	A
Freeman, Paul L.	DSC	A
Gallardo, Robert	DSC	A
Garten, Melvin	DSC	A
Gilchrist, Philip J.	DSC	A
Gividen, George M. Jr.	DSC	A
Glaze, J. R.	DSC	A
Gore, William E.	DSC	A
Gray, John E.	DSC	A
Griffin, Albert F. Sr	DSC	A
Halterman, Roscoe C.	DSC	A
Hanes, Wallace M.	DSC	A
Hanna, Mark J.	DSC	A
Harris, William A.	DSC	A
Harvey, George U.	DSC	A
Hayward, Richard W.	DSC	M
Haywood, Richard W.	DSC	A
Hemphill, John A.	DSC	A
Hernandez, Rodolfo P.	MOH - A	A
Hill, John G.	DSC	A
Hilliard, Frederick E. R.	NC	M
Hudner, Thomas J. Jr.	MOH - N	N

Ingman, Einar H.	MOH - A	A		Moses, Lloyd R.	DSC	A
Jackson, Willis	DSC	A		Mueller, Harold P.	DSC	A
Jenkins, Reuben E.	DSC	A		Murphy, Daniel Michael	NC	M
Johnson, Harold K.	DSC	A		Murphy, James F.	DSC	A
Jones, Donald R.	NC	M		Murphy, John M.	DSC	A
Jones, Jack R.	NC	M		Murphy, Raymond G.	MOH - N	M
Jones, Robert E.	DSC	A		Myers, Reginald R.	MOH - N	M
Jordan, Earle H. Jr.	DSC	A		Nehls, Edwin E.	DSC	A
Josey, Claude Kitchin	DSC	A		Nichol, Bromfield B.	DSC	A
Kahoohanohano, Anthony T.	MOH - A	A		Nickerson, Herman Jr.	DSC	M
Kapaun, Emil J.	MOH - A	A		Nonnweiler, Edward C.	DSC	A
Keeble, Woodrow W.	MOH - A	A		O'Brien, George H.	MOH - N	M
Keenan, Joseph F.	NC	N		Orr, Robert H.	DSC	A
Kelso, Jack W.	MOH - N	M		Orsulak, Edmund T.	NC	M
Kestlinger, Robert S.	DSC	A		Parr, Ralph S.	DSC	A
Kouma, Ernest R.	MOH - A	A		Parsley, Jimmie R.	DSC	A
Kozares, Victor	DSC	A		Petro, George E.	NC	M
Ladd, James Von K.	DSC	A		Phoenix, Earl C. Jr.	DSC	A
Lauer, Richard F.	DSC	A		Polley, Paul N.	NC	N
Lawrence, James F.	NC	M		Powell, Herbert Butler	DSC	A
Lederer, Edward R.	DSC	A		Psihas, George P.	DSC	A
Ledford, James H.	DSC	AF		Puller, Lewis B.	DSC	M
Lee, Chew-mon	DSC	A		Puller, Lewis B.	NC	M
Lee, Kurt C.-E.	NC	M		Read, Beverly M.	DSC	A
Lippman, Gordon J.	DSC	A		Reusser, Kenneth L.	NC	M
Litzenberg, Homer L.	NC	M		Rhodes, Roger J.	DSC	A
Litzenberg, Homer L.	DSC	M		Rhotenberry, R. M.	DSC	A
Lonsford, Charles A.	DSC	A		Richards, J. C.	DSC	A
Lopez, Erasmo G.	DSC	A		Roberts, Robert D.	DSC	A
Louder, Joseph J.	NC	M		Rodriguez, Joseph C.	MOH - A	A
Lounsburg, G. W.	NC	N		Rosser, Ronald E.	MOH - A	A
Lowe, Frank E.	DSC	A		Roush, John N. Jr.	DSC	A
Loyd, Frank R. Jr.	DSC	A		Roy, Franklin D.	NC	M
Lukas, Frank W.	DSC	A		Rubin, Tibor	MOH - A	A
MacArthur, David W.	DSC	AF		Ruffner, Clark Louis	DSC	A
MacLeod, Norman E.	DSC	A		Russ, Joseph R.	DSC	A
Macy, Jack E.	DSC	M		Schauer, Ernest J.	DSC	A
Mamula, George	DSC	A		Serrano, Roberto	NC	N
Mason, Donald	NC	N		Shilling, Winford A.	DSC	A
Mausen, John E. Jr.	NC	N		Shouldice, D'Arcy V.	NC	N
McCloskey, Paul N. Jr.	NC	M		Siegert, Frank	DSC	A
McCraney, William P.	DSC	A		Sigmund, Louis J.	NC	M
McCullough, Richard R.	DSC	A		Simanek, Robert E.	MOH - N	M
McDaniel, William T.	DSC	A		Sitler, Ross E.	DSC	A
McGahn, Patrick T. Jr.	NC	M		Sitter, Carl L.	MOH - N	M
McKim, John S.	DSC	A		Southall, James B.	NC	M
Michaelis, J. H.	DSC	A		Spicer, William H.	DSC	A
Middlemas, John N.	DSC	A		Stone, Cletus H.	NC	N
Miller, Wilfred D.	DSC	A		Stone, James L.	MOH - A	A
Millett, Lewis L	DSC	A		Stratemeyer, George E.	DSC	AF
Millett, Lewis L.	MOH - A	A		Svehla, Henry	MOH - A	A
Mize, Ola L.	MOH - A	A		Tamez, Rudolph	DSC	A
Monagham, John T.	DSC	A		Teeters, Bernard G.	DSC	A
Montez, Benito Jr.	DSC	A		Terrell, Ernest P.	DSC	A

Thomas, Gerald C.	DSC	M
Thornton, John W.	NC	N
Tolbert, Jack P.	DSC	A
Van Orman, Chester W.	DSC	A
Wallace, William C.	DSC	A
Walls, Claude R.	DSC	A
Ward, Joseph M.	NC	M
Wawrzyniak, Stanley J.	NC	M
Weisgerber, William D.	NC	M
Whear, Roger G. Jr.	NC	N
White, Millard C.	DSC	A
Wilson, Frank E.	NC	M
Wolf, Wilmot H.	NC	M
Woolley, Earl K.	DSC	A
Zanin, John B.	DSC	A

Vietnam War 1962–1975

Abernathy, Joe V.	DSC	A
Abood, Edmond P.	DSC	A
Adkins, Bennie G.	MOH - A	A
Ajdukovich, George	NC	N
Allen, Lawrence W.	DSC	A
Allen, Yale G.	NC	M
Alley, Lee B.	DSC	A
Allison, John V.	AFC	AF
Altazan Kenneth A.	NC	M
Ames, Lawrence J.	DSC	A
Anderson, Webster	MOH - A	A
Archibald, Robert S.	DSC	A
Armstrong, Russell P.	NC	M
Aronhalt, Charles E.	DSC	A
Baca, John P.	MOH - A	A
Bahnsen, John C. "Doc"	DSC	A
Bailey, Henry M.	DSC	A
Bailey, Otis	DSC	A
Baker, John F. Jr.	MOH - A	A
Baker, Walter L.	DSC	A
Baldwin, Norman Earl	DSC	A
Ballard, Donald E.	MOH - N	N
Barber, William B.	NC	N
Bargewell, Eldon A.	DSC	A
Barnes, Brice H.	DSC	A
Barnum, H. C. Jr.	MOH - N	M
Barrett, James J.	NC	M
Barrett, John J.	NC	M
Batcheller, Gordon D.	NC	M
Baxter, William Purnell	DSC	A
Beach, Martin H.	DSC	A
Bechtel, Herbert J.	DSC	A
Beikirch, Gary B.	MOH - A	A
Bell, Christopher Hiawatha	DSC	A
Benavidez, Roy P.	MOH - A	A
Bennett, Steven L.	MOH - AF	AF

Benoit, Ronald R.	NC	M
Bensen, John O.	DSC	A
Benson, John O.	DSC	A
Bercaw, William E.	DSC	A
Bernardo, Peter R.	DSC	A
Biggin, Donald M. Jr.	DSC	A
Binkoski, Vic	DSC	A
Binns, Ricardo C.	NC	M
Birchim, James D.	DSC	A
Black, Arthur N.	AFC	AF
Blair, John D. IV	DSC	A
Bode, John R.	AFC	AF
Bouchard, Thomas D.	DSC	A
Boyd, Charles G.	AFC	AF
Brady, Eugene R.	NC	M
Brady, Patrick H.	DSC	A
Brady, Patrick H.	MOH - A	A
Brandtner, Martin L.	NC	M
Breland, Artis	DSC	A
Brickel, James R.	AFC	AF
Brindel, Charles L.	DSC	A
Briscoe, Charles H.	DSC	A
Britton, Warner A.	AFC	AF
Brock, Bobby Q.	DSC	A
Broughton, Jacksel M.	AFC	AF
Brown, Walter Ronald	DSC	A
Bucha, Paul W.	MOH - A	A
Buchanan, Richard W.	NC	M
Burbank, Kenneth R.	DSC	A
Burke, Robert C.	MOH - N	M
Burns, Leon R.	NC	M
Burroughs, William D.	AFC	AF
Burrow, George D.	DSC	A
Bustamante, Manuel C.	DSC	A
Cain, Jerry A.	DSC	A
Caldwell, William R.	AFC	AF
Campbell, Keith A.	DSC	A
Campbell, Thomas A.	AFC	AF
Capodanno, Vincent R.	MOH - N	N
Caristo, Fredrick J. G.	DSC	A
Carnes, Edward L.	DSC	A
Carpenter, Michael F.	DSC	A
Carrizales, Daniel A.	DSC	A
Carter, Hilliard	DSC	A
Carter, Marshall N.	NC	M
Carter, Tennis H.	DSC	A
Carter, William R.	AFC	AF
Cavaiani, Jon R.	MOH - A	A
Cecil, Gerald T.	DSC	A
Cheatham, Ernest C. Jr.	NC	M
Chenoweth, Ted	DSC	M
Cherry, Fred V.	AFC	AF
Chervony, Eddie E.	DSC	A
Childers, Richard L.	DSC	A

Guarino, Timothy S.	NC	M	Johnson, John C.	DSC	A
Guay, Robert P.	NC	M	Jones, William A.	MOH – AF	AF
Gustafson, Gerald C.	AFC	AF	Jordan, Daniel Walter	DSC	A
Guy, Theodore W.	AFC	AF	Joubert, Donald L.	DSC	A
Hackney, Duane D.	AFC	AF	Judkins, Roy E.	DSC	A
Hackney, Hunter F.	AFC	AF	Kalen, Herbert D.	AFC	AF
Hackworth, David H.	DSC	A	Kasler, James	AFC	AF
Hagemeister, Charles Chris	MOH – A	A	Kelley, Edwin C.	NC	M
Haig, Alexander M. Jr.	DSC	A	Kelley, Gordon F.	DSC	A
Hall, Billie A.	DSC	A	Kelly, Ross S.	DSC	A
Harding, James C.	AFC	AF	Keltner, Neil L.	DSC	A
Harper Tony	DSC	A	Kennedy, Herman J.	DSC	A
Harr, Gerry A.	DSC	A	Kennedy, Johnnie M.	NC	M
Harrington, Myron C. Jr.	NC	M	Kennedy, LeLand T.	AFC	AF
Haszard, Sidney S. "Hap"	DSC	A	Kennedy, Leslie D.	DSC	A
Hattersley, Roger K	DSC	A	Kettles, Charles S.	DSC	A
Hayenga, William E. Jr.	NC	N	Keys, William M.	NC	M
Hayes, Daniel J.	NC	M	Kimura, Donald K.	DSC	A
Hazelbaker, Vincil W.	NC	M	Kingston, Robert C.	DSC	A
Hazelip, Charles R.	DSC	A	Kinnard, Donel C.	NC	N
Helmick, Robert F.	DSC	A	Kizirian, John	DSC	A
Henderson, Donald L.	DSC	A	Klinger, Vernon L.	DSC	A
Herbert, Robert S.	NC	N	Knight, Robert Clyde	DSC	A
Herrera, Fernando Q.	DSC	A	Koch, Robert A.	DSC	A
Hibbs Robert J.	MOH – A	A	Kotite, Richard S.	DSC	A
Hibbs, Robert J.	MOH – A	A	Kunz, Anthony Edmund	DSC	A
Hilgers, John Jack W.	NC	M	Lambers, Paul R.	MOH – A	A
Hoapili, John	NC	M	Landry, Robert M.	DSC	A
Holleder, Donald	DSC	A	Lang, George Charles	MOH – A	A
Hollingsworth, James F.	A		Lawrence, William	DSC	A
Hopkins, James R.	AFC	AF	Lawton, John P.	DSC	A
Hoptkins Perry C.	DSC	A	LeBas, Claude G.	NC	M
Horinek, Ramon A.	AFC	AF	LePeilbet, Andrew R.	DSC	A
Hosking, Charles Ernest Jr.	MOH – A	A	Ledbetter, Walter R. Jr.	NC	M
Houghton, Kenneth J.	NC	M	Ledfors, Fredrick D.	DSC	A
Howard, Jimmie E.	MOH – N	M	Lewis, John J.	DSC	A
Howard, Robert L.	MOH – A	A	Lindemann, Edward W.	DSC	A
Howard, Robert L.	DSC	A	Liteky, Angelo J.	MOH – A	A
Hudson, Claude K.	DSC	A	Livingston, James E.	MOH – N	M
Hughes, George W.	DSC	A	Livingston, Lawrence H.	NC	M
Hunter, Russell L.	DSC	A	Lowery, Steven M.	NC	M
Jackson, Joe M.	MOH – AF	AF	Lownds, David E.	NC	M
Jacobs, Jack H.	MOH – A	A	Lutchendorf, Thomas E.	DSC	A
Jaehne, Richard L.	NC	M	Lynch, Allen James	MOH – A	A
James, Alan C.	NC	N	MacVane, Matthew C.	NC	M
James, Kirk J.	DSC	A	Magouryk, James R.	DSC	A
Jenkins, Wilbur G.	DSC	A	Malone, George M.	NC	M
Jennings, Delbert O.	MOH – A	A	Maloney, George A.	DSC	A
Johnson, Dallas W.	DSC	A	Manglona, Martin A.	DSC	A
Johnson, Dean Raymond	DSC	A	Mann, Bennie H. Jr.	NC	M
Johnson, Harold E.	AFC	AF	Mansfield, Gordon H.	DSC	A
Johnson, James H.	DSC	A	Mari, Louis A.	DSC	A
Johnson, James L.	NC	M	Marlantes, Karl A.	NC	M
Johnson, Jesse L.	DSC	A	Marm, Walter Joseph Jr.	MOH – A	A

Martin, Cecil Harvey	NC	N	Nelson, Charles Edward	DSC		A
Marx, Donald L.	AFC	AF	Nelson, James R.	NC		N
Mason, Larry Buren	AFC	AF	Nguyen, Kiet V.	NC	RV	N
Mayer, Frank H.	DSC	A	Northrop, Ralph A.	DSC		A
Mayor, Robert G.	DSC	A	Norton, John J.	NC		M
Mayton, James A.	NC	N	Novosel, Michael J.	MOH - A		A
Maywald, Phillip V.	AFC	AF	O'Brien, Joseph J.	NC		M
McCaffrey, Barry H.	DSC	A	O'Dell, Eugene J. Jr.	DSC		A
McCarthy, James R.	AFC	AF	O'Mara, Oliver E.	AFC		AF
McCarthy, Thomas W.	DSC	A	O'Sullivan, Christopher J.	DSC		A
McCauley, Bertram W.	NC	M	O'Sullivan, John I.	DSC		A
McClean, Michael A.	DSC	A	Orsini, Donald A.	DSC		A
McDermott, Michael A.	DSC	A	Otto, William Frederick	DSC		A
McDougald, Lacy Jr.	DSC	A	Panian, Thomas C.	NC		M
McEnery, John W.	DSC	A	Parker, George W. Jr.	DSC		A
McEwen, Robert M.	NC	N	Parr, Ralph S.	AFC		AF
McGinnis, Edward G.	DSC	A	Patterson, James H.	DSC		A
McGonagle, William L.	MOH - N	N	Patton, George S. III	DSC		A
McGowan, Arthur J. Jr.	DSC	A	Payne, Keith	DSC	RA	A
McInerney, James E. Jr.	AFC	AF	Peck, Millard A.	DSC		A
McKeown, Ronald E.	NC	N	Peczeli, Joseph S.	NC		M
McKibben, Ray	MOH - A	A	Pence, Charles "Charlie"	DSC		A
McMahon Thomas J.	MOH - A	A	Peoples, Leon	DSC		A
McNichol, John J.	DSC	A	Perry, Michael Phillip	DSC		A
McTasney, John B.	AFC	AF	Peters, Lawrence D.	MOH - N		M
Meadows, Richard J.	DSC	A	Petersen Danny J.	MOH - A		A
Mehr, Richard L.	AFC	AF	Phelps, John G.	NC		M
Merkerson, Willie Jr.	DSC	A	Piatt, Louis R.	NC		M
Miles, Martin C.	DSC	A	Pierpan, Herbert E.	NC		M
Milius, Paul Lloyd	NC	N	Pittman, Homer L. Jr.	DSC		A
Miller, Franklin D.	MOH - A	A	Pittman, Richard A.	MOH - N		M
Miller, Phillip E.	DSC	A	Pless, Stephen W.	MOH - N		M
Miller, Richard L.	DSC	A	Poulson, Leroy N.	NC		M
Millsap, Walter G.	DSC	A	Powell, Thomas E.	DSC		A
Minatra, John D.	DSC	A	Price, Donald S.	AFC		AF
Mize, John D.	AFC	AF	Primmer, Frank G.	DSC		A
Modrzejewski, Robert J.	MOH - N	M	Pritchard, Paul M.	DSC		A
Monahan, Frederick G.	NC	M	Pryor, Robert D.	DSC		A
Monroe, Charles H.	NC	M	Quick, Claude Jr.	DSC		A
Montgomery, Robin L.	NC	M	Ragin, William D. H.	DSC		A
Moore, Douglas Eugene	DSC	A	Ramirez, Ramiro	DSC		A
Moore, Harold G. Jr.	DSC	A	Randall, Michael Eugene	DSC		A
Moore, Joseph W.	DSC	A	Ranger, Michael B.	DSC		A
Morris, Charles B.	MOH - A	A	Rankin, Howard F.	DSC		A
Morris, Melvin	DSC	A	Rau, Raymond R.	DSC		A
Morris, Wayne H.	DSC	A	Ray, Ronald E.	MOH - A		A
Mullen, William J.	DSC	A	Reeves, Thomas M.	DSC		A
Mulloy, James E. Jr.	NC	M	Reilly, Donald J.	NC		M
Murphy, Kenneth E.	DSC	A	Rice, Robert C.	DSC		A
Murphy, Robert C.	DSC	A	Richards, Thomas A.	NC		M
Murray, John D.	NC	M	Richardson, Dennis M.	AFC		AF
Murray, Robert C.	MOH - A	A	Riensche, Harold A.	NC		M
Myers, Richard J.	DSC	A	Riley, Ronald J.	DSC		A
Nedolast, Daniel A.	DSC	A	Rinaldo, Richard J.	DSC		A
Neil, Michael I.	NC	M	Rios, Adolph	DSC		A

Ripley, John W.	NC	M	Stuckey, James L.	NC	M
Risner, Robinson	AFC	AF	Sullivan, Daniel F.	NC	M
Robinson, David B.	NC	N	Swanson, Jon E.	MOH - A	A
Robinson, William P.	AFC	AF	Sweet, Richard S.	DSC	A
Rocco, Louis R.	MOH - A	A	Sykes, Larry W.	DSC	A
Rodela, Jose	MOH - A	A	Taft, David A.	NC	M
Rogers, Bernard W.	DSC	A	Taft, John K.	DSC	A
Rogers, Charles C.	MOH - A	A	Talley, Joel E.	AFC	AF
Rogers, James D.	DSC	A	Taylor, James Allen	MOH - A	A
Rollins, Dale F.	DSC	A	Taylor, James Thompson Jr.	DSC	A
Romine, Richard E.	NC	M	Taylor, Ronald S.	DSC	A
Rose, Gary M.	DSC	A	Teevens, Richard P.	DSC	A
Rubin, Kenneth E.	DSC	A	Terry, Gilbert N.	DSC	A
Sabo, Leslie Halaxz	MOH - A	A	Terry, Ronald T.	DSC	A
Saracino, Frank DePaul	DSC	A	Thacker, Brian Miles	MOH - A	A
Sargent, Ruppert Leon	MOH - A	A	Thornton, Michael E.	MOH - N	N
Scher, Donald M.	DSC	A	Thornton, Michael Edwin	MOH - N	N
Schlottman, James C.	DSC	A	Thurman, Jerry W.	DSC	A
Schungel, Daniel F.	DSC	A	Tilley, Leonard W.	DSC	A
Schurr, Harry W.	AFC	AF	Timmons, James	NC	M
Schweitzer, Robert L.	DSC	A	Tissler, John G.	DSC	A
Scott, James A. III	DSC	A	Tolson, John J. III	DSC	A
Scott, Travis H. Jr.	AFC	AF	Tomcik, Dennis C.	DSC	A
Seath, Ned E	NC	M	Tomlinson, Raymond F.	DSC	A
Severson, Daniel J.	DSC	A	Tonsetic, Robert L.	DSC	A
Sexton, Merlyn A.	NC	M	Totten, Clifford R.	DSC	A
Shea, Thomas J. M.	DSC	A	Towles, Robert L.	DSC	A
Shields, Marvin Glen	MOH - N	N	Trautman, Konrad W.	AFC	AF
Shortman, Phillip V.	DSC	A	Trent, Herman L.	DSC	A
Silverstein, William I.	DSC	A	Tucker, Gary L.	DSC	A
Slater, Albert C. Jr.	NC	M	Turner, Robert E.	AFC	AF
Sleigh, Duncan B.	NC	M	Underwood, Victor C.	DSC	A
Sloat, Donald P.	MOH - A	A	Vampatella, Philip V.	NC	N
Smith, Chester B.	NC	N	Vann, John Paul	DSC	A
Smith, Jack Rae	DSC	A	Vargas, Jay R.	MOH - N	M
Smith, Mark A.	DSC	A	Vaughan, Denny R.	DSC	A
Smith, Ray L.	NC	M	Versace, Humbert R.	MOH - A	A
Snyder, Robert A.	DSC	A	Villanueva, David O.	DSC	A
Soppe, Ronald J.	DSC	A	Villarreal, Raul	DSC	A
Sowell, Ronald	DSC	A	Wagner, Louis C. Jr.	DSC	A
Spaulding, Frederick L.	DSC	A	Walden, Darrell Edward	DSC	A
Speer, Paul H.	NC	N	Walden, Jerry T.	DSC	A
Speers, Max Dale	DSC	A	Waldrop, Andrew H. Jr.	DSC	A
Sperling, Richard A.	DSC	A	Walkabout, Billie B.	DSC	A
Spinaio, Edward W.	DSC	A	Walker, James R.	NC	N
Spitz, James D.	DSC	A	Walker, Robert H.	DSC	A
Springer, Charles A.	DSC	A	Walker, Wesley F.	DSC	A
Stahl, Mykle E.	NC	M	Wanat, George K. Jr.	DSC	A
Stark, Peter M.	DSC	A	Wandke, Richard D.	DSC	A
Starr, William J.	DSC	A	Ward, William H.	DSC	A
Stayton, Norman B.	NC	N	Wasco, Joseph Jr.	DSC	A
Steimel, Gregg Francis	DSC	A	Washington, Johnny Lee	DSC	A
Stewart, Harvey E.	DSC	A	Watkins, Patrick N.	DSC	A
Stockdale, James B.	MOH - N	N	Watts, Albert R.	DSC	A
Stone, Raymond E.	DSC	A	Webb, James H. Jr.	NC	M

Weise, William	NC	M
Welch, Albert C.	DSC	A
Weseleskey, Allen E.	NC	N
Westphal, Warren R.	NC	N
Wetzel, Allan R.	DSC	A
Wetzel, Gary G.	MOH - A	A
Wetzel, Gary G.	DSC	A
Weyand, Fred C.	DSC	A
Whatley, Wayne N.	AFC	AF
Whitaker, Ira E.	DSC	A
Whitehead, John B. III	DSC	A
Whitehead, Rudolph L.	DSC	A
Whitesides, Richard LeBrou	AFC	AF
Whitted, Jack G.	DSC	A
Wijas, Rodney J.	DSC	A
Wilbanks Hilliard	MOH - AF	AF
Williams, Jack L.	DSC	A
Williams, James Elliott	NC	N
Williams, James Elliott	MOH - N	N
Williams, Robert S.	NC	M
Wishik, Jeffrey	DSC	A
Wofford, Travis	AFC	AF
Wolford, Grover G.	DSC	A
Wood, Daniel	DSC	A
Wood, Patrick H.	AFC	AF
Woods, Luther	DSC	A
Worley, M. G.	DSC	A
Worrell, Rowland H. III	AFC	AF
Wright, Garth A.	AFC	AF
Wright, Larry D.	DSC	A
Wright, Raymond R.	MOH - A	A
Wynn, Edward H.	NC	M
Yano, Rodney J. T.	MOH - A	A
York, Glen P.	AFC	AF
Zinser, Harry J.	NC	N

Persian Gulf War 1991

Johnson, Paul T.	AFC	AF
Kurth, Michael M.	NC	M
Ray, Eddie S.	NC	M

Somalia 1992–1993

| Gordon, Gary I. | MOH | A |
| Wilkinson, Timothy A. | AFC | AF |

War on Terrorism/Afghanistan 2003

Abbate, Matthew T.	NC	M
Axelson, Matthew Gene	NC	N
Bass, Stephen	NC	N

Chapman, John A.	AFC	AF
Chontosh, Brian R.	NC	M
Coffman, James H. Jr.	DSC	A
Copeland, Willie L. III	NC	M
Dietz, Danny	NC	N
Fonseca, Luis E. Jr.	NC	N
Gutierrez, Robert	AFC	AF
Hollenbaugh, Donald R.	DSC	A
LeHew, Justin David	NC	M
Lollino, Joseph L.	DSC	A
Martinez, Marco A.	NC	M
McGinnis, Ross A.	MOH - A	A
Miller, Robert J.	MOH - A	A
Mitchell, Mark E.	DSC	A
Monti, Jared C.	MOH - A	A
Montoya, Scott C.	NC	M
Murphy, Michael P.	MOH - N	N
O'Connor, Brendan W.	DSC	A
Perez, Joseph B.	NC	M
Rhyner, Zachary J.	AFC	AF
Shaw, Eric B.	DSC	A
Slabinski, Britt K.	NC	N
Smith, Paul Ray	MOH - A	A
Snith, Paul Ray	MOH - A	A

Iraqi Freedom

Adlesperger, Christopher S.	NC	M
Atkins, Travis W.	DSC	A
Cooper, David F. Jr.	DSC	A
Corbin, Todd J.	NC	M
Crawford, Barry F.	AFC	AF
Donald, Mark L.	NC	N
Dunham, Jason	MOH - N	M
Haerter, Jordan C.	NC	M
Halbisengibbs, Jarion	DSC	A
Jackson, Walter B.	DSC	A
Kraft, Jarrett A.	NC	M
McDade, Aubrey L. Jr.	NC	M
Mitchell, Robert J. Jr.	NC	M
Monsoor, Michael A.	MOH - N	N
Mooi, Joshua R.	NC	M
Nein, Timothy F.	DSC	A
Oropeza, Erik	DSC	A
Sanford, Stephen C.	DSC	A
Waiters, Christopher B.	DSC	A
Williams, Gregory D. Jr.	DSC	A
Wilson, Justin A.	NC	N
Wooldridge, Clifford M.	NC	M
Workman, Jeremiah W.	NC	M
Yale, Jonathan T.	NC	M
Yoakum, Keith	DSC	A

Enduring Freedom XIX

Eberle, William N.	DSC	A
Manoukian, Matthew P.	NC	N
Wyckoff, Charles E.	DSC	A

Special Legislation

Entrekin, Emery L.	NC	M

Unknown

Claud,	NC	N/A
Dorian, Paul T.	NC	N
Harman, Walter E.	NC	N
Kerns, Paul	NC	M
Mamas, John	NC	N/A
McCanna, Edward M.	NC	N/A
Pearsons, John C.	DSC	A
Petty, Alfred C.	DSC	A
Reed, William A.	NC	N
Suberg, Fred H.	NC	N
Vanderpyl, Ellis C.	DSC	AF

Legion of Valor Museum Volunteer Staff

Alvarez, Ruben
Azevedo, Louis
Bill Biggers,
Boudreau, Linda
Casillas, Leonard
Casillas, Leslie
Chavez, Ronald
Cristando, Frank
Fabela, Jesse
Fusinato, David
Harris, Mike
Hill, Floyd Sam
Horg, Harold
Hudson, Harold
Jones, Judy
Ledford, David
Lee, Ray
Machado, Fred
Newland, Don
Poulter, Richard
Specht, Bob
Svelik, Ed
Teniente II, Carlos
Terrazas, Chuck
Traeger, Les
Wells, Stan

Retired Staff Members

Bruno, Nick
Colmenero, Ramon
Crenshaw, Willie
Doctor, Alan
Eckenrod, Gerry
Gentile, Tom
Gless, Frank
Hokr, Frank
Tanaka, Carolyn
Trevino, Juan

Deceased Staff Members

Aivazian, Barkley
Aivazian, Gail
Anderson, Jack
Barcus, Paul
Barkman, Sam
Coleman, Forrest
Cramer, Paul
Crumpacker, Bill
Doi, Ben
Harrison, Bill
Hayes, Bob
Fries, Gerhardt
Frint, Clifford
Ginther, Don
Hayes, Ken
Hill, Art
Hills, Warren
Isogawa, Hiro
Kalfayan, Sam
Laub, Tom
Lopez, Carlos
McMahan, George
Maguire, Warren
Martinusen, Gil
Monges, Charles
Newton, David
Moore, Ampless
Nichols, Jess
Odell, Bob
Powell, Don
Raymer, Q. T.
Scovell, Rolf
Shamshoian, John
Stephens, Charles
Stokem, Fred
Winslow, George
Dunlavy, Harry